G-D'S PHYSICS

*A New Scientific Paradigm for
the Twenty-First Century*

Jehonathan Bentovish (Bentwich), Ph.D.

G-D'S PHYSICS
A NEW SCIENTIFIC PARADIGM FOR THE TWENTY-FIRST CENTURY

iUniverse books may be ordered through booksellers or by contacting:

iUniverse
1663 Liberty Drive
Bloomington, IN 47403
www.iuniverse.com
844-349-9409

The cover drawing portraying the Hebrew letter Yud was produced by the famous Jewish artist Nachshon from Kiryat Arba, Israel (all rights reserved). This drawing can be purchased online at:

ISBN: 978-1-5320-9037-0 (sc)
ISBN: 978-1-5320-9038-7 (hc)
ISBN: 978-1-5320-9039-4 (e)

Library of Congress Control Number: 2021902794

Print information available on the last page.

iUniverse rev. date: 02/11/2021

This book is dedicated to Rabbi Menachem Mendel Schneerson (1902–1994), the great Lubavitcher Rebbe, whose teachings and life's mission was to bring the world toward a state of moral and spiritual perfection; in other words, <u>Geula</u>, as termed by the Jewish tradition and wisdom. It was his mission to make us all open our eyes to see the presence of G-d in everything around us and in our own personal moral, purposeful, self-driven spiritual lives.

It is dedicated to my dear father, Professor Zvi Bentwich, who gave me a personal example of excellence and set me out to discover how to become a true scientist.

This book is also dedicated to my dear beloved mother, Dr. Tirza Bentwich, whose endless love and faith in me have enabled me to discover this new scientific theory—G-d's Physics—that advances physics and science ever closer toward an all-embracing truth.

This book is written out of great love and gratitude to my beloved wife, Shulamit Bentovish, whose unbounded love, faith, encouragement, and trust have made this book possible, and has changed my life profoundly!

It is also dedicated to my dear beloved children, Shoham, Netanel Yossef, and Neumi Tirza Shulamit. May you all grow to embrace this new profound, faithful, grateful, and awe-inspiring realization of the one singular higher-ordered G-d reality, who creates, sustains, cares, and loves all human beings and encourages us to grow toward fulfilling our highest moral and divine nature.

It is also dedicated to Mr. Brian Fisher who encouraged me to grow as an individual.

I would like to thank my dear friend Motti Ben Mordechai and my dear friends Pinchas Elyahu (Allen) and Tamar Mietla and Dvir Even Chen for supporting me through trying times. I would also like to deeply thank Prof. Shlomo Kalish for his unwavering support of us in trying times.

This article is also dedicated in memory of dear beloved Mrs. Diana Raz, who shed so much light and Goodness in the lives of so many couples but whose own life was stumped at such an early age leaving behind four innocent children, may her Memory Blessed and may her Soul ascend to Paradise (where she belongs)…

This book is also dedicated to all human beings in hope and prayer that the new G-d's physics paradigm of twenty-first-century physics may open our eyes to see the presence of G-d and his continuous creation, caring, and moral oneness that underlies, evolves, and drives our entire physical universe toward a state of moral, spiritual, and physical perfection—<u>Geula</u>.

—Jehonathan Bentovish (Bentwich), PhD

PREFACE

We now stand at a historic time in which twenty-first-century physics, and <u>Science</u> more generally, is undergoing a profound paradigmatic shift from the old twentieth-century Material-Causal Paradigm underlying Einstein's Relativity Theory and Quantum Mechanics to the new Computational Unified Field theory Paradigm. This points at the existence of a singular higher Universal Consciousness Reality, which continuously creates, sustains, dissolves, and reproduces the entire physical universe many billions of times per second! It is therefore befitting to call this new Computational Unified Field Theory G-d's physics, which is the topic of this profound new book.

I wrote this book out of a strong wish and sense of mission (*shlicus*) to explain as much as possible in simple terms this profound new understanding of the physical universe in which we live, and indeed of our very significant part within it. As human beings, we possess the most expansive form of consciousness and are therefore *expected* to play a *very significant* role in the perfection of the world, morally, spiritually, and physically in the light of this new scientific understanding. It is quite clear that the old world as we know it would cease to exist with the discovery of this new G-d's physics paradigm of twenty-first century theoretical physics, and <u>Science</u> more generally. This is simply because our whole conception and understanding of the physical universe—and of our own human consciousness within it—is undergoing a profound and exciting change with the discovery of G-d's Physics! This book follows the publication of over forty peer-reviewed scientific articles and a special issue published by *Global Journals* entirely dedicated to this new <u>Computational Unified Field Theory</u>'s G-d's Physics. As will be scientifically shown in this book, the new scientific understanding of the universe is that it was not created by a "Big-Bang" nuclear event; neither is it being run "accidently" by mere physical interactions between massive objects and "space-time", as assumed by Einstein's Relativity Theory. Nor can the empirically observed accelerated expansion of the physical universe be attributed to the concepts of "dark matter" or "dark energy", the existence of which cannot be proven and, in any event, is negated by the G-d's Physics new paradigm.

Instead, what stands at the center of this new G-d's Physics paradigm for twenty-first-century theoretical physics is its profound discovery of a singular higher-ordered "Universal Consciousness Reality" that solely creates, dissolves, recreates, and evolves every spatial pixel in the universe at the incredible rate of c^2/h" = 1.36^{-50} seconds! In other words, this happens many billions of times per second. Indeed, the discovery of this new higher-ordered Universal Consciousness Reality and the new G-d's Physics Paradigm associated with it is both *exciting* and *promising*. Our universe as well as our own human world undergoes an extremely significant metamorphosis from being viewed as a mere material-physical (arbitrary) physical reality toward a new divinely governed, morally embedded, purposeful, and meaningful human existence. As shall be seen throughout this book, our whole human existence and lives, as well as the world in which we live, are being transformed into the new higher-ordered G-d's Physics singular Universal Consciousness Reality that "knows" all past, present, and multiple (possible) futures but, nevertheless, endows us human beings with a "Free Moral Choice", encouraging us and teaching us to use our Free Moral Choice capacity to better our own personal human characters and lives and to partake in the great purpose and goal of this singular higher Universal Consciousness Reality—in other words, "G-d"—to steer the world toward the realization of the great moral, spiritual, and physical perfection appreciating the Goodness and Wisdom of this sole "G-d Reality".

It is not by chance but rather by Personal Providence (*hashgacha pratit*) that the publication of *G-d's Physics* comes out precisely on אלול חי, the Jewish birth date of two "Great Lights"—two of its recent centuries' great Chassidic leaders, the Alter Rebbe and the Baal-Shem-Tov, who, following the great Jewish tradition and wisdom, emphasized that the whole of creation is being continuously created and recreated by

G-d and that the purpose of human life and existence is to acknowledge the presence of G-d, glorify and thank Him, and lead a meaningful and purposeful life, including observing the "Seven Noah Commandments", moral observances, and studying the greatness of G-d, which will lead to a state of perfection (Geula) in the world. They also taught humanity that nothing is by chance; rather, it is all ordained and orchestrated by this singular higher G-d Reality whose sole aim is to uplift humanity, as individuals and as a group, toward this perfected state of existence (Geula) in which there will be complete harmony and peace in the world, a morally and physically perfected world pervaded by humanity's occupation with the unifying recognition and knowledge of this singular G-d Reality!

The most illustrious leader of this Jewish Chassidic Geula movement to perfect the world and to reach a state of moral, spiritual, and physical perfection focusing on G-d's Presence and existence in the world is the great Rabbi Menachem Mendel Schneerson (born in 1902), the Lubavitecher Rebbe, to whom this book is dedicated. May his beautiful and profound vision, as well as that of all other Jewish Fathers, Sages, and Leaders, be fulfilled now, and may this book constitute another chain in this inevitable fulfillment of G-d's' Geula of the world!

Jehonathan Bentovish (Bentwich),

ח"י אלול (תשע"ט), Zefat

INTRODUCTION

A Paradigmatic Shift in Twenty-First-Century Physics

Science has reached another pivotal point along its development. It is equivalent to the Paradigmatic Shift that occurred precisely one hundred years ago with the confirmation of Einstein's General Relativity Theory through the validation of Relativity's prediction regarding the perihelion of Mercury by the sun's curvature of its traveling pathway. This is because now, as then, there seems to arise a strong need for a basic Paradigmatic Shift from the Old Paradigm of Relativity Theory and Quantum Mechanics toward the discovery of a New Paradigm that would be able to resolve the apparent theoretical inconsistency that exists between <u>Relativity Theory</u> and <u>Quantum Mechanics,</u> and would also explain a series of phenomena that cannot be resolved by either of these systems.

Indeed, perhaps a good starting point for our journey toward the discovery of the Computational Unified Field Theory's New Paradigm for twenty-first-century physics is to review the state of theoretical physics at the turn of last century prior to Einstein's 1905 and 1915 "New" Paradigm, Relativity. At the turn of the twentieth century, there existed two primary pillars of modern physics: Newtonian Classical Mechanics and Maxwell's Electromagnetic Theory. However, these two pillars of nineteenth-century physics were not theoretically consistent, and in addition, there existed a fundamental problem revolving around the concept of the "ether," which was essential for both Newton's Classical Mechanics as well as for Maxwell's Theory, but yet could not be detected empirically. Multiple experiments attempted to detect this purely hypothetical ether, but all failed to experimentally verify its existence. Perhaps the most famous of these experimental attempts to detect the ether substance was the Michelson-Morley experiment, which could not detect the existence of the ether. Interestingly, numerous theoretical "excuses" were given for this principle empirical inability to detect this elusive ether substance, including far-fetched hypothetical explanations wherein the speed of the observer shortens or lengthens the actual measuring device proportionally to its velocity, which results in the supposed inability of the measuring apparatus to measure the expected differences in the light beam's velocity relative to the assumingly pervading ether substance. Indeed, this is where Einstein's genius thinking came into the picture: he could have simply asserted that, if the purely hypothetical ether substance could not be detected experimentally, then it should be discarded as superfluous or nonexistent! Instead, Einstein stipulated that a new Relativistic Paradigm had to be recognized based on a few simple theoretical postulates.

Thus, simply through Einstein's recognition of the essential need for a Paradigmatic Shift and his willingness to discard one of the primary assumptions of the old Newtonian/Maxwellian paradigms, he set modern twentieth-century physics on an entirely new pathway toward discovering, and ultimately validating, the General Theory of Relativity. It therefore seems that twenty-first-century theoretical physics finds itself in a state akin to that of twentieth-century physics prior to Einstein's Relativity Paradigmatic Shift: first, the two primary pillars of Relativity Theory and Quantum Mechanics seem contradictory to each other; for instance, the Relativistic Model assumes a strict cause-and-effect relationship between any given event and its transmission of a light signal that must pass through Space-Time to reach another corresponding (relativistic) observer. In contrast, in Quantum Mechanics, there exist instances such as the phenomenon of Quantum Entanglement, which seem to contradict such cause-and-effect physical relationships wherein the measurement of one of two "entangled particles" apparently affects instantaneously the complimentary measurement value of the other "entangled particle" without any time lapse given for the passage of the light signal in between these two "entangled particles"! Also, equivalently to the inability of nineteenth-century Newtonian/Maxwellian Models to detect the ether substance, accompanied by their inability to discard this purely hypothetical ether concept, it is suggested that, currently, the Old Paradigms of Relativity Theory and Quantum Mechanics find it very difficult to let go of the purely hypothetical concepts of "dark matter" and "dark energy" despite the inability to detect them empirically, even though there have been numerous attempts to do so.

To better understand the real underlying dynamics behind this apparent stubbornness of twenty-first-century physics to let go of twentieth-century physics' Old Paradigm of Relativity Theory and Quantum Mechanics, it is helpful to study what Thomas Kuhn, one of the famous philosophers of twentieth-century Science, had to say about the evolution of Science. Kuhn wrote a very influential book in 1962 titled *The Structure of Scientific Revolutions* in which he discovered that Science, as any human endeavor, alternates between phases of "Standard Science" in which a given scientific discipline agrees to research and advances the scientific knowledge based upon an agreed Scientific Paradigm, and phases in which this given Old Paradigm no longer suffices to explain or account for all known phenomena within that given discipline and therefore calls for a Paradigmatic Shift in the evolution of Science! Kuhn argued that, even though the Standard Science phase may be useful for advancing our scientific knowledge within a given scientific discipline at a particular given time, the usefulness of this Standard Science phase inevitably reaches its own limitations at a certain point in time. It is at this point in time, argued Kuhn, that the alternating phase of a Paradigmatic Shift is called for; indeed, the appearance of such a Paradigmatic Shift broadens the scope of our scientific understanding within a given discipline and enables Science to discover a more exhaustive theoretical understanding of the physical reality. Indeed, the interesting part of Kuhn's revolutionary analysis of the way in which Science evolves is that he discovered a basic human fallibility that has to do with scientists' own belief systems that greatly influence the way they operate. Put simply, Kuhn discovered that scientists, as do all ordinary human beings, possess a certain belief system that they hold dear. They find it difficult to let go of this belief because of the basic human tendency to hold on to the familiar and be somewhat reluctant to replace it with a new and unfamiliar way of looking at the world. Therefore, when Science reaches a pivotal turning point along its natural course of evolution that calls for a Paradigmatic Shift, Kuhn argues, scientists behave in much the same manner as all other human beings behave in the face of the unknown; that is, we'd rather cling to our old ways of thinking and believing than change our basic beliefs and assumptions about the world and our own lives.

Two simple historic life examples may be helpful to elucidate this basic human tendency to cling to the familiar and to resist change. The first is the known story relating to Columbus's attempt to find a shorter route to India for which he approached numerous potential financial patrons for funding for his adventurous planned journey. To his surprise, he found that most of his potential patrons refused to fund such an audacious journey due to their innate fear of the unknown. They were all convinced that, beyond the visible horizons, the world ended! They believed that Columbus and his three ships would simply fall off the edge of the world when they reached those horizons, and they would be swallowed by ferocious beasts! Once we realize that, during the time of Columbus, the common belief was that the world was flat, which implied that one could fall off it, along with the understanding of the basic innate human fear of the unknown, then we can understand why most of the affluent potential patrons in Columbus's time could not agree to fund his voyage, which nevertheless ultimately led to the discovery of North America. Interestingly, it was the *open-mindedness* of Queen Isabel of Spain that prompted her to fund his adventurous journey from her own private funds, and this made possible his historic journey.

What may we learn, then, from this intriguing historic example of human beings' innate tendency to avoid the unknown? Or, how, you may wonder, is this historic example relevant to our deeper understanding of Science's seemingly intrinsic difficulty to undertake a Paradigmatic Shift at a particular pivotal point along its evolutionary development?

Well, perhaps reverting to one of Einstein's famous quotes may be helpful here: "Sometimes I wonder how did it come to pass that I developed the Theory of Relativity; I think it is because most people wonder about 'space' and 'time' etc. when they're children and by the time they've become adults they've 'figured it out.' But, because my intellectual development was retarded I continued to think about these matters as an adult."

Yes, Einstein's utterly modest yet sincere answer reveals an important part of his secret for success. It was his innocent, childlike open-mindedness that enabled him to break through and venture further than any of his contemporary scientists. Indeed, this surprising childlike streak in his personality along with his unique way of thinking were already recognized by some of his biographers who noted that, where his contemporaries were hesitant and fearful to make the inevitable leap from the old Newtonian Classical Mechanics Paradigm toward the New Paradigm of the Relativity Theory due to their conservative nature and outlook, Einstein's rebellious nature made him inclined to move ahead and, indeed, pushed him to gladly challenge the acceptable norms; that is, the Standard Paradigm of Newtonian Mechanics.

So, what we can gather from this whole historical analysis of Queen Isabella's open-minded and courageous commitment to fund Columbus's adventurous journey, and, more specifically, from Einstein's rebellious, open-minded willingness to discard old belief systems and embrace new ways of looking at the world? We know that it takes both open-mindedness and courage to enable Science, and indeed Humanity as a whole, to evolve further in its expanding comprehensive understanding of the universe and the physical reality in which we live.

Getting back to our current, urgent need for a Paradigmatic Shift in twenty-first century theoretical physics and Science more generally, we see that Science has reached a dead end in its current theoretical understanding of physical reality. We cannot accept a situation in which the two major pillars of modern physics—Relativity Theory and Quantum Mechanics —seem to contradict each other!

Imagine a scenario in which an aircraft pilot hovering over Buckingham Palace sends us photographs of this entire royal mansion, including its marble stones, sculpted greenery, golden enhancements, and so forth. While, in another scenario, an observer walking along the front of the same palace sends us photographs that showed the mansion as a run-down hut! Indeed, this seemingly impossible scenario of two apparently contradictory perspectives of the same royal Buckingham Palace is quite equivalent to the seemingly impossible state of twenty-first-century physics in which our macroscopic picture of the physical universe depicted by the Relativity Theory seems strikingly contradictory to our microscopic portrayal of the physical reality provided by Quantum Mechanics. Simply put, Relativity declares that the physical universe is orderly, predictable, and elegant, governed by strict causal laws whereas Quantum Mechanics portrays a physical reality that is random and even chaotic. This, of course, seems to contradict the strict causal order described by the Relativity Theory.

No wonder the great Einstein said (in his famous quote): "G-d does not play with *dice*." Moreover, he was unwilling to accept Quantum Mechanics, of which he was the original father, as a complete theory. Indeed, Einstein was ceaselessly preoccupied with his unfailing quest to discover a unifying field theory that would bridge this seemingly impossible gap between the causal, predictable universe of Relativity Theory and the chaotic, unpredictable subatomic realm of Quantum Mechanics. It is, therefore, perhaps historic justice toward Einstein, who is considered one of the two greatest scientists the world has ever seen (the other being Isaac Newton), that the new twenty-first century's Scientific Paradigm that was shown capable of resolving this apparent contradiction between Relativity Theory and Quantum Mechanics is called the Computational Unified Field Theory. In fact, it is named after Einstein's admirable, almost prophetic quest for such a "Unified Field Theory" almost one hundred years ago!

To perhaps make this urgent need for a twenty-first-century theoretical physics for a basic Paradigmatic Shift clearer, imagine an "alien scientist" arriving to our dear planet Earth and sitting in on a scientific conference with the leading physicists of the world, who might be from MIT, Princeton, Oxford, and other highly respected places of learning and scientific progress. Imagine this alien scientist asking our leading theoretical physicists to simply explain or describe <u>Science</u>'s contemporary basic understanding of the way the universe is structured, or the laws by which it operates. Now, imagine this being's utter surprise and disbelief upon hearing a response from these top physicists of planet Earth; namely, that they really do not know where up to 95 percent of all the mass and energy in the universe exists!

Yes, at some point along their delineation of what modern physics actually *knows* about the universe, they would have to reveal the embarrassing truth that, according to the Relativity Theory, in order to account for the empirically observed accelerated expansion of the universe, there should have existed within the universe 95 percent more mass and energy than is currently observed and known to exist. In other words, our current General Relativity Model of the universe fails to account for up to 95 percent of all the mass and energy that is believed to exist in the universe. In scientific terms, the scientists would try to explain to the advanced alien scientist that the "missing" mass and energy that simply *cannot be observed* today are given the name of "dark matter" and "dark energy". But nonetheless, in the eyes of this alien scientist, this would still mean that <u>Science</u> simply cannot explain where 95 percent of all the mass and energy in the universe is!

It doesn't take an Einstein to figure out what would be the resulting expression on the face of this alien scientist. He would undoubtedly show utter surprise and disbelief! In polite terms, he would have to inform those leading theoretical physicists of the world that, if that was humanity's current scientific model of the universe, then our scientific model simply *doesn't work!* This is because, the alien scientist would simply explain, real <u>Science</u> is not interested in purely hypothetical postulates; that is, postulates that cannot be *proven experimentally* or at least given some credence based on valid empirical measurements.

Of course, this alien scientist would be right! In much the same manner that Einstein discarded the purely hypothetical ether concept because it could not be verified empirically, so do the purely hypothetical, at this point, "dark matter" and "dark energy" concepts have to be discarded as nonexistent. But if, indeed, <u>"dark matter"</u> and <u>"dark</u>

energy" are discarded, then our current model of <u>Relativity Theory</u> simply does not hold as valid for explaining the whereabouts of 95 percent of all matter and energy in the universe, and it may therefore be considered inadequate for explaining the universe. This is not to speak about the earlier-mentioned intrinsic problem of the principle apparent contradiction that exists between Relativity's deterministic, causal model and <u>Quantum Mechanics</u> ' probabilistic, non-causal model of the universe. So, the inevitable conclusion of the alien scientist, as well as our own conclusion, should be that the current Old Paradigm of twentieth-century <u>Relativity Theory</u> and <u>Quantum Mechanics</u> is simply inadequate to explain the universe, and we therefore must urgently look for a broader, more expansive New Paradigm that would resolve the principle apparent theoretical inconsistency between <u>Relativity Theory</u> and <u>Quantum Mechanics</u> as well as offer a reasonable new explanation for the accelerated expansion of the physical universe. Such a New Paradigm may shine a new light on a series of other related unexplained physical phenomena!

Perhaps one final word for this (long) introduction to our fascinating journey to uncover the New Computational Unified Field Theory's offer to <u>Science</u>; It offers Science an entirely new and awe-inspiring, higher-ordered perspective on the origination, sustenance, dissolution, and evolution of our entire physical universe, many billions of times per second! It may be helpful, once again, to ponder Einstein's modest yet profound remark regarding the desired fate for of his remarkable Relativity Theory—one hundred years onward in the distant future, which is *now!* Einstein was asked what he wished for the fate of his <u>Relativity Theory</u> in one hundred years, and whether he believed that it would hold valid after that time span. He modestly replied: "I do not believe that <u>Relativity Theory</u> would hold as the final truth in 100 years ... I only hope that it would be seen as a 'special-case' in a broader scientific understanding"!

In other words, the great Einstein gave us the "green light" to evolve in our Scientific understanding beyond the limitations of his <u>Relativity Theory</u> and also of <u>Quantum Mechanics</u> toward a broader more exhaustive conceptualization of the physical reality and the universe in which the <u>Relativity Theory</u> and <u>Quantum Mechanics</u> would appear as special cases.

So, let us now embark upon this fascinating, awe-inspiring journey to discovering the new Computational Unified Field Theory twenty-first-century New Paradigm of the universe, emboldened by Einstein's own blessing and characteristic rebellious open-mindedness to discard what is superfluous and advance courageously towards discovering the new, broader truth that <u>Science</u> and humanity are so eager to unveil.

CHAPTER 1

A Universe from Above?

In order to better understand what may be the nature of the necessary <u>Paradigmatic Shift </u>for twenty-first century's theoretical physics, let us first realize the gist of the Old Paradigm of twentieth-century Physics, which is rooted in both <u>Relativity Theory </u>and <u>Quantum Mechanics</u>.

Perhaps another metaphor may be helpful to elucidate the essential nature of twentieth-century physics, rooted in these systems. It is said that King Solomon, who is referred to as the "wisest of men", could explain any matter in up to three thousand metaphors simply because he could adjust his great wisdom to the specific level of his listener.

Imagine you're being asked to lift yourself up from the ground simply by pulling on your hair. Obviously, this is impossible! Archimedes is known to have said: "Give me a point outside of Earth—and I shall lift it up in the air."

A famous Jewish statement proclaims: "A prisoner cannot free himself from prison."

The key point to be noted from these scenarios and metaphors is that it is simply impossible to manipulate any object or person from within the system in which it exists; we cannot lift ourselves from the ground on which we're standing; neither can we lift the earth while we are standing on it! This simple truth sounds so indisputable that the intelligent reader would probably wonder why I bother to state this obvious truth.

Well, I'm stating these common-sense scenarios and metaphors simply because, in a nutshell, that is exactly what <u>Relativity Theory</u>

and <u>Quantum Mechanics</u> try to do—they ineffectively and impossibly attempt to "lift themselves by their hair"!

Really?

Yes, in both disciplines, there is an attempt to determine the dynamics of a physical system from within that system!

Take, for example, the Theory of Relativity theory. Einstein's equations that express its most generalized form attempt to determine the movement of planets, suns, stars, and other massive, or less massive, objects simply based on their interactions with each other, or with the more abstract concept of Space-Time, which, simply put, would be the "bending" of the "fabric" of space by massive objects.

One explanation of this delicate dance between massive objects and their curvature of the fabric of space and time uses a trampoline metaphor: Imagine a trampoline in the middle of which is placed a heavy mercury ball. This weight would obviously cause the trampoline's delicate membrane to distend and partially cover the heavy mercury ball. Now imagine that we toss a series of small marbles onto the trampoline's membrane. They would swirl down around the sunken mercury ball in the center region of the trampoline. They would seem to be gravitating toward that mercury ball, right? Well, this metaphor portrays roughly the curvature of space-time as caused by the presence of heavy objects (represented by the mercury ball in this scenario). Einstein's equations go further to explain that this very same curvature of space-time (the sunk-in structure of the trampoline's membrane caused by the presence of the mercury ball) also affects the movement of that mercury ball! So, according to Relativity Theory, there is a constant "dance" or interplay between the curvature of the trampoline membrane caused by the mercury ball and the movement pathways of that very same mercury ball (or of the other smaller marbles) based on the curvature of the trampoline membrane.

How does this trampoline metaphor help us to understand the basic problem with twentieth-century's physics paradigm—the one based on both the <u>Relativity Theory</u> and <u>Quantum Mechanics</u>? Simply put, the basic problem with twentieth-century physics in the case of the <u>Relativity Theory</u> is that it attempts to determine this delicate dance between certain massive objects, which are assumed to cause the curvature of space-time, and the effects of this curved space-time on the traveling pathways of those and other massive (or not-so-massive) objects from *within* the direct interactions between those massive objects and the fabric of Space-Time! To use the trampoline metaphor, this would be equivalent to a situation in which the trampoline membrane functions *by itself*; in other words, it places the heavy mercury ball at its center causing the membrane to form into the curvature around it, and also tosses the small marbles onto membrane. Also, it determines the traveling pathways of the marbles around the depression in the membrane caused by the mercury ball in its center!?

Obviously, when we hear the equivalence of the trampoline metaphor to Einstein's General Relativity equations, we find it absurd! We know that the trampoline cannot place the mercury ball on its membrane; neither can it toss the marbles onto the membrane. We know that a *person* has set up the trampoline, stretching the membrane between a series of metal springs. A person has also placed the ball and marbles onto the membrane. So it sounds almost absurd to say that the Relativity Theory would assume that this trampoline membrane would *itself* place the mercury ball at its center, or that It would *itself* toss the marbles onto its own surface!

How is this possible? (I'm sure you're asking!)

Well, the surprising answer is that, often in Science as well as in other human undertakings, we sometimes fail to observe the obvious! Einstein once remarked: "'Common-Sense' is only that which is 'common' [i.e., habitual] to the 'senses'"! In other words, this truly great scientist was warning us not to take for granted something that seems valid only because that's how we've been accustomed to seeing it. This ties, by the way, to his earlier quoted "self-reflection" regarding the particular reason that he developed Relativity, which was his rebellious lack of acceptance for "known" truths such as the nature of space, time, energy, and mass. Instead, he required his own independent inquiry and analysis of these basic constituents of the physical reality. So, it is suggested that the limitations of the twentieth-century Old Paradigm of Physics—embodied both in the Relativity Theory and Quantum Mechanics — is its failure to detect its own basic self-referential assumption; in other words, its intrinsic assumption that the curvature of Space-Time is caused by a direct physical interaction with massive objects. Indeed, such a material, causal assumption would be equivalent to the trampoline metaphor scenario in which the trampoline membrane is assumed to set its own surface, place the mercury ball at its center, and also determine the precise traveling pathways of the marbles upon its surface… Or it may be said that it is equivalent to the previous example of a man trying to pull himself up by his own hair or Archimedes's inability to lift the earth while still standing upon it.

Perhaps one final conceptual equivalence can be stated in this context from the realm of logic and mathematics. It comes from most likely the greatest mathematician and logician of the twentieth century, Kurt Gödel. Gödel discovered a fundamental intrinsic limitation for the whole of Logic and Mathematics, termed "Gödel's Incompleteness Theorem"; it basically states that, no matter how complex any mathematical or logical system may be, it would run into terrible problems if a self-referential "Liar Paradox" were inserted within it! A Liar Paradox is a sentence such as this one: "This sentence is a lie!"

If we look at this Liar Paradox—this sentence is a lie!—we can immediately see that it inevitably leads to an intrinsic contradiction because, if it is true, then its statement that it is a lie constitutes a contradiction, and if it is a lie, then its own statement that it is a lie implies that it is true, which, once again, constitutes a contradiction to its statement: it is a lie! Gödel's groundbreaking discovery was that, once you allow any mathematical or logical system to include such a self-referential Liar Paradox, then this inevitably leads to a breakdown of that system. So, this led logicians and mathematicians to create axiomatic logical-mathematical laws that prohibit the use of any such self-referential statements, thereby safeguarding any breakdown of any logic and mathematics. It is perhaps noteworthy to mention the fact that Gödel's ingenious proof demonstrated that, no matter how complex any hypothetical mathematical system might be, it cannot function if a self-referential negative statement (such as the Liar Paradox) is included within this system! The important take-home message from Gödel's seminal work in logic and mathematics is that we cannot determine the physical relationships within any physical system from within that system!

So, we come to the conclusion that one of the basic problems that exist with the Old twentieth-century "Material-Causal" Paradigm is its attempt to determine the physical relationships that exist between massive objects such as the sun, planets, galaxies, and so forth, and space-time *from within* their direct physical interaction. We saw that, based on the trampoline metaphor, this attempt to determine the physical relationships between massive objects and the fabric of Space-Time from within their direct physical interaction is problematic. And we received additional converging evidence from Gödel's incompleteness theorem, which also indicates that attempting to determine the given physical relationships that exist within a given physical system from within that system leads to serious problems and, so, should be strictly avoided. We therefore identified the old twentieth-century physics Paradigm and called it the Material-Causal Paradigm, which assumes that it is possible to determine the physical relationships in a given physical system from within it. We then reached the inevitable conclusion that this Material-Causal assumption leads to inevitable problems and must be replaced and broadened by a New Paradigm that is likely to include a new understanding that, *in order to determine any physical relationships that exists within a given physical system, it is necessary to compute the physical relationships from outside the system!*

This, then, is the computational "Duality Principle" or more generally termed the *"Universal Computational Principle"!*

Indeed, one of the key initial theoretical postulates that has led to the discovery of the computational unified field theory is the computational Duality Principle (subsequently generalized as the Universal Computational Principle), which essentially asserts that, in order to determine the physical relationships between any two entities or factors, it is necessary to have a higher-ordered computational system or principle that embeds these two factors within it. An analysis of both the Relativity Theory and Quantum Mechanics models from a higher-ordered new computational perspective has led to the conclusion that both possess a computational flaw: both models attempt to determine the physical relationships between multiple factors from *within* their direct physical relationship, and this, as we've already seen, inevitably leads to problematic situations, as shown by Gödel's incompleteness theorem, leading to a breakdown of the logical-mathematical system and is therefore prohibited.

In the case of the Relativity Theory, the Duality Principle indicates that it is not possible to determine the physical relationships between a given relativistic observer and a corresponding space-time, energy-mass phenomenon from within their direct physical relationship. This applies to both Relativity Theory's general attempt to determine the physical relationships between any such space-time, energy-mass phenomenon and a corresponding array of possible different relativistic observers, and more specifically, Einstein's General Relativity's equations' attempt to determine the curvature of space-time throughout the physical universe based on its direct physical interaction with massive objects, or conversely to determine the traveling pathways of such massive objects based on their direct physical interaction with curved Space-Time.

Therefore, the Computational Unified Field Theory postulated that there must exist a singular, higher-ordered Universal Computational Principle that simultaneously computes the physical relationships between any two or more pixels throughout the entire physical universe, and that is external to all these spatial pixels, which comprise the entire physical universe! Indeed, the discovery of this singular, higher-ordered Universal Computational Principle represents a radical shift from the old Material-Causal Paradigm of twentieth-century physics because it recognizes the fact that the entire physical universe doesn't exist independently or objectively, but is rather continuously dependent upon the constant computation, sustenance, and evolution by this singular higher-ordered Universal Computational Principle. This is because, in Relativity Theory, there exists a basic material-causal assumption that every possible relativistic space-time, energy-mass phenomenon exists objectively and continuously, but that it is only the relativistic measurements of each of these phenomena that may differ across different relativistic observers; for example, those that travel at different velocities relative to the given phenomenon.

Let's use a practical example to clarify this basic material-causal assumption of the Relativity Theory and also, as we'll see shortly, underlying Quantum Mechanics. Imagine that we are observing an explosion that is taking place within a coal mine tunnel. According to the Relativity Theory, the precise time this explosion took place would be measured differently by different relativistic observers traveling at different speeds, say a pilot in a fighter jet and a pedestrian on a highway, both of whom are traveling away from this explosion, but at different speeds. This is because, due to Relativity's assertion that the speed of the light beam emanating from this coal mine explosion and reaching each of these different relativistic observers who are traveling at different speeds is constant (in other words, the same for all observers), then necessarily the time it would take for the light beam to reach each of these observers would be different: it would take longer for the light beam to reach the rapidly progressing fighter jet pilot than it would take for it to reach the slowly progressing pedestrian. So, necessarily, the temporal measurement of the pedestrian would yield an earlier temporal value of when precisely this coal mine explosion took place relative to the temporal value of the fighter jet pilot. Hence, Relativity discovered that the time values of any given relativistic event differs according to the velocity of the particular given relativistic observer, so that the same event would be measured as occurring at different times for different relativistic observers. The same applies, according to Relativity Theory, to the three other basic physical features of space, mass, and energy of any given space-time or energy-mass phenomenon that has respective values that also differ for different relativistic observers. Note, however, that, regardless of the particular relativistic values of any given event, such as the coal mine explosion, Relativity Theory assumes that the *actual* coal mine explosion, as well as all its resulting phenomena (such as its emission of a light beam or other physical ricochets), represents a real constant phenomenon.

In contrast, the Computational Unified Field Theory's new paradigm advocates a new and different—broader, more exhaustive, and higher ordered—understanding of the physical universe wherein the physical reality exists only *transiently* and *phenomenally*; in other words, *is noncontinuous*. That is because, according to the Computational Unified Field Theory, the singular, higher-ordered Universal Computational Principle's simultaneous computation of all exhaustive spatial pixels in the universe occurs for each consecutive universal frame of the universe at the incredible—almost inconceivable—rate of $c^2/h = 1.36^{-50}$

per second! Simply put, this means that billions of billions of times per second, this singular, higher-ordered Universal Computational Principle produces (computes) the entire physical universe as one simultaneous, three-dimensional universal frame "picture," and that in between any two such consecutive universal frames, the entire physical universe "dissolves" back into this singular, higher-ordered Universal Computational Principle! So this means that the physical universe and all its various phenomena, including our coal mine explosion example, do not exist permanently or continuously, but only transiently during each consecutive universal frame, and they cease to exist in between any two such consecutive universal frames! Indeed, this new Computational Unified Field Theory's conception of the physical reality presents an entirely new physical universe that does not exist constantly or continuously, but only transiently and phenomenally, and which is continuously being created, then dissolved, then recreated and evolved by this singular higher-ordered Universal Computational Principle. In fact, due to this entirely new conception of the physical universe as existing only during each consecutive universal frame but not in between any two consecutive universal frames, the new Computational Unified Field Theory's paradigm reached the inevitable conclusion that the only thing that we may regard as "real" and "constant" is this singular, higher-ordered Universal Computational Principle, whereas the entire physical universe must be regarded as only a transient, phenomenal manifestation of the singularity of this Universal Computational Principle!

So, let us recap our new, twenty-first-century Physics Paradigm of the physical reality—The Computational Unified Field Theory. And let us see how it differs from the old Material-Causal Paradigm, which underlies both the Relativity Theory and Quantum Mechanics. The Material-Causal Paradigm assumed that the physical universe exists constantly and continuously, but our measurements of particular phenomena within it may vary between different relativistic observers, relative to their speed and other factors. In contrast, our new A-Causal Computation Paradigm of the Computational Unified Field Theory assumes that the entire physical universe does not exist constantly or continuously but, rather, is being continuously produced, dissolved, recomputed, and evolved by this singular higher-ordered Universal

Computational Principle many billions of times per second! In order to complete the Computational Unified Field Theory's new portrayal of the physical universe, let us review how this new A-Causal Computation Paradigm differs also from the Quantum Mechanics model, which is also based on the Material-Causal twentieth-century physics paradigm.

In a nutshell, Quantum Mechanics also assumes that the subatomic world exists continuously and permanently, but that only our measurements of particular subatomic target particles may differ according to the specific measurements of any target particle. Let's take a concrete example in order to better grasp the understanding of the Quantum Mechanics Material-Causal Paradigm of how the subatomic world exists and operates: Suppose we wish to measure the whereabouts of a particular subatomic target particle. We can do that by shooting another subatomic probe particle at this measured target particle. But Quantum Mechanics teaches us that, by doing this, we may alter the target particle's energetic value! So, imagine two go-carts in a children's playground arena—one green and one red. Imagine that we are interested in measuring the precise location of the green go-cart relative to gridlines painted on the floor of the arena. The important point we're trying to demonstrate is that, if our only way of determining the precise location of the green go-cart is to send the red go-cart out to hit the green target go-cart and then bounce back to the edge of the arena, then the more precise we wish this measurement to be, the faster the red go-cart must go. But it is clear from this simple go-cart example that the faster the measuring red go-cart's speed, then the harder it will hit the target green go-cart, knocking it off course, and proportionately the more we will impact (offset or change) the original speed of the green go-cart whose location we are trying to determine. In this way, Quantum Mechanics stipulates that each of our measurements of any given subatomic target produces complimentary measurement accuracy constraints in such a manner that, if we try to increase our measurement accuracy for the target particle's spatial location, we decrease proportionally our ability to measure its energy value, and vice versa. Or, if we wish to increase our measurement accuracy of the target's temporal value, we proportionately decrease that target's measurement accuracy of its mass value. So, we obtain one of a few odd features in Quantum Mechanics involving an interdependency of the target particle's spatial location and energetic measurement accuracy levels, as well as an interdependency of the target's mass and temporal values. Another oddity of Quantum Mechanics relates to its assumption that, prior to the measurement of the target particle by the probe particle, the target particle is assumed to be dispersed all along a probability wave function, which could be represented by our go-cart example: the green go-cart could be potentially occupying almost any part of the arena floor grid before our measurement of where it actually is, but once we actually carry out a subatomic measurement of where it is—by shooting the red go-cart (subatomic probe particle) at it—through their direct clash the entire hypothetical probability wave function (the potential of the target green go-cart to occupy any potential spot on the grid)—collapses (is negated) to a single complimentary space-energy or mass-time location.

When we look at all these oddities, along with some others which we'll encounter subsequently, it is no wonder that Einstein, who was the initial father of Quantum Mechanics and was later joined by other physicists, expressed on multiple occasions that Quantum Mechanics is *"incomplete"!* Yes, Einstein said that it is not that Quantum Mechanics is "wrong"; rather, it is "incomplete" and the prospective discovery of a satisfactory Unifying Field Theory, over which he labored for over thirty years, but still could not complete himself, would clarify and ultimately resolve the apparent oddities. He believed that Quantum Mechanics and the Relativity Theory would exist within the more extensive Unifying Field Theory; in fact, Quantum Mechanics and the Relativity Theory could be said to represent "special cases" within the integral more exhaustive Unifying Field Theory. Indeed, it is suggested that this is precisely what's being obtained through the discovery of the new Computational Unified Field Theory's A-Causal Computation Paradigm of twenty-first-century physics.

But, regardless of the specific oddities of Quantum Mechanics and their satisfactory resolution through the Computational Unified Field Theory's A-Causal Computation Paradigm, which will be presented later on, we've reached the point at which we can clearly discern the principle difference between the old twentieth-century physics' Material-Causal Paradigm of Relativity Theory and Quantum Mechanics and new the twenty-first century's Computational Unified Field Theory's A-Causal Computation Paradigm.

Simply put, in both Relativity Theory and Quantum Mechanics, any given physical phenomenon, as well as the existence of the entire physical universe, is based on the direct physical interactions between particular physical elements such as the direct physical interaction between a given relativistic observer moving at a specific speed, and a specific space-time, energy-mass phenomenon, or between a specifically chosen subatomic probe element and a corresponding subatomic target element. More generally, Relativity Theory describes the physical universe as existing and operating based on the direct physical interactions between a given Space-Time that is curved by particular massive objects, or conversely the determination of the traveling pathways of those massive objects by the curvature of Space-Time. Quantum Mechanics, on the other hand, describes the existence and operation of the physical universe as instigated by the direct physical interaction between all possible subatomic probe elements, which is assumed to cause the collapse of their corresponding subatomic target elements' probability wave function, that yields singular, complimentary space-energy or time-mass measured values of all potential subatomic target particles.

Hence, the physical reality and physical universe described by the old twentieth-century Material-Causal Paradigm stems from the direct physical interactions of curved Space-Time and massive objects in Relativity Theory, or from the direct interaction between a given set of selected subatomic probe elements and their corresponding set of collapsed subatomic target particles. In contrast, the new A-Causal Computation Paradigm of the Computational Unified Field Theory postulates that the existence of any hypothetical spatial pixels in the universe—as well as of the entire physical cosmos—is made possible only based on the operation of the singular higher-ordered Universal Computational Principle's simultaneous computation of each and every spatial pixel in the universe for each minimal time point giving rise to the extremely rapid series of Universal Frames constituting the entire physical universe. Hence, the physical universe exists, according to the A Causal Computation Paradigm, not as an objective physical reality that arises from any direct physical interactions between any given set of relativistic space-time and massive objects, or of selected subatomic probe elements and corresponding collapsed target particles, but rather as solely arising from the singular, higher-ordered Universal Computational Principle's extremely rapid computation of all spatial pixels comprising the entire physical universe for each consecutive universal frame. Consequently, the physical universe ceases to exist as a permanent objective reality, but is rather seen as a transient phenomenal manifestation of the singular constant reality of this higher-ordered Universal Computational Principle, or as we'll see later, as a singular Universal Consciousness Principle, which exists both during each consecutive universal frame as well as in between any two consecutive universal frames!

So, we see that our known physical universe undergoes a fundamental metamorphosis from existing as an objective, independent reality that arises from the direct physical interactions between Space-Time and massive objects or between subatomic probe elements and corresponding target particles toward a new realization that the entire physical universe and every spatial pixel constituting it exists only as a phenomenal transient manifestation of the singular, higher-ordered Universal Computational Principle, which produces, sustains, and dissolves (in between any two consecutive universal frames) and evolves every such spatial pixel comprising the existence, operation, and evolution of our entire physical universe billions times per second! The next necessary step in our new understanding of this new physical universe (from above!) is to investigate the real A Causal nature of this new physical universe.

CHAPTER 2

A New A-Causal Universe

The existence of causality is perhaps the most fundamental building block of our everyday lives as well as of the basic conception by <u>Science</u> of the way the universe functions. Our cars ignite in the morning when we must rush to our workplace because we turn the switch on. We become sick because a virus invades our system. We aim to improve our salary by applying for a better job. Science tells us that our universe was created by a "Big-Bang" nuclear event that accidently also created our burning sun and our own small, blue planet Earth. Science also tells us that our own human species was created through a particular cause-and-effect cascade of events wherein only those animals that were compatible with their environment managed to survive and give birth to offspring, which, together with certain chance mutations—accidental arbitrary changes in the genetic composition of these offspring—resulted in the selection of the fittest in terms of their compatibility to the environment.

In fact, we're so habituated and conditioned to this basic framework of thinking that it easy for us to believe that everything in this universe functions based on a material cause and effect, and it almost becomes impossible for us to conceive of any other a-causal kind of relationships.

How could anything function, in fact, if it is not caused by another factor?

Perhaps we need another helpful metaphor that can illustrate the possibility of such a-causal relationships. Imagine a cinematic film depicting a glass jar being broken by the impact of a hammer, which consequently leads to the spillage of the water that had been contained in the jar. Now, if I were to ask you what caused the breaking of the jar and the subsequent spillage of the water, your answer would certainly be that it was the impact of the hammer upon this glass jar, right?

But, you'd probably be surprised to discover that, if we were to closely analyze the series of cinematic film frames comprising this short film, we would find out that there doesn't exist any such cause-and-effect physical relationship between the impact of the hammer and the breaking of the glass jar or the subsequent water spillage.

Yes, because an analysis of each of the consecutive film frame comprising this film scenario would reveal that no one film frame or series of film frames shows any direct physical interaction between the hammer and the glass jar! This is simply due to the fact that, in each of the consecutive frames, all the comprising spatial pixels are presented simultaneously, thereby negating the very possibility of the existence of any physical interaction or cause-and-effect physical relationships between the hammer and the glass jar! Moreover, we realize that in between any two consecutive film frames, there exists only pure light from the projector so that there is no transference of any material entities or the possibility of the existence of any cause-and-effect physical relationships that can pass across frames.

So, you may wonder why what we see and perceive is a clear cause-and-effect physical relationship that seems to exist between the hammer impacting, the jar breaking, and the water spilling.

Perhaps it is appropriate to mention, once again, Einstein's remark that common sense is only that which is common to the senses, or his earlier quoted self-reflection relating to the deeper reason that enabled him to discover the theory of relativity: Einstein refused to look at things according to the conventions that he had been taught; rather, he continued to wonder about and investigate the nature of space, time, energy, and mass as a child might do because it is not necessarily the way things seem or the way we perceive things that determines their real or deepest truth. When we look at this imagined series of film frames and closely analyze their real nature, we realize that no single frame or series of frames shows any real physical interaction, much less so any cause-and-effect physical relationships between the hammer and the glass jar!

All that truly exist is the serial presentation of these consecutive film frames, which seem to present a growing spatial proximity of the location of the glass jar and the hammer until they're presented adjacent to each other, and subsequently there is a film frame in which the water is presented not within the glass jar, but rather outside it, spilled over the surface of the table together with a depiction of shattered glass pieces spread over the table. So, we reach the inevitable conclusion that, despite the apparent depiction of a clear cause-and-effect film scenario that seems to indicate that it was the impact of hammer upon the glass jar that caused it to break and the water to spill, in reality no such cause-and-effect physical relationships exists! Instead, what exists is a series of film frames that are sequenced in such a manner as to give the impression that the hammer impacted the glass jar. So it only *seems* that the hammer caused the breakage.

We use this cinematic film metaphor in order to demonstrate that what seems to constitute purely causal physical relationships is truly achieved by a higher-ordered a-causal arrangement of the series of film frames by the editor of the film. So, now that we're equipped with this metaphor's new higher-ordered a-causal account of what seems to constitute a material-causal physical reality, we revert back to the Computational Unified Field Theory's new model of the universe, which is also based upon such an a-causal fundamental new understanding: we already saw that this theory led to the existence of a singular, higher-ordered Universal Computational Principle that simultaneously computes (or produces) all the exhaustive spatial pixels in the universe through its production of an extremely rapid series of universal frames. This simultaneous production of all the spatial pixels in the universe at the incredible rate of billions of billions ($c^2/h = 1.36^{-50}$) of times per second produces what may be somewhat equivalent to a standard cinematic film, albeit with some significant differences. Therefore, we can use the film metaphor to begin to understand the basic a-causal nature of the Universal Computational Principle's production, dissolution, and evolution of the physical universe at the incredible rate of many billions of times per second.

Let's take, for example, two basic tenets of the old Material-Causal Paradigm of twentieth century's Relativity Theory and Quantum

Mechanics. According to General Relativity, the universe was created by an initial Big-Bang explosion that created all the planets, galaxies, mass, and energy in the physical universe. But, if we apply our new, higher-ordered understanding wherein, for each consecutive universal frame, all the spatial pixels comprising the entire physical universe are being recreated simultaneously out of the singular, higher-ordered Universal Computational Principle, and then are dissolved back into this singular Universal Computational Principle in between any two such consecutive universal frames, then we immediately realize that the basic Big Bang model of Relativity Theory cannot stand. This is simply because we see that in no single universal frame, or multiple universal frames, can there exist any such cause-and-effect physical relationship between an assumed initial Big Bang explosion and the production of planets, galaxies, energy, or mass! If we analyze, for instance, the initially assumed first universal frame or frames, we realize that all the spatial pixels comprising the entire universe (depicting the initial Big Bang explosion) were necessarily computed (or produced) simultaneously by the singular higher-ordered Universal Computational Principle. This means that, for the first universal frame (created by the singular Universal Computational Principle), there could not have existed any cause-and-effect relationship such as, for example, between the assumed initial Big Bang explosion and the creation of planets, galaxies, mass, or energy! The same principle negation of the existence of any cause-and-effect physical relationships between any two or more spatial pixels comprising the first Big-Bang universal frame obviously applies also for all consecutive universal frames. In fact, it applies for any past, present, or even future universal frames comprising the entire physical universe, which cannot tolerate or include any real cause-and-effect physical relationships!

A more accurate description of the physical universe would be to say that the universe was not created by an initial Big Bang explosion, but rather that it is being continuously created, dissolved, recreated, and evolved many billions of times per second by the singularity of the Universal Computational Principle. Indeed, let's take a closer look at the mechanics of how this singular, higher-ordered Universal Computational Principle computes (or creates) every spatial pixel comprising the entire physical universe at each consecutive universal frame many billions of times per second. Let's revert to our cinematic film metaphor in order to try to explain the manner in which this singular Universal Computational Principle computes the four basic physical features of space, energy, mass, and time for each spatial pixel in the universe for each consecutive extremely rapid universal frame.

Imagine seeing a film depicting a ferocious F-35 combat aircraft zooming through the sky. If I were to ask you if the aircraft exhibits any speed (or energy), you'd surely say that it exhibits a tremendous velocity, right? You may even go so far as to measure this mighty aircraft's tremendous speed across the screen, which could also be calculated relative to the considerable distance of the observed plane from the recording camera. Intriguingly, however, if I were to slow down the rolling of the film and ultimately halt it altogether and insist upon analyzing or even measuring the velocity or energy of the aircraft for each consecutive film frame, we'd find out that, in fact, no velocity or energy is depicted in any single frame.

Yes, to our utter astonishment, we'd find out that no speed or energy is depicted on any film frame. So, the F35 aircraft does not exhibit any speed or energy! How could that be?

Well, this is simply due to the fact that our *perception* of the F35's ferocious speed arises only from the plane's great displacement across the series of film frames! Despite the *appearance* of the aircraft's tremendous speed, in truth, its apparent velocity arises only from its displacement across the series of film frames. We therefore reach the inevitable conclusion that, within the Cinematic Film Metaphor, energy (or speed) is computed as the degree of displacement of any given object across a series of frames.

How is space (or spatial values) computed within the cinematic film scenario? Take, for instance, the spatial extension of your dining table. Within the Cinematic Film Metaphor, why does your dining table not shrink or expand from one film frame to another? It's obvious that the constancy of the film's dining table, in terms of its spatial extensions, is obtained based on its consistency across the various film frames. The fact that the dining table doesn't change its spatial dimensions in the film is due to the computation of the degree of consistency in terms of its number of constituting spatial pixels across the film frames. So, we find out that space—or an object's spatial measures—is computed based on an object's frame consistency across a series of consecutive film frames.

Interestingly, we find that, within the Cinematic Film Metaphor, there seems to exist an inverse and converse computational relationship between the computation of an object's energy and space measurements (or values) within a film setting. This is because we compute an object's energy, or speed, value based on its degree of displacement (inconsistency) across a given series of frames, whereas we compute that object's spatial extension or space value based on that object's frame consistency. So, surprisingly, we find that, within the Cinematic Film Metaphor, the spatial and energetic values of an object are inversely related. They are computed as the degree of consistency or inconsistency of an object's degree of displacement relative to the frame. In much the same manner, it can be shown that, within this Cinematic Film Metaphor, the computation of mass and time are also inversely related—computed as the degree of consistency or inconsistency of a given object in terms of its composition across a series of film frames. Imagine, for instance, seeing a movie depicting the historic Olympic Games in Berlin in 1936 depicting Jesse Owens's triumphant victory in the hundred-meter sprint. Now imagine that this film is being projected in slow motion: the progression of time appears to slow down. We immediately realize that the depiction of time within a film setting is simply calculated based on the degree of change in any given object's composition across frames. The greater the degree of change in any given object's composition across a given number of film frames, the more time has elapsed. Therefore, when our Jesse Owens Olympic Games film is projected in slow motion, time seems to slow down.

If we were to project a film depicting one of the greatest sages the Jewish people have known in recent times, the Lubavitcher Rebbe, seated without any change across a series of film frames, then time would stop still altogether within the film itself! Even though our perspective on time would still have time moving on, since our own wrist watches would still be ticking, our heartbeats would most likely be hastened by seeing this great Jewish Sage Leader (or seeing Jesse's historic triumph—not only physical but also moral).

These examples clearly show us that time is calculated in the film as the degree of change in an object's composition across a series of film frames. Conversely, we can create a film scenario wherein a given object is presented in a faint hue in any single film frame, but when it is being presented repeatedly across a large number of film frames, the boldness of that object would be increased! So this example also clearly demonstrates that the equivalent of an object's mass is computed as a function of the degree of an object's consistent presentations across a series of frames. Therefore, within this Cinematic Film Metaphor, we discover intriguing new computational relationships between the physical features of space and energy as computational measures of the degree of consistency (stability) or inconsistency (displacement) in any given object's presentation relative to the entire frame; and, likewise, we find that the computational measure of the degree of such consistency or inconsistency in any given object's composition across a series of film frames yields that object's apparent mass or time values.

Indeed, this Cinematic Film Metaphor proved quite helpful in explaining at least some of the attributes and intriguing new discoveries made by the Computational Unified Field Theory. According to the Computational Unified Field Theory's new A-Causal Computation Paradigm of twenty-first century theoretical physics, the singular, higher-ordered Universal Computational Principle simultaneously computes for each spatial pixel comprising the entire physical universe at every minimal time point universal frame its four respective physical features of space, energy, mass, and time. And it does so by similarly computing the degree of consistency (stability) or inconsistency (displacement or change) of any given object, either relative to the entire frame, which gives rise to the computational measures of space and energy respectively, or relative to the actual composition of the object, which produces the computational measures of mass and time.

So, when we perceive or even measure the velocity of the F35 aircraft, in truth, it merely represents the Universal Computational Principle's computation of that F35 aircraft's displacement across a series of universal frames.

Or, when we hold in our hands a heavy mercury ball, its great mass arises as a result of the Universal Computational Principle's computation of the number of times the ball is being presented consistently across a series of universal frames, say, as opposed to the number of consistent presentations of a feather across the same number of universal frames.

Yes, as surprising as it may sound, one of the special predictions of this new A-Causal Computation Paradigm is that, if we were to measure and compare, side by side, the number of universal frames across which our mercury ball (or iron atom) appears relative to the number of equivalent universal frames across which the feather (or, say, a light hydrogen atom) would appear in, we would be stunned to find out that the mercury ball (or iron atom) would appear across a much greater number of universal frames than the feather (or hydrogen atom).

You are probably shouting, "How could this be?"

Well, the simple answer is that it's all happening all so quickly. The singular, higher-ordered Universal Computational Principle computes and produces an extremely rapid series of Universal Frames at such an incredible rate (many billions of times per second) that our ordinary senses cannot fathom that some objects, or indeed atoms, do not appear in all the frames (such as our imaginary feather or lighter hydrogen atom) while others do (such as the mercury ball or iron atom).

By the way, a similar scientific leap occurred a hundred years ago with the Paradigmatic Shift from Newton's Classical Mechanics to the (then "new") Relativity Theory Paradigm of 20th Century Theoretical Physics, which was also associated with a need for much more advanced technological measurements. It was found that Newtonian (Classical Mechanics) was accurate for standard physical measurements of objects traveling at standard speeds, but once objects begin traveling at much greater velocities, approaching the speed of light, Newtonian Mechanics was found to be inadequate to describe the behavior of the physical reality. So, it was only with the technological advancement of Science (and Physics particularly) that it was discovered that computations made using Newtonian Classical Mechanics can be seen as approximations, "special cases" pertaining to nonrelativistic speeds within the broader theoretical framework of the Relativity Theory. Indeed, the full empirical validation of some of the surprising new discoveries of Relativity Theory could be validated only empirically with the advent of more advanced technological capabilities for measuring the behavior of relativistic moving objects. Similarly, it is suggested that, for an empirical validation of the current "G-d's Physics" Paradigmatic Shift of the twenty-first-century Theoretical Physics brought about by the Computational Unified Field Theory, it is necessary to use the more advanced subatomic accelerator technology capable of measuring extremely rapid temporal measurements. Thus, for example, measuring one of the special predictions of the New G-d's Physics Paradigm (Computational Unified Field Theory) regarding the appearance of relatively more massive iron atoms across a greater number of Universal Frames than lighter hydrogen atoms is something that could be possibly detected in one of the advanced subatomic accelerators but could not have been detected a hundred years ago technologically.

Thank G-d, initial empirical validation for the A-Causal Computation Paradigm was already supplied through the accidental discovery of what's known as the "Proton Radius Puzzle" phenomenon. This refers to the measurement of the radius of the nucleus of a hydrogen atom in two different situations. In the standard hydrogen atom, the nucleus is comprised of one (positively charged) proton, one (negatively charged) electron, and one (neutrally charged) neutron. In the modified hydrogen atom, the negatively charged electron is replaced with another negatively charged particle called a muon, which is approximately a hundred times heavier than the electron. Surprisingly, the proton radius puzzle phenomenon relates to the fact that, when we measure the radius of the nucleus of the standard hydrogen atom and compare it to the radius of the modified hydrogen atom, we are surprised to find that the diameter of the modified hydrogen nucleus (to which the muon sinks) is approximately one hundred times smaller than the diameter of the nucleus of the standard hydrogen atom (surrounded by the electron). This is known as the "Proton Radius Puzzle" since this dramatic decrease in the diameter of the muon nucleus relative to the diameter of a standard nucleus cannot be accounted for by either Relativity Theory or Quantum Mechanics.

However, intriguingly, this precise empirical finding was previously predicted as one of the critical predictions of the Computational Unified Field Theory! You see, as we mentioned earlier, when Science reaches such pivotal turning points along its evolutionary development—a need for a basic <u>Paradigmatic Shift</u>—one of the key methods through which the shift may be affected is based on the empirical validation of a certain critical prediction/s of the new paradigm, which opposes corresponding predictions of the old paradigm. Indeed, this happened precisely a hundred years ago with the empirical confirmation of Einstein's bold critical prediction regarding the much greater perihelion curvature of Mercury's pathway then as predicted by Newtonian classical mechanics (the old paradigm) due to the sun affecting the curvature of Space-Time, which was predicted to affect Mercury's perihelion pathway around the sun. Once Einstein's Relativity Theory's unique critical prediction was validated empirically (through Eddington's famous 1919 Solar Eclipse expedition), <u>Science</u> accepted Einstein's new <u>Relativity Theory</u> Paradigm practically overnight! It is suggested that precisely the same revolution is taking place currently in twenty-first-century Theoretical Physics, precisely one hundred years after the last Paradigmatic Shift brought about by Einstein's Relativity Theory!

Yes, based on the Computational Unified Field Theory's new A Causal Computation Paradigm's unique specific prediction regarding its new computational definition of "mass" as the singular, higher-ordered Universal Computational Principle's computation of any given object's consistent presentations across a series of universal frames, the <u>Computational Unified Field Theory</u>'s unique critical prediction predicted that relatively more massive particles (such as muons) would be measured as more "spatially consistent" than less-massive particles (such as electrons), which precisely conforms to those observed Proton Radius Puzzle's empirical findings. So, in effect, these Proton Radius Puzzle findings confirm unequivocally the <u>Computational Unified Field Theory</u> new paradigm's critical prediction as more valid than the corresponding predictions of either <u>Relativity Theory</u> or <u>Quantum Mechanics</u>, thereby crowning the <u>Computational Unified Field Theory</u> as the appropriate New Paradigm for twenty-first-century Physics!

Of course, there exist a select few other unique critical predictions that are specific to the <u>Computational Unified Field Theory</u>'s New Paradigm that differ from the old Material-Causal Paradigm of <u>Relativity Theory</u> and <u>Quantum Mechanics</u>. These include the possibility to "reverse time" as well as the appearance of relatively more massive particles (such as the muon particle) across a much greater number of universal frames' fine temporal measurements relative to the number of universal frames across which a lighter (electron) would be detected, as well as the disappearance of all measured subatomic particles between any two consecutive universal frames! Indeed, some of these intriguing, and even provocative, unique critical predictions will be discussed in subsequent chapters, including some of their potentially far-reaching theoretical implications. But the fact of the matter is that, based on this initial Proton Radius Puzzle phenomenon's empirical validation of one of the unique critical predictions of the Computational Unified Field Theory, twenty-first-century Theoretical Physics is embracing its new A-Causal Computation Paradigm as more valid and more exhaustive than the old Material-Causal Paradigm of both Relativity Theory and Quantum Mechanics.

Another exciting measurement of one of the Computational Unified Field Theory's time-sensitive critical predictions is taking place as this book goes into print for the first time. The Jewish New Year, Rosh Hashanah, is a time interval wherein, according to the Computational Unified Field Theory's unique "Collective Human Consciousness Focus Hypothesis theoretical postulate, it is possible for a concerted focus of millions of Jews around the world to affect the singular, higher-ordered Universal Consciousness Principle in terms of its non-continuous expansion of the universe.

So, what's the gist of this new emerging A-Causal Computation picture of the physical universe that is brought about by the Computational Unified Field Theory model?

First of all, we see that there cannot exist any real cause-and-effect physical relationships in the universe, whether on the big scale of Relativity Theory or the smaller scale of Quantum Mechanics. This is simply because, as we've seen, the discovery of the singular, higher-ordered Universal Computational Principle's *simultaneous* computation of every spatial pixel in the universe (for each consecutive universal frame) does not allow for any physical relationships to exist, including any cause-and-effect relationships at any single universal frame or multiple universal frames. Even more so, we realize that, since the entire physical universe dissolves in between any two consecutive universal frames, there cannot be any physical effects passing from one universal frame to another. This means that Physics' old Material-Causal Paradigm's conception of the physical universe as created by an initial Big Bang explosion or as evolving based on the direct physical interaction of purely hypothetical "dark matter" or "dark energy" with galaxies, planets, and other heavenly entities cannot hold any longer. It also means that General Relativity's famous Einstein Equations that describe the evolution of the physical universe based on the direct physical interactions of massive objects' curvature of space-time and conversely postulates that such curved Space-Time dictates the traveling pathways of such massive objects is strictly negated. Instead, what we're left with is an entirely new picture of the physical universe as being continuously created (computed) simultaneously for each exhaustive spatial pixel comprising the entire physical cosmos many billions of times per second by the singular, higher-ordered Universal Computational Principle, based on its computation of the four basic physical features of space, energy, time, and mass for each consecutive universal frame.

Finally, as odd as it may sound to our Material-Causal-habituated minds, our entire physical universe and all the apparently physical objects which we're so dearly attached to *do not exist continuously or independently of this singular higher-ordered Universal Computational Principle's operation.* Yes, based one of the fascinating additional theoretical postulates of this new Computational Unified Field Theory's A Causal Computation Paradigm, termed the "Computational Invariance Principle", we realize that only the singular, higher-ordered Universal Computational Principle may be considered as "real" and "permanent", whereas the reality of the entire physical cosmos as comprised by these four basic, apparently physical features of space, energy, mass, and time may only be deemed "phenomenal" and "transient", since they only exist during each consecutive universal frame, which is solely produced by this singular, higher-ordered Universal Computational Principle, but cease to exist (in other words, dissolve) in between any two consecutive universal frames. Whereas this singular, higher-ordered Universal Computational Principle exists constantly and unchanged both during its sole computation of the entire physical universe for each consecutive universal frame (including its simultaneous computation of each spatial pixel comprising this physical universe), as well as exists solely without the presence of any physical universe in between any two consecutive universal frames. Therefore, the Computational Invariance Principle postulates that only this singular higher-ordered Universal Computational Principle may be regarded as "permanent" and "real", whereas the whole physical universe, comprised of those four basic physical features of space, energy, mass, and time, may only be regarded as "transient" and "phenomenal", and as merely representing a manifestation of this singular Universal Computational Principle (reality).

It is therefore perhaps fitting to complete this chapter by relating this amazing new discovery of the singular existence of this Universal Computational Principle to some of the older findings of some of the Jewish sages (*tzadikim*) and prophets who also discovered and propounded the existence of a singular, higher G-d reality beginning from the Jewish Nation's father, Abraham, who lived 3831 years ago and who discovered the existence of the singular, higher G-d; through the "Great Eagle" of Jewish thought and wisdom, the great Maimonides, a medieval Jewish philosopher, who declared that the "foundation of all foundations and the pillar of all pillars" of wisdom is to know that there exists a primary, singular G-d Reality and that this primal G-d Reality creates all that exists. And all that exists does exist only based on its true existence...

This famous idea was given to us by one of Judaism's greatest seers and sages, Maimonides, in his introduction to the *Mishne Torah Hilchot Yesodei Hatorah*, which was written 842 years ago! In fact, this amazing discovery regarding the sole existence of a singular, higher-ordered G-d Reality was propounded some 1800 years ago by the foremost of Jewish Kabbalah and author of *The Book of Zohar*, Rabbi Shimon Bar Yochai ("Rashbi"), and later on further expounded upon and developed by the Holi Ari, Rabbi Yiztchak Luria ben Shlomo Ashkenazi, 1437 years ago, which led to the further expounding and development of this singular higher Truth by the two "Great Lights", the two great Jewish Sages, the sacred Baal Shem-Tov who lived before 319 years and who discovered the incessant creation and recreation of the world by this singular higher

Jehonathan Bentovish (Bentwich), Ph.D.

G-d existence (quoted by the Leubavitch Library in the *Keter Shem Tov*, Part B, תא-ב), and then further delineated by the great Alter Rebbe, Rabbi Schneur Zalman (who lived 207 years ago) who wrote the famous sacred *Tanyah*, which specifically mentions this constant enlivening of the world and all its constituting creatures (chapters מא and מו). Remarkably, this book is being published at the Jewish date of their birth (תשעט חי אלול) precisely at the Jewish date of the birth of these two great lights. Indeed, the Alter Rebbe's sacred *Tanyah* became the cornerstone for the Chassidic Chabad Jewish World Movement, and through the series of Lubavitcher Rebbe's leading to the great Rebbe Yossef Yitzchak Schneersohn, the Rayatz, and the following sacred Lubavitcher Rebbe, Rabbi Menachem Mendel Schneerson, leading the whole Jewish Nation who all expressed the same singular, higher-ordered existence of G-d's Reality that continuously produces, dissolves, and reproduces the entire physical universe, and called for the immediate fulfillment of G-d's "Geula" (redemption) in תשא Jewish year. These great Jewish leaders continuously express their true knowledge that the Jewish Torah must be found to coincide with the latest discoveries of Science and that it is paramount that the whole wide world acknowledge this singular higher truth, and accordingly live a perfected moral and spiritual life, leading to G-d's "Geula" (redemption) of the world!

May it be the case that what's been discovered, investigated, and studied for over two thousand years by the Jewish sages, prophets, and seers is now being rediscovered through Science's most advanced technological probing of the physical universe, both at the microscopic subatomic level of the minutest particles, as well as at the largest macroscopic scale indicating the accelerated expansion of the physical universe.

CHAPTER 3

The New Twenty-First Century's G-∂'s Physics

We stand, it seems, at the brink of a completely new era in <u>Science</u>'s development where the apparently strict boundaries that exist between <u>Science</u> and Religion, and even Philosophy, are being completely dissolved. This is because, as we've already seen, instead of the twentieth-century Material-Causal Physics Paradigm, which assumed that the universe exists as a material entity created by an initial Big Bang explosion and evolving based on the direct physical interactions between massive objects, which are assumed to cause the curvature of space-time, which, in turn, determines the traveling pathways of these massive objects, the new twenty-first-century Theoretical Physics A-Causal Computation Paradigm completely alters our basic conceptions of the origin and sustenance of the universe and also its continuous dissolution (in between any two consecutive universal frames) and reproduction, all by the singular, higher-ordered Universal Computational Principle, many billions of times per second!

In fact, toward the end of the previous chapter, we reached another "shocking" new realization stemming from the Computational Unified Field Theory's new A Causal Computation Paradigm. This is based on the Computational Invariance Principle theoretical postulate: accordingly, only the singular, higher-ordered Universal Computational Principle exists "invariantly" (that is, constantly) both during its sole simultaneous computation of each spatial pixel for each consecutive universal frame, and also solely exists in between any two such consecutive universal frames, without the presence of any physical universe that dissolves back into this singular Universal Computational Principle in between any two consecutive universal frames! Whereas the whole physical universe exists only during each consecutive universal frame, but dissolves in between any two consecutive universal frames…. Therefore, only the singularity of this Universal Computational Principle may be regarded as constant and independent whereas the whole physical universe is seen as representing only a "transient" and "phenomenal" manifestation of this singular Universal Computational Principle.

In fact, further development of this intriguing Universal Computational Principle theoretical postulate has led to the discovery of a closely related additional Universal Consciousness Principle postulate which reveals that, in truth, since this singular, higher-ordered Universal Computational Principle is shown to possess all the characteristic features of a universal consciousness, this singular Universal Computational Principle is really a Universal Consciousness Principle.

Let us first explain how the Universal Computational Principle possess all the characteristics of a Universal Consciousness; we will then advance further toward a more refined Universal Consciousness Principle postulate of the Computational Unified Field Theory, which will completely revise our basic conception of the physical universe as a material entity. But, perhaps, in order to better understand the equivalence of the Universal Computational Principle with a novel Universal Consciousness Principle, let's revisit our Cinematic Film Metaphor. Imagine watching the adventure scene in which James Bond 007 escapes down a curvy canyon road in his legendary silver Aston Martin sports car. I'd hate to spoil your enjoyment of Bond's phenomenal ability to escape almost any tense danger and then brush it off with a winning smile or a chauvinistic gesture, but imagine for a moment that you slow down this lively film progression so much that you begin to notice that, in between any two consecutive film frames, there appears a pure white light. Now, let's compare this cinematic film to our Computational Unified Filed theory's model. Take, for example, the fact that, in between any two consecutive film frames there only exists the pure beam of light from the projector. This implies that, within the Cinematic Film Metaphor, there cannot pass any material object or pixel of even any physical effect between one film frame and its consecutive frame. When we examine the equivalence of this fact as it applies to the Computational Unified Field Theory, we notice that there is a slight difference between the two: the consecutive film frames continue to exist even when they're not being actively presented (they're stored on a length of celluloid film, for example) but this is not the case with the Computational Unified Field Theory.

Yes, since in the case of the Computational Unified Field Theory, the Universal Computational Principle is postulated to compute each spatial pixel comprising the entire physical universe during each consecutive universal frame, but dissolves all these spatial pixels in between any two consecutive universal frames, there is no real physical existence or continuity to any of the spatial pixels in between any two consecutive universal frames. Instead, we realize that the only possible existence or, indeed, continuity of any single or multiple spatial pixels or objects comprising our entire physical universe is solely based on a consciousness-like quality of the singular, higher-ordered Universal Computational Principle. This is because the only manner in which any such physical traits or features of any exhaustive spatial pixel can pass or even continue to exist from one film frame to a consecutive film frame is based only on the singular, higher-ordered Universal Computational Principle's memory or retention of each of the universe's spatial pixels characteristics, and that in fact this singular higher-ordered Universal Consciousness Principle also evolves each of these exhaustive spatial pixels in the universe from one universal frame to its consecutive frame!

Think about the consecutive presentation of, say, a baby across a series of universal frames. We know that the baby's cells are dividing and its organs are growing and evolving, but this can take place only based on the singular, higher-ordered Universal Computational Principle's memory, retention, dissolution, and reproduction, and evolution of each of the baby's sets of bodily pixels across a series of universal frames. So, we reach the inevitable conclusion that this singular, higher-ordered Universal Computational Principle must necessarily possess Universal Consciousness computational properties!

Jehonathan Bentovish (Bentwich), Ph.D.

Yes, the entire physical universe and every spatial pixel found within it can exist only based on the continuous computation, dissolution, recomputation, and evolution by this singular, higher-ordered Universal Consciousness Principle, not as any objective or independent physical reality. Think, for instance, of one object that you like. For this example, we'll say it's your car. Ordinarily, you believe that your car exists objectively or independently. You bought it with your hard-earned money, and it's yours. And it will continue to exist as long as you don't sell it or (G-d forbid) something happens to it, right? But when we take into account the astonishing new findings of the new A-Causal Computation Paradigm of twenty-first-century theoretical physics, our whole conception and understanding of the physical reality—and your precious car—changes dramatically! Your car cannot pass from one universal frame to its consecutive one because it simply dissolves back into the singularity of the Universal Consciousness Principle many billions of times per second. ($c^2/h=1.36^{-50}$ per second!)

It is, no doubt, quite an astonishing revelation that the existence of the entire physical universe and every constituting spatial pixel within it is made possible only from one universal frame to another solely by the consciousness power of the singular, higher-ordered Universal Consciousness Principle. This is simply because all the spatial pixels comprising the entire physical cosmos dissolve back into this singular Universal Consciousness Principle in between any two consecutive universal frames; and the only means through which each of these spatial pixels continue to exist from one universal frame to its consecutive frame is solely due to the memory, retention, and evolution of each of the specific spatial pixels by the Universal Consciousness Principle. Indeed, when we probe deeper into this new and fascinating understanding and appreciation of the intricacy of the physical universe—not existing as an objective independent physical reality, but rather as entirely dependent upon the continuous memory, retention, dissolution, recreation, and evolution of each exhaustive spatial pixel constituting the entire physical cosmos many billions of times per second by the singular higher-ordered Universal Consciousness Principle—we come into a profound feeling of awe and even reverence towards this Universal Consciousness Principle!

Indeed, this new profound revelation coincides with teachings of two of Judaism's great sages and religious giants over the past few centuries, the Baal-Shem Tov, Rabbi Israel ben Eliezer, and the Alter Rebbe, Rabbi Schneur Zalman. Both of these tremendous Jewish seers discovered and taught that physical reality—everything in the universe—is being continuously created, dissolved, and recreated by G-d, and that if it were not for this continuous act and will of G-d, the whole universe would dissolve back into nothingness. Interestingly, these two sages saw that the entire physical reality is being enlivened every second by G-d's divine power and intelligence. It is indeed quite baffling that this Jewish Kabbalistic conception of the physical universe is so similar to the A-Causal Computation Paradigm of twenty-first-century Theoretical Physics. The reason that I mention the Alter Rebbi is that he states that one way to reach a sense of love and reverence for G-d is to look at His infinite wisdom. Interestingly, when I stumbled across knowledge of the infinite intelligence overseeing, computing, dissolving, recreating, and evolving every spatial pixel throughout the physical universe, I felt precisely such profound and deep feelings of awe, reverence, and love for this singular higher G-dly presence. We'll see that, according to the A Causal Computation Paradigm, as well as according to the Baal Shem Tov and the Alter Rebbi, there is no chance in the universe but rather personal providence, which is complete personal care and guidance to each human overseen and acted upon by G-d.

Perhaps in order to share with interested readers a sense of this profound personal experience that I have discovered, I'll repeat the example that I use in large conferences in which I am asked to present this <u>Computational Unified Field Theory</u>'s new A Causal Computation Paradigm. I ask the audience members to close their eyes and imagine their Torah (Bible) room where they sit and study. I ask them to imagine and focus their minds on all the books in this room and try to list all the titles of the books. Obviously, people find this task almost impossible. Then I go one further step and ask them to imagine all the letters in all these books. That's clearly impossible for any ordinary human being!

Now, I revert this example to the capacity of the singular, higher-ordered G-d's Universal Consciousness Principle reality. I explain that, according to the A Causal Computation Paradigm, this singular, higher-ordered G-d's Universal Consciousness Principle reality must remember, retain, dissolve, recreate, and even evolve every spatial pixel throughout the entire physical cosmos many billions of times per second! Indeed, this new conception of the singular, higher-ordered Universal Consciousness Principle—G-d—is utterly inconceivable for our limited intelligence and understanding so it inevitably leads us to a complete new sense of awe, reverence, and even love toward this singular, higher-ordered Universal Consciousness Principle, just as the great Alter Rebbi wrote in his famous and sacred *Tanya*.

Indeed, to complete the profoundness of the discovery of this new singular, higher-ordered G-d Universal Consciousness Principle as far as the A-Causal Computation Paradigm goes, let me mention one further theoretical postulate of the Computational Unified Field Theory, which I mentioned earlier. It is termed the Universal Consciousness Principle. According to this new theoretical postulate, the only principle that exists constantly both during the production of the extremely rapid series of universal frames, and every spatial pixel comprising the entire universe depicted by them, as well as solely existing in between any two consecutive universal frames, is this singular, higher-ordered Universal Consciousness Principle. Yes, the entire physical universe and every spatial pixel comprising it exists only during each consecutive universal frame as computed for the four basic physical features of space, time, energy, and mass solely by the singular Universal Consciousness Principle, but not in between any two universal frames! Therefore, this new Universal Consciousness Principle postulate deduces that there exists only one constant and continuous Universal Consciousness Principle—G-d—which constitutes the sole reality of the world and, as we'll see, also beyond it! In other words, the entire physical universe is seen as existing only as a manifestation of the singular, higher-ordered Universal Consciousness Principle, which exists invariantly (constantly and continuously) rather than independently (or objectively) by itself. Once again, this is because it is realized that its existence is only transient and phenomenal; it exists only during each consecutive universal frame as being produced by this singular Universal Consciousness Principle but ceases to exist in between any two consecutive universal frames wherein only the singular, higher-ordered <u>Universal Consciousness Principle</u> continues to exist…

Perhaps another small, everyday metaphor may be useful here. When I was driving from Jerusalem to Zichron-Yaakov in Israel, one day, early, just before dawn, I found myself behind a large semi-tractor-trailer truck covered in glaring white canvas. Since it was still dark outside, I could see the canvas cloth cover only every time the truck passed below one of the many streetlights spaced along the freeway. But, when it was between the streetlights, it would disappear from my view. At that moment, it struck me that, while the truck exists all the time and did not change, for me, as the observer, it existed only when it was lit up by the streetlights. Upon further reflection, I realized that this could serve as an everyday metaphor for the A Causal Computation Paradigm's <u>Universal Consciousness Principle </u>because, just as the truck appeared to me to exist only when it passed beneath a streetlight, so our entire physical universe appears to exist only during each consecutive universal frame, and it seems to disappear in between any two consecutive universal frames. But, just as we realize that the truck continued to exist in between the streetlights, even though I could not see it, so we realized that the singular, higher-ordered <u>Universal Consciousness Principle</u> exists continuously both during its sole production of each consecutive universal frame as well as in between any two such frames (without the presence of any physical universe)! So, in fact, the singular <u>Universal Consciousness Principle</u> constitutes the only real reality, which manifests as the physical universe during the universal frames, but also continues to exist without the physical universe in between each two consecutive universal frames…

What is significant regarding this new scientific discovery of the singularity of the <u>Universal Consciousness Principle</u> is the fact that this <u>Universal Consciousness Principle</u>—G-d—can exist without the presence of the physical universe as well as manifesting as the physical universe during its production of each consecutive universal frame. This new finding is significant since it begins to portray the physical universe as being entirely dependent upon and solely produced by the singular, higher-ordered <u>Universal Consciousness Principle</u>—G-d—whereas it is not dependent upon the existence of the universe. Therefore, the

Jehonathan Bentovish (Bentwich), Ph.D.

A-Causal Computation Paradigm scientific understanding shifts the focus of twenty-first-century physics from the old Material-Causal Paradigm of Relativity Theory and Quantum Mechanics towards a new G-d's Physics—the investigation and delineation of the higher-ordered attributes and operations of the singular Universal Consciousness Principle which creates, dissolves, reproduces, and evolves every spatial pixel in the physical universe many billions of times per second!

Indeed, perhaps a good starting point for discovering and gaining a better understanding of the mechanics of this singular, higher-ordered Universal Consciousness Principle's simultaneous production, dissolution, reproduction, and evolution of every spatial pixel in the universe is to revert back to its computation of the four basic physical features of space, time, energy, and mass for each consecutive universal frame. Earlier, we used a Cinematic Film Metaphor to illustrate this singular higher-ordered Universal Consciousness Principle's computation of each of the four basic physical features. We came to the conclusion that the singular, higher-ordered Universal Consciousness Principle simultaneously computes the physical features of energy and space as a computational measure of the degree of displacement (inconsistency) or lack of displacement (consistency) of any given object across a series of universal frames, and conversely, that this Universal Consciousness Principle computes the physical features of the time and mass values of any given object based on its computation of the degree of inconsistency (number of times a given object is presented inconsistently across a certain number of universal frames) or consistency (the number of times that object is presented consistently across that number of universal frames). Indeed, when this is illustrated through the Cinematic Film Metaphor, we can make sense of the fact that the speed (or energy) of an F35 aircraft can be computed based on the degree of its displacement from one frame to another, and that by contrast, its wing's length must remain consistent in terms of the number of spatial pixels comprising it across a given series of film frames. Or likewise, that we could create a special film scenario in which the darkness (hue) of a given object would be based on the number of times the object is presented consistently across a series of film frames, which would correspond to the computation of its mass value. Conversely, the time

— 34 —

value of a given object in the film could be computed as the degree of changes in the object's composition across a given number of film frames.

But, once again, when we translate this into the corresponding singular higher-ordered <u>Universal Consciousness Principle</u>'s (G-d's) computation of these four basic physical features of the physical reality, our basic understanding of the origination, dissolution, sustenance, and evolution of our entire physical universe (so many billions of times per second) is completely revised. First of all, we realize that, as real and material as the basic four physical elements of space, time, energy, and mass may appear to us, this new and profound discovery of the A-Causal Computation Paradigm completely alters our understanding of their basic nature and existence. Indeed, so far, Physics viewed these four basic physical features as existing quite independently and objectively from each other. True, <u>Relativity Theory</u> found that there exist certain physical relationships between specific physical features such as, for instance, space and time as a four-dimensional continuum; for example, that the velocity of a given relativistic observer affects his or her respective measurements of the space-time value of a given event, and that these Space-Time values are related to each other. But still, the basic concepts of space and time remain quite independent of each other. Likewise, general <u>Relativity Theory</u> taught us that mass may curve Space-Time, but this basic Material-Causal assumption has already been shown to be challenged by the new A-Causal Computation Paradigm due to the Universal Consciousness Principle's *simultaneous* computation of all spatial pixels comprising the entire physical universe for each consecutive universal frame, thereby negating the very possibility of the existence of any such material-causal physical relationships. Moreover, in any event, the basic conception of mass and Space-Time still remains independent of one another except that each is assumed to cause an effect in the other, which again has been negated by the A Causal Computation Paradigm. Likewise, in <u>Quantum Mechanics</u>, the basic conception is that these four physical features are assumed to be separate from each one another, even though the probabilistic interpretation of <u>Quantum Mechanics</u> assumes that there exists particular Material-Causal physical relationships between the two "complimentary pairs" (Heisenberg's uncertainty principle): space and energy or mass and time. Thus, Quantum Mechanics assumes that, if, for instance, we wish to increase the accuracy level of our measurement of the subatomic target's spatial location, we need to increase the energy level of the measuring probe (subatomic particle), thereby proportionally decreasing our measurement accuracy for the target's energy value. Likewise, if we wish to increase the measurement accuracy level of the subatomic target's mass value, we are assumed to cause a proportional decrease in that target's temporal accuracy measurement level. Once again, the A-Causal Computation Paradigm of the Computational Unified Field Theory negated the possibility of the existence of such material-causal physical relationships between the subatomic probe and target particles in which, based on their assumed direct physical interaction, an increase or decrease in the accuracy level of one of the probe's complimentary pairs would lead to a proportional decrease in the target's complimentary pair's accuracy level of measurement. This happens simply because, according to the A Causal Computation Paradigm, there cannot exist any such material-causal physical relationships between the subatomic probe and target elements because of the simultaneity of the Universal Consciousness Principle's computation of both of the subatomic particles as well as of any other exhaustive spatial pixel for each consecutive universal frame.

So, we see that, in contrast to the old twentieth-century Material-Causal Paradigm, which views the four basic physical features of space, energy, mass, and time as separate and existing independently of one another and possessing an objective physical reality, and as affecting one another, the new G-d's Physics discards this basic assumption and teaches us that the whole physical universe is only a manifestation of the singularity of the higher-ordered Universal Consciousness Principle, which manifests as the entire physical universe during it's extremely rapid computation of each spatial pixel that comprises it—many billions of times per second—and solely remains without the presence of the physical universe in between any two consecutive universal frames. We call this A-Causal Computation Paradigm G-d's Physics simply because, in contrast to the old Material-Causal Paradigm of twentieth-century's Relativity Theory and Quantum Mechanics, which assumed that the world exists objectively as an independent objective physical reality, the <u>Computational Unified Field Theory</u>'s new A-Causal Computation Paradigm points to the existence of a singular, higher-ordered <u>Universal Consciousness Principle</u> that solely computes every spatial pixel in the universe many billions of times per second, giving rise to the extremely rapid series of universal frames, but which also exists independently of the physical universe in between any two such consecutive universal frames. Indeed, it probably is some sort of a "historical justice" that, in contrast to the old Material-Causal Paradigm whose final product may be the recent discovery of the Boson-Higgs "G-d particle", the new and real G-d's Physics' discovery of the singularity of the higher-ordered, nonmaterial, noncausal <u>Universal Consciousness Principle</u>—G-d— completely discards the objective-independent reality of the entire physical universe, including all its assumed subatomic particles, as merely representing a transient phenomenal manifestation of this singular higher-ordered <u>Universal Consciousness Principle</u>. This is because, whereas the old Material-Causal Paradigm assumes, for instance, that the recently discovered Higgs-Boson "G-d particle" imparts mass to all other subatomic particles, therefore cynically terming it as the "G-d particle," the A-Causal Computation Paradigm completely revises our conception of the entire physical universe as being solely produced (computed) dissolved, reproduced, and evolved many billions of times per second by the sole singular, higher-ordered <u>Universal Consciousness Principle</u>, which is termed as G-d!

It may also be "historic justice" that one of <u>Science</u>'s giants—Albert Einstein—stated that "G-d does not play dice" when referring to <u>Quantum Mechanics</u>' odd, apparently merely probabilistic interpretation of the physical reality. Indeed, Einstein spent the entire second half of his illustrious scientific career attempting to find such a "G-d's Physics" that would completely unify the apparently contradictory <u>Relativity Theory</u> and <u>Quantum Mechanics</u> and encapsulate in one singular equation the whole of creation in both its microscopic subatomic and macroscopic relativistic aspects as well as point at G-d's existence and manifestation through the beauty and magnanimity of the entire physical universe.

Indeed, it is with a special tribute to this truly great scientist, who could not accept a situation in which the two basic pillars of twentieth-century theoretical physics—<u>Relativity Theory</u> and <u>Quantum Mechanics</u>—seemed to contradict one another and who relentlessly pursued his quest for such a Unified Field Theory that would restore consistency and harmony back to physics. He also deeply believed and sensed the presence of a higher-ordered divine presence, which is why I called my theory the Computational Unified Field Theory. Up until his physical death—even on his deathbed—Einstein was seeking to find that singular, higher-ordered Unifying Field Theory equation, which would also somehow point at G-d's presence and creation of the physical universe. With that bold belief that there must exist a singular higher-ordered (G-d's) reality which solely produces, sustains, and evolves the entire physical universe, Einstein kept on going, relentlessly pursuing his quest for truth. Despite the fact that almost of all his contemporary physicists continued to criticize and belittle his bold attempt to expand and transcend old twentieth-century Material-Causal Physics, Einstein went courageously solely by his deep faith and conviction that there must exist such a singular higher-ordered (G-d's) reality that could be proven through a Unifying Field Theory.

In doing so, Einstein seems to have joined some of Judaism's greatest Fathers and Mothers, Sages, Philosophers, and Seers. For example, the legendary Abraham strictly refused to accept that the world was governed simply by Nature's apparently dominant forces of the sun and the moon reasoning that any material or physical entity is limited, meaning that it possesses a beginning and end and therefore could not create or sustain the magnanimity of creation. Moses recognized the singular G-d who created the world and who also imparted His Moral Commandments to Humanity. The sacred Rashbi, Rabi Shimon Bar-Yochai, discovered the singular G-d reality, which also manifests as the apparent pluralistic multifarious physical reality and existence.

It therefore seems as if the cutting-edge discoveries in twenty-first-century Theoretical Physics coincide with some of the deepest truths revealed by Judaism's Fathers, Mothers, Prophets, and Sages. How could that be? Interestingly, one of the most profound sacred books in Judaism was written by Rabi Shimon Bar Yochai whose day of remembrance was just celebrated by hundreds of thousands of Jews in Mt. Meron, Israel. In his famous book, *The Book of Zohar* (meaning the Shining Light, which is the basis for all Kabalah and Chassidic profound wisdom) he predicted—in the second century—that, toward this time in history, there would be an outpouring of both scientific knowledge and new discoveries as well as an opening and worldwide dissemination of this profound inner Kabalistic and Chassidic spiritual knowledge. Indeed, from a Kabbalistic Chassidic Jewish standpoint, these two basic forms of human knowledge—scientific knowledge stemming from the outer aspects of human consciousness born from purely Intellectual and sensory data, and the more inner spiritual sources of inspiration, prayer and connection with G-d—must ultimately point at the same singular truth regarding the singularity of G-d's existence and manifestation as the physical universe.

Let's get back to <u>Science</u>'s new twenty-first-century G-d's Physics. We reached the inevitable conclusion that the entire physical universe, including every spatial pixel comprising it, is computed simultaneously by the singular higher-ordered <u>Universal Consciousness Principle</u> many billions of times per second. When we began probing deeper into the possible mechanics of this new G-d's Physics—<u>Computational Unified Field Theory</u>'s new A Causal Computation Paradigm—we discovered that what seem to be the four separate basic physical features of space, energy, mass, and time are, in truth, only the secondary computational by-products of the singular, higher-ordered <u>Universal Consciousness Principle</u>'s (G-d's) simultaneous computation of the degree of displacement or consistency in any given object (space and energy), or number of consistent or inconsistent presentations of a given object's composition across a series of universal frames. So, according to this new singular higher-ordered G-d's Physics, space and energy or mass and time do not exist as separate independent objective physical features, but rather are seen as only manifestations of the singular, higher-ordered <u>Universal Consciousness Principle</u>'s simultaneous computation of each exhaustive spatial pixel's two complimentary computational measures of frame—consistent (space) or inconsistent (energy) or object—consistent (mass) or inconsistent (time) values. Indeed, this profound new discovery of the A-Causal Computation Paradigm of the inseparability of these four apparently independent physical features from the singularity of the <u>Universal Consciousness Principle</u> has led to their complete integration within a singular "Universal Computational Formula" as secondary integrated computational byproducts of the <u>Universal Consciousness Principle</u>'s simultaneous computation of each exhaustive spatial pixel in the universe.

Universal Computational Formula (UCF):

$$
{}^{\prime}\left\{ \begin{array}{c} c^2 \\ \\ — \\ \\ h \end{array} \right\} \quad \text{UF's } \{\text{ת}...\text{מ}...\text{א}\} \qquad \begin{array}{ccc} = & \underline{s} & {}^{*} & \underline{e} \\ \\ & t & {}^{*} & m \end{array}
$$

Note: The singular higher-ordered Universal Computational Principle—represented by the Hebrew letter *Yud* (י)—simultaneously computes all spatial pixels in the universe comprising each consecutive universal frame that already exists in a potential from within the Universal Computational Principle's "Supra-Spatial-Temporal Reservoir" of all past, present, and multiple possible future Universal Frames (represented by the Hebrew letters from א through מ to (ת depending on the Moral Choice of each Individual Human Consciousness (individual) as computing and integrating these four basic physical features of space and energy, mass, and time at the incredible rate of: $c^2/h = 1.36^{-50}$ second for all spatial pixels comprising the entire physical universe for each consecutive universal frame.

In a nutshell, this new Universal Computational Formula completely integrates these four basic physical features of space, energy, mass, and time as secondary computational byproducts of the singular <u>Universal Consciousness Principle</u>'s simultaneous computation of every spatial pixel in the universe at the incredible rate of 1.36^{-52} seconds! It thereby fulfills Einstein's dream of integrating all physical features and operation of the entire physical universe within a singular mathematical formula while pointing at the dependency of the entire physical universe upon the singular, higher-ordered <u>Universal Consciousness Principle</u>'s existence—G-d's existence. This newly discovered G-d's Physics Universal Computational Formula also confirms Einstein's deep-seated intuition and faith that "G-d does not play dice"; in other words, that there exists a constant Divine "Personal Providence" behind this <u>Universal Consciousness Principle</u>'s (G-d's) precise computation, dissolution, recomputation, and evolution of each exhaustive spatial pixel in the universe many billions of times per second! And even though it would probably take us an entire book to begin to grasp the awe-inspiring appreciation and love for this <u>Universal Consciousness Principle</u>'s inconceivable Infinite Intelligence, including the intricacies of this <u>Universal Consciousness Principle</u>'s Personal Providence, Moral Principle, universal evolution, and human consciousness evolution, we can already begin sensing that <u>Science</u>'s new G-d's Physics entirely transforms our whole conception of the physical universe as created, dissolved, sustained, recreated, and evolved solely by the singular higher-ordered <u>Universal Consciousness Principle</u>: G-d!

CHAPTER 4

G-d's Physics: Explaining the Universe from Without

So, now that we've begun to understand the basic Paradigmatic Shift that is currently taking place within twenty-first century Theoretical Physics—from the old twentieth-century Physics' Material-Causal Paradigm underlying Relativity Theory and Quantum Mechanics to G-d's Physics "Computational Unified Field Theory's" new A Causal Computation Paradigm—we come to revisit and reconsider the broader theoretical implications of this new A-Causal Computation Paradigm upon Physics, and more generally upon the whole of Science, and our basic understanding of the origin, sustenance, and development of our universe.

Perhaps the most natural place to begin our scientific journey is with a review of Science's conception of the origin of the physical universe, its sustenance, and its evolution. As we've already noted, the old Material-Causal Paradigm of twentieth-century Physics assumed that the universe was created by an initial chance Big Bang explosion that created all the matter and energy in the universe, thereby producing all the known stars, galaxies, suns, and planets, including our own solar system. It is perhaps noteworthy to mention that, at the get-go of our discussion, we included the profound insight of the Lubavitcher Rebbe regarding the very possibility of our intricate and extremely precise physical universe with all its billions of planets, suns, galaxies, and stars, all organized with such profound accuracy, complexity, beauty, and elegance.

The Lubavitcher Rebbe gave the example of a human being entering an extremely complex factory—say, one that manufactures F35 aircraft. The visitor would gaze at all the innumerable units of the factory, with hundreds of workers, computers, and telephones all communicating with each other to enable the production of an extremely complex parts of the aircraft: fuselage, wings, engine, computer systems, missiles, and so forth. We cannot imagine that this awe-struck human being would gaze at all these extremely complex manufacturing systems, communication systems, and other highly intelligent integrated systems and even fathom the possibility that all this had been created by an arbitrary explosion! *Right?* Well, the great Lubavitcher Rebbe similarly proclaimed that it would be as inconceivable to even entertain the impossible postulate that the whole of creation—our entire extremely beautiful and intricate, elegant physical universe with its myriad of suns, planets, galaxies, birds, plants, human beings, and so forth—was produced by a chance explosion.

To fully grasp this great modern sage's profound insight, let's connect it with the latest discoveries of our <u>Computational Unified Field Theory</u>'s new A Causal Computation Paradigm. We've seen that, according to this new G-d's Physics conceptualization, every spatial pixel in the physical universe is computed *multiple billions of times per second simultaneously* by the singular, higher-ordered <u>Universal Consciousness Principle</u>! We've similarly seen that, according to G-d's Physics' A Causal Computation Paradigm, any material cause-and-effect physical relationship between any of these innumerable trillions of exhaustive spatial pixels is negated; in other words, for any single or multiple successive universal frames, which are all created simultaneously. This simply means that, whether it be for that first special universal frame depicting a hypothetical Big Bang explosion or the second, third, millionth, or billionth universal frame, at no single universal frame is it ever possible for any material-causal physical relationships to exist because for each of these successive universal frames the Universal Consciousness Principle simultaneously computes all of the spatial pixels comprising any of these universal frames...

Let's revert to our Cinematic Film Metaphor and take a close look at the rollout of the Big Bang model. Imagine the first universal frame in which we see a small tennis ball–sized concentration of all the mass in the universe. We see it as a very small lump of extremely concentrated mass centered in the vast void. Now let's move on to the second universal frame in which the Big Bang explosion is depicted. We see the lump light up with an explosion. Then we gaze at the third, fourth, and consecutive Universal Frames in which we supposedly see further and further expansion of this initial Big Bang explosion, and eventually we see the creation of more and more suns, galaxies, and bundles of energy and mass.

Now, let's really halt this Big Bang explosion film and closely look at the connection between the succession of universal frames. Surprisingly, we find that really there could not have been any Big Bang explosion, and therefore no creation of all the suns, planets, energy, mass, galaxies, and so forth as far as the progression of Universal Frames is concerned. This is simply because, when we halt the "film" that depicts this hypothetical Big Bang, we see that, in order for such a Big Bang explosion to take place, there has to be an expansion of the hypothesized nuclear explosion ricochets, including suns, planets, galaxies, and other heavenly bodies from the first frame to the second, third, and then successive frames. But, as we've seen from our Cinematic Film Metaphor, in between all the film frames, there exists only a pure light so that no material entities or effects can pass from one frame to another. In our new G-d's Physics A Causal Computation Paradigm, this is equivalent to the dissolution of all exhaustive spatial pixels comprising the entirety of the physical universe back into the singularity of the <u>Universal Consciousness Principle</u>in between any two consecutive universal frames. So, in truth, there cannot have existed any such Big Bang explosion which created all the suns, planets, galaxies, and other components in the universe.

Really? So what, then, is the alternative explanation provided by the new G-d's Physics A-Causal Computation Paradigm for the origins of the physical universe, its sustenance, dissolution, and evolution with its innumerable number of suns, planets, galaxies, and so forth, all orbiting with such profound coordination, beauty, intelligent life, and other wonders, so many not yet discovered?

Well, according to the A Causal Computation Paradigm, every spatial pixel in the universe is being computed, dissolved, recomputed, and evolved many billions of times per second! So, obviously, there cannot exist any cause and effect for an initially assumed Big Bang explosion that was supposed to occur at the initial universal frame and cause a continuing expansion of the entire physical universe throughout the cascade of ensuing universal frames. Instead, the new G-d's Physics paradigm asserts that it is only the continuing operation of this singular higher-ordered Universal Consciousness Principle that can account for the continuing existence, sustenance, dissolution, re-creation, and evolution of the entire physical universe so many billions of times per second.

But, perhaps we should note that the discovery of this G-d's Physics highlights a deeper and more profound new realization that shines and revises all our up-to-date basic scientific understanding of the world: By the very fact that our entire physical universe dissolves in between any two consecutive universal frames (many billions of times per second), we reach the profound new realization that there cannot exist any cause-and-effect relationships between any two or more exhaustive spatial pixels existing either in the same universal frame or, indeed, across any two consecutive or even nonconsecutive universal frames! So, this means that the New G-d's physics A-Causal Computation Paradigm negates not only the Big Bang assumption and model, but much more generally all material-causal physical relationships that exist within physics and Science more generally.

Let's review the old Material-Causal Paradigm of twentieth-century physics and replace it by G-d's physics new A-Causal Computation twenty-first-century Physics Paradigm. According to the old Material-Causal Paradigm underlying both Relativity Theory and Quantum Mechanics, the physical universe was created by a Big Bang explosion. This, as we've seen, is negated by G-d's physics A Causal Computation Paradigm: the universe could not have been created by an explosion because every exhaustive spatial pixel in the universe is dissolved and then recreated many billions of times per second with each consecutive universal frame. So we reach the inevitable conclusion that the entire physical cosmos is being solely created, dissolved, recreated, and evolved many billions of times per second solely by the power of the singular, higher-ordered Universal Consciousness Principle. Next, General

Jehonathan Bentovish (Bentwich), Ph.D.

Relativity teaches us that the universe continues to evolve like a gigantic trampoline membrane comprised of the Space-Time fabric that is curved by the massive objects such as suns, planets, galaxies, and so forth, which, in turn, determines the traveling pathways of these massive objects will take. Once again, Einstein's general <u>Relativity Theory</u> is anchored in the basic Material-Causal Paradigmatic assumption that it is the direct physical interaction between certain massive objects and the fabric of Space-Time that causes Space-Time to be curved. Or, conversely, according to the same Einstein equations, that it is the direct physical interaction between this curved Space-Time and those massive objects that causes the massive objects to travel in their particular orbits. So, you can imagine a gigantic cosmic trampoline carrying out a fine interactive dance between massive objects and curved Space-Time, which goes on and unfolds the physical universe's evolution. One may add the purely hypothetical <u>"dark matter"</u> and <u>"dark energy"</u> concepts, which are hypothesized to account for up to 95 percent of all matter and energy in the universe, but yet cannot be detected empirically despite numerous attempts. When placed within the theoretical framework of Einstein's General Relativity's equations, these purely hypothetical concepts of <u>"dark matter"</u> and <u>"dark energy"</u> are assumed to cause the accelerated expansion of the physical universe due to their direct physical interaction with some of the galaxies, stars, and other elements of the universe.

But, since, as we've already seen, there cannot exist any such cause and effect between any two or more exhaustive spatial pixels existing either in the same or different universal frames, the entire Material-Causal assumption underlying Einstein's General Relativity's gigantic Space-Time trampoline (of course, this is a metaphor) cannot stand. Instead, we must embrace the new G-d's Physics' A Causal Computation Paradigm, which points at the existence of a singular higher-ordered <u>Universal Consciousness Principle</u> that is solely responsible for the origination, sustenance, dissolution, recomputation, and evolution of each spatial pixel in the universe! This new A Causal Computation Paradigm—G-d's Physics—brings about a profound change in the way we view and understand the physical universe and the way in which it was formed and is sustained and evolved. This is because, instead of our conditioned old Material-Causal Paradigm, which assumes that the physical universe exists based on its preceding material causes—a Big Bang explosion, "dark matter" or "dark energy" pushing the galaxies further and further away, massive objects causing the curvature of space-time, and so forth—the new A-Causal Computation Paradigm teaches us that the physical universe does not operate by itself and is not created or caused by earlier interactions taking place within it.

I have published more than forty scientific articles relating to this new G-d's Physics. One particular article is entitled "Explaining the Universe From Without." Indeed, it teaches that, since every spatial pixel throughout the physical universe is being continuously created, dissolved, recreated, and evolved by the singularity of this Universal Consciousness Principle, the entire physical universe may be explained only from outside it by the singular, higher-ordered Universal Consciousness Principle. Indeed, a result of this new profound Paradigmatic Shift from the old Material-Causal Paradigm to the new A Causal Computation Paradigm, our whole conception and understanding of the origin, sustenance, and evolution of the physical universe is completely altered. The universe could not have been created by a Big Bang explosion because there cannot exist any cause-and-effect physical relationships between any two or more spatial pixels in the universe, in any of the universal frames! The universe's observed accelerated expansion cannot be the result of any purely hypothetical "dark matter" or "dark energy" because there cannot exist any such cause-and-effect physical relationships between these elements, which have not been proven to exist.

Another scientific article that I wrote was called "Dark Matter and "Dark Energy" May Be Superfluous." This was reminiscent of Einstein's seminal scientific article in which he similarly termed that the "ether concept" was superfluous. Indeed, there exist some similarity between Einstein's discarding of the purely hypothetical ether concept of pre-Einstein's Newtonian classical mechanics and the old Material-Causal Paradigm of General Relativity Physics' purely hypothetical concept of "dark matter" and "dark energy". In both cases, the "ether" and "dark matter" and "dark energy" concepts could not be detected empirically despite numerous experiments to do so. Therefore, ultimately, the concepts had to be discarded as superfluous; in other words, nonexistent.

In the current case of general Relativity Theory, the basis for negating the existence of these purely hypothetical concepts of "dark matter" or "dark energy" is the discovery of the singularity of the Universal Consciousness Principle, which *simultaneously* computes every spatial pixel in the universe with each consecutive universal frame many billions of times per second! We reach the inevitable conclusion that there cannot exist any material-causal physical relationships between such hypothetical concepts as "dark matter" or "dark energy" as well as the accelerated expansion of the universe because all the exhaustive spatial pixels in the universe are *simultaneously* computed billions of times per second by the singularity of the Universal Consciousness Principle. And all these spatial pixels comprising the entirety of the physical universe are completely dissolved in between any given universal frame and the next consecutive universal frame.

Think about the impossible state at which twentieth-century Theoretical Physics found itself prior to the Paradigmatic Shift of the new Computational Unified Field Theory's A-Causal Computation G-d's Physics when up to 95 percent of all the energy and mass that are hypothesized to exist in the universe as "dark matter" and "dark energy" could not be detected experimentally. In simple terms, this implies that the old Material-Causal Paradigm underlying both Relativity Theory and Quantum Mechanics simply "crashes down". Once again, as I noted earlier, if an alien scientist came to discuss this embarrassing state of affairs of the old Material-Causal Paradigm Theoretical Physics with the top physicists of our planet Earth, our physicists would have to admit that our old Material-Causal Paradigm of General Relativity can account for only approximately 5 percent of all the mass and energy in the physical universe!? The alien scientist would surely discard our old Material-Causal Theoretical Physics Paradigm model of the universe as unsatisfactory!

What, then, is the alternative explanation of the new G-d's Physics Paradigm for the accelerated expansion of the physical universe? What replaces the discarded hypothetical "dark matter" and "dark energy" concepts? Surprisingly enough, G-d's Physics boldly stipulates that it is only due to the singular, higher-ordered Universal Consciousness Principle's accelerated addition of the number of spatial pixels comprising each consecutive universal frame that gives rise to the empirically observed accelerated expansion of our physical universe. So, it is not "dark matter" or "dark energy" that can explain the accelerated expansion of the universe. Remember that up to 95 percent of all mass and energy constituting the physical universe cannot be found! Rather, a completely higher-ordered new explanation regarding the Universal Consciousness Principle's accelerated number of additional spatial pixels (for each consecutive universal frame that it produces) accounts for the universe's accelerated expansion rate.

Perhaps in order to somewhat abate the potential "shock" to our ordinary everyday perception and understanding of our Material-Casual physical universe delivered by the singular, higher-ordered G-d's Physics A Causal Computation Paradigm, let's use once again our Cinematic Film Metaphor. Think about our James Bond film and the cascade of events in which our dear Bond hero is involved. Could we attribute, for instance, Bond's success in evading the dangerous missiles shot at his black Aston Martin to his skillful maneuvering of the car along the curvy, narrow, and steep roads through the hills and canyons? Well, even though this is perhaps what *seems* to be the case when we're engrossed in viewing this nerve-racking film, upon further reflection, we must accept the inevitable truth that there cannot exist any type of real causality found within the film's depiction of James Bond's fascinating adventures! This is because, in between any two consecutive film frames there exists only the projector's pure light. And, as we noted earlier, there cannot exist any cause-and-effect physical relationships either within the same film frame (since all the spatial points comprising any single frame are computed *simultaneously*) or indeed across any two consecutive film frames in between which all the spatial pixels are dissolved back into the pure light. In the case of this Cinematic Film Metaphor, it is perhaps easier to understand the nonreality or only apparent perception of any cause-and-effect occurrences taking place within this James Bond film. We realize that, in reality, any apparent causality found in Bond's film is really produced by the film's editor's selection of a particular succession of film frames giving us the *perception* of a cause-and-effect scenario. We realize, by our analysis of the film's mechanics, that no real cause-and-effect physical relationships could exist within the film because of the pure light between each frame.

A bit more challenging, perhaps, is our acceptance of the noncontinuity and noncausality of the operation of our physical universe. But, once again, let's be guided by Einstein's great observation that common sense is only that which is common to the senses. This means that we should not allow our old preconceived ideas to clutter our pure, objective scientific inquiry into the true nature of the universe.

We acknowledged the inability of the old Material-Causal Paradigm to account for 95 percent of all matter and energy in the world as well as the principle theoretical contradiction that seems to exist between the two pillars of old twentieth-century physics: <u>Relativity Theory</u> and <u>Quantum Mechanics</u>. We were inevitably led to recognize and accept the new A-Causal Computation G-d's Physics Paradigm. We noted the Cinematic Film Metaphor's equivalent depiction of the entire physical universe's existence solely as produced by the singular, higher-ordered <u>Universal Consciousness Principle</u>'s continuous computation, dissolution, recomputation, and evolution of each and every exhaustive spatial pixel in the universe many billions of times (1.36^{-50}) per second! We realized that, between any two such extremely rapid universal frames, only this singular, higher-ordered <u>Universal Consciousness Principle</u> exists; all apparently real spatial pixels comprising the entire physical universe dissolve in between all universal frames. So, we must also accept the inevitable conclusion regarding this singular, higher-ordered <u>Universal Consciousness Principle</u>'s A-Causal Computation of each consecutive universal frame. This means that, just as in the Cinematic Film Metaphor in which we realized that it wasn't James Bond's skillful maneuvering of his Aston Martin that caused him to evade the many bullets and missiles shot at him, but rather the film editor's arrangement of the series of film frames that make, for example, Bond's car seem to be evading the flying bullets and missiles, so, the Universal Computational Principle's new A-Causal Computation G-d's Physics postulates that there cannot exist any cause and effect between any material pixels existing in one universal frame and any consecutive frame; rather, the entire physical universe is being created, dissolved, recreated, and evolved multiple billions of times per second and, therefore, that any apparent cause-and-effect physical relationships are, in truth, produced solely by the singular, higher-ordered <u>Universal Consciousness Principle</u>.

We see that the physical universe was not created by an initial Big Bang explosion; rather, it is being produced (computed) simultaneously for each spatial pixel many billions of times per second. The cause for the existence, sustenance, dissolution, and evolution of the entire physical universe and every spatial pixel or object or phenomenon within it is only this singular, higher-ordered <u>Universal Consciousness Principle</u>! In fact, as we've seen, according to the <u>Universal Consciousness Principle</u>, one of the more advanced theoretical postulates of the Universal Consciousness Principle is there truly exists only one singular <u>Universal Consciousness Principle</u>, and it exists both during the production and manifestation of each consecutive universal frame as the physical universe, and also solely exists, without the presence of any physical universe, in between each consecutive frame.

This profound new <u>Universal Consciousness Principle</u> implies that we can no longer talk about the physical universe in terms of its own Material-Causal physical interactions as apparently caused by particular physical interactions such as relativity's assumed Big Bang initial explosion. This is negated by the A Causal Computation Paradigm. Additionally, we can no longer assume the purely hypothetical existence of <u>"dark matter"</u> or <u>"dark energy"</u> as causing the accelerated expansion of the universe. This is also negated by the A Causal Computation Paradigm—G-d's physics—because it utterly rejects the existence of any cause-and-effect relationships between any two or more spatial pixels existing either in the same or different universal frames. Likewise, Einstein's General Relativity's basic Material-Causal assumption assumes that the evolution of the universe is caused by massive objects curving Space-Time, and also that the traveling pathways of these massive objects is caused by the curvature of Space-Time. This has also been negated by the new A-Causal Computation Paradigm assertion regarding the <u>Universal Consciousness Principle</u>'s simultaneous computation of all spatial pixels in the universe.

Another principle negated by the A-Causal Computation Paradigm is the premise of the Second Law of Thermodynamics, which assumes that the "entropy" level within the universe or any smaller physical system found within it must increase with the progression of time. In simple terms, this means that the entire physical universe is doomed to die or diminish with time. The A-Causal Computation Paradigm also negated this additional manifestation of the old Material-Causal Paradigm based on its principle negation of the existence of any material-causal physical relationships between any two or more spatial pixels that exist either in the same universal frame or in different frames. G-d's Physics' A-Causal Computation Paradigm negated this law based on its negation of the existence of any cause-and-effect relationships between the level of entropy that exists in one given universal frame to the corresponding level of entropy that exists in any consecutive universal frame and that is assumed to increase across frames. Once again, in simple-terms, this means that the old Material-Causal Physics Paradigm's assumption that the universe was created by a chance explosion and is marching on toward its inevitable death is negated by the new G-d's Physics A Causal Computation Paradigm!

So, contrary to the old Material-Causal Paradigm, which underlies both <u>Relativity Theory</u> and <u>Quantum Mechanics</u>, the new G-d's Physics A-Causal Computation Paradigm views the physical universe not as being created or caused by any material-interactions or any Material-Causal physical relationships found within the physical universe; rather, it was originated and is operated, sustained, and evolved solely by the existence of the singular, higher-ordered <u>Universal Consciousness Principle</u>. This basic shift from a Material-Causal universe to the singular, higher-ordered <u>Universal Consciousness Principle</u> highlights an extremely important turning point in the evolution of <u>Science</u> represented by this new G-d's Physics A Causal Computation Paradigm: it may be said to represent the shift from a Materialistic-Reductionistic perspective that is the attempt to explain any given physical phenomenon in the world or even the entire universe through its breakdown into smaller and smaller constituting elements to a higher-ordered expansive <u>Science</u>.

In order to better comprehend this pivotal turning point in the development of <u>Science</u>, let's look at another metaphor that Leonardo de Vinci is said to have conceived. Leonardo lived during the time of the very early stages of the budding of Cartesian <u>Science</u>. Toward the end of the Renaissance—that beautiful period of time of Humanity's blossoming of the arts—Leonardo was relating to those ridiculous "materialists"—that is, scientists! He presented a metaphor about the manner in which these "materialistic" scientists were attempting to explain a blossoming beautiful, fragrance-filled cherry tree. He said that, in order to explain the beauty and complexity of the tree, the materialistic scientists would first pluck its beautiful pink flowers. Then they would strip the gentle, lively, bright-green leaves from the tree. Then they would cut off all the branches and remove the bark. Finally, they would tear the powerful roots out of the ground. By the time the scientists would have organized all the parts of this magnificent cherry tree within a box, they would think that they understood what the cherry tree was. This is the problem—not to say folly—of the old Material-Causal Scientific Paradigm because it attempted to explain any given physical phenomenon by breaking it down to its constituting elements. The problem is that this Materialistic-Reductionist breakdown is a never-ending process, and it doesn't really explain a given phenomenon, but rather makes us escape further away from a real understanding of the actual phenomenon and its real meaning and significance. This is perhaps illustrated best with the recent discovery of the A Causal Computation Paradigm. Through the discovery of the singular, higher-ordered Universal Consciousness Principle's *simultaneous computation* of all spatial pixels in the physical universe (for each minimal time-point universal frame), the A-Causal Computation—G-d's Physics—realized that there cannot really exist any such Material-Causal physical relationships between any two or more spatial pixels in the universe. This undermined the very basis for the old Material-Causal Paradigm, which assumed that we can explain any physical phenomenon as well as the entire universe based on the analysis of its constituent physical interactions.

This, no doubt, represents a pivotal turning point along the evolutionary development of Science in that it negates the basic assumption that it is possible to explain the physical universe by breaking it down to its more elementary causal physical interactions. But, if, as G-d's Physics A-Causal Computation Paradigm asserts, there cannot really exist any such Material-Causal or cause-and-effect physical interactions between any two spatial pixels existing either in the same or consecutive Universal Frames due to the simultaneous computation of all spatial pixels by the singular, higher-ordered <u>Universal Consciousness Principle</u>, and their complete dissolution back into the singular, higher-ordered <u>Universal Consciousness Principle</u> between any two consecutive universal frames, then we have to replace the old impossible Material-Causal Paradigm with G-d's Physics' A Causal Computation Paradigm's description of the operation and the higher-ordered qualities of the singular <u>Universal Consciousness Principle</u>!

Indeed, in this new and profound realization of G-d's Physics A Causal Computation Paradigm, it is realized that it is not possible to explain the physical universe, or indeed any of its constituting spatial pixels, from within it—through any wrongly assumed physical interactions. Rather, we can explain it *only* from *without*. This completely transforms our old Material-Causal Paradigm's basic understanding of the physical universe—its origin, sustenance, and evolution! As we've already seen, it undermines and negates the very possibility of the Big Bang model's assumption regarding the existence of an initial explosion that created the physical universe. It negates the existence of <u>"dark matter"</u> or <u>"dark energy"</u> causing the empirically observed accelerated expansion of the universe. It undermines Einstein's General Relativity's equations that assume cause-and-effect physical relationships between certain given massive objects and their curvature of Space-Time, and conversely assumes that the traveling pathways of these massive objects are determined by this "curved" space-time. Instead, using the <u>Universal Consciousness Principle</u>, the physical universe can now be seen as being continuously created (computed) at each of its spatial pixels many billions of times per second, which solely exists in between any two consecutive Universal Frames without the presence of the physical universe and also exists, computes, and manifests as each spatial pixel in the universe during each consecutive universal frame!

On the subatomic quantum mechanical level, this profound G-d's Physics A-Causal Computation Paradigm portrays an entirely new and different conception of physical reality. Instead of the Material-Causal Paradigm's <u>Quantum Mechanics</u> assumption that any given subatomic target particle exists in a potential form as a dispersed probabilistic wave function, which is collapsed into a singular complimentary (energy-space or mass-time) value as caused by its direct physical interaction with another corresponding subatomic probe element, the new G-d's Physics A-Causal Computation Paradigm asserts that it is not possible for any such Material-Causal (direct) physical interactions to exist between the subatomic probe and target elements because of the *simultaneity* of the singular, higher-ordered <u>Universal Consciousness Principle</u>'s computation of all exhaustive spatial pixels in the universe for each consecutive universal frame. Instead, the A-Causal Computation Paradigm postulates that the singularity of this higher-ordered <u>Universal Consciousness Principle</u> simultaneously computes all single spatial-temporal particles or multiple spatial-temporal wave entities, which are embedded within the broader exhaustive universal frame perspective, which is computed at the incredible rate of $c^2/h = 1.36^{-50}$ per second!

I mention this latter G-d's physics A-Causal Computation negation of the Material-Causal Paradigm's <u>Quantum Mechanics</u> account and succinctly outline the new alternative theoretical explanation of G-d's Physics just as another indication that the Material-Causal Paradigm of twentieth-century Physics is no longer adequate to account for the multifarious physical phenomena discovered in the universe. With the discovery of the new G-d's Physics' A Causal Computation Paradigm, we realize that our previous Material-Causal Paradigm's attempt to explain the physical universe from within has reached its limitations and that it must give way to the G-d's Physics A Causal Computation Paradigm's entirely novel and much more expansive explanation of the physical universe as being continuously computed, dissolved, recreated, and evolved many billions of times per second at each of its constituting spatial pixels by the singularity of the <u>Universal Consciousness Principle</u>!

CHAPTER 5

The Universal Consciousness Principle Science of G-d's Physics

We now come to an important phase in our journey toward a broader understanding of the G-d's Physics' A-Causal Computation Paradigm of twenty-first century Theoretical Physics; that is, after negating the Material-Causal Paradigm of <u>Relativity Theory</u> and <u>Quantum Mechanics,</u> we are ready to fully embrace the new G-d's Physics A-Causal Computation Paradigm and its entirely novel, broader, and awe-inspiring understanding of the physical universe—its origin, sustenance, dissolution, and evolution as a manifestation of the singular, higher-ordered <u>Universal Consciousness Principle</u>.

Once again, it may be helpful to revisit the ideas of the great Jewish sage and philosopher, Maimonides, who analyzed and described the necessary steps leading to a finer and more accurate description and ultimate realization of Truth. The great Maimonides stated that, in order to reach truth, we need to negate all that is *not* truth! He discovered that, in a sense, truth cannot be grasped although it may be experienced! Indeed, by discarding that which is not true, Maimonides came to the inevitable conclusion that there exists only one singular, higher-ordered reality by which all other things exist. This is amazingly similar to the singular, higher-ordered <u>Universal Consciousness Principle</u> stipulated by the A Causal Computation Paradigm.

I mention this magnificently simple yet profound method discovered by Maimonides for uncovering truth not only because his philosophical investigation led him toward the discovery of a singular, higher-ordered G-d, but also because this very method of discarding what's untrue in order to enable us to discover what's true is precisely what describes the evolution of <u>Science</u> from the old Material-Causal Paradigm to the new A Causal Computation Paradigm, which constitutes a complete revision of our basic understanding of the physical universe. As I mentioned earlier, Abraham also reached this inevitable truth that there must exist a singular higher-ordered G-d who is solely responsible for the governance, creation, and sustenance of everything in the universe.

So, let's describe in depth the full scope and beauty of the new G-d's Physics' conception of the universe, its origin, its sustenance, and its evolution, which has been published in over forty scientific articles and books. What we've already seen so far is that each of the constituting spatial pixels in the entire physical universe is computed simultaneously by the singular, higher-ordered <u>Universal Consciousness Principle</u>. We've also noted that this singular <u>Universal Consciousness Principle</u> possesses three Computational Dimensions, two of which—Framework and Consistency—compute together the four basic physical features of space and energy (framework-consistent or inconsistent computations) or mass and time (object-consistent or inconsistent computations).

Now, let us weigh your cell phone and determine that it weighs probably about 100 grams. So, according to this new G-d's Physics A Causal Computation Paradigm, the weight of an object originates from the singular, higher-ordered <u>Universal Consciousness Principle</u>'s computation of the number of times that, say, this cell phone appears across a given number of universal frames. Yes, your cell phone's weight does not exist objectively; rather, it is actually being computed by this singular <u>Universal Consciousness Principle</u> in terms of the number of times that it appears across a given number of universal frames. To make it clearer, if we were to contrast the weight of your cell phone to the weight of, say, a feather, we would find that, according to G-d's Physics, the cell phone would appear in many more Universal Frames than the feather. Because, according to G-d's Physics, the weight of an object arises purely as a function of the <u>Universal Consciousness Principle</u>'s computation of the number of consistent, or same, presentations of that object across a given series of universal frames!

Jehonathan Bentovish (Bentwich), Ph.D.

Indeed, one of the unique predictions of the G-d's Physics as opposed to Relativity Theory or Quantum Mechanics is that, if we are to take a massive particle, such as a muon, and compare it to a less-massive particle, such as an electron, then we could measure the massive muon particle across a much greater number of universal frames than we would need to measure the less-massive electron! Surprisingly, a closely related phenomenon called the Proton Radius Puzzle confirmed the unique predictions of the Computational Unified Field Theory G-d's Physics. The Proton Radius Puzzle relates to the unexplained empirical findings by the Material-Causal Paradigm underlying Relativity Theory and Quantum Mechanics wherein the more massive muon particle is found to be measured much more consistently in terms of its spatial measurement accuracy and smaller spatial size than the less-massive electron particle, thereby closely validating the unique predictions of G-d's Physics as opposed to the predictions of both Relativity Theory and Quantum Mechanics.

It is perhaps important to note that it is precisely this type of experimental validation of the unique predictions of Relativity Theory, as opposed to the even older Newtonian (Classical) Mechanics Paradigm that led to the triumph of Relativity Theory. Back then, Einstein figured out one critical prediction for which the measurements of this new Relativity Theory Paradigm would differ from the predictions of the old Newtonian Mechanics. This had to do with Einstein's predicted doubled degree of curvature of Mercury's perihelion orbit around the sun relative to the degree of curvature predicted by Newton's Mechanics. This double-figure curvature of Mercury's perihelion predicted by Einstein's Relativity Theory was due to Relativity's new explanation of the curvature of space-time by massive objects, an example of which is the strong curvature of Mercury's perihelion.

To me, it is exciting that we now stand at the onset of the empirically confirmed new understanding of the entire universe. It is the new Computational Unified Field Theory A Causal Computation Paradigm—G-d's Physics. The entire universe is being computed at an incredible rate of 1.36^{-50}—many billions of times per second! And contrary to the old Material-Causal Paradigm, the weight, for example, of a more massive muon particle is not the result of the number of subatomic particles that constitute it, but rather the result of the singular higher-ordered <u>Universal Consciousness Principle</u>'s computation of the number of times that it is being presented across a given number of universal frames. This can be compared to the measurement of a relatively less-massive electron.

Indeed, according to this new G-d's Physics not only the mass of a particle, or any given object, but also its three other basic physical features are computed by this singular, higher-ordered <u>Universal Consciousness Principle</u>. In fact, one of the other exciting and uniquely critical predictions of the A-Causal Computation Paradigm is related to the possibility of time reversal! Yes, contrary to the Material-Causal Paradigm's conceptualization of time as flowing only in one direction, the A-Causal Computation— G-d's Physics—paradigm postulates that it is possible to reverse time! In both <u>Relativity Theory</u> and <u>Quantum Mechanics</u>, time may flow only in one direction, from the past to the future; it cannot flow from the future to the past. In Relativity Theory, this stems from the principle negation of the possibility to pass the speed of light, which therefore prohibits the capacity of any relativistic observer catching on to any past event light picture or recording. In <u>Quantum Mechanics</u>, the irreversibility of time stems from its assumption that the target particle's probability wave function collapses into a singular, complimentary space-energy or mass-time value following its direct physical interaction with the corresponding subatomic probe particle. Because of this, it is not possible to uncollapse the already collapsed singular complimentary target value back into the multifarious uncollapsed probability wave function values. So, in effect, according to the Material-Causal Paradigm underlying both <u>Relativity Theory</u> and <u>Quantum Mechanics</u>, time may flow only in only one direction—from the past into the present and on to the future.

But, surprisingly, according to A-Causal Computation, time reversal is possible. This stems from the new computational definition of time according to the A-Causal Computation G-d's Physics paradigm. Interestingly, time is defined as any given object's degree of change, or inconsistency, across a given series of universal frames. We learned earlier through the Cinematic Film Metaphor that if, for instance, we were to present the precise same film frame repeatedly for say one minute, during that minute, time would appear to stand still. Note that, even though we, as viewers, would still most likely sense time passing during this odd one minute of static image because we would be noticing progressive changes around us—our heartbeats, our cell-phones beeping, birds tweeting, and so forth. But, strictly speaking, from within the film scenario itself, time would appear to have stopped still.

So, we realize, through the Cinematic Film Metaphor, that time is a function or a measure of the degree of changes or inconsistency in objects. Indeed, according to the <u>Computational Unified Field Theory</u>, the singular, higher-ordered <u>Universal Consciousness Principle</u>'s computation of time for each spatial pixel in the universe is based on the <u>Universal Consciousness Principle</u>'s computation of the degree of inconsistency or number of changes in that particular object across a series of universal frames. Moreover, this computation of time for each spatial pixel may be characterized based on the directional changes taking place from one frame to its consecutive frame, so that the unidirectional passage of time is characterized by the particular changes taking place in a given object from one frame to the next or across a series of film frames.

Take, for example, a film's depiction of the life of a sheep from its birth through its childhood, mature years, and finally on to death. We could characterize this sheep's life cycle from birth to death by the particular changes taking place in each of its constituting spatial pixels throughout its existence. The surprising discovery made by the A-Causal Computation Paradigm is that it is possible to reverse time by rolling the film backward. Within the Cinematic Film Metaphor, this isn't difficult to imagine. We've all seen films projected in reverse. For example, a broken glass vase, with all its myriad thousand little pieces, is reassembled into the beautiful shining vase it once was before it was shattered. So, it should be possible, according to the A-Causal Computation G-d's Physics Paradigm, to similarly reverse time in our physical universe based on an equivalent manipulation of the electromagnetic spatial pixels comprising any given object across a certain number of universal frames. In that way, an object's past universal frames (electromagnetic) spatial values would be recreated, thereby effectively reversing time for that object.

Perhaps another word regarding the divergence of the A Causal Computation Paradigm's conception of time from the Material-Causal Paradigm's conception of time would be helpful at this point. The great Einstein simply described his revolution of our basic conception of time through an explanation of what time is and, specifically, what simultaneity means to us. Einstein gave the illustrative example of a man sitting at a train station at seven o'clock, when, of course, the long hand of the big clock at the station would point to the twelve and the small hand would point at the seven. The man asks the simple question, "What would it mean if we were to say that a certain event, such as an explosion taking place, say, a hundred miles away from this train station occurred just as the train station clock indicates seven o'clock?" Einstein's ingenious, simple, yet profound reasoning was that such a simultaneous occurrence of the explosion and the long hand of the clock reaching the twelve would depend on the time it would take the light rays emitted by the explosion to reach the train station's clock. Yes, Einstein stated that, if the explosion's light rays reached the clock precisely when the long hand reached the twelve, we could conclude that these two events were simultaneous, or that they occurred at the same time! This then led Einstein to his famous analysis, associated with Relativity Theory, indicating that, therefore, time, as well as space, and ultimately Space-Time as a unified four-dimensional continuum must be relative. Now imagine a supersonic jet flying somewhere in the vicinity of the explosion. If the explosion takes place a hundred miles away from the train station, and we measured the simultaneity of the explosion-related light rays to both the train station's clock and the supersonic jet's clock, we might be surprised to find out that the simultaneous time measurements indicated by the train station clock and by the jet's clock would differ significantly. In other words, the time of the explosion would be measured differently by the stationary clock at the train station than it would be by the moving clock in the jet. This is simply because the explosion's light rays would reach the jet after they reached the train station and would therefore be measured as occurring later by the jet than by the train station. So, Einstein taught us that time is relative to the speed of the observer—relative to the constancy of the speed of light. But, still, time exists as a real objective physical feature of the reality; only it's specific measurement depends on the velocity of the relativistic observer.

Likewise, in <u>Quantum Mechanics,</u> time represents an objective measurement produced by the direct physical interaction between the subatomic probe and the target's probability wave function, which collapses the probability wave function into a singular complimentary time-mass value. Still, like the relativistic dependency of the measurement of the time value upon the velocity of the observer, in <u>Quantum Mechanics,</u> the accuracy level of the time measurement critically depends on the selection of the probe's accuracy level in terms of increasing its complimentary accuracy of the mass value, which decreases the accuracy level of the time measurement, or vice versa decreasing the accuracy level of the measurement of the complimentary mass value, which increases the accuracy level of the time measurement. Nevertheless, time itself exists as an objective Material-Causal reality. This is perhaps most apparent with <u>Quantum Mechanics</u>' assumption regarding the collapse of the subatomic target's probability wave function as caused by its direct physical interaction with the subatomic probe element, which yields the singular complimentary space-energy, mass-time values. Again, it is solely based on the direct physical interaction between the subatomic probe and the target elements that the measurement of the target's singular collapsed complimentary values are obtained, including the target's time value.

So, according to both <u>Relativity Theory</u> and <u>Quantum Mechanics,</u> the measurement of time is an objective measure that is produced through the direct physical interaction between a given relativistic observer and a particular space-time, energy-mass event or phenomenon (according to the <u>Relativity Theory</u>) or through the direct physical interactions between the subatomic probe and target elements (according to <u>Quantum Mechanics</u>). And in both of these models, the objective measurement of time is also unidirectional—it can flow only from the past to the present and on to the future, but not vice versa.

However, according to the new A Causal Computation Paradigm— G-d's Physics—time as well as the other three physical features (mass, energy, and space) do not exist objectively or permanently; rather, they are continuously being computed simultaneously for each spatial pixel comprising the entire physical cosmos: dissolved, recomputed, and evolved many billions of times per second by the singular, higher-ordered Universal Consciousness Principle!

So time doesn't exist as an objective constant physical reality, but is rather seen as a transient phenomenal reality that is being computed, dissolved, and recomputed by the only permanent and continuous reality of the <u>Universal Consciousness Principle</u>. To put things in the proper theoretical perspective of the A Causal Computation Paradigm, the entire physical reality and physical universe—including its four basic physical features of time, mass, energy, and space—is seen as existing only transiently and phenomenally as it is continuously being computed, dissolved, recomputed, and evolved so many billions of times per second by the singular <u>Universal Consciousness Principle</u>. In fact, as we've seen, according to one of the more advance theoretical postulates of the <u>Computational Unified Field Theory</u>, the <u>Universal Consciousness Principle</u> postulate, the entire physical universe is viewed as only a transient phenomenal manifestation of the real and constant <u>Universal Consciousness Principle</u>, which exists both during its simultaneous computation of each exhaustive spatial pixel in the universe at the incredible rate of 1.36^{-50}—many billions of times per second, and also solely exists without the presence of the physical universe in between any two consecutive universal frames.

Therefore, our conception of the possibility of time reversal is also made possible through the A Causal Computation Paradigm; this is contrary to both the relativistic and quantum models. If time, as well as mass, energy, and space, do not exist as objective constant physical realities but rather as transient phenomenal computational byproducts of the singular, higher-ordered <u>Universal Consciousness Principle</u>, then by understanding the manner in which this <u>Universal Consciousness Principle</u> computes time, we can find a way to reverse time! As we've shown, by manipulating the electromagnetic spatial values of any given biological object, we can reverse its growth and aging processes and reverse time for that particular object. Conceivably, we can, in this way, even abolish death! I've written about this in one of the more than forty scientific articles that were published as special issues in international physics journals dedicated solely to the dissemination of the <u>Computational Unified Field Theory</u>. I list the articles at the end of this book.

The key point to note with regards to the A-Causal Computation Paradigm and its basic alteration of <u>Science</u>'s conception of the physical universe is that time, mass, space, and energy are no longer conceived of as constituting an objective constant physical reality; rather, they are seen as plastic elements computed by the singular, higher-ordered <u>Universal Consciousness Principle</u>. They exist only as transient phenomenal manifestations of the real and constant <u>Universal Consciousness Principle</u>. The physical universe does not exist objectively and continuously; in fact, according to the <u>Computational Unified Field Theory</u> <u>Universal Consciousness Principle</u>, it may be said that the *physical universe does not exist as an independent objective reality, but rather as a transient phenomenal manifestation of the singular <u>Universal Consciousness Principle</u>!* Yes, this new conception of the universe brings about a complete revision of <u>Science</u>'s basic understanding of the world as well as, specifically, our unique place as human beings possessing Individual Human Consciousness that is connected with the <u>Universal Consciousness Principle</u>. We will soon address this further.

When we take into consideration our earlier insights regarding the A Causal Computation Paradigm, indicating that there cannot exist any cause-and-effect physical relationships, or even physical interactions, between any two or more spatial pixels existing either within the same or different universal frames, and that the entire physical universe dissolves in between any two consecutive universal frames, we reach the inevitable and logical conclusion that the evolution of the world cannot be caused or explained based on any physical interactions within the world; rather, it may be accounted for through the operation and characterization of the singular <u>Universal Consciousness Principle</u>.

Let's take as a striking example the case of <u>Science</u>'s old Material-Causal Paradigm's theoretical explanation of Darwin's Natural Selection Principle regarding the evolution of biological species. According to Darwin's principle, the evolution of all the biological species—all plants and animals, including human beings—is caused by chance alterations in the genetic composition of each organism that results in an improved capacity for that genetically changed organism to adapt to and survive within its specific environment relative to all other equivalent organisms that did not undergo such a chance genetic change (mutation) and therefore had less chance of surviving and passing on to their offspring their genetic material.

Let's use a simple example to illustrate Darwin's natural selection principle's theoretical explanation of the evolution of biological species. Darwin traveled to the Galapagos Islands where he encountered iguanas, which are large vegetarian reptiles. He noted that, on some islands, iguanas possessed a relatively longer neck than iguanas other islands. He then hypothesized that the biological process through which these longer-necked iguanas developed their longer necks was based on the combination of two factors: One, chance genetic changes (mutations) occurred in one of the iguanas that led to the development of a longer neck for descendants of that particular iguana. Two, a chance drastic change in climate in that island during that year led to death through famine of all the short-necked iguanas on that island, leaving a few long-necked, genetically altered or mutated, iguanas, which would be the only iguanas capable of passing long-necked characteristics along to descendants. In a nutshell, Darwin stated that the evolution of any given species is caused by a combination of chance genetic changes combined with chance drastic changes in the environment.

However, the basic problem with Darwin's natural selection theory is that, according to A-Causal Computation—G-d's Physics—there cannot exist any Material-Causal physical interactions between any organisms and their environment—not between any chance genetic changes and any biological phenomenal changes such as the growth of a longer neck. This is simply because, according to the A Causal Computation Paradigm, the singular Universal Consciousness Principle *simultaneously computes every exhaustive spatial pixel in the universe* for each consecutive universal frame. So, there cannot exist any cause-and-effect physical interaction between any two or more exhaustive spatial pixels in either the same or different universal frames. This negates the basic Natural Selection Principle Material-Causal assumption.

So, according to the A Causal Computation Paradigm, there cannot exist any physical interaction between the long- or short-necked iguana and its environment because they are being presented simultaneously in each consecutive universal frame. In fact, they are dissolved in between any two universal frames back into the singularity of the <u>Universal Consciousness Principle</u>, which produces, dissolves, reproduces, and evolves them. This means that, according to the G-d's Physics paradigm, the evolution of short- or long-neck iguanas has nothing to do with chance genetic mutations or with the chance occurrence of famine on one particular island but not on adjacent islands. The evolution of the various species may only be the result of the singular, higher-ordered <u>Universal Consciousness Principle</u> computation, dissolution, recomputation, and evolution of every exhaustive spatial pixel in the physical universe from one universal frame to another!

This means that, in the case of Darwin's Natural Selection Principle, the A Causal Computation Paradigm—G-d's Physics—of twenty-first-century <u>Science</u> completely alters our basic understanding of how and why species evolve: it completely *negates the possibility of chance genetic mutations and chance environmental changes as the cause for the evolution of species, instead pointing at the singularity of the <u>Universal Consciousness Principle</u>'s computation, dissolution, recomputation, and evolution of all exhaustive spatial pixels in the universe as the sole cause for the evolution of species!*

It is, indeed, fortunate that we chose to focus on Darwin's natural selection principle as an example to explain G-d's Physics of twenty-first-century physics and <u>Science</u> because it represents a prime example of the basic metamorphosis that the old Material-Causal Paradigm of twentieth-century physics' <u>Relativity Theory</u> and <u>Quantum</u> Mechanics is undergoing in favor of the new G-d's Physics' higher-ordered, singular <u>Universal Consciousness Principle</u>!

The Material-Causal Paradigm assumed that any physical event or phenomenon can be explained as caused by specific interactions between particular material entities or physical interactions such as the assumed Big-Bang explosion causing the creation of the universe, or the evolution of the physical universe being caused by the curvature of space-time by massive objects and their respective traveling pathways being caused by this curved space-time, or indeed Darwin's Material-Causal Natural Selection Principle's explanation of the evolution of species as caused by their direct interaction with the environment and the direct interaction between hypothesized chance genetic mutations and phenomenal biological changes in individuals. However, G-d's Physics negates the very possibility of any such Material-Causal physical relationships or interactions, instead pointing at the only possible explanation for physical events or phenomena: the singular higher-ordered <u>Universal Consciousness Principle</u>, which computes, dissolves, recomputes, and evolves every spatial pixel in the universe many billions of times per second!

So, <u>Science</u> now embarks on an exciting new journey. We will be leaving behind an apparently arbitrary Material-Causal universe created by a chance Big Bang explosion and apparently expanding at an accelerated rate by arbitrarily assumed <u>"dark matter"</u> and <u>"dark energy"</u> that is, it is ultimately assumed (by the old Material-Causal Paradigm), going to lead to the universe's arbitrary death when all the suns die out and energy in the universe is used up, based on the (earlier mentioned) Second Law of Thermodynamics. Because this will be shown to be negated by the new G-d's Physics, we will be entering an entirely new promising G-d's Physics Paradigm that reformulates our basic understanding of the physical universe as existing only as a transient phenomenal manifestation of the singularity of the higher-ordered <u>Universal Consciousness Principle</u>, which simultaneously computes, dissolves, recomputes, and evolves every spatial pixel in the universe many billions of times per second according to its own singular, higher-ordered laws and characteristics. Indeed, the second half of this book will be dedicated to discovering these new, exciting, and even awe-inspiring new features, characteristics, and laws of this singular, higher-ordered <u>Universal Consciousness Principle</u> which originates, sustains, and evolves the manifestation of the beautiful, moral, and purposeful cosmos in which we live!

CHAPTER 6

A Multiple-Future, Dynamic-Equilibrium Principle Universe

As we take our journey of discovering the unique features and characterizations of this new singular, higher-ordered Universal Consciousness Principle, we begin with the realization that the root of time must be anchored at this higher-ordered Universal Consciousness Principle instead of existing as an independent, objective reality, as we've seen in the last chapter. Indeed, one of the primary considerations that led to the discovery of the Computational Unified Field Theory's G-d's Physics Universal Consciousness Principle was implicitly related to this root cause of time and the transitory phenomenal nature of the physical universe.

Remember that we've mentioned the two closely related Computational Invariance Principle and Universal Consciousness Principle theoretical postulates. Essentially, these two theoretical postulates of the Computational Unified Field Theory indicate that the physical universe and all its constituent spatial pixels exist both during each consecutive universal frame that it produces as well as in between any two such consecutive universal frames in which only the singular, higher-ordered Universal Consciousness Principle exists. However, the physical universe itself, including all its constituting spatial pixels, exists only during each consecutive universal frame but not in between any two universal frames! This "shocking" new realization that the entire physical universe exists only temporarily during the universal frames but not in between the frames therefore led to the Universal Consciousness Principle postulate that states that the very existence of the physical universe may only be considered as a temporary phenomenal manifestation of the real constant singular reality of the Universal Consciousness Principle!

More and more, we reach the inevitable conclusion that the old Material-Causal Paradigm of Science, characterized by twentieth century's relativistic and quantum models, must give way to our new, exciting, and even awe-inspiring G-d's Physics' A Causal Computation Paradigm, which views our physical universe not as existing independently and constantly, but rather as being entirely dependent upon—entirely computed by—and in fact merely a manifestation of the singular Universal Consciousness Principle...

Indeed, perhaps the first step in our journey toward discovering the new and unique characterizations of this singular, higher-ordered Universal Consciousness Principle is to recognize the fact that this reality must retain, compute, dissolve, and evolve every spatial pixel in the universe many billions of times per second.

Let's revert back to the Cinematic Film Metaphor and slow down the rapid progression of the film frames to the point that we are able to notice that there exists a flash of pure light between any two consecutive film frames. All the spatial pixels comprising one film frame dissolve into this light and are then reproduced, either precisely the same in the subsequent frame or changed or evolved. In fact, I have learned that, in the film industry, there is a production worker whose job it is to inspect all the objects comprising the sequence of a given film scenario to ensure that none of the objects disappears or changes unexpectedly. An example would be an actor dropping a water bottle. This might appear ultimately in the film as the water bottle suddenly appearing out of nowhere! This outside observer who inspects the film frames in our metaphor is parallel to the Universal Consciousness Principle!

The Computational Unified Field Theory's G-d's Physics A-Causal Computation Paradigm is somewhat equivalent to our Cinematic Film Metaphor. In our universe, all the spatial pixels comprising one universal film frame dissolve in between each frame back into the Universal Consciousness Principle. The human film analyzer inspects the contents of consecutive *physical* frames; however, in the <u>Universal Consciousness Principle</u>, the various universal frames do not exist physically! We must accept that, according to the new A Causal Computation Paradigm, the physical reality does not exist as an independent reality; it exists only as a transient phenomenal manifestation of the singularity of the <u>Universal Consciousness Principle</u>! This means that each consecutive universal frame doesn't continue to exist as a physical reality in between any two consecutive universal frames but rather completely dissolves back into the singularity of this <u>Universal Consciousness Principle</u>.

Indeed, the amazing new realization that we can derive from the Cinematic Film Metaphor is that no external human consciousness exists to inspect, or to remember, retain, reproduce, and evolve all the spatial pixels that comprise the entire physical universe at each consecutive universal frame. So, the dissolution of every spatial pixel comprising any given universal frame and its retention, reproduction, and evolution in the consecutive universal frames entirely depends on the operation of the singular, higher-ordered <u>Universal Consciousness Principle</u>. But this means that all the spatial pixels comprising any universal frame must be retained as the series of past universal frame, which comprise the physical universe during all past universal frames by this singular higher-ordered Universal Consciousness Principle!. Moreover, somewhat parallel to the job of the film inspector in our metaphor, in order to reproduce all the spatial pixels comprising the entire physical universe, it is necessary for the <u>Universal Consciousness Principle</u> to remember and then evolve each spatial pixel in the subsequent frames…

So, the emerging questions are: What are the <u>Universal Consciousness Principle</u>'s laws that determine the evolution of the universal frames? And how are all the past, present, and future Universal Frames stored, reproduced, and evolved?

Well, one of the fascinating new discoveries of G-d's Physics is that, within the <u>Universal Consciousness Principle</u>, there exists a "bank" of all past, present, and future universal frames which is called: the Universal Consciousness Principle's "Supra-Spatial-Temporal Reservoir". In fact, the amazing new law discovered by G-d's Physics is called the "Dynamic Equilibrium Moral Principle"; it pertains to the dynamics and operation of this Supra-Spatial Temporal Reservoir of all past, present, and future universal frames! As we've seen, *there exists only one singular Universal Consciousness Principle* underlying all spatial pixels in the universe, and all these spatial pixels represent only a manifestation of the singular Universal Consciousness Principle. And this singular, higher-ordered Universal Consciousness Principle is also characterized by its "Good Will Hypothesis", which is its inherent nature. It is a tendency to do good, assist, and take care of all living things, and be interested in their evolution toward the Universal Consciousness Principle's full complete Perfection. Therefore, this new Dynamic Equilibrium Moral Principle states that the unified Universal Consciousness Principle operates under an inherent law that prohibits any "immoral balance" created or chosen by any Individual Human Consciousness. In fact, it corrects or balances any such attempt. This is simply due to the fact that, from the singular higher-ordered perspective of the Universal Consciousness Principle, all Individual Human Consciousness is comprised of integral parts of the unity and singularity of this Universal Consciousness Principle, which represents a singular whole. So, in the same manner that we could not even imagine a situation in which our right hand would voluntarily inflict pain on our left hand, the Universal Consciousness Principle resists and balances any attempt by one Individual Human Consciousness to inflict pain or suffering upon another Individual Human Consciousness. This new and amazing discovery of the Universal Consciousness Principle's Dynamic Equilibrium Moral Principle is tied to the fact that our Individual Human Consciousness possesses a "free-choice" capacity to make Moral decisions and choices; hence, when our free-will Individual Human Consciousness makes (G-d forbid) an immoral choice to consciously inflict pain or suffering upon another Individual Human Consciousness, any such infliction of pain must be counterbalanced by equivalent suffering to the Individual Human Consciousness that caused the initial pain.

Another metaphor may be useful to explicate the Dynamic Equilibrium Moral Principle. Picture, if you will, an elastic trampoline membrane coved by small marbles. Now imagine that there is a solid metal bar connecting two opposite marbles. Imagine that one of these two marbles decides to "inflict pain" upon the other marble by pushing the solid metal bar into the marble. Given the fact that these two marbles are placed on the same elastic trampoline membrane, we can see that any such "aggressive" movement by one of the marbles against the other would automatically create an opposite reaction in which the marble under attack would exert negative "aggressive" force upon the first "aggressive" marble, right? This metaphor elucidates the basic rationale behind G-d's Physics newly discovered Dynamic Equilibrium Moral Principle. In the same manner that it is suggested that the elastic trampoline membrane has an intrinsic tendency toward balancing any pain inflicted upon one marble by any other marble because of their mutual connection with the single elastic membrane, so it is suggested that the singular, higher-ordered Universal Consciousness Principle possesses an innate tendency toward balancing any immoral choice of any element of Individual Human Consciousness! In other words, the Dynamic Equilibrium Moral Principle indicates that at least one of the important factors determining the computation, sustenance, and evolution of all the spatial pixels comprising any series of Universal Frames is based on the singular Universal Consciousness Principle's innate tendency to correct or balance any immoral choice made by any element of Individual Human Consciousness inflicted upon another such element.

What this means is that, contrary to the old Material-Causal Paradigm's basic explanation of all physical occurrences or events as being caused by certain preceding physical interactions, the Computational Unified Field Theory's G-d's Physics proclaims that, since all the spatial pixels comprising any universal frame dissolve in between any two consecutive universal frames, and there is no physical effect that can pass from one universal frame to its consecutive frame, one of the important factors that can explain the sustenance, recomputation, and evolution of each exhaustive spatial pixel from one universal frame to another is this newly discovered Dynamic-Equilibrium Moral Principle, which explains the occurrences, events, and evolution in human life as related to the moral or immoral choices that every human being makes!

Let's take a concrete example. Imagine a situation in which a certain human being faces a specific moral choice. Our hero is the CEO of a high-tech company. He is rushing to an extremely important board of directors' meeting in which he is expected to present the total earnings of the company over the past year and consequently is also expected to be awarded a special prize of recognition for the financial success of the company. The only thing is that, while he is zooming in his dark-blue Jaguar XJ to this important meeting, a terrible accident causes him to get stuck in a traffic jam. He does not know how long the time delay will be, but he realizes he may be late to his important board meeting. What does he do then? One choice is to take a risk by maneuvering his car and making an illegal U-turn against the oncoming traffic, thereby endangering the oncoming cars and pedestrians. This may be considered an immoral choice, which may enable him to reach his coveted lucrative board meeting on time but comes with the dangerous price of risking other people's safety, or even lives, G-d forbid. Or, he could choose to put aside his own self-centered interests for a while and go out of his way in order to potentially save human lives. This would be the right moral choice. He could even offer his own fast car to rush an injured pedestrian to the hospital when he realizes the ambulance might be delayed. Yes, if our real hero opts to act in this manner, he would risk missing his meeting and may potentially give up a significant rise in his salary, or even be fired following his potential embarrassing absence from the important meeting. Nevertheless, he would have made a highly moral *good* choice.

Now, according to our understanding of the new higher Universal Consciousness Principle's Dynamic Equilibrium Moral Principle, the singular, unitary Universal Consciousness Principle retains the two alternative choices—moral and immoral—one of which was made by our hero. He could have chosen to inflict pain upon another Individual Human Consciousness, which constitutes another integral segment of the same singular Universal Consciousness Principle, or (much better) he could have chosen to bestow goodness upon another such Individual Human Consciousness of the unitary singular whole Universal Consciousness Principle! The new tantalizing discovery made by the A Causal Computation Paradigm—G-d's Physics—is that the choices—moral and immoral—that can be made by an Individual Human Consciousness in any universal frame actually determines the execution of one of multiple potential futures, all of which are stored within the Supra-Spatial Temporal reservoir, the "bank" of all past, present, and future Universal Frames stored within the <u>Universal Consciousness Principle</u>!

Imagine our hero chose the undesirable immoral choice—to make an illegal and potentially dangerous U-turn in order to reach his lucrative board meeting where expected to receive a significant prize and financial gains. According to the new Dynamic Equilibrium Moral Principle, by making such an immoral choice and potentially inflicting pain or suffering on the injured individuals who needed his assistance, and even potentially hitting another car or pedestrian, our hero would set in motion a "moral correction" and "moral balancing" action by the <u>Universal Consciousness Principle</u> singular reality. This could manifest almost instantaneously; for example, through an unexpected turn of events in which someone at the board meeting might disclose a previously undisclosed immoral or unprofessional situation for which this CEO is directly responsible, which would lead to a unanimous vote to fire the CEO immediately. Or, the correcting balance could manifest after a while—say two or three years later on after our hero has already retired as a wealthy man—but then he contracts a severe disease or he is involved in a car accident and finds himself in the same situation in which he chose to act immorally, and would therefore have to experience the same pain or suffering that he inflicted upon others. On the other hand, if our hero had risen to the occasion and opted to act morally, then, according to the new Dynamic Equilibrium Moral Principle, the singular higher-ordered <u>Universal Consciousness Principle</u> would also record and retain that moral choice and remunerate our hero either instantaneously when the board members recognize his noble and courageous act and reward him for it, or after a while, say a few years later, when he would be offered a lucrative prize or higher position, even if initially our CEO hero lost his job and suffered a trying period of time for a few years, at the end of which his courageous story would see the light of day.

Now, why is this new Dynamic Equilibrium Moral Principle significant? Well, because it starts portraying an entirely new and fascinating picture of our physical reality and even the entire physical universe. We now see it governed not by chance physical interactions, but rather as motivated by our own human moral and immoral choices.

The physical reality is not blind to our moral motivations and actions, but is rather propelled and mobilized by them! Succinctly stated, this new Computational Unified Field Theory's A Causal Computation Paradigm—G-d's Physics—carries the basic dynamics governing the evolution of our universe, which is continuously computed, dissolved, recomputed, and evolved. It is not based on any Material-Causal physical interactions; rather, it is driven by the singularity of the Universal Consciousness Principle, which possesses the basic Dynamic-Equilibrium Moral Principle, which views each Individual Human Consciousness—individual human being—as an integral part of it, therefore acting incessantly to balance and correct any immoral imbalance so that if any pain and suffering inflicted upon one of its constituting parts by an aggressive part, the aggressive part will experience an equivalent amount of pain and suffering.

The Dynamic Equilibrium Moral Principle also gives us an entirely new picture of the evolution of our physical universe and our everyday physical reality as being continuously computed, dissolved, and re-produced by the singularity of the Universal Consciousness Principle, as we've seen, many billions of times per second. We understand that what seems to us as a solid physical reality in fact merely represents the enactment or production of a series of universal frames of the past, present, and multiple futures, solely based on our own moral or immoral conscious choices...

So, from now on when we see an unfortunate event—a disease, an accident, an act of deceit or violence—or, conversely, a fortunate event— good health, a safe existence, an act of kindness—we will immediately realize that the circumstance was not caused merely by material factors but rather by a deeper Universal Consciousness Principle's Dynamic Equilibrium Moral Principle! If we witness or experience (G-d forbid!) a car accident, for example, we would no longer just blame an oil spill on the road, a reckless driver, or even the driver's sleepiness, even though each one of these factors could have caused the accident. We would know that the real underlying cause of the accident must the balancing act of the singular, higher-ordered Universal Consciousness Principle's Dynamic-Equilibrium Moral Principle. Yes, the discovery of this principle revises our basic old Material-Causal twentieth-century

Physics Paradigm's conception of the world as being governed by mere physical interactions, instead returning the full weight of our moral responsibility to our shoulders as mature conscious human beings. We realize that, in everything that happens to us in life—our family members' health, wealth, and happiness; our relationships with other people; the good or bad events that happen to us—all depend on our moral or (G-d forbid) immoral choices. If we could but glance at the singular higher-ordered perspective of the <u>Universal Consciousness Principle</u>'s Supra-Spatial Temporal Reservoir bank of all past, present, and multiple future scenarios and realize in what precise manner this singular <u>Universal Consciousness Principle</u> computes and balances its inherent Dynamic Equilibrium Moral Principle to allow each Individual Human Consciousness (human being) to experience the fruits of his or her own good (moral) or bad (immoral) choices, we would be completely overwhelmed by a feeling of awe and reverence at the magnanimity and infinitude of this singular <u>Universal Consciousness Principle</u>'s wisdom, love, and beauty.

Yes, imagine looking even at the computation of a single such Individual Human Consciousness: in order to compute the happenings and occurrences of just one human being out of more than seven billion, in his or her life, we would have to compute all that individual's moral choices from the earliest age when conscious choice is possible. And, if we believe in the soul's reincarnation, then we would have to take into account also all that human-being's soul's previous incarnations' moral and immoral choices! Imagine just looking at that individual's experiences of health or happiness. Remember our CEO's single choice between assisting the car accident's victims or opting to pursue his own selfish interests? Even just for that single moral or immoral choice, the <u>Universal Consciousness Principle</u> would have to compute or balance all the subsequent universal frames that would allow this Individual Human Consciousness to experience the same degree and intensity of that goodwill or misfortune that it caused for another human being. And bear in mind that this singular, higher-ordered <u>Universal Consciousness Principle</u> would have to also take into account in its computation of that individual human being's multiple future occurrences with multiple other people, each one according to the particular merit or demerit and its intensity, so that over the long run, it could balance and even out the experiences of those other individuals (good or bad) in such a manner that the single human being we chose to focus on would also reap the benefits of his or her own good or bad moral choices toward each of these myriad human beings that it comes into contact with every day over the course of a lifetime or even additionally over multiple previous lifetimes. Now multiply this by seven billion human beings…

Obviously, the complexity and infinite wisdom involved in computing all past, present, or multiple future Universal Frames for each of the seven billion or more human beings that are continuously interacting with each other is inconceivable!

Now, we will add in another new discovery, which is introduced for the first time in this book an idea that ties in with the Jewish concept of *teshuva*, which is a sincere feeling of remorse for one's immoral actions and an accompanying sincere attempt and obligation to try one's best *not* to repeat such immoral action. This would lead to an eradicating of any immoral action of an individual human being from all past universal frames. In fact, it would replace them with the opposite moral choices that that individual could have chosen, at least in terms of the singular Universal Consciousness Principle's Dynamic Equilibrium Moral Principle's computation for that individual. In Jewish Chassidic thought, this is thought of as a person's misdeeds transformed into good deeds, as considered by G-d. Indeed, when we view this from the perspective of the A Causal Computation Paradigm, the Universal Consciousness Principle as one singular whole computing all past, present, and multiple futures universal frames, we realize that, according to the new Dynamic Equilibrium Moral Principle, there exists a real possibility of "teshuva"; that is, a real possibility of rectifying all past misdeeds and turning them into past good deeds, thereby preventing the Dynamic Equilibrium Moral Principle's need to balance or teach any Individual Human Consciousness.

In other words, according to the new G-d's Physics A Causal Computation Paradigm, initially we saw that the singular higher-ordered Universal Consciousness Principle contains a bank of all past, present, and multiple future Universal Frames with the Dynamic Equilibrium Moral Principle serving as the means for determining any given individual human being's selected future based on his or her moral or immoral choices. Depending on our behavior, we might win the lottery or gain any other significant benefit; conversely, we might suffer from (G-d forbid) any number of unfortunate occurrences because of our immoral choices. Good and bad circumstances in our lives are not due to any chance physical or material factors! Hence, our moral choices constitute a key determining factor for the quality of our lives and the good or bad experiences we shall experience. But, the good news is that, since this singular, higher-ordered Universal Consciousness Principle possesses an intrinsic Goodwill element that wants to bestow goodness and happiness, health and abundance upon all creatures – human beings (animals and plants), it is postulated by the A-Causal Computation Paradigm that there is a special power of "teshuva" that constitutes another compassionate means through which this singular Universal Consciousness Principle(G-d) has provided us with the possibility of rectifying any immoral choices or misdeeds that we've done through our sincere regret and conscious choice to try and not repeat any such behaviors in the future. Thus, instead of having to experience the same degree of suffering or pain that we consciously inflicted upon another human being, which is the means through which this singular, higher-ordered Universal Consciousness Principle, G-d would teach us and balance the Dynamic Equilibrium principle's basic underlying harmony and unity of the Universal Consciousness Principle, we are given another improved means for rectifying the immoral balance that we've created in the singularity of the Universal Consciousness Principle modifying the Dynamic Equilibrium Moral Principle by making teshuva; that is, by making a conscious effort and prayer of regretting our misdeeds and making a conscious decision to not repeat that behavior. In fact, we make an effort to act in an opposite manner, which would bring good deeds into the world. In this manner, the singular, higher-ordered Universal Consciousness Principle would allow us to avoid having to experience the same suffering or pain that we brought unto others; in fact, we would then ourselves reap the future benefits as if we had opted to act morally instead of immorally in the past.

This means that our moral or immoral choices not only determine which of several multiple potential futures would be selected for us, but also, if we opt to make a sincere "teshuva", this would rectify and alter our past misdeeds into good deeds, thereby erasing and rewriting our past, which therefore would also alter and select one of several good futures based on our teshuva-based moral choice. So, this means that, at the very center or apex of our life's journey, our moral choices, character, and deeds would stand tall! They would select one of multiple futures based on our moral or immoral choices. More philosophically, this new conception of G-d's Physics places as the very center of our new, much more expansive understanding of the physical universe not only the singular, higher-ordered Universal Consciousness Principle, but also our own Individual Human Consciousness and the moral or immoral choices it makes. This is very reminiscent of Maimonides's inspiring and enlightening statement that we should view ourselves always in such a state wherein every small moral choice can tilt the whole world as well as oneself toward a good or bad state or future. So, instead of the world existing materially and independently of our own moral choices, the world and all its occurrences becomes intimately connected with our own Individual Human Moral Choices! Indeed, as we'll see in the next chapter, Human Consciousness has a very special and unique role and place in the entire evolution of the universe from this new singular, higher-ordered perspective of the Universal Consciousness Principle.

But, perhaps one last key point to be discussed relating to the striking and surprising resemblance of the Dynamic Equilibrium Moral Principle to some of Judaism's Chassidic revelations has to do with our moral obligations stemming from the discovery of the new G-d's Physics Dynamic Equilibrium Moral Principle. Remember the small, everyday metaphor of the impossibility of our right hand inflicting pain upon our left hand? It is obvious from own human experience that we would never willingly inflict pain to ourselves! Now, once we started gaining a deeper and higher understanding of the singular, higher-ordered Universal Consciousness Principle, which constitutes the only singular reality that exists constantly and continuously, both during each consecutive universal frames that it computes at the incredible rate of many billions of times per second, as well as solely existing in between any two such consecutive universal frames, and became familiar with one of its key characteristics—the Dynamic Equilibrium

Moral Principle, which views all Individual Human Consciousness as integral elements much as we regard our right and left hands as integral parts of our entire human body—we reach the inevitable new realization that we cannot inflict pain upon another human being! Because we begin to understand that the Universal Consciousness Principle regards all Individual Human Consciousness as integral parts of its entirety, and therefore prohibits us from inflicting pain or suffering upon each other.

This brings us to the surprising discovery of Judaism's proclamation of the Seven Commandments of Noah: 1) worshipping G-d only, 2) respecting G-d, 3) forbidding killing, 4) forbidding incest, 5) forbidding stealing, 6) forbidding eating any living animal, 7) enforcing a legal system relating to these seven commandments. Surprisingly, many of these commandments deal with the enactment of our newly discovered Universal Consciousness Principle's Dynamic Equilibrium Moral Principle; that is, the need to not inflict pain or suffering upon another human being (or animal)! Other commandments address the need to recognize and worship or pray and to maintain gratitude and reverence toward G-d.

Indeed, the Lubavitcher Rebbe, the greatest Jewish sage of our time, declared that the fulfillment of the Noah's Commandments and their dissemination throughout the whole world would create a good and secure future for the world. He regarded their dissemination and support throughout the world as a key task for our generation. Indeed, when Science now reaches the fortunate and inspiring discovery of the existence of a singular, higher-ordered unified Universal Consciousness Principle and its intrinsic propensity of Goodwill—a unitary integrated Dynamic Equilibrium Moral Principle—we are entering a completely new era of Human Redemption, "Geula" in Jewish terms. We will recognize that we are all integral parts of the same singular Universal Consciousness Principle, and we will profit from a basic understanding that we must act wisely and not harm any other Individual Human Consciousness as integral parts of G-d's creation. We will know that, by respecting these universal moral laws, we in fact are selecting for ourselves as well as for others a better future from among multiple morally based futures. We will reach one of the high points along our upward scientific-spiritual journey wherein we realize that our own human existence and our extremely important choices—moral and immoral—do matter; in fact, the moral choices tilt whole world for the better (and the immoral choices tilt it for the worse).

We realize that the Universal Consciousness Principle notices and cares about each of our moral choices and encourages us to choose morally. The singular Universal Consciousness Principle's unfathomable power and intelligence enables it to be responsible for computing, creating, dissolving, and recreating every single spatial pixel in the universe, including all Humanity, all plants, and all animals, many billions of times per second. The Dynamic Equilibrium Moral Principle has an amazing and inspiring capacity to calculate each of the myriad of individual human beings' multiple moral and immoral choices, thereby selecting the specific future for each human being as he or she interacts with all other human beings across the innumerable past, present, and future universal frames. We stand with indescribable awe, humility, and reverence toward the wisdom, intelligence, and compassion of this singular, higher-ordered Universal Consciousness Principle, which is willing even to reorganize each individual's future based on his or her sincere teshuva—asking for forgiveness and making a decision to change his or her way morally. We may not—and indeed cannot—fully understand the unfathomable considerations and computations of this singular higher-ordered Universal Consciousness Principle as it appears in our own personal lives or in the lives of others who are close to us, but we are promised and reassured that this singular G-d Reality cares, listens, and watches over each of us with infinite love and affection. It is All Goodness, and therefore everything that it produces in our lives is for the better, and we should therefore keep an open minded and remain grateful, reverent, and trusting toward it. Pray and believe that it always will take us toward our better future and growth, and indeed steer the whole world towards its Morally, Spiritually and even Physically Perfected State of "Geula" (Redemption)...

CHAPTER 7

The Reversed-Time Goal Hypothesis

The new G-d's Physics opens up a whole new perspective for our basic understanding of the physical universe as well as our own human existence within it; indeed, what we've already seen is that the universe was not created or caused by an initial Big Bang explosion; neither are its components propelled perpetually outward by "dark matter" or "dark energy", neither of which can be proven to exist. In fact, we've just begun to realize that the way in which this physical universe functions or operates and evolves has much more to do with the specific characterizations of this singular, higher-ordered Universal Consciousness Principle than it does with any Material-Causal physical interactions or even laws. Thus, for instance, we've noticed that one of the key characteristics of the Universal Consciousness Principle is its Dynamic Equilibrium Moral Principle. So, we realize that if, for instance, a certain individual contracts a serious disease or is injured in an accident (G-d forbid), the negative outcome may have more to do with that person's past immoral decisions and actions rather than being solely caused by certain Material-Causal agents such as his or her genes or the existence of an agent that caused illness or accident.

Again and again throughout the upward-ascending journey we've shared in this book, we've endeavored to discover and understand the depth and wonders of twenty-first century's new Computational Unified Field Theory A Causal Computation Paradigm—G-d's Physics as we've termed it! We must momentarily stop to digest, reflect upon, and really understand the full meaning and significance of Science's new A-Causal

Computation Paradigm and singular <u>Universal Consciousness Principle</u>, which solely exists as a continual consistent reality in opposition to the old Material-Causal Paradigm through which our human minds have become so habituated to view and comprehend the world. How can it be that the physical universe at large and our own physical reality in which we live and function is not real? How can it be that our old scientific Material-Causal Paradigm, to which we have become habituated, is unsatisfactory in explaining how everything works? Surely we know that, if we light a candle with our lighter, then the burning of the candle's wick is caused by its direct physical contact—or interaction—with the flame of that lighter. Right? Yes—that's how *it seems!*

But, if we remind ourselves of our Cinematic Film Metaphor and its depiction of the shattering of the glass jar as apparently caused by the impact of the heavy hammer, and we remember that, as real as that cause-and-effect scenario may seem at the time that we're watching the film, when we halt the progression of the film, we immediately realize that there cannot exist any such cause-and-effect physical relationships between the hammer and the glass jar. In fact, there can't be such a relationship between any two spatial pixels comprising any number of film frames because we see that all these spatial pixels comprising any film frame are presented simultaneously, and because there cannot be any transference of any spatial pixels or any effect between any two consecutive film frames, there exists only the pure light of the projector between any two such consecutive lights. When we translate this new realization derived from the Cinematic Film Metaphor into the <u>Computational Unified Field Theory</u>'s new A-Causal Computation model, we realize that, even though the physical world and the physical universe at large seem so real and solid, when we take into account the A-Causal Computation model, which teaches us that, in fact, every spatial pixel comprising the whole physical universe is being continuously computed, dissolved, recomputed, and evolved many billions of times per second, and that in between any two such consecutive Universal Frames the whole physical universe dissolves back into the singular <u>Universal Consciousness Principle</u>, we must reach the inevitable conclusion that, even though the physical reality that we're so accustomed to seems so real, solid, and stable, it does not exist, in fact, as an independent and constant physical reality. Everything in our universe exists only as manifestations of the singular, higher-ordered <u>Universal Consciousness Principle</u>, which exists consistently both during each consecutive universal frame as solely computing, dissolving, and evolving each and every spatial pixel in the universe and also existing solely, without the presence of the physical universe, in between any two consecutive universal frames…

Perhaps the small, everyday life metaphor that I shared earlier relating to my own experience when I was driving behind a truck that was covered in white canvas as I drove in the dark between Jerusalem and Zichron-Yaacov in Israel may once again be helpful here. The highway I traveled is lined with streetlights that are spaced every hundred meters or so. What I actually saw was an alternating appearance and disappearance of the back of that white truck. I seemed to be seeing rapid flashes of the white truck interspersed with blackness that suggested the "disappearance" of the truck. To a naïve novice observer of this scenario, the scene would surely appear as if there are two alternating realities—one of the white truck and the other of blackness when the truck was not visible. But, for us mature adults, the reality of the situation appears very clear; in fact, there exists only one singular reality of the canvas-covered truck, which nevertheless seems to appear and disappear due to the presence of the streetlights! This small, everyday life metaphor can shed some light for us when we're trying to grasp the big <u>Paradigmatic Shift</u> of the A Causal Computation Paradigm—G-d's Physics. This is because, in much the same manner that the truck remains constant whether we see it under the streetlights or whether we don't when it is in between any two consecutive streetlights, so does the singular <u>Universal Consciousness Principle</u> exist consistently and constantly whether it is when the <u>Universal Consciousness Principle</u> computes each consecutive universal frame or whether it is in between any two consecutive Universal Frames in which the entire physical universe dissolves back into the singularity of the <u>Universal Consciousness Principle</u>, which remains solely without the presence of the physical universe.

Yes, as hard as it may be for us fully grasp and accept, the only transitory or temporary existence of the physical universe exists only as a manifestation of the singular reality of the <u>Universal Consciousness Principle</u>. This is an inevitable conclusion drawn from the acceptance of the A Causal Computation Paradigm! More and more, we have to adapt and adjust to this new way of looking at the world that twenty-first-century Theoretical Physics is revealing to us: the old Material-Causal Paradigm of twentieth century's <u>Relativity Theory</u> and <u>Quantum Mechanics</u> assumed several incorrect premises: 1) Physical reality can be explained based on mere cause-and-effect physical interactions such as the Big Bang explosion creating the physical universe. 2) <u>"dark matter"</u> and <u>"dark energy"</u> are causing the accelerated expansion of the universe. 3) Einstein's General Relativity equations suggest that the universe evolves through a direct physical interaction between massive objects such as suns, galaxies, and so forth, causing a curvature of space-time, and this curved space-time causes or determines the traveling pathways of those massive objects.

This old Material-Causal Paradigm has to give way to the new A Causal Computation Paradigm's new conception and understanding of the physical universe as being created and recreated many billions of times per second, being dissolved back into the singular <u>Universal Consciousness Principle</u> in between any two consecutive universal frames. So, the new picture we obtain of this wondrous, awe-inspiring singular <u>Universal Consciousness Principle</u> is one in which there really exists only the singular <u>Universal Consciousness Principle</u>. We see that our cherished world and universe exists only as a manifestation of this singular <u>Universal Consciousness Principle</u>. As we've already seen, we have to brush away any old Material-Causal assumptions as there cannot exist any such cause and effect, or in fact any real physical interactions at either the macroscopic relativistic level or at the microscopic quantum level because all spatial pixels comprising any universal frame are computed simultaneously by the singular <u>Universal Consciousness Principle</u>, and the entire physical universe dissolves in between any two consecutive universal frames, so there cannot be any transferences of any such cause and effect or even of any exhaustive spatial pixel across frames.

What we arrive at is an entirely new A-Causal Computation G-d's Physics physical universe that is really only a manifestation of the singular <u>Universal Consciousness Principle</u> that is being continuously produced, dissolved, reproduced, and evolved many billions of times per second. Indeed, one of the amazing new facets of this singular <u>Universal Consciousness Principle</u>'s conception of the physical universe and of <u>Science</u> in general is that we no longer can rely on any of the old Material-Causal scientific laws to explain any physical phenomenon; rather, we must discover the new higher-ordered characteristics of this singular reality of the <u>Universal Consciousness Principle</u>.

One of the amazing new characteristics of this singular, higher-ordered <u>Universal Consciousness Principle</u> is the Dynamic-Equilibrium Moral principle, which governs the real underlying cause for the <u>Universal Consciousness Principle</u>'s intrinsic balancing of any immoral action propagated by one Individual Human Consciousness toward another Individual Human Consciousness. Now we're poised to discover all the new fascinating facets, characteristics, and features of this singular, higher-ordered <u>Universal Consciousness Principle</u>, which was discovered by the new G-d's Physics. First, stemming from the fact that the entire physical universe dissolves in between any two consecutive universal frames and that there cannot be any material entity or any physical interaction in between any two consecutive universal frames, the A-Causal Computation Paradigm asserts that all the physical laws governing the universe—both at the macroscopic relativistic level as well as at the microscopic quantum level—do not bind or constrain this singular, higher-ordered <u>Universal Consciousness Principle</u>. In other words, the <u>Universal Consciousness Principle</u> possesses an element of "Free-Will" that is not bound or constrained by any laws or physical limitations!

Think about the fact that all spatial pixels comprising any universal frame dissolve back into this <u>Universal Consciousness Principle</u> in between any two consecutive frames. This means that, even though it may seem to us that a certain particle or planet exists consistently at a certain spatial location or endowed with a certain energetic level, or that certain physical laws exist, these concepts are all negated by the A Causal Computation Paradigm. These laws include gravity, magnetic attraction, Relativity's assumed curvature of Space-Time by massive objects, the creation of the physical universe by an initial Big

Bang nuclear event, and the assumption by Quantum Mechanics that a target's probability wave function collapses due to its direct physical interaction with another subatomic probe.

There exists only one singular, higher-ordered Universal Consciousness Principle, which appears as the physical universe during each of its computed consecutive universal frames and exists solely without the presence of the physical universe in between any two consecutive frames. This Universal Consciousness Principle is not bound or constrained by any physical laws; rather, the entire existence, dissolution, recreation, and evolution of the physical universe and all its constituent elements, laws, and occurrences may be explained only through an analysis and understanding of the special characteristics of this singular Universal Consciousness Principle.

Hence, the new A-Causal Computation Science developed from the Computational Unified Field Theory advocates an entirely new conception of the physical universe, thus negating the old Material-Causal Paradigm of twentieth-century Relativity Theory and Quantum Mechanics. This new Science reveals that the universe was not created by a chance Big Bang explosion; rather, it is being continuously created, dissolved, recreated, and evolved by the Universal Consciousness Principle. The physical universe is not evolved through chance direct physical interactions between massive objects such as suns, planets, black holes, and so forth or space-time, or between subatomic probe elements that interact and cause the collapse of the subatomic target probability wave function. The new A Causal Computation Paradigm— G-d's Physics— asserts that the whole creation, dissolution, recreation, and evolution of every spatial pixel throughout the entire physical universe many billions of times per second is guided by the Universal Consciousness Principle's goal of evolving and expressing more and more the expansive and unlimited nature of the Universal Consciousness Principle. Yes, according to G-d's Physics, the evolution of the physical universe is guided by an inherent tendency of this singular Universal Consciousness Principle to express itself through increasingly broader and more expansive forms, both as it manifests through the evolution from inanimate objects to animate plants and animals, culminating in this evolution appearing in human beings, and ultimately to the appearance of an expansive human consciousness, which is a state of Individual Human Consciousness that is inseparable from the full expansiveness of the Universal Consciousness Principle...

Yes, one of the amazing and exciting new discoveries made by G-d's Physics is that the entire evolution of the biological forms is purposeful and is propagated by the singular Universal Consciousness Principle goal to create a Morally, Spiritually and even Physically Perfected "Geula" state of the World in which human beings will be capable of appreciating, revering, and manifesting the highest understanding of the singularity of this Universal Consciousness Principle. As we've seen previously, the A-Causal Computation Paradigm negates Darwin's natural selection principle due to its reliance upon the material-causal assumption of the existence of direct physical interactions between certain organisms and their environment, which leads to the extinction of the less-compatible organisms to their environment as opposed to the survival of the more compatible organisms. Indeed, it was previously shown that, due to the simultaneity of the Universal Consciousness Principle's computation of each and every spatial pixel in the universe for each consecutive universal frame, and the dissolution of the entire physical universe in between any two consecutive Universal Frames that there cannot exist any such material-causal physical interactions between any compatible or incompatible organism and its environment, much less so any cause and effect between the environment and its assumed causal effects on the survival or extinction of any given organism or species. However, the new discoveries of G-d's Physics are not only that the evolution of the species is not the result of Darwin's chance genetic mutations accompanied by a natural selection of the most compatible organisms to their directly interacting environment, but also that the appearance of increasingly more evolved or more expansive forms of the singular Universal Consciousness is purposeful and represents an intrinsic part of the program that this Universal Consciousness Principle possesses.

In fact, according to G-d's Physics, there are at least two additional manifestations of G-d's intrinsic tendency to manifest increasingly a growingly expansive nature apart from a tendency to create ever more conscious and expansive forms of inanimate and animate elements: plants and animals, including human beings, and the expansive human consciousness state in which a human being is inseparable from the Universal Consciousness Principle, including in its capacity to compute and affect any exhaustive spatial pixel in the physical universe in much the same manner that this <u>Universal Consciousness Principle</u> simultaneously computes the whole physical universe.

The first instance relates to the accelerated rate of the universe 's expansion. In contrast to the old Material-Causal Paradigm's explanation of this accelerated expansion rate of the universe as caused by <u>"dark matter"</u> and <u>"dark energy"</u>, G-d's Physics postulates that this expansion is due to the singular <u>Universal Consciousness Principle</u>'s accelerated increase of the number of constituting spatial pixels comprising each consecutive universal frame such that each consecutive universal frame comprises a larger more elaborate universe! One may say that this G-d's <u>Universal Consciousness Principle</u> is expressing more and more its infinite intelligence and unlimited nature, and it is allowing the most evolved expression of this singular, higher-ordered <u>Universal Consciousness Principle</u>; that is, the ability of human beings to detect, appreciate, and even revere the magnanimity of this <u>Universal Consciousness Principle</u>.

Yes, according to G-d's Physics, there exists a general goal-oriented process that characterizes the <u>Universal Consciousness Principle</u>'s growing tendency to express and manifest its expansive, Moral, Goodwill, caring nature along with the evolution of the universe, the evolution of all biological forms, the growing awareness of human beings toward the Dynamic-Equilibrium Moral Principle, and even <u>Science</u>'s new G-d's Physics Paradigm pointing at the existence of only one singular, higher-ordered <u>Universal Consciousness Principle</u>.

One of the most recently discovered theoretical postulates of G-d's Physics is called the "Reversed-Time Goal Hypothesis". This Universal Consciousness reality may organize all the constituting past, preset, and multiple future universal frames existing within its Supra-Spatial Temporal Reservoir bank from the future's ultimate goal of the <u>Universal Consciousness Principle</u> of expressing itself within the physical universe in an apparent manner so that human beings would all be aware of the <u>Universal Consciousness Principle</u> as the only reality existing within the physical universe and beyond it. That ultimate redemption in Judaism and Hassidic thought is known as "Geula"! It looks backwards to all preceding past and present universal frames so that the existence of all objects, plants, and animals, including human beings, is planned so that they would ultimately lead to that singular <u>Universal Consciousness Principle</u>(G-d) manifesting in the world through its <u>Geula</u>: total and complete redemption.

Interestingly, these latest exciting and awe-inspiring discoveries of the A-Causal Computation Paradigm theoretical physics of the twenty-first century—G-d's Physics—are strikingly similar to some of the prophetic and mystical statements and wisdom found within Jewish Hassidic and Kabbalistic thought. In *The Book of Zohar*, which Rabbi Shimon Bar Yochai wrote some 2500 years ago while hiding from the Romans in a cave in Mount Meron, the author states that, toward the eighteenth century, there would be a sudden strong awakening of scientific discoveries describing the physical universe, and in parallel, there would be a strong Kabbalistic Hassidic awakening. He also wrote that this would ultimately lead to their unification in the clear discovery of the singular <u>G-d Reality, (Universal Consciousness Principle</u>), which constitutes the only real reality existing in the world! Indeed, according to Hassidic Jewish thought, like the latest discoveries of G-d's Physics, the entire goal and purpose of G-d's creation of the world is to manifest fully within the physical reality of our world and universe. The entire universe is being constantly and continuously created and recreated by the singular G-d's reality, and this singular G-d's reality drives the entire evolution of the world toward a recognition of its singular existence in the world and human beings' growing-awareness toward His singular Goodwill, Moral, caring existence, and their inevitable reverence, gratefulness, prayer, and studying of His Torah (Biblical writings given to the Jewish people).

What are we to do with these latest scientific discoveries, which are strikingly similar and parallel to the Hassidic proclamations and infinite wisdom? First, I believe that the latest discoveries of G-d's Physics awakens an indescribable sense of awe, wonder, and reverence and may even awaken a strong sense of gratitude and prayer toward this newly discovered singular <u>Universal Consciousness Principle</u>, which creates, dissolves, recreates, and evolves every spatial pixel in the universe at the unfathomable rate of many billions of times per second. We must come to realize that we, as human beings, and in fact everything around us and even as far from us as the distant edges of the universe, do not exist independently or continuously but rather exist only temporarily and completely dependent upon the singular existence of the higher-ordered <u>Universal Consciousness Principle</u>. Also, in fact, we and everything around us exist only as a manifestation of this singular <u>Universal Consciousness Principle</u>. This manifests in us a sense of awe, astonishment, and reverence. It makes us humble, grateful, and respectful. It makes us realize that we are all integral parts of this singular united reality. We realize that this singular, higher-ordered <u>Universal Consciousness Principle</u> also possesses an intrinsic Dynamic Equilibrium Moral Principle that cares and diligently works in order to restore "moral balance" toward any of our immoral actions and goes out of its way to remunerate us for any good moral actions we may take. When we realize that this singular, higher-ordered <u>Universal Consciousness Principle</u> cares about our intentions, moral (or immoral) actions, that it wishes us to appreciate it's Goodwill, infinite Love, Compassion, and Wisdom in teaching us to become better, more moral human beings and ultimately to be aware of the oneness of all creation and to be reverent, appreciative, and grateful toward G-d, we may experience a great sense of joy, humbleness, reverence, moral responsibility, and indescribable awe and gratitude as well as a great desire to study, realize, and get closer and closer toward a greater appreciation of <u>Universal Consciousness Principle</u>.

It may be therefore most appropriate to close this first volume of *G-d's Physics* by mentioning the inspiring living truth of some of the greatest Jewish sages and prophets expressing and praying for our current discovery and appreciation of the singular <u>Universal Consciousness Principle</u> G-d's Physics. Maimonides asserted that, toward the end of times, the whole preoccupation of the world would be only to study G-d's existence and know Him to the best of our abilities. The Baal Shem Tov's and Alter Rebbi's discovered and delineated G-d's incessant creation and dissolution of the world—also based upon our moral or immoral choices and our responsibility to correct and prefect our own human nature and character and the world in which we live!

Jehonathan Bentovish (Bentwich), Ph.D.

The Lubavitcher Rebbe prophetically emphasized that <u>Geula</u> (redemption) is already here; we only have to "open our eyes and see it"! Every small positive action that we make, any good deed will bring this <u>Geula</u> ever closer and closer! For Jews, these are the 613 Mitzvas we are commanded to observe, and for non-Jews, these are the Seven Commandments of Noah they are responsible to follow.

CHAPTER 8

Living with G-∂'s Physics

As we're getting close to completing our initial journey, which will be continued and elaborated upon further in the second and third volumes of *G-d's Physics*, the interested reader must be asking, What do I do with this dramatic change in our world view of the universe and our physical reality? Why is this Important for me? How is it relevant for my own life? (By the way, this is precisely what the second volume of *G-d's Physics* will try to address!)

What do these startling discoveries means for us as individual human beings? What do they mean for the world in which we're living?

Well, first of all, we must come to realize some important revelations: 1) The world in which we're living is not physical but, rather, spiritual. 2) The world is being continuously created, dissolved, recreated, and evolved many billions of times per second by the singular, higher-ordered Universal Consciousness Principle. 3) This Universal Consciousness Principle is All Goodness and is characterized by Free-Will rather than bound by any of our physical limitations. 4) Its primary motivation is to do good to us and evolve Humanity and the whole wide world towards its ultimate Goal of a Morally, Spiritually and even Physically Perfected "Geula-State" World (including all inanimate elements such as stones, the entire Earth, the planets, and so forth). 5) All the Universal Consciousness Principle wants to do is help us evolve toward expressing our full human potential; that is, to realize that we are not separate from it and are responsible to partake an important role in "perfecting" the world towards it ultimate "Geula" state of existence! It wants to help us expand our human consciousness—our vision—to understand that the entire physical universe doesn't exist as an independent physical reality but rather as a manifestation of the singularity of the <u>Universal Consciousness Principle</u>.

These revelations surely lead us to a sense of wonderment and awe and perhaps even reverence and gratitude toward this All-Giving, All-Goodness singular <u>Universal Consciousness Principle</u>.

Our transformation is perhaps much like a scenario in which children grow up within a beautiful palace without realizing that the immaculate gorgeous rooms; the delicious, highly nutritious food; the clean, elegant clothing that are all prepared and provided for them every day without fail are *not* natural operations of the beautiful palace, created by themselves. Rather they are orchestrated by the almighty king of the beautiful palace who abandons all his other royal commitments just to take care of his beloved children and make sure that they are being looked after in the best possible manner. How would these pampered children feel when they discover that, in fact, all their royal needs, comforts, and enjoyments are not "natural occurrences" or natural operations happening "by themselves" by the very existence of the palace, but rather that they are provided lovingly and personally by the almighty king who governs and rules his immaculate, infinite kingdom, and that his powers and intelligence are infinite. And yet, this almighty king takes a special interest and individual care of his young children. We can immediately realize that these privileged children would be so delighted and almost awestruck by an incredible sense of surprise, gratitude, and wonderment to go from a state of complete ignorance of the existence of a king to a new realization that all their wonderful benefits did not happen by chance, but were rather preordained, arranged, planned, orchestrated, and well organized long before their birth and into the present and will continue into the future. All the tiniest details of these children's development—clothes, living quarters, education, all the people they would meet, the tests and trials they would go through—were all planned out ahead of time, all immaculately thought through by this singular higher almighty king, whose sole motivation was to enable these children to become the best human beings possible expressing their full appreciation and gratitude and assistance to the king in turning this palace into a shining appreciation and presence of this Almighty King!

This metaphor is taken from one of the great Chassidic Kabbalistic books, the sacred *Tanyah* written in the late eighteenth century by the great sage, Schneur Zalman. His writing depicting the special relationships between the Jewish soul and G-d, kindling a sense of awe, respect, and great love toward G-d, the Almighty King!

This Chassidic metaphor teaches a lesson that seems very relevant for us as we come to a full appreciation of the deeper meaning and implications of the discovery of G-d's Physics new <u>Scientific Paradigm</u>. We come to appreciate the fact that our entire existence is solely dependent upon the creative power of G-d, which sustains us, which dissolves and recreates us many billions of times each second. Additionally, we appreciate that this higher-ordered G-d reality plans ahead of time, from our infancy to our mature age, all our past, present, and multiple futures, which manifest depending on our moral choices. That this higher G-d reality deeply cares about our moral and immoral choices because it is All Goodness, because it knows that every Individual Human Consciousness is a part of it; therefore, all human beings are in oneness: one united whole, pure, good, harmonious manifestation of this singular G-d Reality! Then we must come into a sense of awe, admiration, great surprise, gratitude, and even love and reverence toward this Beautiful, Perfect, All-Goodness singular, higher-ordered G-d reality!

We also invariably develop a sense of wonder and feel a great need and urgency to know more about this higher-ordered, singular, All-Goodness, Moral G-d reality upon which our entire existence and that of our planet and universe depends!

Imagine a scenario in which you find yourself alone in a tiny wooden sailing ship. A great, ferocious typhoon is tossing the boat, and you sense that your very life is at great risk. You automatically start praying and asking G-d to intervene—to watch over you and save your precious life! Now imagine that the minute you pray with all your Soul, the typhoon quiets down and disappears and you can suddenly see that the terrible life-threatening storm was actually created and sustained only by G-d and that, the minute you prayed with all your heart and soul, G-d Himself appeared and immediately made the terrible typhoon evaporate. How would you feel? Surely, you'd fall on your knees. Out of sheer gratitude and faith, you would express an indescribable feeling of gratitude that your life had been saved by the wonderful Life-Giving Pure Goodness of G-d, right?

Once again, this Chassidic metaphor brings us toward a full living appreciation of G-d's Incredible Goodness and indescribable Compassion and caring for our insignificant, tiny existence—in comparison with the vast typhoon in an endless ocean, the entire cosmos (and even beyond that!). And yet this singular infinite G-d Reality stopped the world just for you! He halted the incredible force of nature represented by the ferocious typhoon just so that you could live.

This everyday life metaphor represents our growing awareness of our complete dependency upon the Grace and Goodness of G-d's sole, All-giving reality. In truth, *we are completely dependent* upon G-d's incessant creation, dissolution, recreation, and evolution of every cell in our bodies, every second in our lives. The physical world, our bodies, our health, and every small (good or bad) event that happens in our lives—not only over the last day, but since our birth and up till this very moment, and in fact, to our old age and beyond—everything, every moment, every past, present, and possible future event in our lives, every cell, every breath is all being given to us as an unfathomable present from this singular, All-Goodness, Infinite Wisdom, G-d Reality!

This sounds so overwhelming, so unbelievable, so good. This Goodness and Care, Wisdom and Ultimate Perfection is surely beyond our wildest dreams.

So, how do we live in the light of this Great Light, Immense Love, Infinite Caring, and Wisdom that watches over us and cares about and plans every small step in our lives—all to protect us, to guide us toward a better and more evolved existence and an appreciation of the presence and goodness and the morality and magnanimity of this G-d Reality?

This is where, once again, the great Jewish sages and prophets, Chassidic and Kabbalistic seers, can come to our aid. A full description and deeper understanding of the incredible depth, meaning, joy, and excitement born from this new light shed by G d's physics will be fully described in the next volume of *G-d's Physics*. For now, let us know that the sages and prophets taught the world that there is a deeper meaning and purpose to human life and existence; in a nutshell, they told us that G-d is All Goodness, that He created the world so that human beings can live Morally Perfected lives. He gave all human beings the Seven Commandments of Noah on which they must build their lives, including recognizing G-d's Goodness as well as thanking Him and revering Him for all the innumerable presents He has bestowed upon us. He showed us that life is Sacred and that we must not harm any other human being. We must try as much as we can to assist each other, to perfect our moral nature and character traits. We should therefore begin living our lives with a deep sense of gratitude, meaning, and purpose. Every moment of life counts – that we're in fact give the precise number of days and years that are necessary in order to fulfill our Life's Mission and Purpose. We are never alone; G-d is always with us, closer than our very breath. He ordains, creates, summons, and plans every moment, every occurrence in our incredibly precious lives in order to assist us to grow and evolve, to contribute to the world our special skills and goodness. Every human being living on this planet is as unique as the uniqueness of the whorls on the fingertips of each individual—no two are alike, and all these precious souls are sent to the world to kindle G-d's Light in the world!

And if, for some reason, we find ourselves in a "bad" or "unfortunate" situation in which we think or feel that (G-d forbid) we have been "left alone" or that we are being "punished" or that we have no hope, we must know and believe that everything that happens in our lives and in the world can take place only because this All-Goodness singular Reality of G-d wants it to happen! This is based on the knowledge that everything that happens to us is *not* "by chance"; it happens by "Personal Providence"! This is a Chassidic revelation by the great Jewish sage the Baal Shem Tov, the founder of the Chassidic Movement. G-d is All Goodness; that's His very nature. And He is also All Powerful and All Intelligent, so we must revise our thinking and, accordingly, our feelings to know and believe that, even in those times or situations in which we feel that we're being given "unfortunate" or "rough" or "negative" conditions or experiences, as the Baal Shem Tov said: "even the falling of a leaf in the middle of a forest can only take place because

G-d wishes to protect a small vulnerable worm from the dangerous rays of the sun". So, we're led to the inevitable conclusion that we're never alone; we're always being protected and guided, and even during those apparently "dark times", really G-d is only "washing away" our moral wrongdoings, "cleaning us", perfecting us, preparing us for a better and more harmonious and balanced moral, purposeful existence! This latter simile is again taken from the Alter Rebbe, Rabbi Schneur Zalman, one of the descendants and followers of the Baal Shem Tov (in his famous Sacred "Tanyah" Book).

Indeed, we are being led now toward a new bright future in which the Light of G-d will be continuously revealed by twenty-first century Science's G-d's Physics, a Physics Paradigm that has discovered that there is only one bright and shining reality of G-d's Universal Consciousness! The whole creation of the universe—not back so many years, but *now*, every billionth of a billionth of a billionth of a second—is purposeful, meaningful and being created through the sheer Will and Goodness of this singular higher reality of G-d's Universal Consciousness, purely out of His desire to enable the whole of creation—and mostly human beings—to evolve and to see and appreciate the Goodness, Morality, and Magnanimity of G-d's presence and existence, and accordingly to live a sacred, joyful, and meaningful life!

CHAPTER 9

Science Converges with Jewish Chassidic Thought

It is indeed quite amazing that the newest developments and discoveries in twenty-first-century Theoretical and Experimental Physics are found to converge with some of the ancient insights and profound wisdom of Jewish Chassidic and Kabbalistic knowledge. Take, for instance, the basic notion of the <u>Computational Unified Field Theory</u>'s A-Causal Computation Paradigm that the entire universe is being continuously created, dissolved, recreated, and, evolved many billions of times per second. This represents one of the basic tenets of Jewish Chassidic Kabbalistic thought: in the ancient Jewish Psalms, King David wrote "He who reproduces the whole world in his Goodness every day!" And in Chassidic-Kabbalistic thought, it was explained by Rabbi Shimon Bar Yochai in *The Book of Zohar* and further developed and explained by the Baal Shem Tov that G-d reproduces the entire universe every second, stemming from His All-Goodness. Intriguingly, one of the central discoveries and themes of the Baal Shem Tov was the concept of "Personal Divine Providence", which states that any occurrence taking place in the physical world can only manifest due the precise determination and Goodwill of G-d. The Baal Shem Tov is known to have given the simile of a single leaf falling from a tall tree, tossing and turning so many times until it precisely falls gently to cover the small body of a little worm, which was "praying to G-d" to save it from the dangerous heat. The Baal Shem Tov explained that G-d plans and cares and watches over every small detail in the world including the smallest praying worm and a tiny leaf that is summoned as a shield for it.

Indeed, as we have learned, the A Causal Computation Paradigm—G d's physics—also dictates that, since there cannot exist any cause-and-effect relationship between any two or more spatial pixels existing either in the same or other universal frame, and given the impossibility of the transference of any physical effects across any two universal frames due to the dissolution of all spatial pixels comprising any such universal frame in between any two subsequent universal frames, we conclude that the singular <u>Universal Consciousness Principle</u> exists beyond space and time, energy or mass and also exists beyond causality. The <u>Universal Consciousness Principle</u> exists both during each consecutive universal frame as solely computing and producing all spatial pixels comprising the entire physical universe during that frame, as well as solely existing without the presence of any physical universe in between any two consecutive frames. Therefore, since this singular, higher-ordered <u>Universal Consciousness Principle</u> is not bound by any causality, this also led G-d's physics to the profound realization that the singular <u>Universal Consciousness Principle</u> must be characterized solely through its own intrinsic Free-Will properties. Surprisingly, two of its intrinsic properties were found to be its Moral Principle—the Dynamic-Equilibrium Principle—and it's Goodwill, All-goodness properties!

So, we reach the surprising discovery that some of the latest discoveries of twenty-first-century Theoretical Physics' new A Causal Computation Paradigm—G d's Physics—very similarly converge with the Chassidic Kabbalistic key notions of Morality and compassion, caring, and love along with G-d's Good-Will. According to Chassidic thought, the entire goal and purpose of G-d's creation of the universe and our own world is to allow human beings to evolve and to recognize G-d's presence. Our purpose is to worship and to serve Him, to make this world an appropriate abiding place for His moral, just, pure, and divine presence in the world. One manifestation of this singular higher-ordered G-dly order and presence are the Seven Commandments of Noah, which instruct all human beings to maintain the basic moral order and code in the way that human beings treat each other (and even animals). Beyond that, it is a major Goal, purpose, and driving force behind the whole of creation and evolution of the world by G-d to bring Humanity in general toward a state of redemption (Geula) in which the whole of Humanity would embrace, recognize, and study G-d's presence; develop a sense of gratitude and reverence and prayer toward His All Goodness; and maintain the G-d-given Seven Commandments of Noah as a basic Moral code. Indeed, one of the major hallmarks of "Geula"—Divine Redemption—ultimately taking place in the world is the discovery of G-d's presence in the world, which could very well occur through the current Paradigmatic Shift in twenty-first-century Theoretical Physics' Computational Unified Field Theory's A-Causal Computation—G d's Physics!

G d's Physics proclaims that there exists only one singular, higher-ordered Universal Consciousness Principle, which continuously computes (creates), dissolves, recomputes, and evolves every spatial pixel throughout the entire physical universe many billions of times per second. This singular Universal Consciousness Principle computes all past, present, and multiple future universal frames containing all spatial pixels of the entire physical universe at each such past, present, or future minimal time point frame. And this sole and singular Universal Consciousness Principle's computation of each such past, present, future universal frame is dependent upon our own individual moral choices, which the Universal Consciousness Principle cares so much about because its basic Dynamic Equilibrium Moral Principle is constantly "balancing" and "correcting" any "moral imbalance" that is the result of one Individual Human Consciousness inflicting pain or suffering upon another, or conversely, it corrects an imbalance that is the result of one individual choosing to do a good deed or perform a moral act ("teshuva"). This precise and special care, compassion, and Good-Will of the Universal Consciousness Principle is so clear and apparent in the A-Causal Computation Paradigm wherein it knows and computes the past, present, and multiple future occurrences and events that affect the development and evolution of each individual human being, each small insect, and even each individual microbe, atom, or molecule! This is all geared toward its All-Goodness, All-giving, Free-Will wish to evolve all beings, and especially human beings, toward reaching the full understanding, appreciation, and glorification of G-d's presence,

Goodness, and Purpose to create a Moral and just world, a world in which G-d's Presence is felt, recognized, and adored and which brings a deep sense of humility and endless gratitude.

We see that this new striking and amazing G d's physics opens our eyes to a new world—a universe that is Sacred and Divine where no entity is really "separate" from the singular, higher-ordered <u>Universal Consciousness Principle</u>! Nothing that we do is separate from this <u>Universal Consciousness Principle</u>—G-d. In fact, every one of our small actions determines our own positive or negative future experiences as well as the outcome of the whole world. And, in a sense, we really do not possess any real "free choice", at least in the long run, because this singular, higher-ordered <u>Universal Consciousness Principle</u>(G-d) would not let us make immoral choices without teaching us later on that those choices do not reflect the right way to act or to grow. On the contrary, this <u>Universal Consciousness Principle</u> encourages us every billionth of a billionth of a second to change for the better, to evolve as He does with all inanimate as well as animate entities toward becoming a fully evolved human being, one who sees G-d everywhere, one who senses that there does not exist any objective reality, any world or object, plant, animal, or even human being that is not really G-d's—<u>Universal Consciousness Principle</u>'s—manifestation!

When we wake up in the morning and see our children, our life partners, our neighbors and friends, or even strangers in the street, we realize that it is really only a manifestation of this singular, higher-ordered <u>Universal Consciousness Principle</u>—G-d—standing in front of us! We immediately begin changing, "opening our eyes", as the great Lubavitcher Rebbe declared! We can no longer ignore the "other". We must embrace, love, and honor each other—human beings, animals, and even plants—and our entire dear planet because it is all but a manifestation of the one and singular divine G-d, that infinitely Wise, Moral, Caring, and Loving G-d whose sole Goal is to assist us to realize His Presence, Love, and Care. And we therefore begin feeling love and an indescribable awe, reverence, humility, and infinite gratitude toward this singular Divine G-d Reality. We feel an indescribable sense of hope, faith, gratitude, and prayer toward this unlimited Greatness, Goodness, beauty, and Wisdom that governs, creates, dissolves, recreates, and evolves every spatial pixel in the universe—every tiny cell in our bodies, every spilt second of our life journeys from our birth (or even long before that) until our departure from the physical universe. This divine, unlimited infinite wisdom (and beyond!), love, morality, and caring G-d reality is there with us, attending to all our physical and spiritual needs, always trying to assist us to evolve to "open our eyes". Indeed, the great Lubavicther Rebbe devoted every moment of his divine life toward awakening all human beings and humanity as a whole to rapidly awaken, open our eyes, see and behold G-d's presence everywhere in the world. He urged human beings to become Moral, Good, and Perfected and to fulfill our own Life Journeys and, even more importantly, to fulfill G-d's Purpose of creating a Just, Moral, harmonious, and Divine World in which His presence would become as "real" as our flesh and bones, a real Divine Redemption "Geula" in this physical world of ours!

REFERENCES

Bentwich, J. 2003. "The Cognitive 'Duality Principle': A Resolution of Major Scientific Conundrums." In Vol. 1 of *Science, Cognition and Consciousness; The Proceedings of the International Conference of Philosophy and Cognitive Sciences*, edited by Li Ping, Xiang Chen, Zhang Zhilin, and Zhang Huaxia. Jiangxi People's Press.

Bentwich, J., H. Benveniste, D. A. Ziegler, P. A. Maletic-Savatic, D. Filipek, N. Kennedy, V. S. Makris, S. Caviness, and M. R. Herbert. 2005. "Rightward Volume Asymmetry in Mentalizing Networks in Autistic Cerebral Cortex." Presentation at the International Meeting for Research on Autism (IMFAR), Boston, May 5–7, 2005.

Bentwich, J. 2006a. "The 'Duality Principle': Irreducibility of Sub-Threshold Psychophysical Computation to Neuronal Brain Activation." *Synthese* 153 (3): 451–55.

———. 2006b. *Universal Consciousness: From Materialistic Science to the Mental Projection Unified Theory*. Bloomington, IN: iUniverse.

Bentwich, J., E. Dobronevsky, S. Aichenbaum, R. Shorer, R. Peretz, M. Khaigrekht, R. G. Marton, and J. M. Rabey. 2011b. "Beneficial Effect of Repetitive Transcranial Magnetic Stimulation Combined with Cognitive Training for the Treatment of Alzheimer's Disease: A Proof of Concept Study." *Journal of Neural Transmission* 118, no. 3 (March): 463–71.

Bentwich, J. 2012a. "Harmonizing Quantum Mechanics and Relativity Theory." In *Theoretical Concepts of Quantum Mechanics,* 515–50. London: Intech.

———. 2012b. "Theoretical Validation of the Computational Unified

Field Theory." In *Theoretical Concepts of Quantum Mechanics,* 551–98. London: Intech.

———. 2013a. "The Theoretical Ramifications of the Computational Unified Field Theory." In *Advances in Quantum Mechanics,* 671–882. London: Intech.

———. 2013b. "The Computational Unified Field Theory (CUFT): A Candidate Theory of Everything. In *Advances in Quantum Mechanics,* 395–436. London: Intech.

———. 2014 *What If Einstein Was Right?* Amazon Kindle.

———. 2015a. "The Computational Unified Field Theory (CUFT): A Candidate 'Theory of Everything.'" In *Selected Topics in Application of Quantum Mechanics.*

———. 2015b. "On the Geometry of Space, Time, Energy, and Mass: Empirical Validation of the Computational Unified Field Theory." In *Unified Field Mechanics: Natural Science Beyond the Veil of Spacetime.*

———. 2016. "The 'Computational Unified Field Theory': A Paradigmatic Shift." *Research & Reviews: Journal of Pure and Applied Physics.*

———. 2017a. "The Computational Unified Field Theory: Could 'Dark Matter' & '"dark energy"' be 'Superfluous'?" Special issue, *SciFed Journal of Quantum Physics.*

———. 2017b. "The Computational Unified Field Theory: Explaining the Universe from 'Without.'" Special issue, *SciFed Journal of Quantum Physics.*

———. 2017c. "The Computational Unified Field Theory: A New Acausal Computation Physics." Special issue, *SciFed Journal of Quantum Physics.*

———. 2017d. "The 'Computational Unified Field Theory' (CUFT) May Challenge the 'Big Bang Theory.'" Special issue, *SciFed Journal of Quantum Physics.*

———. 2017e. "Can the 'Computational Unified Field Theory' (CUFT) Challenge the Basic Laws of Conservation?" Special issue, *SciFed Journal of Quantum Physics.*

———. 2017f. "The Computational Unified Field Theory (CUFT): Time 'Reversal' May Be Possible." Special issue, *SciFed Journal of Quantum Physics.*

———. 2017g. "The Computational Unified Field Theory (CUFT) Transcends Relativity's Speed of Light Constraint." Special issue, *SciFed Journal of Quantum Physics.*

———. 2017h. "The Computational Unified Field Theory's New Physics: Transcending Space, Time and Causality." Special issue, *SciFed Journal of Quantum Physics.*

———. 2017i. "A 'Supra-Spatial-Temporal Universal Consciousness Principle.' *Research & Reviews: Journal of Pure & Applied Physics,* Special issue: *The Computational Unified Field Theory (CUFT)—A Paradigmatic Shift in Twenty-First Century Physics.*

———. 2017j. "A New Science: An Infinite Omniscient Dynamic-Equilibrium Universal Consciousness Principle." Special issue, *SciFed Journal of Quantum Physics.*

———. 2017k. "The Computational Unified Field Theory (CUFT) Challenges Darwin's 'Natural Selection Principle'!" Special issue, *SciFed Journal of Quantum Physics.*

———. 2017l. "The Computational Unified Field Theory (CUFT) Challenges the Second Law of Thermodynamics." Special issue, *SciFed Journal of Quantum Physics.*

———. 2017m. "The Computational Unified Field Theory (CUFT): An Empirical and Mathematical Validation of the 'Computational Unified Field Theory.'" Special issue, *SciFed Journal of Quantum Physics.*

———. 2017n. "The Computational Unified Field Theory (CUFT) New Science." Special issue, *SciFed Journal of Quantum Physics.*

———. 2018a. "Review: The Computational Unified Field Theory (CUFT) New Universe." Special issue, *The Global Journal of Science Frontier Research* 18 (8-A).

———. 2018b. "The Computational Unified Field Theory (CUFT): What is 'Time'?" Special issue, *The Global Journal of Science Frontier Research* 18 (8-A).

———. 2018c. "The Universal Consciousness Principle's Camouflage: The Physical Universe!" Special issue, *The Global Journal of Science Frontier Research* 18 (8-A).

———. 2018d. "The Computational Unified Field Theory (CUFT) Epilogue: Can Human Consciousness Affect the Cosmos?"

Special issue, *The Global Journal of Science Frontier Research* 18 (8-A).

———. 2018e. "Testing the Computational Unified Field Theory's (CUFT) Differential-Critical Predictions: The Higgs-Boson Particle May Not Exist Continuously!" Special issue, *The Global Journal of Science Frontier Research* 18 (8-A).

———. 2018f. "The Double-Faceted Universal Consciousness Principle: A Theoretical Review." Special issue, *The Global Journal of Science Frontier Research* 18 (8-A).

———. 2018g. "Letter to the Editor: "dark matter" May Not Exist." Special issue, *The Global Journal of Science Frontier Research* 18 (8-A).

———. 2018h. "The Computational Unified Field Theory's (CUFT) Epilogue: Possible Reversal of the Arrow of Time and Abolishment of Death." Special issue, *The Global Journal of Science Frontier Research* 18 (8-A).

———. 2019a. "The Computational Unified Field Theory's (CUFT) New Universe." Special issue, *The Global Journal of Science Frontier Research* 19 (6).

———. 2019b. "The Computational Unified Field Theory's (CUFT) Goes Beyond the 'Standard Model': 'G-d's Physics.'" Special issue, *The Global Journal of Science Frontier Research* 18 (8-A).

———. 2019c. "A Call for Cosmologists and Experimental Physicists: Empirical Validation of the 'Computational Unified Field Theory' (CUFT) New Paradigm through 'Time-Sensitive' Astronomical and Subatomic Measurements." Special issue, *The Global Journal of Science Frontier Research* 19 (6).

———. 2019d. "The 'Computational Unified Field Theory' (CUFT): Redefining Mass, Gravity and the Physical Universe." Special issue, *The Global Journal of Science Frontier Research* 19 (6).

———. 2019e. "Astronomical Validation of the Computational Unified Field Theory (CUFT) 'Critical Prediction' and Resolution of the 'Universe's Accelerated Expansion Rate Enigma' (UAERE)." Special issue, *The Global Journal of Science Frontier Research* 19 (6).

———. 2019f. *Global Journals.* https://globaljournals.org/GJSFR_Volume19/E-Journal_GJSFR_(A)_Vol_19_Issue_6.pdf.

Bentovish (Bentwich), J. 2020a. "'G-d's Physics' (CUFT) New 'Atom' and Purposeful Universe!" *Advances in Theoretical & Computational Physics* 3 (2): 50–58.

Bentovish (Bentwich), J. 2020b. "An Urgent Need for 'G-d's Physics' New Twenty-First-Century Paradigm's Empirical Validation." *Advances in Theoretical & Computational Physics* 3 (2): 59–65.

Lubavitcher Rebbe, *Likkutei Sichot,* ליקוטי שיחות, מערכת אוצר החסידים קה'ת היכל תשיעי-"שער שלישי" בשלשלת האור של. New York: Otzar HaChassidim.

Maimonides. "Hilchot Yesudy Torah" Chapter 1.

Yochai, Rabbi Shimon Bar (Rashbi). *The Book of Zohar.*

Zakay, D. and J. Bentwich. 2013. Tricks & Taps of Perceptual Illusions in Mythomanians: The Nature of Deception and Self-Deception (Editor: M. Myslobodsky).

Zalman, Rabbi Schneur (Alter Rebbe). *Tanya: The Book of the Intermediates (Likutei Amarim).* New York: Otzar HaChassidim.

Rabbi Yossef Yitzchak ("Harabi HaRAYATZ"), "לתשובה לאלתר לגאולה", "לאלתר", "תשא" Jewish Year.

'G-d's Physics New 21st Century Paradigm: From "Law" to "Mercy"!

Bentovish (Bentwich) Jehonathan, Ph.D.[1]*

Dr. Bentovish is affiliated with Zefat Academic College, Zefat, Israel.

*Note: Dr. Bentovish is currently seeking the most appropriate leading Academic Institute to assist him in carrying-out further necessary empirical validation and Theoretical elaboration of his New Twenty-first Century New 'G-d's Physics' Paradigm.

Dr. Bentovish (Bentwich) e-mail is: drbentovish@gmail.com.

Abstract

Twenty-first Century Physics is undergoing a Major "Paradigmatic-Shift" from the Old "Material-Causal" Paradigm to the New "A-Causal Computation" (ACC) Paradigm associated with the "Computational Unified Field Theory" (CUFT), also called: "G-d's Physics". Based on the CUFT's discovery of a new singular higher-ordered "Universal Computational/Consciousness Principle" (UCP) which simultaneously computes every exhaustive spatial pixel in the universe for each consecutive "Universal Frame" (UF) at the incredibly rapid rate of "c^2/h" $= 1.36^{-50}$ (sec')! this New 'A-Causal Computation' Paradigm of 21st Century Theoretical Physics dramatically revises some of the basic assumptions underlying the Old "Material-Causal" Paradigm: It challenged and revised the "Big-Bang" Model, Einstein's Equations, and discarded "dark-matter" and "dark-energy" as being "superfluous" (i.e., non-existent!) due to the UCP's simultaneous computation of all exhaustive spatial pixels for each consecutive UF's frame/s! Based on another "Computational Invariance Principle" postulate of this New 21st Century 'G-d's Physics' Paradigm asserting that only the UCP may be regarded as "computationally-invariant", whereas the four basic physical features of "space", "energy", "mass" and "time" can only be considered as "transient", "phenomenal" ("computationally-variant") manifestations of this singular higher-ordered UCP; it is derived that the entire physical universe is governed solely based on the characteristics of this singular higher-ordered "Universal Consciousness Reality" (UCP) – one of which is "Goodwill", e.g., the propensity to sustain all Life, to bestow "Goodness" and evolve the entire universe towards an ultimate Perfected State (Physically, Morally and Spiritually), called "Geula" in Jewish Tradition.

1) Introduction: Twenty-first Century Physics 'G-d's Physics' Paradigmatic-Shift! "Paradigmatic-Crisis"

Twenty-first century Theoretical Physics finds itself in a basic "Paradigmatic-Crisis" akin to the state of Physics over 100 years ago, e.g., prior to Einstein's 1905 & 1919 Relativity Theory "Paradigmatic-Shift"!? In order to perhaps better understand the basic nature, dynamics and "evolution" of Science, we have to revert back to Thomas Kuhn's famous historic analysis of the "Structure of Scientific Revolutions" (1962): what Kuhn discovered was that Science does not evolve "linearly", i.e., continuously within the same Scientific Paradigm – rather, it evolves through alterations between periods of "Standard Science" in which a particular Scientific discipline advances its knowledge based on a given known Scientific Paradigm, and periods in which that 'Standard Paradigm' does not suffice, any longer to adequately describe the physical reality and a 'New Paradigm' is called for in order to account for accumulating "unexplained phenomenon" (by the Old 'Standard Paradigm') and which can resolve any major "Theoretical Inconsistencies" that exist in the Old Paradigm! Kuhn also brought Science into the awareness that scientists are (after all) human-beings who seem to be "afraid" of making such necessary "Paradigmatic Shifts"!? Nevertheless, Science has to evolve and provide Humanity with an ever closer understanding of Truth, and it does so by a rigorous Scientific Method combining replicable empirical data and logical (mathematical) explanations!

2) G-d's Physics New Paradigm: From "Reductionism" to "Exhaustiveness"!

The New 'G-d's Physics' Paradigm seems to extend (and transcend) the strict confining boundaries of the Old 'Material-Causal' Paradigm; This is because wherein the Old 'Material-Causal' Paradigm advocated that it only based on direct physical interactions between certain "massive objects" and their curvature of "Space-Time" – that the dynamics and evolution of the physical universe can be explained, or that it is only based on the direct physical interaction between a given subatomic "probe" element and a corresponding subatomic target's "probability wave function" – that this target's 'probability wave function' "collapses" into a singular (measured complimentary) target value is arrived at; according to the New 'G-d's Physics' Paradigm, there cannot exist any such direct physical interaction – e.g., either at the macroscopic relativistic level or at the microscopic subatomic quantum level; simply because the singular (higher-ordered) "Universal Computational/ Consciousness Principle" (UCP) simultaneously computes all exhaustive spatial pixels in the universe for each consecutive Universal Frame/s (UF's)!? Moreover, as stated above (and previously), since the New 'G-d's Physics' (Computational Unified Field Theory, CUFT) Paradigm postulates that the entire physical universe "dissolves" "in-between" any two consecutive UF's frames (back into the singularity of the UCP), therefore there cannot be any "transference" of any "physical effects" or any "material-entity" across any two consecutive UF's frames!

This was indeed the basis for 'G-d's Physics' New Paradigm's rejection and negation of the basic 'Material-Causal' assumptions underlying RT's and QM's Old Paradigm, including: the 'Big-Bang' Model, which assumes that the whole universe originated (or was "caused" by) an initial nuclear explosion – which is assumed to have created all "suns", galaxies, planets, space, mass energy etc. The 'Big-Bang' Model was challenged and rejected based on the UCP's simultaneous computation of every exhaustive spatial pixel in the universe for each consecutive UF's frame – which negates the very possibility of any direct physical interaction between any two (or more) exhaustive spatial pixels comprising the entire physical universe! And also due to the complete "dissolution" of the entire physical universe "in-between" any two consecutive UF's frames – which also negates the possibility of the transference of any 'physical effects' or any 'material-entities' across consecutive UF's frames, e.g., such as the continuous expansion and "expulsion" of the Big-Bang's assumed initial nuclear explosion and ensuing continuous creation- and expansion- of the whole (observed) physical universe! Likewise, this New 'G-d's Physics' Paradigm also challenged Einstein's Equations' basic 'Material-Causal' assumption wherein the continuous evolution of the physical universe is "caused" by the direct physical interactions between given "massive objects" and their "curvature" of "Space-Time", and vice versa that the determination of the "travelling-pathways" of these "massive" and other less-massive objects is "caused" by the "curvature of Space-time"!? This is once again, due to the simultaneity of the UCP's computation of all exhaustive spatial pixels in the universe for each consecutive UF's frame/s – which negates the very possibility of the existence of any such direct "physical interactions" or "physical effects" of those 'massive objects' and their assumed "curvature of Space-Time" or between the assumed 'curved Space-Time' and its determination of the massive/ less massive objects 'travelling-pathways'!? In the same manner the purely hypothetical concepts of "dark-matter" and "dark-energy" have been completely rejected as "superfluous", i.e. "non-existent"! This is because the emergence of these (purely hypothetical) "dark-matter" and "dark-energy" concepts is associated with the empirically observed accelerated expansion of the physical universe – which is assumed to be "caused" by the presence of "dark-matter" or "dark-energy"!? But, if indeed the UCP simultaneously computes each exhaustive spatial pixel in the universe (for each consecutive UF's frame/s with the entire physical universe "dissolving" back into the singularity of the UCP "in-between" any two consecutive UF's frames), then there cannot exist any such "material-causal" direct physical relationships between these (purely hypothetical) "dark-matter" and "dark-energy" entities and the accelerated expansion of the entire physical universe!? Finally, the basic 'Material-Causal' assumption underlying QM's Model, wherein any measurement of any given subatomic 'target's probability wave function' involves the "collapse" of the target's 'probability wave function' is also directly being challenged by the New 'G-d's Physics' Paradigm: this is once again due to its insistence upon the UCP's simultaneous computation of all exhaustive spatial pixels in the universe (e.g., for each consecutive Universal Frame/s – with the entire physical universe being "dissolved" in-between any two such consecutive UF's frames back into the singularity of the UCP); Therefore, there cannot really exist any direct physical interaction between the subatomic 'probe' and 'target's (probability wave function) – at any single or multiple UF's frames, and there cannot be any "transference" of any "physical effect" taking place following any such ("non-existent) direct physical interaction between the subatomic 'probe' and 'target' elements – and the supposed "collapse" of the probability wave function (in a subsequent UF's frame/s)!?

We therefore see that the basic "materialistic-reductionistic" assumption underlying the Old 'Material-Causal' Paradigm of both RT & QM is greatly challenged (and in fact negated!) by the New 'G-d's Physics Paradigm; we acknowledge the fact that this Old 'Material-Causal' Paradigm basic assumption wherein the origination- dynamics and evolution- of the physical universe, or any subsystem of it is determined based on direct physical interactions between relativistic "massive" objects and their curvature of 'Space-Time' (and vice versa the determination of the "travelling-pathways" of these "massive" or "less-massive" objects based on this curved 'Space-Time'); or at the subatomic level, the assumption that any observed subatomic "phenomenon" is the result of the "collapse" of the subatomic target's 'probability wave function' as "Caused" by its direct physical interaction with another corresponding subatomic "probe" element; that this basic 'Material-Causal' assumption is "invalid" – as there cannot exist any such direct physical interaction/s between any two (or more) exhaustive spatial pixels existing either in the same- or different- Universal Frame/s, and moreover there cannot exist any "transference" of any "material effect" or any "material-entity/ies" across two consecutive UF's frames (as all exhaustive spatial pixels in the universe "dissolve" in-between any two consecutive UF's frames!); This New 'G-d's Physics' basic challenging- and revision- of the Old 'Material-Causal' Paradigm basic assumption indeed was shown to possess far-reaching theoretical ramifications: first, it challenged the basic "Big-Bang" Model wherein the physical universe was created by an initial 'Big-Bang' nuclear explosion, e.g., as there could not have been any direct physical interaction/s between any such 'Big-Bang' nuclear explosion and any creation of any "massive-objects", suns, galaxies, planets, energy, space, etc.- either in the first- second- or any other consecutive Universal Frame/s!? Likewise, General Relativity's Einstein's Equations' description of the curvature of 'Space-Time' by massive objects and it's determination of the travelling pathways of these massive objects was also negated by this New 'G-d's Physics' (CUFT) Paradigm. Similarly, the existence of "dark-matter" or "dark-energy" was also rejected and negated as "superfluous" or "non-existent" based on the impossibility of the existence of any such "material-causal" direct physical interactions between any such (purely hypothetical) "dark-matter" or "dark-energy" and any single or multiple exhaustive spatial pixels comprising the entire physical universe due to the simultaneity of the UCP's computation of all exhaustive spatial pixels in the universe for any consecutive Universal Frame/s!

In contrast, the New 'G-d's Physics' Paradigm forces us to expand our "theoretical gaze" towards the higher-ordered singular "Universal Computational/Consciousness Principle" (UCP) – which can alone be responsible for the empirically observed relativistic, quantum or indeed UCP's "exhaustive" phenomena, laws etc.; If indeed, the New 'G-d's Physics' Paradigm is valid, then there cannot exist any relativistic or quantum subatomic direct (or even indirect) physical interactions between any two (or more) exhaustive spatial pixels existing either in the same- or different- UF's frames, as they are all simultaneously computed by the singular higher-ordered UCP! Therefore, instead of the Old 'Material-Causal' Paradigm which can only "reduce" any physical (relativistic or quantum) "phenomenon" to a subset of direct physical interactions comprising this phenomenon, the New 'G-d's Physics' Paradigm steers Physics (and Science, more generally) in the opposite theoretical direction of expanding- and raising- the theoretical explanation of any apparently "physical" phenomenon towards it singular higher-ordered UCP underlying computation of all exhaustive spatial pixels comprising the entire physical universe (for each "minimal time-point" UF's frame/s)!

3) The "Cinematic-Film Metaphor" & "Computational Invariance Principle"

In order to better perhaps understand the gist of this New 'G-d's Physics' Paradigm, e.g., and its transcendence of the Old 'Material-Causal' "reductionistic" Model, it is appropriate to mention two key theoretical postulates of this New 'G-d's Physics' Paradigm: a) The "Cinematic-Film Metaphor"; b) The "Computational Invariance Principle";

a. **The 'Cinematic-Film Metaphor':** attempts to illustrate the UCP's computation of the series of UF's frames comprising all exhaustive spatial pixels comprising the entire physical universe (for each consecutive UF's frame/s) through its comparison to the dynamics of a standard 'Cinematic-Film' mechanics: It indicated that in much the same manner that we could measure the "velocity" (or "energy") of any given object in the film based on a computation of the degree of its "displacement" across a series of UF's frames, as opposed to our measurement of its (unchanging) "spatial-dimensions" as the number of spatial-pixels which remain "constant" across a given number of film-frames; And akin to our film's potential measurement of the "temporal-value" of any given event or phenomenon (such as a man walking in the film) – which we could "slow-down" if we were to project the film's frames in a "slow-motion" mode in which the number of changes taking place in that man walking would be decreased and hence the "time-value" that seemed to have elapsed would be "slowed-down" as well; hence the "time-value" of that given phenomenon (of the man walking) would depend on the number of changes taking place within that object ("man walking") across a given number of film-frames... Conversely, we could create a "film-scenario" in which the perceived "mass" of any given object would be computed based on the number of times that object has been presented "consistently" (e.g., in the same manner) across a given number of film-frames (thereby "increasing its hue"); Indeed, this

'Cinematic-Film Metaphor has been utilized in order to convey two (out of three) UCP's basic "Computational Dimensions", e.g., of "Framework" ('frame' vs. 'object'), 'Consistency' ('consistent' vs. 'inconsistent') – which when combined give rise to the four basic physical features of 'space' and 'energy', and 'mass' or 'time': it was suggested that the UCP simultaneously computes for all exhaustive spatial pixels in the universe these four basic physical features as: 'frame' – 'consistent' ('space') or 'inconsistent' ('energy'), or 'object' – 'consistent' ('mass') or 'inconsistent' ('time') UCP computations! This amazing discovery led to the complete unification of these apparently "distinct" physical features of the universe within a singular UCP "Universal Computational Formula":

Universal Computational Formula (UCF):

$$\left\{ \begin{array}{c} ַc^2 \\ \underline{\quad} \\ h \end{array} \right\} \quad \text{UF's} \{ה...מ...א\} \qquad \begin{array}{c} \underline{s \ * \ e} \\ t \ * \ m \end{array}$$

(**Note**: herein the singular higher-ordered UCP – represented by the Hebrew letter "Yud" ("י") simultaneously computes all exhaustive spatial pixels in the universe comprising each consecutive Universal Frame/s (UF's) which already exist in a "potential-from" within the UCP's "Supra Spatial-Temporal Reservoir" of all "past", "present" and multiple possible "future/s" UF's (represented by the Hebrew letters from "א through "מ" to "ת)" depending on the Moral Choice of each Individual Human Consciousness – as computing and integrating these four basic physical features of "space" and "energy", "mass" and "time", at the incredible rate of: "c^2/h" = 1.36^{-50} sec'!)

Indeed, one of the fascinating facets of this New 'G-d's Physics' Paradigm is its far-reaching new understanding that these four basic physical features of the universe do not exist as "independent" (albeit "interconnected") features – but in fact represent four complimentary aspects of the UCP's singular (simultaneous) computation of the degree of Frame/Object & Consistent/Inconsistent computation for each and every exhaustive spatial pixel in the universe, e.g., comprising the series of UF's frame/s! No longer are *only* "space" and "time" connected (e.g., Space-Time) and "energy" and "mass" equivalent (e.g., "$E = Mc^2$"); and "mass" assumed to "curve" "Space-Time" (e.g., as expressed in Einstein's equations); instead, for the first time in Theoretical Physics, all of these four basic physical features are found to be mere secondary computational properties of the singular UCP's simultaneous computation of the degree of "change" (consistency) or "lack of change" (inconsistency) computed for each exhaustive spatial pixel – pertaining to its own comprising features ('object'), or as relating to its features relative to the entire Universal-Frame ('frame')!Moreover, as shown previously, this singular, higher-ordered UCP 'Universal Computational Formula' (UCF) completely integrates fundamental 'relativistic' and 'quantum' features as integral parts of the UCF (as expressed in its "Relativistic" and "Quantum" Formats, delineated previously).

In this regard, the discovery of 'G-d's Physics' New Paradigm may also be said to fulfill "Einstein's vision" (e.g., and more generally Kuhn's delineation of the structure and nature of "Paradigmatic-Shifts") – wherein both Relativistic and Quantum laws and features are seen to comprise only "special-cases" within the broader scope of 'G-d's Physics' New Paradigm's theoretical framework...

Perhaps one more important aspect of this 'Cinematic-Film Metaphor' may be worth mentioning (at this point) – regarding its explanation of the depiction of a (massive) "Mercury Ball" impacting a (delicate) "Glass-Jar" filled with water, which seems to "cause" the spillage of the water element (unto the floor); when watching such a given "film-scenario" of the 'Mercury-Ball' impacting the 'Glass-Jar', which seems to "cause" the spillage of the water – we are immediately under the impression that there exists clear "cause" and "effect" (direct) physical relationships between the impact of the 'Mercury-Ball' and its "causing" of the breakage of the 'Glass-Jar' and the subsequent spillage of the water... But, according to this 'Cinematic-Film Metaphor's' deeper analysis we find that – if we are to inspect each individual "film-frame" (and even more so – the intermittent "pure-light" found "in-between" every two consecutive frames), we will notice that there cannot exist any real direct physical interactions between this 'Mercury-Ball' and 'Glass-Jar' – at none of these consecutive 'film-frames'!? This is because at none of these individual film-frames can there exist any direct physical interactions between any two (or more) exhaustive spatial pixels comprising the entire film-frame/s, as they are depicted simultaneously!? Indeed, when we examine closely the raid succession of these individual film-frames, we find that even though the relative 'spatial-configuration' of these 'Glass-Jar' and 'Mercury-Ball' is presented in ever greater 'spatial-proximity' across the series of film-frames (e.g., until their spatial "identification" in the particular film-frame in which the "Mercury-Ball' impacts the 'Glass-Jar'), still since these two objects are presented simultaneously in each film-frame, there cannot really exist any direct physical interaction/s between them! Indeed, the impossibility of the existence of any direct physical interactions between these two 'Mercury-Ball' and 'Glass-Jar' objects becomes even more apparent when we consider the fact that "in-between" any two consecutive film-frames, the entire film-frame "dissipates" (or "dissolves") into the "pure-light" that is presented, we realize that in reality, there cannot be any "transference" of any "physical effect" or even any "physical entity" across any two consecutive film-frames!

The implied understanding derived from this 'Cinematic-Film Metaphor' regarding the New 'G-d's Physics' Paradigm is quite significant (and far-reaching): it implies that even though it may seem that certain physical "laws", "relationships" or even "phenomenon" exist at the relativistic or quantum levels – i.e., such as Einstein's Equations Relativistic "cause" and "effect" relationships between the existence of certain "massive objects" and their "curvature of Space-Time", or such as the assumed Quantum Mechanical "collapse" of the 'target's probability wave function' as "caused" by it being "impacted" by the corresponding subatomic 'probe' element; we realize through this 'Cinematic-Film Metaphor' that in reality there cannot exist any such "real" direct physical relationships between any relativistic or quantum objects, particles, laws or phenomena!? Instead, when we follow (closely) the implied meaning of the 'Cinematic-Film Metaphor, we realize that it is only based on the Film's Director's "arrangement" of the particular order and "spatial-proximities" found in the series of UF's frames that gives rise to our "perceived impression" that there exist certain "relativistic" or "quantum" "phenomenon", "relationships" or even "laws"!? In other words, the Film's Director's arrangement of the particular series of film-frames, depicting the ever closer "spatial-proximity" of those 'Mercury-Ball' and 'Glass-Jar' give us (the "viewers" of the film) the impression as if there exists a "cause" and "effect" physical relationship/s between the impact of the 'Mercury-Ball' unto the 'Glass-Jar' which "caused" its "breakage" and "spillage of water", whereas in reality there doesn't exist any such direct physical relationships, but only the particular arrangement of those 'film-frames' in such a manner that gives us such "cause and effect" impression... In other words, it becomes clear that the UCP's arrangement of the series of Universal Frames (UF's) is such that it gives us the impression that there exist certain "relativistic" or "quantum" phenomenon, relationships or even "laws" – but in truth all that really exists is the UCP's simultaneous computation of all exhaustive spatial pixels comprising the entire physical universe (for each consecutive Universal-Frame), and its particular "arrangement" of these series of UF's frames, which gives us the impression of the existence of certain relativistic or quantum "laws"...

b. **The 'Computational Invariance Principle':** Indeed, this 'Cinematic-Film Metaphor's realization of the only "apparent", "phenomenal" nature of any "relativistic" or "quantum" physical relationships (or even "laws") becomes even clearer based on another key 'G-d's Physics' theoretical postulate termed: The "Computational Invariance Principle", which states that since only the singular, higher-ordered UCP exists "computationally-invariantly" both "during each consecutive UF's frame/s – e.g., as solely computing each exhaustive spatial pixel's four basic physical features (of 'space', 'energy', 'mass' and 'time'), and also solely exists "in-between" any two such exhaustive UF's frames without the presence of any physical universe; whereas the entire physical universe exists only "computationally-variantly", i.e., exists only "during" each consecutive UF's frame/s (as solely being computed by this singular UCP) but "dissolves" back into the singularity of the UCP "in-between" any two consecutive UF's frames, therefore the 'Computational Invariance Principle' asserts that it is only the 'Universal Computational/Consciousness Principle' (UCP) that may be regarded as "real", e.g., existing "invariantly", consistently and continuously whereas the entire physical universe (and all of its constituting exhaustive spatial pixels) may only be regarded as "transient" and "phenomenal" – truly representing only a "manifestation" of the singular Universal Computational/Consciousness Principle" Reality! We therefore reach a "pivotal point" along the development of Science wherein we realize that the entire physical universe exists only as a "transient", "phenomenal" "manifestation" of the singular higher-ordered 'Universal Computational/Consciousness Principle' Reality, termed: the "Universal Consciousness Reality", which exists (invariantly) both "during" its (simultaneous) computation of all exhaustive spatial pixels in the universe for each consecutive

UF's frame/s, and also exists solely (without the presence of the physical universe) "in-between" any two consecutive UF's frame/s!

4) "Supra-Spatial-Temporal Reservoir", "Multiple Future/s" & "Dynamic-Equilibrium" Moral Principle

Indeed, the fascinating discovery of 'G-d's Physics' New 21st century Paradigm's ' singularity of the Universal Computational/Consciousness Principle (UCP) – and its only "phenomenal", "transient" manifestation as the physical universe was also shown to be connected with the discovery of Ten "Hierarchical Laws of Manifestation" which describe the manner in which this singular higher-ordered UCP manifest this physical universe! Thus, for instance, it was shown above and beyond the existence of the physical universe there exist a higher-ordered UCP's "Supra-Spatial-Temporal Reservoir" containing all "past", "present" and multiple (possible) "future/s" UF's frames of the entire physical universe! Based on the discovery of the UCP's novel "Dynamic-Equilibrium" Moral Principle which postulates that since all exhaustive spatial pixels comprising the entire physical universe are in truth only manifestations of the singular (higher-ordered) Universal Computational/Consciousness Principle (UCP); and moreover based on another 'G-d's Physics' theoretical postulate called" the "UCP's Inseparability Principle", which postulates that all Individual Human Consciousness are found to also be inseparable from this singular Universal Consciousness Principle, e.g., as also manifested in the "Deep-Sleep" State of Human Consciousness – and indeed, as manifested through the "special" state of "Expanded Human Consciousness" (in the waking state – for those "rare" of "blessed" individuals in which their Individual Human Consciousness completely identifies with the singularity of the Universal Consciousness Principle, e.g., which can also be described as a "prophetic" state); Therefore, the "UCP's Inseparability Principle" states that in reality all Individual Human Consciousness – comprise integral parts of this singular (higher-ordered) Universal Computational/Consciousness Principle! Therefore, based on this 'UCP's Inseparability Principle' the "Dynamic-Equilibrium" Moral Principle postulate of the New 'G-d's Physics' Paradigm states that since all Individual Human Consciousness – truly constitute integral parts of this singular (higher-ordered) Universal Computational/Consciousness Principle (UCP), therefore the UCP also possesses an intrinsic property (or "Hierarchical Law of Manifestation") stating that in any case that one of these "Individual Human Consciousness" makes a "negative Moral Choice", e.g., inflicting "pain" or "suffering" upon another Individual Human Consciousness, then this would "automatically" create a "balancing-Moral-Effect" instigated by the UCP to choose of multiple possible future/s that would "balance" or "teach" that "inflicting-pain/ suffering" Individual Human Consciousness a "lesson" comprising experiencing precisely the same degree of "negative" suffering/pain as inflicted upon another Individual Human Consciousness...

Another "Trampoline Metaphor" was utilized to convey this profound new theoretical understanding brought about by the discovery of this new "Dynamic-Equilibrium" Moral Principle: According to this 'Trampoline-Metaphor', if we were to imagine a Trampoline, e.g., with its fine-elastic-sheath, and a "solid iron-bar" firmly attached from one point along this 'trampoline-elastic-sheath' to another particular point on this 'Trampoline-sheath'; and if we imagined that one of these two points to which the Iron-Bar is attached "decided" to "inflict-pain/suffering" upon the "other point" (to which the Iron-Bar was attached), such as by pushing ("violently") the Iron-Bar against the "other" ("suffering") point; then we can see that this "unidirectional-violent-force" exerted by the "Inflicting-pain" point upon the "suffering-point" (through the Iron-Bar), would inevitable "cause" a "balancing" counter-force that would inflict the same degree of "pain/suffering" as did experience the "suffering-point"!? In other words, this 'Trampoline-Metaphor' is utilized to convey the simple message that due to the 'UCP's Inseparability Principle' and associated 'Dynamic-Equilibrium' Moral Principle, any "negative force" exerted by one "inflicting-pain" point (e.g., representing a particular Individual Human Consciousness) upon another "suffering-point" (representing another Individual Human Consciousness experiencing a negative "suffering" or "painful" experience) – would necessarily "cause" the singular, unitary 'Universal Consciousness Principle' (represented by the solid-unitary Trampoline-sheath) to create or select one of multiple possible future/s Universal Frame/s that would produce a completely opposite experience by the "inflicting-pain" point (Individual Human Consciousness) to "experience" precisely the same degree of "negative-painful experience" that it inflicted upon another Indivdiaul Human Consciousness – i.e., in order to "teach" or bring to its awareness that All Human Beings (and in fact the entire nature and physical universe) back into a Morally Balanced and Harmonious State!? In this manner, the New 'G-d's Physics' Paradigm (e.g., for the first time in Theoretical Physics!) postulates that there exist in fact multiple possible future/s for each Individual Human Consciousness (e.g., individual); and that for each of these Billions of Individual Human Consciousness – the UCP "selects" one of multiple possible future/s' 'Universal Frame' (UF) that are stored within the UCP's singular higher-ordered "Supra-Spatial-Temporal Reservoir", based on the UCP 'Dynamic-Equilibrium' Moral Principle's computation for "balancing" the 'Moral-Decision/s' of each such Individual Human Consciousness!

Indeed, the discovery of these two "UCP Supra-Spatial-Temporal Reservoir" – encompassing all "past", "present" and "future/s" Universal Frames, and the selection of any given particular "negative" or "positive" Moral-Choice possesses profound new theoretical ramifications pertaining to our basic understanding (and appreciation) of the dynamics of the apparently "physical" reality and universe; No longer can the physical universe be regarded as a "mere physical reality" – which is based on the direct physical interactions between given relativistic "massive-objects" and their "curvature of Space-Time", or between certain subatomic "probe" and "target's (probability wave-function) elements! Instead, the New 'G-d's Physics' Paradigm (of 21st century Theoretical Physics) is seen as computing- "dissolving- "re-computing- and evolving- every exhaustive spatial pixel in the universe many Billions of times each second – creating an extremely rapid series (e.g., "c^2/h" = 1.36^{-50} sec'!) of Universal Frames (UF's) depicting the entire physical universe, which is also realized to be completely "dissolved" back into the singularity of the UCP "in-between" any two consecutive UF's frames! As a matter of fact (as mentioned earlier),

'G-d's Physics' 'Computational Invariance Principle' also indicated that what truly exists is only this singular higher-ordered 'Universal Computational/Consciousness Principle' – which exists both "during" each consecutive UF's frame (as solely simultaneously computing each and every exhaustive spatial pixel comprising the entire physical universe), as well as solely existing "in-between" any two consecutive UF's frames (without the presence of any physical universe)! Not only so, according to 'G-d's Physics' New Paradigm's 'Supra-Spatial-Temporal Reservoir' & 'Dynamic-Equilibrium' theoretical postulates, the UCP's (extremely rapid) computation of the series of Universal Frames (UF's) – does not depend on- or is constrained by- any "material-causal" physical interactions between any relativistic or quantum entities (pixels etc.), but rather depends (among all of the UCP's other ten- Laws of Manifestation) on the Moral-Choice/s that each Individual Human Consciousness makes at any given point in time – which "sets in motion" the UCP's 'Dynamic-Equilibrium' Moral Principle's "balancing" of any such particular "negative" or "positive" Moral Choice as manifesting in the selection of one of multiple possible "future/s" for both the "inflicting-pain" and corresponding "suffering" Individual Human Consciousness… This means that the physical universe does not exist as a "solid-independent" material-causal reality, but rather as a "transient", "phenomenal" manifestation of the singularity of the UCP – with one of its key propensities being the "Dynamic-Equilibrium" Moral Principle's "balancing" all Individual Human Consciousness' Moral Choices – i.e., through the UCP's "selection" (computing) of one of the multiple possible "future/s" for each of the over 7 Billion Individual Human Consciousness (individuals) in the world!? This incredibly complex computing capacity of the UCP which has to "retain" and "compute" – for each time-dependent 'Moral-Choice' carried out by any two (or more) individual Human Consciousness, so that any "Inflicting-suffering" Individual Human Consciousness is "balanced" relative to the "inflicted" Individual Human Consciousness (e.g., and also takes into consideration all of those two (or more) Individual Human Consciousness past actions and Moral-Choices etc.) is (once again) almost "unfathomable"! But, what becomes increasingly clear is that this constant and continuous computation- "dissolution"- re-computing- and evolution- of each exhaustive spatial pixel in the physical universe is completely dependent upon the UCP's higher-ordered Ten-Hierarchical Laws of Manifestation (of which the 'Dynamic-Equilibrium' Moral Principle and UCP's "Multi-Spatial-Temporal Reservoir" constitute two Laws of Manifestation)...

5)   The UCP's "Free-Will", "Goodwill" & "Reversed-Time Goal Hypothesis" ("Geula") Characteristics:

Hence, the New 21st century Theoretical Physics 'G-d's Physics' Paradigm completely revises our basic understanding of the origination-nature and evolution of the entire physical universe: No longer is the physical universe regarded as a mere "mechanical" or "material-causal" entity which originated in an initial nuclear 'Big-Bang' explosion; which is governed by mere relativistic (direct physical) interactions between certain "massive objects" and their "curvature of Space-Time", nor by direct physical interactions between certain given subatomic "probe" and "target's" (probability wave function) entities – which "cause" the "collapse" of this target's 'probability wave function' into a single (complimentary) 'space-energy' or 'time-mass' value!? No longer is the universe's (empirically observed) accelerated expansion attributed to (completely hypothetical) "dark-matter" or "dark-energy" theoretical concepts, neither is the universe assumed to expand into "dissolution" as predicted by the "Second Law of Thermodynamics" (e.g., which assumes that the degree of "entropy" in any given system increases with time)!? Instead, as stated earlier (and previously), the New 'G-d's Physics' Paradigm asserts that the entire physical universe is being continuously "created", "dissolved", "recreated" and "evolved" so many billions of times each second (e.g., "c^2/h" = 1.36^{-50} sec'!) solely based on the singular higher-ordered "Universal Computational/Consciousness Principle" (UCP)! In fact, as mentioned above, 'G-d's Physics' 'Computational Invariance Principle' clearly depicts the entire physical universe as constituting merely a "transient", "phenomenal" manifestation of this singular Universal Consciousness Principle; Indeed, a closely related additional "Universal Consciousness Reality" (UCR) theoretical postulate asserts that since only this singular 'Universal Computational/ Consciousness Principle' (UCP) exists "computationally-invariantly" – e.g., both "during" its sole (simultaneous) computation of all exhaustive spatial-pixels in the universe for each consecutive Universal Frame/s (UF's), and this UCP also solely exists "in-between" any two consecutive UF's frames – without the presence of any physical universe; therefore the 'Universal Consciousness Reality' (UCR) theoretical postulate suggests that in truth all that exists is this singular 'Universal Consciousness Reality' – which manifests as the physical universe "during" its computation of the extremely rapid series of Universal Frames (UF's), and which solely exists without the presence of the physical universe "in-between" any two consecutive UF's frames! Indeed, it is from this singular higher-ordered perspective of this New 'G-d's Physics' Paradigm which negates the possibility of any relativistic or quantum (subatomic) physical interactions (between any two or more exhaustive spatial pixels comprising any single or multiple UF's frames), instead solely attributing the continuous "creation"- "dissolution"- "recreation" and "evolution" of each exhaustive spatial pixel comprising the entire physical universe to the UCP's characteristics – that an entirely new understanding and appreciation of the magnanimity, beauty and complexity of the UCP's continuous creation of the universe arises…

Indeed, a studying of these UCP's "Ten Hierarchical Laws of Manifestation" brings about a new realization that the physical universe does not operate by strict "material-causal" laws, is not governed by mere material-physical interactions, but is rather derived and continuously being "directed" by the UCP's singular higher-ordered dynamics and characterizations: First, we saw that underlying and "driving" the computation of each consecutive UF's frame there is the continuous computation of the UCP regarding each Individual Human Consciousness 'Moral-Choice/s" based on the UCP's 'Dynamic-Equilibrium' Moral Principle's selection of one of multiple possible "Multi-Spatial-Temporal Reservoir's" "future/s" (e.g., as computed by this UCP for the over seven billions Individual Human Consciousness for each of their time-dependent 'Moral-Choices')! Second, as described previously (extensively) regarding these UCP's Ten-'Hierarchical Laws of Manifestation' this singular higher-ordered UCP is also characterized by a "Free-Will" and "Goodwill" intrinsic characterizations! This means that since the entire physical universe is totally dependent upon the continuous computation- "dissolution"- re-creation and evolution- of each and every exhaustive spatial pixel in the universe (for each consecutive UF's frame/s), and based on the abovementioned 'Computational Invariance Principle' and 'Universal Consciousness Reality' theoretical postulates; therefore the "UCP's Free-Will" postulate evinces that this singular Universal Consciousness Reality is not "constrained" or "limited" by any "material-causal" (or any other) physical (relativistic or quantum) "law"! Bearing in mind that the entire physical universe "dissolves" in-between" any two consecutive UF's frames, and that (in truth) the entire physical universe is nothing but a "transient", "phenomenal" manifestation of the this singular higher-ordered UCP or Universal Consciousness Reality (UCR), we realize that this singular higher-ordered UCR "itself" is not constrained by any physical (relativistic or quantum) "laws"!? Moreover, when we take into consideration the UCR's basic fundamental 'Goodwill' and "Reversed-Time Goal Hypothesis" ("Geula") (descried previously), we understand that what's driving this singular higher-ordered UCR is an innate tendency to "Give-Life", to bestow "Goodness", "Happiness", "Harmony", "Peace" and "Moral Perfection" throughout the entire physical universe! The basic "Motivation" of this singular higher-ordered 'Universal Consciousness Reality' is to create and evolve a Universe which expresses ever more expansive and refined "forms" of Life, Moral and Spiritual Peace, Harmony and Perfection, as well as bring Humanity towards such a State of "Geula" – in which the Oneness of all Creation, the Awareness of the Existence of this singular Goodwill, Infinite Wisdom UCR is acknowledged, "seen" and appreciated! This is what's driving the entire evolution of the entire physical universe towards the expression and manifestation of an ever more Conscious and Moral Awareness – from inanimate, animate: plants, animals, human beings – and up to the highest manifestation of the special "expanded" form of Human Consciousness ("prophetic") State... This is what's driving the accelerated expansion of the entire physical cosmos – not as "caused" by any (non-existent, purely hypothetical) "dark-matter" and "dark-energy", but as brought about by this singular higher-ordered "Universal Consciousness Reality" (UCR) which continuously accelerates the number of additional exhaustive spatial pixels comprising each consecutive Universal Frame (perhaps in order for us, Human-beings to detect this Infinite Wisdom and Power of the UCR which increases and accelerates its manifested enlarged universe!); Indeed, as shown previously, this UCR's accelerated expansion of the entire physical universe is moreover dependent upon the "Collective Human Consciousness Focus" hypothesis, which states that it is the 'Collective Human Consciousness Focus' at such "special times" as the Jewish "Rosh-Hashanna" (New Year) in which Millions of Jews pray and focus on this singular higher-ordered 'Universal Consciousness Reality', 'G-d'! that brings about this UCR's "Non-Continuous" addition in the "Accelerated Expansion Rate" (AER) of the physical universe – taking place at each New "Rosh-Hashanna" Jewish Year… Indeed, the New 'G-d's Physics' Paradigm brings us ever closer to the profound new realization that the whole course and development of the universe is governed and "driven" towards the Ultimate Goal of this singular higher-ordered Universal Consciousness Reality (UCR) which is "Geula": a Perfected Moral, Spiritual and even Physical State of the world in which there is complete Peace and Harmony, in which Human-Beings realize their oneness with each other and with this singular UCR, in which Science and Humanity realize the singularity, Magnanimity, Infinite Wisdom and 'Goodwill' of this UCR, 'G-d'!, appreciate- have gratitude towards- and also carry out a Moral, Purposeful Life aimed at the fulfillment of their individual and Collective role in bringing about this Perfected "Geula" State… Viewed in this Light, Science realizes that the whole existence, sustenance and evolution of the entire physical universe, i.e., towards this Ultimate Perfected "Geula" State is seen as representing this singular higher-ordered UCR, 'G-d' "Mercy" towards all Human Beings (and the World at large), rather than the physical universe being governed by strict "material-causal" physical "laws"! May Science and Humanity begin to comprehend and realize this singular "Merciful", "Goodwill" UCR, 'G-d'! and be grateful, aware and strive towards the complete understanding of this UCR's Ultimate "Geula" State – towards which the UCR drives the entire evolution of the physical universe (and may we fulfil our important "role" in bringing about this "Geula" State of Moral, Spiritual and Physical Perfection)!

6)   References

Bentwich, J. (2012a) "Harmonizing Quantum Mechanics and Relativity Theory". *Theoretical Concepts of Quantum Mechanics*, Intech (ISBN 979-953-307-377-3), Chapter 22, pp. 515-550.

Bentwich, J. (2012b) "Theoretical Validation of the Computational Unified Field Theory". *Theoretical Concepts of Quantum Mechanics*, (ISBN 979-953-307-3773), Chapter 23, pp. 551-598.

Bentwich, J. (2013b). "The Theoretical Ramifications of the Computational Unified Field Theory". *Advances in Quantum Mechanics* (ISBN 978-953-51-1089-7), Chapter 28, pp. 671-882.

Bentwich, J. (2013c). The Computational Unified Field Theory (CUFT): A Candidate Theory of Everything. *Advances in Quantum Mechanics* (ISBN 978-953-51-1089-7) Chapter 18, pp. 395-436.

Bentwich, J. (2015). The Computational Unified Field Theory (CUFT): A Candidate 'Theory of Everything'. *Selected Topics in Application of Quantum Mechanics* (ISBN 978-953-51-2126-8) Chapter 6.

Bentwich, J. (2014) *What if Einstein was Right? Amazon Kindle Book Store.*

Bentwich, J. (2015). On the Geometry of Space, Time, Energy, and Mass: Empirical Validation of the Computational Unified Field Theory. *Unified Field Mechanics: Natural Science Beyond the Veil of Spacetime (Proceedings of VIGIER IX Conference, Morgan State University, USA, 16-19 November 2014).*

Bentwich, J. (2016) The 'Computational Unified Field Theory': A Paradigmatic Shift. *Research & Reviews: Journal of Pure & Applied Physics.*

Bentwich, J. (2017a) The Computational Unified Field Theory: Could 'Dark Matter' & 'Dark Energy' be "Superfluous"? *SciFed Journal of Quantum Physics Special Issue.*

Bentwich, J. (2017b) The Computational Unified Field Theory: Explaining the Universe from "Without". *SciFed Journal of Quantum Physics Special Issue.*

Bentwich, J. (2017c). The Computational Unified Field Theory: A New 'A-Causal Computation' Physics. *SciFed Journal of Quantum Physics Special Issue.*

Bentwich, J. (2017d). The 'Computational Unified Field Theory' (CUFT) May Challenge the 'Big-Bang Theory'. *SciFed Journal of Quantum Physics Special Issue.*

Bentwich, J. (2017e). Can the 'Computational Unified Field Theory' (CUFT) Challenge the Basic Laws of Conservation? *SciFed Journal of Quantum Physics Special Issue.*

Bentwich, J. (2017f). The Computational Unified Field Theory (CUFT): Time "Reversal" May be Possible. *SciFed Journal of Quantum Physics Special Issue.*

Bentwich, J. (2017g). The Computational Unified Field Theory (CUFT) Transcends Relativity's Speed of Light Constraint. *SciFed Journal of Quantum Physics, Special Issue.*

Bentwich, J. (2017h). The Computational Unified Field Theory's New Physics: Transcending Space, Time and Causality. *SciFed Journal of Quantum Physics Special Issue.*

Bentwich, J. (2017i). A "Supra-Spatial-Temporal Universal Consciousness Reality'. *Research & Reviews: Journal of Pure & Applied Physics, Special Issue: The Computational Unified Field Theory (CUFT)- A Paradigmatic Shift in 21st Century Physics.*

Bentwich, J. (2017j). A New Science: An Infinite Omniscient Dynamic-Equilibrium Universal Consciousness Reality. *SciFed Journal of Quantum Physics Special Issue.*

Bentwich, J. (2017k). The Computational Unified Field Theory (CUFT) Challenges Darwin's 'Natural Selection Principle'! *SciFed Journal of Quantum Physics Special Issue.*

Bentwich, J. (2017l). The Computational Unified Field Theory (CUFT) Challenges the Second Law of Thermodynamics. *SciFed Journal of Quantum Physics Special Issue.*

Bentwich, J. (2017m). The Computational Unified Field Theory (CUFT): An Empirical & Mathematical Validation of the 'Computational Unified Field Theory'; *SciFed Journal of Quantum Physics Special Issue.*

Bentwich, J. (2017n). The Computational Unified Field Theory (CUFT) New Science; *SciFed Journal of Quantum Physics Special Issue.*

Bentwich, J. (2018a). Review: The Computational Unified Field Theory (CUFT) New Universe: *The Global Journal of Science Frontier Research, Vol. 18 (8-A), Special Issue.*

Bentwich, J. (2018b). The Computational Unified Field Theory (CUFT): What is "Time"? *The Global Journal of Science Frontier Research, Vol. 18 (8-A), Special Issue.*

Bentwich, J. (2018c). The Universal Consciousness Reality's Camouflage: The Physical Universe! *The Global Journal of Science Frontier Research, Vol. 18 (8-A), Special Issue.*

Bentwich, J. (2018d). The Computational Unified Field Theory (CUFT) Epilogue: Can Human Consciousness Affect the Cosmos? *The Global Journal of Science Frontier Research, Vol. 18 (8-A), Special Issue.*

Bentwich, J. (2018e). Testing the Computational Unified Field Theory's (CUFT) Differential-Critical Predictions: The Higgs-Boson Particle May Not Exist Continuously! *The Global Journal of Science Frontier Research, Vol. 18 (8-A), Special Issue.*

Bentwich, J. (2018f). The Double-Faceted Universal Consciousness Reality: A Theoretical Review. *The Global Journal of Science Frontier Research, Vol. 18 (8-A), Special Issue.*

Bentwich, J. (2018g). Letter to the Editor: Dark Matter May Not Exist. *The Global Journal of Science Frontier Research, Vol. 18 (8-A), Special Issue.*

Bentwich, J. (2018h). The Computational Unified Field Theory's (CUFT) Epilogue: Possible Reversal of the Arrow of Time and Abolishment of Death. *The Global Journal of Science Frontier Research, Vol. 18 (8-A), Special Issue.*

Bentwich, J. (2019a). The Computational Unified Field Theory's (CUFT) New Universe. *The Global Journal of Science Frontier Research, Vol. 19 (6), Special Issue.*

Bentwich, J. (2019b). The Computational Unified Field Theory's (CUFT) Goes Beyond the 'Standard Model': "G-d's Physics"?!. *The Global Journal of Science Frontier Research, Vol. 18 (8-A), Special Issue.*

Bentwich, J. (2019c). A Call for Cosmologists & Experimental Physicists: Empirical Validation of the 'Computational Unified Field Theory' (CUFT) New Paradigm through "Time-Sensitive" Astronomical and Subatomic Measurements. *The Global Journal of Science Frontier Research, Vol. 19 (6), Special Issue.*

Bentwich, J. (2019d). The 'Computational Unified Field Theory' (CUFT): Redefining Mass, Gravity & the Physical Universe. *The Global Journal of Science Frontier Research, Vol. 19 (6), Special Issue.*

Bentwich, J. (2019d). Astronomical Validation of the Computational Unified Field Theory (CUFT) "Critical Prediction" & Resolution of the "Universe's Accelerated Expansion Rate Enigma" (UAERE).*The Global Journal of Science Frontier Research, Vol. 19 (6), Special Issue.*

Bentwich, J. (2019e) Urgent Call for Empirical Validation of the Computational Unified Field Theory's (CUFT) New 21st Century 'A-Causal Computation' (ACC) Paradigm. *Acta Scientific Applied Physics, Volume 1(1).*

Bentovish (Bentwich) J. (2020a) **'G-d's Physics'**. In Press. *iUniverse Publication.*

Bentovish (Bentwich) J. (2020a) **'G-d's Physics'**. In Press. *iUniverse Publication.*

Bentovish (Bentwich), J. (2020b). 'G-d's Physics' (CUFT) New "Atom" & Purposeful Universe! *Advances in Theoretical & Computational Physics. Volume 3 (2),* p. 50-58.

Bentovish (Bentwich), J. (2020c). An Urgent Need for "G-d's Physics" New 21st Century Paradigm's Empirical Validation. *Advances in Theoretical & Computational Physics. Volume 3 (2),* p. 59-65.

ב"ה

Fulfilling Einstein's Quest: "G-d's Physics" New Twenty-First Century's Paradigm's Multi-Level Computational Universe

Jehonathan Bentovish (Bentwich), Ph.D.

Note: Dr. Bentovish is seeking scientific collaboration and validation of this New CUFT's 'G-d's Physics' Paradigm's empirical "critical predictions" involving precise Astronomical /Cosmological Measurements as well as time-sensitive Accelerators validations.

Dr. Bentovish (Bentwich) e-mail is: drbentwich@gmail.com.

Abstract:

Twenty-first Century Theoretical Physics is undergoing a "Paradigmatic-Shift" (akin to Einstein's Relativity Theory (RT) "Paradigmatic Shift" over 100 years ago) from the Old "Material-Causal" Paradigm underlying both RT and Quantum Mechanics (QM) to the New "Computational Unified Field Theory" (CUFT), recently called" "G-d's Physics" New Paradigm! This New "G-d's Physics" Paradigmatic-Shift was called for due to the apparent "theoretical inconsistency" between the two "pillars" of the Old "Material-Causal" Paradigm, i.e., RT & QM, as well as the inability of the Old Paradigm to account for up to 95% of all the mass and energy concepts that could not be verified empirically; The New "G-d's Physics" Paradigm is based on the discovery of a singular, higher-ordered "Universal Computational Principle" (UCP) which simultaneously computes all exhaustive spatial pixels in the universe for each consecutive "Universal Frame/s" (UF) at the unfathomable rate of "c^2/h" = 1.36^{-50} (sec'), with the entire universe "dissolving" into the UCP's singularity "in-between" any two consecutive UF's frames! This

New "G-d's Physics" A-Causal Computation Paradigm was shown to challenge, negate and revise some of the most fundamental assumptions of the Old "Material-Causal" Paradigm such as: the "Big-Bang" Model, Einstein's Equations, discarding of "dark-matter" and "dark-energy" as "superfluous" (non-existent!) and QM's "material-causal" assumption regarding the "collapse" of the probability wave function due to its assumed direct physical interaction with another subatomic "probe" element. A few key new "Theoretical Postulates" of the New "G-d's Physics" Paradigm include: the "Universal Computational Formula" shown capable of unifying the Four basic Forces, as well as the four basic physical features of "space", "energy", "mass" and "time", and integrate all key relativistic and quantum laws and relationships. Nevertheless, "G-d's Physics" New "A-Causal Computation" Paradigm points at the complete dependency of the UCP's simultaneous computation of all exhaustive spatial pixels in the universe upon the UCP's "Ten Laws of Hierarchical Manifestation" which include: its Three "Computational Dimensions", "Supra Spatial-Temporal Reservoir", "Dynamic-Equilibrium Moral Principle", "Expansion of Consciousness (Hypothesis)", Collective Human Consciousness Focus (Hypothesis)", "Reversed-Time Goal Hypothesis", "Good-Will" & "Free-Will" characterizations of the UCP; Therefore, the New "G-d's Physics" Paradigm of 21st Century Physics portrays an entirely "New Universe" – which completely depends on the UCP's continuous computation- "dissolution" sustenance- and evolution- of all exhaustive spatial pixels comprising the universe towards the "Ultimate Goal" o a "Perfected: Physically, Morally and Spiritually" State of the World (and Humanity) which realizes the Singularity, "Unity" and "Goodness" of this "Universal Consciousness Reality", called: "Geula" in Jewish Tradition!

1.   Introduction: G-d's Physics New 21st Century Scientific Paradigm

Albert Einstein is considered one of the two greatest Scientists the world has ever known (e.g., the other one being Isaac Newton) and his General Relativity Theory is deemed the greatest intellectual achievement accomplished by any single human-being! Yet his unwavering singular quest towards a "Unifying Field Theory" that will be able to resolve the apparent basic "theoretical-inconsistency" between Relativity Theory (RT) and Quantum Mechanics (QM) (e.g., which he carried on "relentlessly" for the entire second half of his illustrious scientific career) – was viewed by his contemporaries as leading to a "dead-end" and was even construed as indicating that Einstein has "lost his genius"?! Nevertheless, approximately one hundred years since Einstein begun his quest for such a "Unifying Field Theory" Theoretical Physics is increasingly seeking such a "Theory of Everything" which would essentially accomplish Einstein's vision of unifying RT & QM as well as all of the Forces of Nature; Indeed, Einstein's own "vision" was to unify space, time, energy and mass, RT & QM, and the plethora of elementary subatomic particles – within one singular formula, stemming from a higher-ordered theoretical understanding of the nature of the "Field" – which encompasses, integrates and transcends the narrow constraints of the current "Relativistic" and "Quantum" theoretical models… It is no "secret" that quite a few of Einstein's hypotheses and "predictions" were tested and validated empirically many years after his passing in 1955- which has led to multiple Nobel prizes, e.g., including his "visionary" hypothesis of "gravitational waves", "gravitational lensing" etc.!

Amazingly, it seems that Einstein's major quest for a grand "Unifying Field Theory" is being fulfilled by what's considered today as Physics New 21st Century Paradigm, i.e., the "Computational Unified Field Theory" (CUFT), recently also termed: "G-d's Physics" Paradigm! Prior to describing the gist of this New "G-d's Physics" Paradigm (CUFT) and delineating its basic theoretical postulates, it is important to first, capsulate the essence of the "Paradigmatic-Crisis" of 20th Century basic "Material-Causal Paradigm", e.g., underlying both RT & QM and its inevitable ensuing "Paradigmatic-Shift" to the New "G-d's Physics" (CUFT) Paradigm of 21st Century Theoretical Physics: Perhaps the clearest instance indicating the basic "Paradigmatic-Crisis" of 20th Century's Material-Causal Paradigm is the apparent theoretical inconsistency that seems to exist between RT's strict "Speed of Light" barrier for the transmission of any light signal across space and time – as opposed to QM's well known (and empirically validated)

Quantum-Entanglement" phenomenon; according to RT's strict Light Speed Barrier it is not possible for any signal (or any physical effect) to travel- or affect- any other element at a speed greater than the Speed of Light; In contrast, the empirically validate "Quantum Entanglement" phenomenon indicates that a subatomic measurement of any one of Heisenberg's "Uncertainty Principle's" "complimentary pairs", e.g., "space" and "energy", or "time" and "mass" – in one of two "entangled particles" will "instantaneously" determine the other complimentary pair's measurement accuracy level (constraint) in the other "entangled particle" (e.g., separated by a greater distance than can be traversed by a light-signal), thereby clearly "violating" Relativity Theory's strict "light Speed Barrier"!? Additionally, as analyzed and defined by the great Philosopher of Science Thomas Kuhn (1962), the Old "Material-Causal" Paradigm underlying both RT & QM indicated the "clear signs" signifying a "Paradigmatic-Crisis" – as shown by its inability to explain a series of key empirical (or theoretical) phenomena, i.e., perhaps the most "glaring" one is its inability to explain the accelerated expansion of the physical universe, which is attributed to the purely hypothetical concepts of "dark-matter" or "dark-energy", which are assumed to comprise up to 95% of all of the "matter" and "energy" in the universe, but which yet cannot be empirically directly validated (despite numerous attempts to do so)! Moreover, the inability to unify or explain between the three basic "Strong", "Weak" and "Electromagnetic" Forces and the "Gravitational" Force of the Standard Model also indicate a basic "failure" of the Old "Material-Causal" Paradigm to adequately account for the plethora of physical phenomena (existing both in the relativistic and subatomic realms) – clearly calling for a fundamental "Paradigmatic-Shift" in 21st Century Theoretical Physics! Interestingly, once again, Einstein played a major role in demonstrating such a "Paradigmatic-Shift" from the Old "Newtonian Classical Mechanics" towards the (then "new") Relativity Theory and subsequently Quantum Mechanics Paradigm of 20th Century Physics – simply by discarding the "superfluous" (purely hypothetical) "ether" concept which also could not be detected empirically (despite numerous attempts) and postulating a few simple new "Theoretical Postulates";

Similarly, the New "G-d's Physics" Paradigm discarded the purely hypothetical concepts of "dark-matter" and "dark-energy" and introduced several new Theoretical Postulates including:

a. **The "Universal Computational/Consciousness Principle"**

According to the New "G-d's Physics" Paradigm, there exists a singular higher-ordered Universal Computational/ Consciousness Principle (UCP) which *simultaneously* computes every exhaustive spatial pixel in the universe at the unfathomable rate of "c^2/h" = 1.36^{-50} sec'(!) giving rise to an extremely rapid series of "Universal Frames" (UF's) comprising the entire physical universe at every such "minimal time-point", wherein "in-between" any two such consecutive UF's frames the entire physical universe "dissolves" back into the singularity of this UCP! This UCP possesses three "Computational Dimensions", e.g.,: "Framework" ("frame" vs. "object"), "Consistency" ("consistent" vs. "inconsistent") and "Locus" ("global" vs. "local") – two out of which "Framework" and "Consistency" produce the four basic physical features of "Framework" – "consistent" ("space") or "inconsistent" ("energy") and "Object" – "consistent" ("mass") or "inconsistent" ("time) physical features that continuously and simultaneously compute any exhaustive spatial pixel in the universe for each consecutive UF's frame/s! Another key new discovery made by the New "G-d's Physics" (CUFT) Paradigm is its insistence that this singular higher-ordered UCP *simultaneously computes* all of the exhaustive spatial pixels in the universe for each consecutive UF's frame/s at the incredible rate of "c^2/h" = 1.36^{-50} sec'(!); and that "in-between" any two consecutive UF's frames the entire physical universe and all of its constituting exhaustive spatial pixels "dissolve" back into the singularity of this singular higher-ordered UCP!

b. **"G-d's Physics" New "A-Causal Computation" Paradigm**

Based on "G-d's Physics" New Paradigm's discovery that the singular higher-ordered UCP *simultaneously computes* all exhaustive spatial pixels comprising the entire physical universe – for each consecutive UF's frame/s (and that "in-between" any two consecutive UF's frames the whole universe "dissolves" back into the singularity of the UCP), a new "A-Causal Computation" characterization of "G-d's Physics" New Paradigm is acknowledged: essentially, the simultaneity of the UCP's computation of all exhaustive spatial pixels (and their complete "dissolution" "in-between" any two consecutive UF's frame/s back into the UCP) means that there cannot exist any "material-causal" physical interaction between any two (or more) exhaustive spatial pixels existing either in the same- or different- UF's frames! Rather, the same singular UCP computes simultaneously all exhaustive spatial pixels comprising the entire physical universe – which implies that there cannot exist any Relativistic or Quantum "material-causal" physical relationships, interactions, or effects! This negated many of the Old "Material-Causal" (20th Century Physics) Paradigm's basic assumptions underlying both Relativity Theory and Quantum Mechanics, including: the "Big-Bang" Model, Einstein's Equations, discarding of the hypothetical "dark-matter" and "dark-energy" concepts etc.

c. **The "Computational Invariance Principle" & "Universal Consciousness Reality"**

Another key new theoretical postulate of the New "G-d's Physics" Paradigm is the "Computational Invariance Principle" which posits that since only the UCP exists – continuously and consistently both "during" each consecutive UF's frame/s – solely computing (simultaneously) all exhaustive spatial pixels' four basic physical features of "space" and "energy", "mass" and "time", and also singularly exists "in-between" any two consecutive UF's frame/s (without the presence of the physical universe), therefore the "Computational Invariance Principle" theoretical postulate asserts that only this singular UCP may be regarded as "computationally-invariant" existing uniformly and "consistently" – both "during" its computation of each consecutive UF's frame/s and also "in-between" any two consecutive UF's frame/s, whereas the four basic physical features being computed for all exhaustive spatial pixels in the universe may only be regarded as "computationally-variant", e.g., existing only "transiently" and "phenomenally" ("during" each consecutive UF's frame/s but "dissolving" "in-between" any two consecutive UF's frames)! This new (profound) realization of the "Computational Invariance Principle" of "G-d's Physics" New Paradigm is also associated with another new theoretical postulate termed: the "Universal Consciousness Reality" (UCR) which posits that since the whole physical universe (e.g., and all of its constituting exhaustive spatial pixels) is only regarded as "computationally-variant" – existing only "transiently" "during" each consecutive UF's frame/s but "dissolving back into the singularity of the UCR, whereas the singular higher-ordered UCP is considered to be "computationally-invariant" (existing continuously and consistently both "during" each consecutive UF's frame/s as computing each exhaustive spatial pixel's four basic physical features of "space" and "energy", "mass" and "time", as well as solely existing "in-between" any two consecutive UF's frames without the presence of any physical universe); therefore there only exists one singular "Universal Consciousness Reality" which exists consistently and continuously – manifesting as the phenomenal physical universe "during" its computation of every exhaustive spatial pixel of each consecutive UF's frame/s and existing without the presence of the physical universe, in-between any two consecutive UF's frames! Indeed, this new "Universal Consciousness Reality" carries with it a profound alteration of our basic perception and understanding of the physical universe – which ceases to exist as an "objective-independent" reality, and it transformed into the new theoretical understanding that (in truth) the entire physical universe only represents a "phenomenal, transient manifestation" of this singular UCR!

d. **The "Universal Computational Formula"**

Based on "G-d's Physics" (CUFT) New Paradigm's discovery of the Universal Computational/Consciousness Principle (UCP) and its simultaneous computation of all exhaustive spatial pixels comprising each consecutive UF's frame/s it also revealed the existence of an integrated simultaneous computation of all the four basic physical features of "space" and "energy", "mass" and "time" as computed based on two out of the three basic "Computational Dimensions" of the UCP (delineated further below and previously):

Universal Computational Formula (UCF):

$$\left\{ \begin{array}{c} \text{'}c^2 \\[1em] - \\[1em] h \end{array} \right\} \quad \text{UF's } \{\text{ת}...\text{מ}...\text{א}\} \qquad \begin{array}{ccc} = & s & {}^* & e \\[1em] & t & {}^* & m \end{array}$$

wherein the singular higher-ordered UCP – represented by the Hebrew letter "Yud" ("י") simultaneously computes all exhaustive spatial pixels in the universe comprising each consecutive Universal Frame/s (UF's) which already exist in a "potential-from" within the UCP's "Supra Spatial-Temporal Reservoir" of all "past", "present" and multiple possible "future/s" UF's (represented by the Hebrew letters from "א through "מ" to "ת)" depending on the Moral Choice of each Individual Human Consciousness – as computing and integrating these four basic physical features of "space" and "energy", "mass" and "time", at the incredible rate of: "c^2/h" = 1.36^{-50} sec'!

e. **The "Dynamic Equilibrium" Moral Principle & UCP's "Multi Spatial-Temporal Reservoir"**

Another key theoretical postulate of this New "G-d's Physics" Paradigm is the discovery of the UCP's associated "Dynamic-Equilibrium" Moral Principle and its associated "Multi Spatial-Temporal Reservoir" bank of all "past", "present" and multiple possible "future/s" UF's frames based on the "Moral/Immoral Choices" of each Individual Human Being towards another human being; Essentially, due to the "inseparability" of all Individual Human Consciousness (human beings) from this singular higher-ordered "Universal Consciousness Principle" (UCP) the New "G-d's Physics" Paradigm asserts that there is a basic fundamental "Dynamic-Equilibrium" Moral Principle characterizing the operation of this UCP – such that any "immoral-imbalance" created by any "immoral choice" made by any Individual Human Consciousness towards another Individual Human Consciousness is "corrected" and "balanced" by the UCR in a manner in which that Individual Human Consciousness which chose to "inflict pain/suffering" upon another Individual Human Consciousness – the UCP is selecting one of multiple "possible future/s" UF's frame/s in which it will also have to experience the same (nature and degree) of pain/suffering that it inflicted upon the other Individual Human Consciousness in order that it learns and realizes the basic "unity" and "inseparability" of all Individual Human Consciousness from the singular higher-ordered UCP and honors and respects all other such Individual Human Consciousness (just as pointed out by the Alter-Rebbi, Rabbi Schneur-Zalman in his famous Tanyah Book, chapter 32)! Additionally, according to this new "Dynamic-Equilibrium" Moral Principle, since the whole "purpose" of the UCP's associated "Dynamic-Equilibrium" Moral Principle is to "teach", "correct" or "balance" any "immoral-choice/s" of any Individual Human Consciousness so that that Individual Human Consciousness acknowledges and "realizes" it's "unity" with the UCP and inseparability from all other Individual Human Consciousness – so that it could not and would not consider or execute any "immoral-choice/s" toward any other Individual Human Consciousness, therefore there is another possibility carved out by the singular higher-ordered UCP of "teshuva" – e.g., repentance, a sincere regret relating to the "immoral choice" and a conscious decision not to repeat it in the future – which "circumvents" and replaces the need of that Individual Human Consciousness to experience itself the abovementioned "negative future" that is equivalent to its own "wrongdoing"… Finally, this "Dynamic-Equilibrium" Moral Principle may be seen as part of the overall "Goal" of the UCP's constant and continuous origination- sustenance- "dissolution" and evolution- of the entire physical universe – which is to bring the World towards its "Perfected- Geula" State of Moral, Spiritual and even Physical Perfection, in which the oneness and integrity of all creation as part of the singularity of the UCP will be realized and acknowledged by Humanity, see next "Reversed-Time Goal Hypothesis" theoretical postulate;

f.   **The UCR's "Expansive Consciousness Spectrum Hypothesis" & "Reversed-Time Goal Hypothesis"**

Another two profound and key theoretical postulates of the New "G-d's Physics" Paradigm are: the UCR's – "Expansive Consciousness Spectrum Hypothesis" & "Reversed-Time Goal Hypothesis"; the "UCR's Expansive Consciousness Spectrum Hypothesis" stipulates that as part of the UCP/UCR's ultimate Goal of driving the world (and entire universe) towards a "Perfected State" – called "Geula" in Jewish Tradition in which the oneness and unity of all creation as integral parts of the singular higher-ordered UCP/UCR will be recognized by Humanity; the UCR computes- ", "dissolves", "re-computes"- and evolves- the forms manifested by this singular UCP/UCR from "inanimate" matter (e.g., subatomic particles and the entire macroscopic universe) through "animate" forms of plants, then animals then human-beings – which represents the most "expansive" form of Consciousness; and ultimately leads this much "refined" and more "Expansive" form of Human Consciousness towards its ultimate "expanded" manifestations of this singular Universal Consciousness Reality which are expressed in the "expanded form of Individual Human Consciousness" (previously delineated) in which Individual Human Consciousness "expands" to a state in which it is "not separate" and functions in "unity" with the Universal Consciousness Reality (e.g., sometimes related to as states of "Prophecy" such as with Moses!); Another manifestation of this expansion of Individual Human Consciousness occurs also in "special times" and states of "Collective Human Consciousness Focus (Hypothesis" (also delineated below and previously) – such as during the Jewish "Rosh-Hashana" (New Year) time-interval in which Millions of Jews (all over the world) collectively focus on- and pray to- this singular higher-ordered "Universal Consciousness Reality", i.e., "G-d"! As published and delineated previously, this New "G-d's Physics" profound expansive new perspective on the development and evolution of the entire cosmos – including its "inanimate" manifestations of all material compositions, e.g., including the relativistic accelerated expansion of the physical universe as well as all subatomic (quantum) particles, forces and phenomena, all "animate" forms of "plants", "animals" and "human-beings" brings about an entirely new and integrated view on the origination- and evolution- of the physical universe and all biological forms – not as "caused" by any "random" Big-Bang nuclear explosion but as driven and computed by the singular higher-ordered UCR whose sole Goal is to bring the entire physical universe and our own world towards the State of "Geula" Perfection (Morally, Spiritually and Physically); Indeed, the additional "Reversed-Time Goal Hypothesis" theoretical postulate posits that the entire origination of the entire physical universe continuous and constant computation by the UCP (simultaneously) of all exhaustive spatial pixels in the universe for every consecutive UF's frame/s from its onset- in the "first" UF frame and until this date and onwards until the UCP/UCR brings the universe into its ultimate "Goal" of a Perfected: Morally, Spiritually and Physically State; This "Reversed-Time Goal Hypothesis" simply posits that the entire origination-sustenance and evolution of the entire physical universe – is driven by its drive to bring the world towards its ultimate Perfected "Geula" State of Moral, Spiritual and even Physical Perfection (e.g., in which there will not be any longer "death"!); a State in which all Human Being will recognize and realize the oneness of all creation with this singular higher-ordered Universal Consciousness Reality (UCR), and therefore there could not exist any longer any such "negative" phenomena of "violence", "aggression", crimes" or "immoral behavior", and on the contrary Humanity's (and Science's) ultimate recognition of the singular higher-ordered UCR as the sole reality that drives and sustains the entire universe will lead to an attitude of "reverence", "gratitude" and "studying" of this "All-Goodness", "Divine" "Universal Consciousness Reality" ("G-d"!), as anticipated by the great Jewish Sage and Teacher, Maimonides (in his monumental "Mishna-Torah" masterpiece)…

In order to fully appreciate the significance of this New "G-d's Physics" Paradigm of 21st Century Theoretical Physics let us encapsulate the major conceptual differences between the Old "Material-Causal" Paradigm and the New "G-d's Physics" (CUFT) Paradigm: Succinctly stated, the Old "Material-Causal" Paradigm assumed that any relativistic or quantum phenomenon can be explained strictly through direct (or even indirect) physical interaction/s between a finite number of material or physical elements (or forces etc.); Based on this basic "Material-Causal" assumption, the Old "Material-Causal" Model explains the origination of the physical universe as "caused" by an initial "Big-Bang" nuclear event which is assumed to have created all the stars, galaxies, "energy" and "matter" in the universe; Likewise, Einstein's (famous) Equations underlying General Relativity Theory assume that it is the direct physical interaction between certain "massive objects" and "Space-Time" which "causes" the "curvature" of Space-Time, and conversely, that it is this "curved Space-Time" which "causes" or determines the "travelling-pathways" of those "massive objects" and other "less-massive" objects. In a similar manner, Quantum Mechanics explains the dynamics of the subatomic realm based on the same basic "Material-Causal" assumption wherein it is assumed that it is the direct physical interaction between a given subatomic "target's probability wave function" and a corresponding subatomic "probe" element – which "causes" the "collapse" of the target's "probability wave function" into a single (complimentary "energy-space"/"time-mass") value. However, contrary to this Old Material-Causal Paradigm (of RT & QM) basic assumption wherein it is the direct physical interaction between any given relativistic "massive-objects" and "Space-Time" which "causes" the curvature of Space-Time (or conversely that it is this "curved Space-Time" which "causes" the travelling-pathways of these massive/less-massive objects); or that it is the direct physical interaction/s between the subatomic target's "probability wave function" and a corresponding "probe" element – which "causes" the "collapse" of the probability wave function into singular complimentary value; the New "G-d's Physics" (CUFT) Paradigm negates the very possibility of the existence of any such direct physical interaction/s between any two (or more) exhaustive (relativistic or quantum) spatial pixels in the universe – based on the discovery of the existence of the singular higher-ordered UCP which *simultaneously computes* all exhaustive spatial pixels comprising the entire physical universe, e.g., at any minimal-time point "Universal-Frame/s" (UF's) being computed by this singular UCP at the unfathomably rapid rate of "c^2/h" = 1.36^{-50} (sec')! Based upon this profound new discovery of "G-d's Physics" (CUFT's) New Paradigm of the *UCP simultaneous computation* of all exhaustive spatial pixels comprising each consecutive UF's frame/s, this results in "G-d's Physics" New "A-Causal Computation" Paradigm which strictly negates the very possibility of the existence of any direct (or even indirect) physical (or material) interaction/s between any two (or more) exhaustive spatial pixels existing either in the same- of different- UF's frame/s! Moreover, due to "G-d's Physics" postulate that the entire physical universe (e.g., and all of its constituent exhaustive spatial pixels) completely "dissolve" "in-between" any two consecutive UF's frame/s back into the singularity of the UCP, therefore the New "G-d's Physics' A-Causal Computation

Paradigm" principally negates the possibility of the existence of any direct (or indirect) physical interactions between any two (or more) exhaustive spatial pixels existing either in the same- or other- UF's and the impossibility of any "transference" of any physical interaction or effect/s (or any material entities) "in-between" any two consecutive UF's frame/s!

2. "G-d's Physics" Newly Revised Physical Universe!

Hence, the discovery of the New "G-d's Physics" Paradigm completely alters and revises our basic conception and understanding of the origin- nature- sustenance- dynamics- and evolution- of the entire physical universe, e.g., at both its macroscopic ("relativistic") and microscopic ("quantum") computational levels; At the macroscopic level, we realize that the physical universe could not have been "caused" or "created" by an initial "Big-Bang" nuclear event! This is because, according to RT's "Big-Bang" Model, the entire universe, e.g., including all of its suns, galaxies, mass, energy (space and time) have been "caused" or "created" by an initial nuclear explosion – which implies that such a "nuclear event" took place in the "first", "second", "third", etc. UF's frame/s – leading up to the creation of certain mass, energy, suns and subsequent galaxies etc. But since, as stated above (and previously), there cannot exist any such direct (or even indirect) physical interaction/s between any two (or more) exhaustive spatial pixels existing either in the same- or different- UF's frames (e.g., due to the UCP simultaneous computation of all exhaustive spatial pixels comprising every consecutive UF's frame/s and the complete "dissolution" of the entire physical universe "in- between" any two consecutive UF's frame/s), therefore the New "G-d's Physics" Paradigm negates the basic "material-causal" assumption of the Big-Bang Model – instead pointing at the continuous computation- "dissolution"- re-computation- and evolution- of every exhaustive spatial pixel in the universe by the singular higher-ordered UCP for each consecutive UF's frame/s! Likewise, at the macroscopic level, the sustenance and evolution of the physical cosmos – is not governed by General Relativity's Einstein's Equations "material-causal" assumption, but rather "points" at "G-d's Physics" higher-ordered UCP's "A-Causal

Computation" Paradigm! According to Einstein's Equations, the sustenance and evolution of the entire physical cosmos solely depends on the direct physical interactions that exist between certain "massive objects" and "Space-Time", which is assumed to "cause" the "curvature of Space-Time", and conversely, this "curved Space-Time" is assumed to "cause" (or determine) the "travelling-pathways" of those "massive" and other "less-massive" objects; But, once again, due to the "G-d's Physics" New "A-Causal Computation" Paradigm, which principally negates the very possibility of the existence of any such "material-causal" physical interaction/s between any two (or more) exhaustive spatial pixels existing either in the same- or different- UF's frame/s; therefore also Einstein's Equations basic "material-causal" assumption has to be negated! Instead, we reach the inevitable (surprising) theoretical conclusion, wherein what seems as the curvature of "Space-Time" by "massive objects" (and conversely the determination of those "massive/ less-massive objects" as apparently "caused" by this "curved Space-Time") – truly only arises from the UCP singular higher-ordered simultaneous computation of all exhaustive spatial pixels in the universe (for each consecutive UF's frame/s), i.e., based on the discovery of the UCP's "Universal Computational Formula" (UCF) which completely integrates the four basic physical features of "space", "time", "energy" and "mass" for its simultaneous computation of all exhaustive spatial pixels comprising the entire physical universe!

Likewise, "G-d's Physics" New ("A-Causal Computation") Paradigm was also shown to negate the Old "Material-Causal" Paradigm's assumption of the existence of the (purely hypothetical) concepts of "dark-matter" and "dark-energy" – which are assumed to "cause" the accelerated expansion of the physical universe, but which yet cannot be directly detected (despite numerous attempts to do so!) Alike Einstein's "ingenious" discarding of the (purely hypothetical) "Ether" concept of 19th Century Newtonian Mechanics as "superfluous", due to the experimental "failure" to detect the presence of this "Ether" element, "G-d's Physics" (CUFT) New Paradigm also discarded the purely hypothetical concepts of "dark-matter" and "dark-energy" as "superfluous" (e.g., "non-existent"!) due to the inability of numerous experimental efforts to detect those "dark-matter" and "dark-energy" concepts; and due to the New "G-d's Physics" Paradigm's principle negation of the very possibility of the existence of any such direct (or even indirect) "material-causal" physical interactions between any such (purely hypothetical) "dark matter" or "dark-energy" concepts and the various galaxies, stars and planets comprising the entire physical universe – e.g., which is assumed to "cause" the accelerated expansion of the universe!? Instead, the New "G-d's Physics" Paradigm explains the empirically observed accelerated expansion of the physical universe – not as "caused" by any direct (or even indirect) physical interaction/s between any purely hypothetical "dark-matter" or "dark-energy" and any other exhaustive spatial pixels comprising certain elements in the physical universe (such as stars, galaxies "matter" or "energy"), but rather as resulting from the UCP's simultaneous computation of all of the exhaustive spatial pixels comprising the entire physical universe for each consecutive UF's frame/s! Specifically, the New "G-d's Physics" Paradigm explains the accelerated expansion of the physical universe – as arising from the UCP's accelerated addition of the number of exhaustive spatial pixels added to each consecutive UF's frame/s (which it computes simultaneously)!

On the subatomic level, the New "G-d's Physics" Paradigm also greatly challenges the Old "Material-Causal" Paradigm of Quantum Mechanics; instead of QM's "Material-Causal" assumption wherein it is assumed that the subatomic measurement of any given subatomic "target" element's "probability wave function" "collapses" as "caused" by its direct physical interaction with another subatomic "probe" element; Once again, such a "material-causal" assumption is negated by "G-d's Physics" New "A-Causal Computation" Paradigm which negates the very possibility of any such direct physical interactions between any two (or more) exhaustive spatial pixels existing either in the same or different UF's frames! Instead, the New "G-d's Physics" Paradigm postulates that the UCP singular higher-ordered simultaneous computation of all exhaustive spatial pixels in the universe – includes its computation of single- "particle" or multiple- "wave" spatial-temporal entities, which are embedded within the UCP's exhaustive computation of all of the exhaustive spatial pixels comprising the entire physical universe at each minimal time-point UF's frame/s; Hence, as outlined previously, instead of the "collapse" of the target's hypothetical probability wave function based on its direct physical interaction with another subatomic probe element, according to the New "G-d's Physics" Paradigm, the UCP simultaneously computes both the "single spatial-temporal particle" elements and the "multi spatial-temporal wave" elements – which are both embedded within the more exhaustive entire UF's frame/s being computed (simultaneously) by the UCP!

3. "G-d Does Not Play with Dice": "G-d's Physics" UCP's Universal Computational Formula & Hierarchical Laws of Manifestation!

Hence, the New "G-d's Physics" Paradigm entirely revises our basic understanding of the origin- sustenance- and evolution- of the entire physical universe: not as created by an initial "random" Big-Bang nuclear event, nor as being governed by any "material-causal" physical interactions between certain "massive-objects" and "Space-Time" (which are assumed to "curve" Space-Time etc.), nor as being driven by purely hypothetical "dark-matter" and "dark-energy" entities (which are assumed to "cause" the accelerated expansion of the physical universe); Nor is the subatomic realm governed by direct (or indirect) physical interactions between subatomic "probe" and "target's probability wave function" which "causes" the "collapse" of the probability wave function into a singular complimentary (space-energy or time-mass) value?! Instead, the New "G-d's Physics" Paradigm forces Science to accept the basic fundamental discovery of a singular higher-ordered UCP which simultaneously computes all exhaustive spatial pixels in the universe for each consecutive UF's frame/s! Instead, we begin realizing that since there cannot exist any direct (or even indirect) physical interactions between any two (or more) exhaustive spatial pixels in the universe – existing either in the same- or different—UF's frames, and moreover that the entire physical universe "dissolves" in-between" any two consecutive UF's frames, therefore the whole existence, "dissolution", sustenance, and evolution of the entire physical universe cannot be explained through any direct (or even indirect) physical interactions between any two (or more) exhaustive spatial pixels, but may only be explained based on the UCP's singular higher-ordered (simultaneous) computation of all exhaustive spatial pixels in the universe for each consecutive UF's frame/s! Indeed, one of the profound new theoretical postulates of the New "G-d's Physics" Paradigm is the "Computational Invariance Principle" postulate and its closely associated "Universal Consciousness Reality" theoretical postulate: these two new theoretical postulates essentially point out that since only the singular higher-ordered UCP may be considered as "computationally-*invariant*", e.g., existing both "during" its simultaneous computation of all exhaustive spatial pixels comprising each consecutive UF's frame/s, and also solely existing "in-between" any two consecutive UF's frame/s (without the presence of any physical universe); whereas all exhaustive spatial pixels comprising the entire physical universe may only be regarded as "computationally-*variant*", i.e., existing only "during" each consecutive UF's frame as solely being computed by the UCP, but "ceasing to exist" by "dissolving" back into the singularity of the UCP "in-between" any two consecutive UF's frame/s; therefore the "Computational Invariance Principle" postulates that only the singular (computationally-invariant) UCP may be considered as "constant" (and "real"), whereas the entire physical universe may only be seen as "computationally-variant" – that is, as existing only "phenomenally" and "transiently" "during" the UCP's computation of each consecutive UF's frame/s, but "dissolving" back into the singularity of the UCP "in-between" any two consecutive UF's frames! Even more profound is the associated "Universal Consciousness Reality" theoretical postulate which suggests that since only the "Universal Computational/Consciousness Principle" (UCP) is seen as "constant", "continuous" and "unchanging", whereas the "phenomenal", "transient" physical universe exists only as solely produced by this Universal Consciousness Principle (UCP); therefore, we reach the inevitable conclusion wherein there truly exists only one singular higher-ordered "Universal Consciousness Reality" (UCR) – which solely exists "in-between" any two consecutive UF's frames, and which manifests as the physical universe "during" each consecutive UF's frame/s!

Indeed, the discovery of this latter "Universal Consciousness Reality" (UCR) theoretical postulate brings about an amazing new

"Paradigmatic-Shift" from the Old "Material-Causal" Paradigm underlying Relativity Theory and Quantum Mechanics to the New "G-d's Physics" Paradigm, because it unravels the purely "Universal Consciousness Principle's" origination- sustenance- "dissolution" and evolution- of each and every exhaustive spatial pixel in the universe, as well as of the existence of the whole entire universe! Once we realize that according to the New "G-d's Physics" "Universal Consciousness Reality" theoretical postulate the whole existence of the physical universe merely represents a "transient-phenomenal manifestation" of the only "real" singular, higher-ordered "Universal Consciousness Reality" (UCR or UCP) and that the whole universe "dissolves" back into this singular UCR "in-between" any two consecutive UF's frame, then this entirely alters our basic understanding of the true nature of the physical universe (and all of its comprising exhaustive spatial pixels for each consecutive UF's frame/s solely computed by this singular UCR/UCP); we can no longer consider any relativistic or quantum "phenomenon", "entity", "particle" or "force" as existing as an "independent" or "solid" reality – because it is only being computed and sustained by the singular higher-ordered UCP/UCR and it only exists "transiently" "during" each consecutive UF's frame (as solely computed- "dissolved"- and sustained- by this singular UCP/UCR), but "ceases to exist" (e.g., "dissolves" back into the singular existence of the UCR "in-between" any two consecutive UF's frame/s)!? So, we reach the inevitable ("somewhat "shocking") realization wherein the only "real", "solid", "continuous" and "constant" "Reality" is this singular higher-ordered "Universal Consciousness Reality" (UCR) – whereas all relativistic or quantum phenomena, particles, forces or entities (such as suns, galaxies, particles, forces and even "laws") are realized to represent mere "transient-phenomenal manifestations" of this singular higher-ordered UCR which exists constantly and continuously both "during" its (simultaneous) computation of all exhaustive spatial pixels comprising the entire physical universe for each consecutive UF's frame/s, as well as exists solely (without the presence of any physical universe) "in-between" any two such consecutive UF's frame/s!

We therefore "abandon" (and indeed negate) the Old "Material-Causal" Paradigm of 20th Century Physics underlying both Relativity

Theory (RT) and Quantum Mechanics which assumes that any relativistic or quantum "phenomenon", "entity", "force" or even "law" can be explained as "caused" by its direct (or indirect) physical interaction with another given material entity – instead realizing that the only "real" underlying "Reality" which computes- sustains- "dissolves"- and evolves- any relativistic or quantum entity or phenomenon is the singular higher-ordered UCR (or UCP) which simultaneously computes all exhaustive spatial pixels comprising the entire physical universe for each consecutive UF's frame/s! Indeed, this new and profound realization of "G-d's Physics" sounds strikingly similar to Einstein's (almost "prophetic") statement that "G-d does not play with dice"!? Even though Einstein's famous statement was said within his "discontent" with the "probabilistic nature" of Quantum Mechanics, more fundamentally, Einstein's historic statement pointed at his deep "insight" that the entire physical universe may be "guided" or indeed "underlie" by a singular higher-ordered "Divine Power" which directs the dynamics and evolution of the universe... Indeed, the discovery of the New "G-d's Physics" Paradigm of 21st Century Theoretical Physics forces to acknowledge that there cannot exist any "probabilistic" or even "positivistic" direct physical interactions between any two (or more) exhaustive spatial pixels comprising either the same- or different- UF's frame/s, but rather that the only "real Reality" which both (simultaneously) computes all exhaustive spatial pixels comprising the entire physical universe "during" each consecutive UF's frame/s and which continues to exist solely (without the presence of the physical universe) "in-between" any two consecutive UF's frames is this singular higher-ordered Universal Consciousness Reality (UCR or UCP)!

Surprisingly, this new profound discovery of the singular existence of the UCR forces us to acknowledge that this singular UCP/UCR Reality's computation- sustenance- "dissolution" and evolution- of each and every exhaustive spatial pixel comprising the entire physical universe "during" each consecutive UF's frame/s may only be explained based on this singular higher-ordered UCR/UCP "intrinsic characteristics" or "Hierarchical Laws of Manifestation"! As pointed out previously, it is essential to understand that unlike the Old "Material-Causal" Paradigm's "Materialistic-Reductionistic" basic approach which sought to "fragment" and "dissect" any physical phenomenon into more "rudimentary" material elements, e.g., assumed to "cause" or "Explain" the given physical phenomena, entity or "law", the New "G-d's Physics" Paradigm negates and transcends such "Materialistic-Reductionistic" approach since it recognizes the fact that no such "elementary" or "basic" "material" entity, particle, force/s or even "law" can exist "independently" of the singular higher-ordered UCP (or UCR) which solely (and continuously) exists both "during" its simultaneous computation of all exhaustive spatial particles comprising each consecutive UF's frame/s and also exists singularly (without the presence of any physical universe) "in-between" any two consecutive UF's frame/s; On the contrary, as we've seen already, the apparent "transient-phenomenal" existence of each of these "basic subatomic particle/s" or "basic (four) forces" etc. – can only be (truly) explained based on the singular higher-ordered UCP's (UCR's) computation of any exhaustive spatial pixel/s for each consecutive UF's frame/s! We therefore need to outline (once again) those "UCP's Hierarchical Laws of Manifestation" – which unlike the Old "Material-Causal" Paradigm's "Materialistic-Reductionistic" approach actually "ascend"- and become increasingly "comprehensive"- and unitary"- and depend upon each other as higher- and more inclusive- manifestations or characterizations of this singular higher-ordered UCP/UCR!

a. **The UCP's Three "Computational Dimensions": Framework, Consistency and Locus**

The first ("lowest") Law of Manifestation is the UCP's three "Computational Dimensions" of "Framework" (frame/object), "Consistency" (consistent/inconsistent) and "Locus" (global/local), which were shown to produce the four basic physical features of "space" and "energy" (i.e., "frame-consistent" or "frame-inconsistent") or "mass" and "time" (e.g., "object-consistent" or "object-inconsistent") computational measures. This means that the UCP's basic computation of the four basic physical features of the physical universe of "space" and "energy", "mass" and "time" are seen to merely represent

— 153 —

different computational combinations of the UCP's (UCR's) two Computational Dimensions (Framework and Consistency – with the third "Locus" Computational Dimension qualifying these four basic physical features depending on the particular point of view of the "observer", e.g., from within the measured phenomenon or from the perspective of the entire UCP's frame etc.).

b. <u>**The UCP's "Universal Computational Formula" (UCF): Complete Integration of Space, Energy, Time & Space**</u>

The "second" (ascending) UCP's Law of Manifestation is its "Universal Computational Formula" (UCF) which completely integrates those four basic physical features of "space" and "energy", "mass" and "time" – due to the UCP's simultaneous computation of each of those exhaustive spatial pixel's four basic physical features! We find that due to the fact that the UCP simultaneously computes all of those four basic physical features simultaneously for each exhaustive spatial pixel therefore the UCP's "Universal Computational Formula" (UCF) describes the manner in which these four basic physical features are computed simultaneously (for each exhaustive spatial pixel comprising every consecutive UF's frame/s)! As explained previously, we find that this integrated simultaneous computation of the UCP – of those four basic physical features implies that they are truly not "separate" or "independent" of each other, but rather represent integrated- and (in fact) "complimentary" secondary computational "by-products" of the same singular UCP's computation of every exhaustive spatial pixel (in the universe), in terms of it's "Object"/"Frame" – "Consistent"/"Inconsistent" computational measures; As explained previously, for instance, the well-known relativistic "laws" (and relationships), such as between an object's relativistic speed and it's increase in "mass" or "dilation of time" – may be easily explained based on the UCP's simultaneous and integrated computation of any given object's (increased) "Object-consistent" ("mass") value and its (decreased) "Object-inconsistent" ("time") value, or between an object's (increased) "Frame-inconsistent" ("energy") value and its (increased) "Object-consistent" ("mass") value; this is due to the fact that the UCP's computational definitions of any give (exhaustive) spatial pixel's "Object-consistent" ("mass") is converse to its computational definition of that spatial pixel's "Object-inconsistent" ("time"), and likewise due to the UCP's computational definition of any given (exhaustive) spatial pixel's "Frame-inconsistent" ("energy") value is necessarily conversely related to its computational definition of that spatial pixel's "Object-consistent" ("time") value, due to certain UCP's computational constraints set on the "maximal degree of displacement" possible of any given object (e.g., in terms of the number of spatial pixels it may be displaced across any two given consecutive UF's frame/s!) Indeed, in this manner the discovery of "G-d's Physics" "Universal Computational Formula's" complete unification of the four basic physical features of "space" and "energy", "mass" and "time" (as "Frame"-"consistent"/"inconsistent" and "Object"-consistent"/"inconsistent" computational measures) has led not only to the unification of key relativistic and quantum features as integral computational aspects of the UCF, but (perhaps more significantly) also led to a complete unification of space, energy, mass and time as secondary computational integrative aspects of the same unitary singular UCR, including its replication and explanation of key Relativistic and Quantum "law" and relationships such as the "Energy-Mass Equivalence", the "curvature of Space-Time by mass" the "dilation of time" for "relativistic observers" (or for "massive objects") etc. Indeed, one of the recent "striking" new discoveries made through this UCF is its potential accounting for all known (and to be discovered) elementary particles predicted by the Standard Model – as merely representing different computational values embedded within this UCP's "Universal Computational Formula"; as well as unifies between the four basic forces (Weak, Strong, Electromagnetic and Gravitational)! Nevertheless, as pointed out above (and previously), "G-d's Physics" realization of the "Computational Invariance Principle" and especially of the "Universal Consciousness Reality" (UCR) teaches us that none of these "transient-phenomenal" "particles", or "forces" or even four basic physical features (of "space" and "energy", "mass" and "time") may be regarded as "real" continuous "independent" material entities – but are now only seen as transitory manifestations of the singular higher-ordered UCR!

Universal Computational Formula (UCF):

$$\left\{ \begin{array}{c} \text{'}c^2 \\ \\ — \\ \\ h \end{array} \right\} \quad \text{UF's } \{\text{א}...\text{מ}...\text{ת}\} \qquad = \quad \dfrac{s \; * \; e}{t \; * \; m}$$

(**Note:** herein the singular higher-ordered UCP – represented by the Hebrew letter "Yud" ("י") simultaneously computes all exhaustive spatial pixels in the universe comprising each consecutive Universal Frame/s (UF's) which already exist in a "potential-from" within the UCP's "Supra Spatial-Temporal Reservoir" of all "past", "present" and multiple possible "future/s" UF's (represented by the Hebrew letters from "א through "מ" to "ת)" depending on the Moral Choice of each Individual Human Consciousness – as computing and integrating these four basic physical features of "space" and "energy", "mass" and "time", at the incredible rate of: "c^2/h" = 1.36^{-50} sec'!)

c. **The UCP's Supra Spatial-Temporal Reservoir: Multiple Possible Future/s!**

The next "rung" UCP's "Hierarchical-Law of Manifestation" relates to the UCP's computation of all possible "past", "present" and multiple possible "future/s" UF's frame/s which are contained within the UCP's "Multi Spatial-Temporal Reservoir"! Indeed, according to "G-d's Physics" New Paradigm, since there cannot exist any direct (or even indirect) physical interaction/s between any two (or more) exhaustive spatial pixels existing either in the same- or different- UF's frames – but rather the UCP simultaneously computes all of these exhaustive spatial pixels comprising each consecutive UF's frame/s; therefore there exists a "bank" of all "past", "present" and multiple possible "future/s" UF's frame/s which are computed by the UCP and stored within it – which in turn are dependent upon still higher "rung" "Hierarchical-Laws of Manifestation", i.e., such as the "Dynamic-Equilibrium Moral Principle"! It is nevertheless noteworthy to mention (at this point) that this UCP's "Supra Spatial-Temporal Reservoir" transcends "space" and "time" – as it includes all "past", "present" and multiple possible "future/s" UF's, and also that it exhibits a "unitary-integrative-singular" Reality which encompasses all past, present and multiple future/s UF's as a singular Reality which is associated and indeed being affected by yet higher "rungs" of the UCP's "Hierarchical Laws of Manifestation"!

d. **The UCP's "Dynamic-Equilibrium Moral Principle"**

The next ("higher-up") "Hierarchical Law of Manifestation" is the "Dynamic-Equilibrium Moral Principle" which essentially describes one of the basic intrinsic propensities or characteristics of the "Universal Consciousness Reality" (UCR) which relates to its basic "Unitary-Harmonious" nature; i.e., since there exists only one singular higher-ordered UCP/UCR – which exists both "during" it's (simultaneous) computation of all exhaustive spatial pixels comprising each consecutive UF's frame/s and also solely exists (without the presence of any physical universe) "in-between" any two consecutive UF's frame/s, and since this unitary and singular UCR possesses an intrinsic propensity to encourage all "Individual Human Consciousness" (e.g., human beings) to realize their "inseparability" from this singular higher-ordered "Unitary-Harmonious" UCR; therefore the "Dynamic-Equilibrium Moral Principle" represents the UCP's intrinsic tendency towards "balancing" any "moral-injustice" or "immoral choice" made by any given Individual Human Consciousness towards another Individual Human Consciousness! Metaphorically speaking, in the same manner that a healthy human-being would never use their "right hand" to "inflict pain" upon their "left hand" (because they are part of the same human-being), so does this UCP's "Dynamic-Equilibrium Moral Principle" operates to "teach" and "correct" any given Individual Human Consciousness (e.g., person) who opts to inflict "pain" or "suffering" (G-d forbid) upon another Individual Human Consciousness to not repeat such "immoral-choice/s or action/s" based on its computation of an "equivalent negative (pain/suffering)" experienced by the same Individual Human Consciousness that decided to inflict pain upon another Individual Human Consciousness... This means that to the UCP's "Dynamic-Equilibrium Moral Principle" selects one of the multiple possible "future/s" for each Individual Human Consciousness based on its "moral/immoral" choice/s and action/s executed towards any other Individual Human Consciousness – in order to "balance" any "immoral choice/ action" so that that Individual Human Consciousness that chose ('G-d forbid') to inflict pain upon another Individual Human Consciousness would have to "experience" (itself) such a "negative experience" (e.g., of the same degree of "pain"/"suffering" that it inflicted upon the other Individual Human Consciousness). Indeed, as mentioned above (and previously) the "Trampoline-Metaphor" was given wherein if a "metal-bar" was placed on the elastic sheath of a Trampoline such that it "connects" two points (equivalent to two Individual Human Consciousness), and to the extent that one of these two points "chose" to "push and press hard" the metal-bar against the other point – then this would inevitably lead to the other point automatically "pushing back" the metal bar against the "first-point" (which would be a representation of the Dynamic-Equilibrium Moral Principle's "balancing" of any "immoral-choice" made by one Individual Human Consciousness against another Individual Human Consciousness that "automatically" sets in motion the UCR's "balancing" and "teaching" that "inflicting-pain" Individual Human Consciousness having to experience the same "degree" of "pain/suffering" that it inflicted upon the other Individual Human Consciousness)... We therefore see that the selection of one of multiple possible "future/s" UF's for each Individual Human Consciousness is carried out by the UCR – based on the "moral/immoral choice/s" executed by any Individual Human Consciousness at any given point in time towards any other Individual Human Consciousness!? (Obviously, such "incomprehensible", "infinite" Intelligence implied by this UCR's "infinite" capacity to compute and "balance" all of the almost either Billion Individual Human Consciousness towards any other Individual Human Consciousness at any past, present or indeed future/s time/s – may invoke a sense of "wonderment", "awe" and even "reverence" towards this UCR's "Infinite Intelligence" and also its basic "All-Goodness" propensity to "teach" and "harmonize" all Individual Human Consciousness to "respect" and regard any other Individual Human Consciousness as "inseparable" from the same singular higher-ordered "Universal Consciousness Reality"...)

e. **The UCP's "Expansion of Consciousness" (Inanimate & Animate) Hypothesis**

But, even beyond the UCP's "Dynamic-Equilibrium Moral Principle", which computes one of multiple possible "future/s" UF's frame/s for each Individual Human Consciousness based on each Individual Human Consciousness' "selection" of "moral/ immoral choice/s" at each point in time, there exists a more general tendency of the UCP to express ever more "expansive" forms of Consciousness – i.e., from the inanimate forms of "matter" (e.g., including all relativistic and quantum subatomic "particle/s" or "wave", the Four Forces of Nature etc.) through animate: plants, animals and leading up to human-beings (which manifests the most "expansive" form of Consciousness! Even within this most advanced and "Expansive" form of Individual Human Consciousness (e.g., human-beings) there exists a further "Expanded form of Human Consciousness" – in which the Individual Human Consciousness is "inseparable" from the Universal Consciousness Principle (UCP or UCR), which was previously outlined; In this "expanded" form of Individual Human Consciousness the "expanded Human Consciousness" functions in a manner which is equivalent to the functioning of the UCR (e.g., in some respects, at least) – which implies that such "Expanded Individual Human Consciousness" can cognize- know- and even affect- any exhaustive spatial pixel/s in the universe (simultaneously and pertaining to any "past", present" or multiple possible "future/s" UF's frames)! Indeed, as previously outlined this "Expansion of Consciousness" hypothesis implies that there does not exist any real "separation" between the UCP's "driving" of the evolution of Inanimate forms (e.g., relativistic or quantum – including the accelerated expansion of the universe and all Four Forces, basic particles etc.) towards its more expansive expression of animate forms – including the whole presentation of ever more conscious forms of animate: plants, animals and human-beings and up to the most "expanded form of Individual Human Consciousness! Hence, for the first time, Science's New "G-d's Physics" 21st Century Paradigm "bridges the (apparent) gap" between its various sub-disciplines of Physics, Biology and Psychology etc., as comprising one fully integrated process allowing the UCP to express ever more "conscious" and "expansive" forms of manifestation!

f. **The UCP's "Collective Human Consciousness Focus Hypothesis" & Jewish "Rosh-Hashana" (New Year) Non-Continuous Accelerated Expansion Rate Prediction**

The next higher-up "rung" of the Hierarchical Laws of Manifestation is the "Collective Human Consciousness Focus" (hypothesis) which essentially points out that there exists a close connection between a state in which a multitude group of Individual Human Consciousness all focus collectively upon the singular higher-ordered UCP/UCR – in prayer to be "connected" or receive "plentitude" from this singular higher-ordered UCP/UCR, which brings about a "Blessing" or "Plentitude", "Life", "Growth", "Goodness" from this singular higher-ordered UCP/UCR! This "Collective Human Consciousness Focus Hypothesis" explains in what manner this singular higher ordered UCR bestow "Growth", "Expansion", "Life" or "Goodness" upon all of Humanity, and even towards the accelerated expansion of the physical universe! In other words, beyond the previous "Dynamic-Equilibrium Moral Principle's" account of the UCP/UCR's selection of one of multiple possible "future/s" UF's frame/s for each Individual Human Consciousness – in order to "balance" and "teach" each such Individual Human Consciousness to recognize it's inherent "oneness" and "unitary-harmony" with all other Individual Human Consciousness based on their common "inseparability" from this singular higher-ordered UCR and its intrinsic basic "Moral Principle"; Beyond that there arises the question – what may "drive" the UCR's singular higher-ordered Reality to evolve the entire universe and particularly our own Human World and lives and continuously bestow "Life", Health", "Sustenance", "Goodness" to continue to sustain and evolve our physical existence and needs (material and spiritual etc.), as well as sustain and evolve the whole of Life, the various Suns, Galaxies and Universe at large?! Once again, we must remember that according to the New "G-d's Physics" Paradigm, we cannot (any longer) look towards any "material-causal" direct or indirect physical interactions between any two (or more) exhaustive spatial pixels, but rather must look at these higher-ordered "Hierarchical Laws of Manifestation" in order to be able to understand and "explain" the UCR's continuous computation-"dissolution" and evolution of every exhaustive spatial pixel comprising every consecutive UF's frame/s! Indeed, according to this "Collective Human Consciousness Focus Hypothesis" and associated Jewish "Rosh-Hashana" (New Year) "Non-Continuous Accelerated Expansion of the Universe" one of the "reason/s" for the singular higher-ordered UCR's continuous computation- sustenance- and evolution- of the entire physical universe is anchored in- or related to- a State of "Collective Human Consciousness Focus" towards this singular higher-ordered UCR, in which many millions of Individual Human Consciousness direct their focus and Consciousness collectively towards this UCR and pray for the bestowal of "Goodness, "Life", Happiness" etc.!

Indeed, according to one of the unique "Critical Predictions" differentiating the new "G-d's Physics" from the Old "Material-Causal" Paradigm is this particular prediction wherein there will be a "Non-Continuous Accelerated Expansion Rate" at the Jewish Rosh-Hashana (New Year) time-interval wherein the accelerated rate of the universe's expansion rate – observed in each Jewish Year prior to the "Rosh-Hashana" (New Year) will increase in a non-continuous rate ("leap") at the special "two-day" time interval of the New Rosh-Hashana time (and continue at this increased accelerated rate throughout the New Jewish Year) – due to the abovementioned "Collective Human Consciousness Focus Hypothesis", wherein Millions of Jews all over the world pray at this time to the singular higher-ordered UCR, "G-d" for providing them and the world with Life, Health, Growth etc.!

g. **The UCP's "Reversed-Time Goal Hypothesis" ("Geula")**

Indeed, the discovery of the UCP's "Non-continuous Accelerated Expansion of the Universe at the Jewish Rosh-Hashana" special "time-interval" and the UCP's basic "Good-Will" propensity to bestow "Life", "Health", "Happiness", "Fulfilment" is closely related to the UCP's basic "Goal" in creating- sustaining- and evolving the entire physical universe, the "Expansion of

Consciousness" (e.g., including the development of inanimate, animate" plants, animals, human-beings) – all "designed" and "planed" to culminate in the leading up to another "higher" "Hierarchical Law of Manifestation" of the UCP which is called: the UCP's "Reversed-Time Goal (Geula) Hypothesis"! According to this "Reversed-Time Goal Hypothesis (Geula), the UCP's entire series of UF's frames – from the beginning of the manifestation of the inanimate physical universe through its various expressions of ever more expansive forms of animate: plants, animals and human-beings etc. – is all planned and designed initially to lead to the universe's "Perfected Geula" State: Physically, Morally and Spiritually! Indeed, as outlined previously, this Perfected State of "Geula" (e.g., a term signifying complete "Redemption" and "Perfection" in the Jewish Tradition) represents a state of the world in which there exists complete "harmony", "peace", and a basic recognition and gratitude of human-beings towards the basic underlying singular "All-Goodness" "UCR, i.e, "G-d" Reality which continuously sustains and evolves all of Life and the entire universe; Tis state is also typified by the lack of any "violence" or "aggression, the abolishment of "death" and complete peace, harmony and a deep sense of gratitude and appreciation, prayer and studying of this singular higher-ordered Universal Consciousness Reality, "G-d"!

h. **The UCP's "Good-Will" Hypothesis**

The next "higher-up" "Hierarchical-Law of Manifestation" is the basic intrinsic propensity of this singular higher-ordered UCP/UCR of "Good-Will" (hypothesis) which characterizes the UCP's basic "drive" to bestow "Goodness", "Life", "Growth" towards all of Life! This basic "Good-Will" propensity of the singular higher-ordered UCR manifests in its basic sustenance and Life-Giving force to create Life, sustain all of Life, fulfill the basic needs and beyond that create ever more "expansive" opportunities for Life in general and human-beings (in particular) to grow and evolve, to fulfil their full potential and to expand their Moral and Spiritual awareness towards appreciating the Oneness and Singularity of this Universal Consciousness Reality.

i. The UCP's "Free-Will" Hypothesis

Above and beyond all of these UCP's various "Hierarchical Laws of Manifestation" the New "G-d's Physics" Paradigm of 21st Century Theoretical Physics and Science postulates that there exists the most basic "Free-Will" of the UCP – unbound by any "limits" of its creation of the physical universe and all of its various inanimate and animate forms, unaffected by any of the multifarious manifestations of the universe and which transcends even its own "ultimate Goal of Geula"! This entirely "Free-Will" origin of the UCP, nevertheless "cares" about the "Goodness" of Human-beings and all of Life; this is also where the Jewish concept of an unlimited "Compassion and Forgiveness" (e.g., Thirteen Propensities of Mercy") of this UCP manifests and where the basic Jewish concept of "Teshuva" – the ability to ask for "forgiveness" from this singular UCR, "G-d" and to make a "sincere conscious decision" to "not repeat any immoral actions" is made possible (which was also shown to be capable of "altering" and indeed "avoiding" any of the negative possible "multiple future/s" instigated by any Individual Human Consciousness selection of any "immoral action/s", G-d forbid)!

4. "G-d's Physics" Hierarchical Multi-Level Computational Universe – Leading to "Geula"!

We finally come to the fulfillment of Einstein's "quest" towards unifying all of the basic Forces of Nature (e.g., Strong, Weak, Electromagnetic and Gravitational) within one simple "Universal Computational Formula", which was discovered by the New "G-d's Physics" Paradigm of 21st Century Physics! As Einstein foresaw "G-d does not play with dice"! in other words, the whole evolution of the physical universe cannot be explained merely based on direct (or even indirect) physical interactions between any two (or more) exhaustive spatial pixels existing in the same- or different- UF's frame/s! This is because as we've seen based on the discovery of "G-d's Physics" New "A-Causal Computation" Paradigm which *negates* the very possibility of the existence of any such direct/indirect physical interactions between any exhaustive spatial pixels (existing either in the same- or different-UFs frame/s) due to the *simultaneity* of the UCP's computation of all exhaustive spatial pixels comprising each consecutive UF's frame/s and the complete "dissolution" of the entire physical universe "in-between" any two consecutive UF's frame/s! In this manner, the Old "Material-Causal" Paradigm of 20th Century's Relativity Theory and Quantum Mechanics was negated- embedded and (indeed) "transcended" by the New "G-d's Physics" Paradigm which evinced that the only manner in which this newly discovered UCP/UCR may be shown to continuously originate- sustain- "dissolve"- and "evolve" the entire physical universe – is based on its outlining of the "Ten Laws of Hierarchical Manifestation" which lead from the most basic UCP's Three "Computational Dimensions" that simultaneously compute all exhaustive spatial pixels in the universe for each consecutive UF's frame/s, through the UCP's associated "Multi Spatial-Temporal Reservoir" which contains all "past", "present" and multiple possible "future/s" UF's (for each Individual Human Consciousness) – which is being "selected" by the UCP based on its higher-ordered "Dynamic-Equilibrium Moral Principle" based on the "moral/immoral choice" of each Individual Human Consciousness towards any other Individual Human Consciousness (at any point in time) in order to "balance" or "correct" any Individual Human Consciousness "immoral" action/s; Even beyond the UCP's striving to "teach" or "correct" or "uplift" all Individual Human Consciousness towards their internal realization of their "oneness" – as integral and "inseparable" parts of this singular higher-ordered UCR/UCP, the UCR was indeed shown to strive to manifest ever more "expansive" forms of inanimate, then animate: plants, animals, human-beings – and even towards the most "expanded" form of Individual Human Consciousness (in which the Individual Human Consciousness realizes that it is "inseparable" from the Universal Consciousness Reality and therefore can also function in manners somewhat equivalent to the capacity of this singular higher-ordered UCR!); We then realized that according to "G-d's Physics" New Paradigm's Ten Laws of Hierarchical Manifestation, above and beyond the UCP's "Expansion of Consciousness" manifest in its creation of inanimate, animate: plants, animals and human –beings, there is a higher "rung" in which the very "desire" of this UCR to create such "evolving" forms of ever more expansive Consciousness, and to sustain all of Life and the continuous creation (and evolution) of the entire physical universe) is "driven" by the "Collective Human Consciousness Focus (Hypothesis)", which brings about a "renewal" and "Non-Continuous Accelerated Expansion of the Universe" at the Jewish "Rosh-Hashana" special time-interval (in which Millions of Jews pray and focus on the singularity of this UCR, i.e., "G-d" asking for its infinite "Giving of Life, Health, Happiness, Fulfillment etc.".... This "plea" and "prayer" (e.g., Collective Human Consciousness Focus) of so many Jews in the Jewish Rosh-Hashana time-interval which brings about the "renewal" and "evolution" of the entire physical universe, its "Non-Continuous Leap in the Rate of Accelerated Expansion" and indeed the abovementioned evolution and expansion of Consciousness (from inanimate through animate" plants, animals, human-beings and up to the full "expansion" of Individual Human Consciousness as "inseparable" form the Universal Consciousness Reality) – was also seen to arise from UCP's basic fundamental "Ultimate Geula Goal" – of bringing the entire physical universe towards a State of Physical, Moral and Spiritual Perfection! Indeed, according to this higher "Reversed-Time Goal Hypothesis" the UCR's Ultimate "Geula Goal" stands at the very basis of all of its computation of the entire progression of the universe from its very "first" UF frame through its entire "past", "present" and multiple possible "future/s", all geared towards the realization of the "oneness" and "perfection" of all creation as "inseparable" from this UCR; In particular, this "Ultimate Geula Goal" manifests through the realization of human-beings of this "Perfected Physical Moral and Spiritual State", in which there could be no more "disharmony, "wars", strife or aggression – instead, in which all Individual Human Consciousness will realize the "Oneness" and Singularity" of this Universal Consciousness Reality and therefore live in perfect Harmony and Peace with each other... The two highest "rungs" associated with the UCR's Ten Laws of Hierarchical Manifestation are: the UCR's "Good-Will" and "Free-Will" propensities! The "Good-Will" Law of Manifestation simply points at the very fundamental aspect of characteristic of the UCR which tends to Bestow Life, Goodness and all aspects of "Giving" – creating the myriads of galaxies, suns, planets, atoms, inanimate and animate forms of manifestation and aspiring to "evolve" them towards the Perfected State of Geula! The "Free-Will" higher Law of Manifestation teaches us that despite the "Good-Will" propensity and all of the other Laws of Hierarchical Manifestation, at the very "top" aspect of the UCR, the UCR is entirely "free" and "unbound" by any of its Laws of Manifestation – in fact it exists in a manner that is "unbound" and exists "independently" of the entire physical universe and all of creation! Yet at the same time, this primal highest Law od Manifestation is also associated with what Jewish Tradition calls: the Thirteen Propensities of Mercy", which means that due to its "unbounded nature" it can "bypass" and bestow "forgiveness" and renewal of "Life, Hope and Goodness – even for an Individual Human Consciousness which "violated" or performed "immoral actions but then undergoes a complete "teshuva" – remorse, a sincere asking of "forgiveness" and a sincere conscious decision not to repeat any "wrong-doing", which then allows for this highest "Free-Will" & "Thirteen Propensities of Mercy" to "cancel" the otherwise selection of a "negative-correcting" possible "future" UF's frame for any Individual Human Consciousness which made an immoral-choice towards another Individual Human Consciousness!

So, where does all of these UCR's "Ten Laws of Hierarchical Manifestation" lead us, and what new (profound) understanding does this New "G-d's Physics" Paradigm supply Science (and Humanity more generally)? Simply put, it tells us that the whole creation, sustenance and evolution of every exhaustive spatial pixel in the physical universe – from its inception to our present state of the universe is "pre-ordained" and "programmed" by this singular higher-ordered UCR to evolve continuously in the direction of the "expansion of Consciousness" from inanimate matter through animate" plants, animals, human-beings and up to the fully "expanded" form of Individual Human Consciousness, and leading up the "Perfected Geula" State of Humanity and the World (at large) as set by the singular higher-ordered UCR! We suddenly realize that contrary to the Old (20th Century) "Material-Causal" Scientific Paradigm which viewed the origin of the universe by a "chance" "Big-Bang" nuclear explosion, the evolution of the universe as dictated by direct physical interactions between certain "massive objects" and Space-Time and its ongoing accelerated expansion as initiated by (purely hypothetical) "dark-matter" or "dark-energy" concepts; Or at the quantum subatomic level, contrary to the Old Model's conception of the entire physical universe being governed by "probabilistic" direct interactions between subatomic "target probability wave function" elements and corresponding subatomic "probe" elements which cause the "collapse" of this probability wave function into complimentary (space-energy, mass-time) singular value; the New "G-d's Physics" evinces that there are no "chance" direct interactions between either relativistic "massive" entities and "Space-Time", nor between subatomic "target" and "probe" elements – dynamics because all exhaustive spatial pixels in the universe are computed simultaneously by this singular higher-ordered UCR for each consecutive UF's frame, and the whole entire physical universe "dissolves" back into the singularity of the UCR "in-between" any two consecutive UF's frame/s! Instead, we are shown that the only way in which we can theoretically explain both the existence of any relativistic or quantum "force", "law", relationship or "entity", as well as the origin, sustenance and evolution of the entire physical universe – including its inanimate and animate forms is solely based on the discovery of "G-d's Physics" New Paradigm's singular higher-ordered UCR which simultaneously computes every exhaustive spatial pixel in the universe for each consecutive UF's frame/s at the unfathomable rate of "c^2/h" = 1.36^{-50} (sec')! And moreover, that the operation of this singular higher-ordered UCR may only be accounted for based on its "Ten Hierarchical Laws of Manifestation" which culminate in it's basic "Free-Will" and "Good-Will" propensities and are "driven" by its innate Ultimate "Geula Goal" (e.g., "Reversed-Time Goal Hypothesis") which created the entire physical universe from its "onset" towards an "Ultimate Goal" of manifesting ever more "expansive" forms of Consciousness (e.g., from inanimate through animate: plants, animals, human-beings and up to the fully "expanded" forms of Individual Human Consciousness and Collective Human Consciousness Focus expressions) leading up to the "Perfected Geula State": Morally, Spiritually and Physically – in which the Oneness, Unity and Goodness of this singular higher-ordered UCR will be manifested, i.e., in particular in our Human Consciousness and World; A World in which there cannot exist any "wars", "aggression" or "conflict" since all of Humanity will recognize its innate fundamental "Oneness" with this singular "Universal Consciousness Reality", and operate harmoniously towards studying- realizing- and focusing- on this singular UCR, "G-d' Reality with gratitude, appreciation and praying etc.

In this sense, 21st Century Physics New "G-d's Physics" Paradigm may play a critically important role in bringing about this profound Ultimate State of "Geula" by recognizing that there exists a singular higher-ordered UCR force which not only unifies between Relativity Theory and Quantum Mechanics, between the Four basic Forces of Nature, between the four basic physical features of "space", "energy", "mass" and "time", between the evolution of inanimate and animate forms – but is also constantly creating, "dissolving" re-creating and evolving every exhaustive spatial pixel in the universe towards the realization of "G-d's Physics" discovery of what the Jewish Tradition has expounded for thousands of years: that this singular UCR "G-d" Reality is the only reality underlying the entire physical universe and is bringing it ever closer to the current realization of a Perfected (Physically, Morally and Spiritually) "Geula" State in which Science and Humanity will exist in complete Harmony and Peace, in recognition, gratitude and continuous reverence (and prayer and studying) of this "All-Goodness", "All-Giving" singular Universal Consciousness Reality, "G-d"!

2.   References

Bentwich, J. (2012a) "Harmonizing Quantum Mechanics and Relativity Theory". *Theoretical Concepts of Quantum Mechanics*, Intech (ISBN 979-953-307-377-3), Chapter 22, pp. 515-550.

Bentwich, J. (2012b) "Theoretical Validation of the Computational Unified Field Theory". *Theoretical Concepts of Quantum Mechanics*, (ISBN 979-953-307-3773), Chapter 23, pp. 551-598.

Bentwich, J. (2013b). "The Theoretical Ramifications of the Computational Unified Field Theory". *Advances in Quantum Mechanics* (ISBN 978-953-51-1089-7), Chapter 28, pp. 671-882.

Bentwich, J. (2013c). The Computational Unified Field Theory (CUFT): A Candidate Theory of Everything. *Advances in Quantum Mechanics* (ISBN 978-953-51-1089-7) Chapter 18, pp. 395-436.

Bentwich, J. (2015). The Computational Unified Field Theory (CUFT): A Candidate 'Theory of Everything'. *Selected Topics in Application of Quantum Mechanics* (ISBN 978-953-51-2126-8) Chapter 6.

Bentwich, J. (2014) *What if Einstein was Right? Amazon Kindle Book Store.*

Bentwich, J. (2015). On the Geometry of Space, Time, Energy, and Mass: Empirical Validation of the Computational Unified Field Theory. *Unified Field Mechanics: Natural Science Beyond the Veil of Spacetime (Proceedings of VIGIER IX Conference, Morgan State University, USA, 16-19 November 2014).*

Bentwich, J. (2016) The 'Computational Unified Field Theory': A Paradigmatic Shift. *Research & Reviews: Journal of Pure & Applied Physics.*

Bentwich, J. (2017a) The Computational Unified Field Theory: Could 'Dark Matter' & 'Dark Energy' be "Superfluous"? *SciFed Journal of Quantum Physics Special Issue.*

Bentwich, J. (2017b) The Computational Unified Field Theory: Explaining the Universe from "Without". *SciFed Journal of Quantum Physics Special Issue.*

Bentwich, J. (2017c). The Computational Unified Field Theory: A New 'A-Causal Computation' Physics. *SciFed Journal of Quantum Physics Special Issue.*

Bentwich, J. (2017d). The 'Computational Unified Field Theory' (CUFT) May Challenge the 'Big-Bang Theory'. *SciFed Journal of Quantum Physics Special Issue.*

Bentwich, J. (2017e). Can the 'Computational Unified Field Theory' (CUFT) Challenge the Basic Laws of Conservation? *SciFed Journal of Quantum Physics Special Issue.*

Bentwich, J. (2017f). The Computational Unified Field Theory (CUFT): Time "Reversal" May be Possible. *SciFed Journal of Quantum Physics Special Issue.*

Bentwich, J. (2017g). The Computational Unified Field Theory (CUFT) Transcends Relativity's Speed of Light Constraint. *SciFed Journal of Quantum Physics, Special Issue.*

Bentwich, J. (2017h). The Computational Unified Field Theory's New Physics: Transcending Space, Time and Causality. *SciFed Journal of Quantum Physics Special Issue*.

Bentwich, J. (2017i). A "Supra-Spatial-Temporal Universal Consciousness Reality". *Research & Reviews: Journal of Pure & Applied Physics, Special Issue: The Computational Unified Field Theory (CUFT)-A Paradigmatic Shift in 21st Century Physics*.

Bentwich, J. (2017j). A New Science: An Infinite Omniscient Dynamic-Equilibrium Universal Consciousness Reality. *SciFed Journal of Quantum Physics Special Issue*.

Bentwich, J. (2017k). The Computational Unified Field Theory (CUFT) Challenges Darwin's 'Natural Selection Principle'! *SciFed Journal of Quantum Physics Special Issue*.

Bentwich, J. (2017l). The Computational Unified Field Theory (CUFT) Challenges the Second Law of Thermodynamics.*SciFed Journal of Quantum Physics Special Issue*.

Bentwich, J. (2017m). The Computational Unified Field Theory (CUFT): An Empirical & Mathematical Validation of the 'Computational Unified Field Theory'; *SciFed Journal of Quantum Physics Special Issue*.

Bentwich, J. (2017n). The Computational Unified Field Theory (CUFT) New Science; *SciFed Journal of Quantum Physics Special Issue*.

Bentwich, J. (2018a). Review: The Computational Unified Field Theory (CUFT) New Universe: *The Global Journal of Science Frontier Research, Vol. 18 (8-A), Special Issue*.

Bentwich, J. (2018b). The Computational Unified Field Theory (CUFT): What is "Time"? *The Global Journal of Science Frontier Research, Vol. 18 (8-A), Special Issue*.

Bentwich, J. (2018c). The Universal Consciousness Reality's Camouflage: The Physical Universe! *The Global Journal of Science Frontier Research, Vol. 18 (8-A), Special Issue*.

Bentwich, J. (2018d). The Computational Unified Field Theory (CUFT) Epilogue: Can Human Consciousness Affect the Cosmos? *The Global Journal of Science Frontier Research, Vol. 18 (8-A), Special Issue*.

Bentwich, J. (2018e). Testing the Computational Unified Field Theory's (CUFT) Differential-Critical Predictions: The Higgs-Boson Particle May Not Exist Continuously! *The Global Journal of Science Frontier Research, Vol. 18 (8-A), Special Issue.*

Bentwich, J. (2018f). The Double-Faceted Universal Consciousness Reality: A Theoretical Review. *The Global Journal of Science Frontier Research, Vol. 18 (8-A), Special Issue.*

Bentwich, J. (2018g). Letter to the Editor: Dark Matter May Not Exist. *The Global Journal of Science Frontier Research, Vol. 18 (8-A), Special Issue.*

Bentwich, J. (2018h). The Computational Unified Field Theory's (CUFT) Epilogue: Possible Reversal of the Arrow of Time and Abolishment of Death. *The Global Journal of Science Frontier Research, Vol. 18 (8-A), Special Issue.*

Bentwich, J. (2019a). The Computational Unified Field Theory's (CUFT) New Universe. *The Global Journal of Science Frontier Research, Vol. 19 (6), Special Issue.*

Bentwich, J. (2019b). The Computational Unified Field Theory's (CUFT) Goes Beyond the 'Standard Model': "G-d's Physics"?!. *The Global Journal of Science Frontier Research, Vol. 18 (8-A), Special Issue.*

Bentwich, J. (2019c). A Call for Cosmologists & Experimental Physicists: Empirical Validation of the 'Computational Unified Field Theory' (CUFT) New Paradigm through "Time-Sensitive" Astronomical and Subatomic Measurements. *The Global Journal of Science Frontier Research, Vol. 19 (6), Special Issue.*

Bentwich, J. (2019d). The 'Computational Unified Field Theory' (CUFT): Redefining Mass, Gravity & the Physical Universe. *The Global Journal of Science Frontier Research, Vol. 19 (6), Special Issue.*

Bentwich, J. (2019d). Astronomical Validation of the Computational Unified Field Theory (CUFT) "Critical Prediction" & Resolution of the "Universe's Accelerated Expansion Rate Enigma" (UAERE).*The Global Journal of Science Frontier Research, Vol. 19 (6), Special Issue.*

Bentwich, J. (2019e) Urgent Call for Empirical Validation of the Computational Unified Field Theory's (CUFT) New 21st Century 'A-Causal Computation' (ACC) Paradigm. *Acta Scientific Applied Physics, Volume 1(1).*

Bentovish (Bentwich) J. (2020a) *'G-d's Physics'.* In Press. *iUniverse Publication.*

"G-d's Physics": Complete Unification of the Four Basic Forces of Nature & "Geula"!

Jehonathan Bentovish (Bentwich), Ph.D.

Note: Dr. Bentovish is currently seeking the most appropriate leading Academic Institute to assist him in carrying-out further necessary empirical validation and Theoretical elaboration of his New Twenty-first Century New 'G-d's Physics' Paradigm.

Dr. Bentovish (Bentwich) e-mail is: <u>drbentovish@gmail.com</u>.

<u>Abstract</u>

Twenty-first Theoretical Physics is undergoing a major "Paradigmatic-Shift" from the Old "Material-Causal" Paradigm to the New "A-Causal Computation" of the "Computational Unified Field Theory" (CUFT), also recently termed: "G-d's Physics" Paradigm! Contrary to the "Material-Causal" Paradigm which assumes that every physical subatomic or relativistic phenomenon can be explained merely through direct physical interactions between a subatomic "probe" and "target" (probability wave function) elements or between massive objects and their curvature of Space-Time (as described by Einstein's Relativistic Equations); The New "G-d's Physics" Paradigm negates the possibility of any such "Material-Causal" physical relationships due to the *simultaneity* of a singular higher-ordered "Universal Computational/ Consciousness Principle's" (UCP) computation of all exhaustive spatial pixels in the universe for each consecutive "Universal Frames" comprising the entire physical cosmos at every minimal "time-point", e.g., computed at the rate of "c^2/h" = 1.36^{-50} sec'! This New "A-Causal Computation" Paradigm for 21st Century Theoretical Physics opens a plethora of new fascinating possibilities such as the unification of

Relativity Theory and Quantum Mechanics, a complete unification of the four basic physical features of "space" and "energy", "mass" and "time" as secondary integral computational by-products of the UCP's singular operation, the possibility of transcending the strict relativistic "Speed of Light Barrier" for transmission of any signal or physical effect across space and time, "time-reversal" and even the "abolishment of death"! G-d's Physics New Paradigm has also been shown to challenge and revise the basic "Material-Causal" assumption underlying the "Big-Bang" Model, Einstein's Equations, the Second Law of Thermodynamics, discard the purely hypothetical concepts of "dark-matter" and "dark-energy" as "superfluous" (non-existent) and more generally also of Darwin's Evolutionary Natural Selection Principle! This article unifies the Four basic Forces known in Nature as a manifestation of the New "G-d's Physics" Paradigm's evolution of this singular Universal Consciousness Principle's full manifestation – from the limited "Material-Causal" assumption towards its fully expansive and integrated "Perfected" – Morally, Spiritually and even Physically "Geula" (Redemption) State of Humanity and the Universe!

1. Introduction: Twenty-first Century's Physics "Paradigmatic-Shift"!

Twenty-first Century Theoretical Physics finds itself in an "impossible" state in which the two basic "pillars" of Modern Physics, e.g., "Relativity Theory" and "Quantum Mechanics" seem "theoretically inconsistent", up to 95% of all of the mass and energy in the universe cannot be directly "detected" – instead assumed to comprise purely "hypothetical" concepts of "dark-matter" and "dark-energy", and there is an inability to unify between the four basic forces of Nature – i.e., particularly between gravity and the three other forces associated with the subatomic realm! Such a state of Physics obviously calls for a basic "Paradigmatic Shift" as previously described by the famous Philosopher of Science Thomas Kuhn in 1962 stemming from the fact that Science (and Physics) alternates between phases of "Standard Science" in which a particular Scientific discipline advances its knowledge based on the framework of a given "Standard Paradigm", and an alternative "Paradigmatic-Shift" phase in which the foundations of the "Old Standard Paradigm" seem "inconsistent" of each other and there appear a series of "unexplained physical phenomena" which cannot be accounted for by the Old Standard Paradigm and therefore call for a "New Paradigm" that would be able to resolve the (apparent) "theoretical-inconsistency" between the "pillars" the Old Standard Paradigm, account for those "unexplained physical phenomena" and also predict new "Critical Prediction/s" which cannot be accounted for by the Old Standard Paradigm!

Precisely such a state of a "Paradigmatic-Crisis" existed in Theoretical Physics just prior to Einstein's famous 1905 "Annus-Mirabelus" year's discovery of (Special) Relativity Theory and its full acceptance in 1915 following the empirical validation of its unique "Critical Prediction" regarding Mercury's Perihelion's pathway's curvature (doubled value) caused by the Sun's curvature of the fabric of Space-Time around it! We now stand at the brink of precisely such a "Paradigmatic-Shift" in 21st Century Theoretical Physics with the discovery of the New "Computational Unified Field Theory" (CUFT) called" "G-d's Physics" Paradigm shown capable of resolving the apparent principle "theoretical-inconsistency" between Relativity Theory and Quantum Mechanics, alternatively explain the "unexplained phenomenon of "dark-matter" and "dark-energy" based on the discovery of a singular higher-ordered "Universal Computational/Consciousness Principle" (UCP) which simultaneously computes all exhaustive spatial pixels in the universe at the unfathomable rate of "c^2/h" = 1.36^{-50} sec'!

Perhaps most apparent is this basic "theoretical crisis" calling for an immediate "Paradigmatic-Shift" from the Old "Material-Causal" Paradigm to the New "G-d's Physics" (CUFT) Paradigm based on the "glaring" theoretical inconsistencies and unexplained phenomena existing in the Old "Material-Causal" Paradigm which specifically comprise:

a. An apparent "theoretical inconsistency" between Relativity Theory's (RT's) strict "Speed of Light Barrier" and Quantum Mechanics (QM's) "Quantum Entanglement" phenomenon indicating that it may be possible for two "entangled particles" to *instantaneously* affect each other's complimentary physical properties, thereby violating RT's strict theoretical constraint upon the transmission of any signal (or information) across space and time!

b. <u>An inability of the Old "Material-Causal" Paradigm to account for the accelerated expansion rate of the physical universe – assumed to be explained by the purely hypothetical concepts of "dark-matter" and "dark-energy"</u> which are assumed to account for up to 95% of all the mass and energy in the universe, but which could not be detected empirically (despite numerous attempts to do so)!

c. <u>An inability to unify between the Four basic forces of Nature – specifically between the Gravitational Force (of General Relativity Theory) and the other three Quantum Forces (e.g., the Electromagnetic Force and the Strong and Weak Nuclear forces)!</u> Once again this is a manifestation of the principle theoretical inability to unify between RT and QM as indicated by RT's conceptually "different" theoretical account of the Gravitational Force as derived from "massive objects" curvature of "Space-Time" (which, in turn, is assumed to "cause" or determine the "travelling-pathways" of those "massive objects" and other "less-massive" objects) as described by Einstein's Equations; and QM's "Standard Model" depicting and explaining the plethora of subatomic particles existing and specifically explicating the three other basic Forces (e.g., Electromagnetic Force and Strong and Weak Nuclear Forces) – as originating from the specific subatomic physical interactions of these subatomic particles. Metaphorically this apparent principle inability to unify between RT's Gravitational Force and QM's "Standard Model" could be likened to the principle inability to "unify" or "bridge" between "apples and "oranges", representing two separate and "different" entities which do not share any "common characteristics", thereby negating the very possibility of "unifying" them!?

2. "G-d's Physics" New Twenty-First Century's Paradigm

In order to gain a clear theoretical understanding of the necessary "Paradigmatic-Shift" from the Old "Material-Causal" Paradigm to the New "G-d's Physics" Paradigm let us briefly describe some of the key theoretical postulates of this New "G-d's Physics" Paradigm and the manner in which this New "G-d's Physics" Paradigm offers a new (exciting) explanation for all of the Old "Material-Causal" (abovementioned) apparent "theoretical inconsistencies" as well as identifies new unique "Critical Predictions" that differentiate it from the corresponding predictions of the Old "Material-Causal" Paradigm, thereby allowing for a clear empirical validation of this New "G-d's Physics" (CUFT) Paradigm as the new satisfactory Paradigm for 21st Century Theoretical Physics!

a. The "Universal Computational/Consciousness Principle"

According to the New "G-d's Physics" Paradigm, there exists a singular higher-ordered Universal Computational/ Consciousness Principle (UCP) which *simultaneously* computes every exhaustive spatial pixel in the universe at the unfathomable rate of "c^2/h" $= 1.36^{-50}$ sec'(!) giving rise to an extremely rapid series of "Universal Frames" (UF's) comprising the entire physical universe at every such "minimal time-point", wherein "in-between" any two such consecutive UF's frames the entire physical universe "dissolves" back into the singularity of this UCP! This UCP possesses three "Computational Dimensions", e.g.,: "Framework" ("frame" vs. "object"), "Consistency" ("consistent" vs. "inconsistent") and "Locus" ("global" vs. "local") – two out of which "Framework" and "Consistency" produce the four basic physical features of "Framework" – "consistent" ("space") or "inconsistent" ("energy") and "Object" – "consistent" ("mass") or "inconsistent" ("time) physical features that continuously and simultaneously compute any exhaustive spatial pixel in the universe for each consecutive UF's frame/s! Another key new discovery made by the New "G-d's Physics" (CUFT)

Paradigm is its insistence that this singular higher-ordered UCP *simultaneously computes* all of the exhaustive spatial pixels in the universe for each consecutive UF's frame/s at the incredible rate of "c^2/h" = 1.36^{-50} sec'(!); and that "in-between" any two consecutive UF's frames the entire physical universe and all of its constituting exhaustive spatial pixels "dissolve" back into the singularity of this singular higher-ordered UCP!

b. **"G-d's Physics" New "A-Causal Computation" Paradigm**

Based on "G-d's Physics" New Paradigm's discovery that the singular higher-ordered UCP *simultaneously computes* all exhaustive spatial pixels comprising the entire physical universe – for each consecutive UF's frame/s (and that "in-between" any two consecutive UF's frames the whole universe "dissolves" back into the singularity of the UCP), a new "A-Causal Computation" characterization of "G-d's Physics" New Paradigm is acknowledged: essentially, the simultaneity of the UCP's computation of all exhaustive spatial pixels (and their complete "dissolution" "in-between" any two consecutive UF's frame/s back into the UCP) means that there cannot exist any "material-causal" physical interaction between any two (or more) exhaustive spatial pixels existing either in the same- or different- UF's frames! Rather, the same singular UCP computes simultaneously all exhaustive spatial pixels comprising the entire physical universe – which implies that there cannot exist any Relativistic or Quantum "material-causal" physical relationships, interactions, or effects! This negated many of the Old "Material-Causal" (20th Century Physics) Paradigm's basic assumptions underlying both Relativity Theory and Quantum Mechanics, including: the "Big-Bang" Model, Einstein's Equations, discarding of the hypothetical "dark-matter" and "dark-energy" concepts etc.

c. **The "Computational Invariance Principle" & "Universal Consciousness Reality"**

Another key new theoretical postulate of the New "G-d's Physics" Paradigm is the "Computational Invariance Principle" which posits that since only the UCP exists – continuously and consistently both "during" each consecutive UF's frame/s – solely computing (simultaneously) all exhaustive spatial pixels' four basic physical features of "space" and "energy", "mass" and "time", and also singularly exists "in-between" any two consecutive UF's frame/s (without the presence of the physical universe), therefore the "Computational Invariance Principle" theoretical postulate asserts that only this singular UCP may be regarded as "computationally-invariant" existing uniformly and "consistently" – both "during" its computation of each consecutive UF's frame/s and also "in-between" any two consecutive UF's frame/s, whereas the four basic physical features being computed for all exhaustive spatial pixels in the universe may only be regarded as "computationally-variant", e.g., existing only "transiently" and "phenomenally" ("during" each consecutive UF's frame/s but "dissolving" "in-between" any two consecutive UF's frames)! This new (profound) realization of the "Computational Invariance Principle" of "G-d's Physics" New Paradigm is also associated with another new theoretical postulate termed: the "Universal Consciousness Reality" (UCR) which posits that since the whole physical universe (e.g., and all of its constituting exhaustive spatial pixels) is only regarded as "computationally-variant" – existing only "transiently" "during" each consecutive UF's frame/s but "dissolving back into the singularity of the UCR, whereas the singular higher-ordered UCP is considered to be "computationally-invariant" (existing continuously and consistently both "during" each consecutive UF's frame/s as computing each exhaustive spatial pixel's four basic physical features of "space" and "energy", "mass" and "time", as well as solely existing "in-between" any two consecutive UF's frames without the presence of any physical universe); therefore there only exists one singular "Universal Consciousness Reality" which exists consistently and continuously – manifesting as the phenomenal physical universe "during" its computation of every exhaustive spatial pixel of each consecutive UF's frame/s and existing without the presence of the physical universe, in-between any two consecutive UF's frames! Indeed, this new "Universal Consciousness Reality" carries with it a profound alteration of our basic perception and understanding of the physical universe – which ceases to exist as an "objective-independent" reality, and it transformed into the new theoretical understanding that (in truth) the entire physical universe only represents a "phenomenal, transient manifestation" of this singular UCR!

d. **The "Universal Computational Formula"**

Based on "G-d's Physics" (CUFT) New Paradigm's discovery of the Universal Computational/Consciousness Principle (UCP) and its simultaneous computation of all exhaustive spatial pixels comprising each consecutive UF's frame/s it also revealed the existence of an integrated simultaneous computation of all the four basic physical features of "space" and "energy", "mass" and "time" as computed based on two out of the three basic "Computational Dimensions" of the UCP (delineated further below and previously):

Universal Computational Formula (UCF):

$$\left\{ \frac{\text{'c}^2}{h} \right\} \quad \text{UF's } \{ \text{ה}...\text{מ}...\text{א} \} \qquad = \quad \frac{s \quad * \quad e}{t \quad * \quad m}$$

wherein the singular higher-ordered UCP – represented by the Hebrew letter "Yud" ("י") simultaneously computes all exhaustive spatial pixels in the universe comprising each consecutive Universal Frame/s (UF's) which already exist in a "potential-from" within the UCP's "Supra Spatial-Temporal Reservoir" of all "past", "present" and multiple possible "future/s" UF's (represented by the Hebrew letters from "א through "מ" to "ת)" depending on the Moral Choice of each Individual Human Consciousness – as computing and integrating these four basic physical features of "space" and "energy", "mass" and "time", at the incredible rate of: "c^2/h" = 1.36^{-50} sec'!

e. **The "Dynamic Equilibrium" Moral Principle & UCP's "Multi Spatial-Temporal Reservoir"**

Another key theoretical postulate of this New "G-d's Physics" Paradigm is the discovery of the UCP's associated "Dynamic-Equilibrium" Moral Principle and its associated "Multi Spatial-Temporal Reservoir" bank of all "past", "present" and multiple possible "future/s" UF's frames based on the "Moral/Immoral Choices" of each Individual Human Being towards another human being; Essentially, due to the "inseparability" of all Individual Human Consciousness (human beings) from this singular higher-ordered "Universal Consciousness Principle" (UCP) the New "G-d's Physics" Paradigm asserts that there is a basic fundamental "Dynamic-Equilibrium" Moral Principle characterizing the operation of this UCP – such that any "immoral-imbalance" created by any "immoral choice" made by any Individual Human Consciousness towards another Individual Human Consciousness is "corrected" and "balanced" by the UCR in a manner in which that Individual Human Consciousness which chose to "inflict pain/suffering" upon another Individual Human Consciousness – the UCP is selecting one of multiple "possible future/s" UF's frame/s in which it will also have to experience the same (nature and degree) of pain/suffering that it inflicted upon the other Individual Human Consciousness in order that it learns and realizes the basic "unity" and "inseparability" of all Individual Human Consciousness from the singular higher-ordered UCP and honors and respects all other such Individual Human

Consciousness (just as pointed out by the Alter-Rebbi, Rabbi Schneur-Zalman in his famous Tanyah Book, chapter 32)! Additionally, according to this new "Dynamic-Equilibrium" Moral Principle, since the whole "purpose" of the UCP's associated "Dynamic-Equilibrium" Moral Principle is to "teach", "correct" or "balance" any "immoral-choice/s" of any Individual Human Consciousness so that that Individual Human Consciousness acknowledges and "realizes" it's "unity" with the UCP and inseparability from all other Individual Human Consciousness – so that it could not and would not consider or execute any "immoral-choice/s" toward any other Individual Human Consciousness, therefore there is another possibility carved out by the singular higher-ordered UCP of "teshuva" – e.g., repentance, a sincere regret relating to the "immoral choice" and a conscious decision not to repeat it in the future – which "circumvents" and replaces the need of that Individual Human Consciousness to experience itself the abovementioned "negative future" that is equivalent to its own "wrongdoing"... Finally, this "Dynamic-Equilibrium" Moral Principle may be seen as part of the overall "Goal" of the UCP's constant and continuous origination- sustenance- "dissolution" and evolution- of the entire physical universe – which is to bring the World towards its "Perfected- Geula" State of Moral, Spiritual and even Physical Perfection, in which the oneness and integrity of all creation as part of the singularity of the UCP will be realized and acknowledged by Humanity, see next "Reversed-Time Goal Hypothesis" theoretical postulate;

f. **The UCR's "Expansive Consciousness Spectrum Hypothesis" & "Reversed-Time Goal Hypothesis"**

Another two profound and key theoretical postulates of the New "G-d's Physics" Paradigm are: the UCR's – "Expansive Consciousness Spectrum Hypothesis" & "Reversed-Time Goal Hypothesis"; the "UCR's Expansive Consciousness Spectrum

Hypothesis" stipulates that as part of the UCP/UCR's ultimate Goal of driving the world (and entire universe) towards a "Perfected State" – called "Geula" in Jewish Tradition in which the oneness and unity of all creation as integral parts of the singular higher-ordered UCP/UCR will be recognized by Humanity; the UCR computes- ", "dissolves", "re-computes"- and evolves- the forms manifested by this singular UCP/UCR from "inanimate" matter (e.g., subatomic particles and the entire macroscopic universe) through "animate" forms of plants, then animals then human-beings – which represents the most "expansive" form of Consciousness; and ultimately leads this much "refined" and more "Expansive" form of Human Consciousness towards its ultimate "expanded" manifestations of this singular Universal Consciousness Reality which are expressed in the "expanded form of Individual Human Consciousness" (previously delineated) in which Individual Human Consciousness "expands" to a state in which it is "not separate" and functions in "unity" with the Universal Consciousness Reality (e.g., sometimes related to as states of "Prophecy" such as with Moses!); Another manifestation of this expansion of Individual Human Consciousness occurs also in "special times" and states of "Collective Human Consciousness Focus (Hypothesis" (also delineated below and previously) – such as during the Jewish "Rosh-Hashana" (New Year) time-interval in which Millions of Jews (all over the world) collectively focus on- and pray to- this singular higher-ordered "Universal Consciousness Reality", i.e., "G-d"! As published and delineated previously, this New "G-d's Physics" profound expansive new perspective on the development and evolution of the entire cosmos – including its "inanimate" manifestations of all material compositions, e.g., including the relativistic accelerated expansion of the physical universe as well as all subatomic (quantum) particles, forces and phenomena, all "animate" forms of "plants", "animals" and "human-beings" brings about an entirely new and integrated view on the origination- and evolution- of the physical universe and all biological forms – not as "caused" by any "random"

Big-Bang nuclear explosion but as driven and computed by the singular higher-ordered UCR whose sole Goal is to bring the entire physical universe and our own world towards the State of "Geula" Perfection (Morally, Spiritually and Physically); Indeed, the additional "Reversed-Time Goal Hypothesis" theoretical postulate posits that the entire origination of the entire physical universe continuous and constant computation by the UCP (simultaneously) of all exhaustive spatial pixels in the universe for every consecutive UF's frame/s from its onset- in the "first" UF frame and until this date and onwards until the UCP/UCR brings the universe into its ultimate "Goal" of a Perfected: Morally, Spiritually and Physically State; This "Reversed-Time Goal Hypothesis" simply posits that the entire origination-sustenance and evolution of the entire physical universe – is driven by its drive to bring the world towards its ultimate Perfected "Geula" State of Moral, Spiritual and even Physical Perfection (e.g., in which there will not be any longer "death"!); a State in which all Human Being will recognize and realize the oneness of all creation with this singular higher-ordered Universal Consciousness Reality (UCR), and therefore there could not exist any longer any such "negative" phenomena of "violence", "aggression", crimes" or "immoral behavior", and on the contrary Humanity's (and Science's) ultimate recognition of the singular higher-ordered UCR as the sole reality that drives and sustains the entire universe will lead to an attitude of "reverence", "gratitude" and "studying" of this "All-Goodness", "Divine" "Universal Consciousness Reality" ("G-d"!), as anticipated by the great Jewish Sage and Teacher, Maimonides (in his monumental "Mishna-Torah" masterpiece)…

3. "G-d's Physics" Complete Unification of Space, Energy, Mass & Time!

One of the breakthrough discoveries of "G-d's Physics" New Paradigm is its "Universal Computational Formula" which completely unifies between the four basic physical features of "space" and "energy", "mass" and "time" – as integral, secondary computational by-products of the singular higher-ordered UCP simultaneous computation of all exhaustive spatial pixels in the universe! Indeed, it is important to note that whereas (General) Relativity Theory integrates between "space" and "time" (as a unitary four dimensional "Space-Time" continuum) and between "energy" and "mass" (e.g., through its famous "Energy-Mass Equivalence": "$E = Mc^2$"), as well relates the "curvature of Space-Time" by "massive objects" and conversely describes the "travelling-pathways" of those "massive" and "less-massive" objects based on this assumed curvature of "Space-Time"; still there lacks a complete unification between those four basic physical features comprising the physical universe! Likewise, in Quantum Mechanics, there exist fine interrelationships found between Heisenberg's "Uncertainty Principle's" "complimentary pairs" of "space and energy" or of "mass and time" – e.g., wherein increasing the measurement accuracy of any one of these pairs elements (for instance increasing the measurement accuracy level of the "spatial localization" of any given subatomic target element proportionally decreases that target's "energy level" measurement accuracy); But, in both Relativistic and Quantum Mechanical Models those four basic physical features of "space", "energy", "mass" and "time" remain conceptually "separate" from each other. In contrast, G-d's Physics New Paradigm completely integrates these apparently "separate" physical features based on the singularity of the UCP's simultaneous computation of them as integral elements within the Universal Computational/Consciousness Principle's computation of the degree of "Consistency" (consistent/inconsistent) of each exhaustive spatial pixel in the universe – pertaining to its "Framework" (e.g., relative to the entire "frame" or just to an "object's" internal constitution): Indeed, the newly discovered "Universal Computational Formula" completely integrates these four basic physical features of the physical universe – as the UCP's incredibly rapid ("c^2/h" = 1.36^{-50} sec'!) computation of each exhaustive spatial pixels' degree of "Frame" – "consistent" (space") or "inconsistent" ("energy") level!

Universal Computational Formula (UCF):

$$\left\{ \frac{\text{`c}^2}{h} \right\} \quad \text{UF's } \{\text{ת}...\text{מ}...\text{א}\} \qquad = \quad \frac{s \quad ^* \quad e}{t \quad ^* \quad m}$$

wherein the singular higher-ordered UCP – represented by the Hebrew letter "Yud" ("י") simultaneously computes all exhaustive spatial pixels in the universe comprising each consecutive Universal Frame/s (UF's) which already exist in a "potential-from" within the UCP's "Supra Spatial-Temporal Reservoir" of all "past", "present" and multiple possible "future/s" UF's (represented by the Hebrew letters from "א through "מ" to "ת")" depending on the Moral Choice of each Individual Human Consciousness – as computing and integrating these four basic physical features of "space" and "energy", "mass" and "time", at the incredible rate of: "c^2/h" = 1.36^{-50} sec'!

What's critical to note (at this point) is that these four basic physical features of the physical universe cease to exist as "separate" or "independent" material entities – from the UCP's singular higher-ordered (completely integrated) computation of the degree of consistency or inconsistency pertaining to each exhaustive spatial pixel's "frame" or "object" values (e.g., across a series of consecutive UF's frames)! Thus, for instance, G-d's Physics New Paradigm teaches us that the famous Relativistic "Energy-Mass Equivalence" arises not from the transformation of certain mass related physical properties (such as particular "radioactive" features of certain elements) into proportional energy emission levels – but rather from the UCP's singular (simultaneous) computation of any given object's "frame-inconsistent" values which also necessarily corresponds to that object's UCP computed "object-consistent" ("mass") values!? In other words, the real "reason" for the existence of Relativity's discovered "Energy-Mass Equivalence" arises from the UCP's integral simultaneous computation of any given object's "mass" properties, e.g., its "object-consistent" value and that object's "frame-inconsistent" values; since the greater that object's "displacement-value" (energy computed level) across a given series of UF's frames, necessarily the greater also is its "object-consistent" "mass" computed value (due to the UCP intrinsic computational constraint set upon the maximal degree of "displacement" possible for any object across a series of consecutive UF's frames, as described previously!); Similarly, Relativity's curvature of "Space-Time" by "massive objects" is not "caused" by any direct physical interaction between such "massive objects" and the fabric of "Space-Time" – since as explained above (and previously) there cannot exist any such direct (or even indirect) physical interactions between any two (or more) exhaustive spatial pixels existing either in the same- or different- UF's frames! Instead, according to the UCP's novel Universal Computational Formula complete integration of those four basic physical features of "space" and "energy", "mass" and "time" the apparent "curvature" of "Space-Time" arises from the UCP's "differential" computation of regions in which there are "massive objects" which therefore appear in most (if not all) consecutive UF's frames – as opposed to "less massive" objects that appear in only some of those consecutive UF's frames, therefore leading to those "less massive" objects not occupying the adjacent regions to those "massive objects", i.e., "consistently" across a series of subsequent UF's frames! As explained and delineated previously this leads to what appears as the "curvature of Space-Time" around "massive objects"?!

In fact, the discovery of this new "Universal Computational Formula" fully integrates between those four basic physical features in such a manner that it is no longer possible to differentiate them from the singular integrated and complimentary simultaneous computation of the UCP – of every exhaustive spatial pixels in the universe for each consecutive UF's frame! This is because even the very computational definitions of each of these four basic physical secondary computational by-products (e.g., features) of this singular higher-ordered UCP reveals to us that they merely represent complimentary (integrated) facets of the UCP's singular higher-ordered computation of the degree of "consistency" or "inconsistency" – in any given "object" (e.g., "mass" or "time") or relative to the entire "frame" (i.e., "space" or "energy"), see bellow computational definitions of each of these four basic physical features computed simultaneously by the UCP for each exhaustive spatial pixel comprising any single (or multiple) consecutive UF's frame/s!

We thus reach the inevitable conclusion that "G-d's Physics" New Paradigm's discovery of the "Universal Computational Formula's" complete integration of the four basic physical features of "space" and "energy", "mass" and "time" as secondary (integrated) computational by-products of the UCP's singular higher-ordered computation of any exhaustive spatial pixel's "frame" – "consistent" ("space") or "inconsistent" ("energy"), or "object" – "consistent" ("mass") or "inconsistent" ("time") values offers an entirely new broader (exciting) theoretical framework pertaining to our basic understanding of the physical universe than the Old "Material-Causal" Paradigm of Relativity Theory (RT) and Quantum Mechanics (QM); As a matter of fact, these two RT & QM "pillars" of the Old Material-Causal Paradigm have been shown to comprise "special-cases" within this newly discovered "G-d's Physics" "Universal Computational Formula" (UCF):

As can be glanced from the two respective Relativistic and Quantum Formats of this novel UCF, certain key elements within RT such as its "Energy-Mass Equivalence" ($E = Mc^2$) and Quantum's "Uncertainty Principle's" "complimentary pairs" appear as particular elements within the UCF's more generalized and comprehensive formula! Indeed, this new UCF completely integrates – not only those four basic physical features of space, energy, mass and time as secondary integrative computational by-products of the UCP's singular (simultaneous) computation of all exhaustive spatial pixels in the universe; but also completely integrates and unifies between RT & QM as integral "special-cases" within the UCP's exhaustive description of the UCP's simultaneous computation of all exhaustive spatial pixels in the universe at the incredible rate of "c^2/h" $= 1.36^{-50}$ sec'! It was thus shown in what manner does the UCP's UCF's computation integrates between its "relativistic" computation of "single spatial-temporal particle" features together with QM's computation of "multi spatial-temporal wave" characteristics – as embedded within "G-d's Physics" exhaustive UCP's (simultaneous) computation of all exhaustive spatial pixels in the universe embedded within each consecutive UF's frame/s (at the unfathomable rapid rate of "c^2/h" $= 1.36^{-50}$ sec'! mentioned above)! In fact, some of the potentially far reaching theoretical ramifications of this new "G-d's Physics" Paradigm are its alternative theoretical explanations of General Relativity's assumed "curvature of Space-Time by massive objects" – and its associated newly discovered unique capacity to completely unify between the four fundamental forces in Nature!

As hinted above (and delineated previously), according to the New "G-d's Physics" Paradigm, the curvature of "Space-Time" cannot be "caused" by the presence of certain "massive objects"! This is simply because since all exhaustive spatial pixels comprising the entire physical universe are being computed simultaneously by this singular higher-ordered UCP (for each consecutive UF's frame/s) there cannot exist any such "Material-Causal" physical relationships between any two (or more) exhaustive spatial pixels existing in the same UF frame – including obviously between any "massive object/s" and the fabric of "Space-Time"! And since according to the New "G-d's Physics" Paradigm the whole entire physical universe "dissolves" "in-between" any two consecutive UF's frames there cannot also be in "transference" of any "physical effect" (or any "material entity") across any two consecutive UF's frame/s! Instead, according to the New "G-d's Physics" Paradigm, the apparent "curvature" of "Space-Time" is only produced through the UCP's Universal Computational Formula's production of a series of consecutive UF's frames – based on the more "consistent" presentations of relatively more "massive" objects then "less-massive" objects across a given series of UF's frames, which therefore gives the "impression" or "appearance" of relatively more "stable" ("consistent") regions in the series of UF's frames – as opposed to the relatively "less massive" objects which do not occupy such "stable" ("consistent") points allocated across the series of UF's frames, thereby giving rise to the appearance of an apparent "curvature of Space-Time around massive objects"…

More fundamentally (and generally), the "Paradigmatic-Shift" from the Old "Material-Causal" Paradigm to the New "G-d's Physics" Paradigm brings about a basic change in Physics' most basic assumptions: instead of the Old "Material-Causal" basic assumption wherein it is assumed that any material-physical (relativistic or quantum) phenomenon can be explained merely in terms of certain direct (or indirect) "material-causal" physical interactions – the New "G-d's Physics" Paradigm teaches us to abandon this "material-causal" assumption in favor of the singular higher-ordered UCP simultaneous computation of every exhaustive spatial pixel in the universe comprising the extremely rapid series of UF's frames! This basic "Paradigmatic-Shift" from the Old "Material-Causal" Paradigm towards the New "G-d's Physics" Paradigm's discovery of the singular higher-ordered UCP's simultaneous computation of every exhaustive spatial pixels comprising the entire physical universe (for each consecutive UF's frame/s) was indeed already shown to revise some of our most basic ("material-causal" assumptions) of 20th Century Theoretical Physics: Hence, "G-d's Physics" New Paradigm was shown to negate the "Big-Bang" Model, Einstein's Equations' "material-causal" assumption regarding the "curvature of Space-Time as caused by the presence of massive objects", Quantum Mechanics' "material-causal" assumption regarding the subatomic particle's "collapse of the probability wave-function" as "caused" by its direct physical interaction with a corresponding subatomic probe element; discarded the very existence of "dark-matter" and "dark-energy" purely hypothetical concepts – as "superfluous" (i.e., non-existent) due to the empirical inability to detect it coupled with it's basic "material-causal" assumption assuming that it is the direct physical interaction between these purely hypothetical "dark-matter" and "dark-energy" concepts that "causes" the accelerated expansion of particular galaxies and the universe (more generally)! Indeed, the basic theoretical breakthrough discovered by "G-d's Physics" New Paradigm is that none of these Relativistic or Quantum Mechanical phenomenon can be explained based on such a "G-d's Physics" newly discovered singular higher-ordered UCP's simultaneous computation of every exhaustive spatial pixel comprising the entire physical universe (at each consecutive UF's frame/s at the incredible rate of "c^2/h" = 1.36[-50] sec'!)

The universe was not created by an initial "Big-Bang" nuclear event because that would imply that at those "first", "second", "third", etc. UF's frames there existed a direct physical interaction between certain exhaustive spatial pixels comprising those "i...n" frames which "expanded" the evolving universe and created further "suns", galaxies, matter and energy etc. which is negated by "G-d's Physics" discovery of the simultaneous computation of each of the universe's exhaustive spatial pixels for each consecutive UF's frame/s and its complete "dissolution" back into the singularity of the UCP "in between" any two consecutive UF's frames! Likewise, the New "G-d's Physics" Paradigm negates the very possibility of the "collapse" of the target's assumed "probability wave function as "caused" by its direct physical interaction with another corresponding subatomic "probe" particle once again because there cannot exist any such direct physical interaction between any two exhaustive spatial pixels existing in any single (or multiple) UF's frames. For the same reason, "G-d's Physics" New 21st Century Paradigm negates General Relativity's Einstein's Equations' assumed "curvature of Space-Time" as "caused" by the presence of certain "massive objects" (or the converse "material-causal" assumption encapsulated in those Einstein's Equations indicating that it is this "curvature of Space-Time by massive objects" which "causes" or determines the travelling-pathways of those and other less massive objects) – due to the UCP's *simultaneous* computation of every exhaustive spatial pixel comprising the entire physical universe for each consecutive UF's frame/s and the complete "dissolution" of the physical universe "in-between" any two such consecutive UF's frames which negates the possibility of any such "material-causal" physical interactions!

4. Unifying the Four Basic Forces of Nature: Discovery of "G-d's Physics" New Universal Computational Formula!

Instead, the manner in which the New "G-d's Physics" Paradigm offers an alternative theoretical explanation for all of those Relativistic or Quantum phenomena is solely based on the newly discovered "Universal Computational Formula" (UCF, above mentioned) which simultaneously computes the four basic physical features of "space" and "energy", "mass" and "time" of each exhaustive spatial pixel/c comprising the entire physical universe (of each consecutive UF's frame/s) – as secondary computational by-products of the UCP's singular computation! This also means that the four basic forces of Nature – i.e., the Weak and Strong Forces, and the Electromagnetic Force and the Gravitational Force are all solely derived and produced by this singular higher-ordered UCP's UCF description of the UCP's simultaneous computation of each of the universe's exhaustive spatial pixels four basic physical features of "space" and "energy", "mass" and "time" – as "frame's" or "object's" – "consistent" or "inconsistent" computations! This is where we have to closely analyze and realize "G-d's Physics" UCP's new computational definitions of each of these Four Forces – which solely relies upon the singular higher-ordered UCP's computation of the various forms of "energy", i.e., including any of these three "Weak", "Strong" and "Electromagnetic" Forces, and of "mass" – e.g., which gives rise to what appears as the "Gravitational" Force, as manifesting through the UCP's (abovementioned) "Universal Computational Formula"! As noted above (and previously), the UCP's computation of *any type of "energy"* is computed by this singular higher-ordered UCP as the degree of "displacement" of any (relativistic or quantum) object relative the coordinates of the entire Universal Frame/s across a series of UF's frames; this means that the "root" for all three "Strong, Weak and Electromagnetic Forces is the UCP's computation of their degree of "displacement" across a given series of UF's frames! Moreover, based on the complete integration of those four basic physical features comprising any exhaustive spatial pixel in the universe through the UCP's Universal Computational Formula (UCF), therefore the entire array of subatomic particles described by the Standard Model – amongst which those Three Nuclear Forces operate are exhaustively described by the UCP's UCF! Indeed, the multifarious different levels of electromagnetic charge, mass, energy values etc. of each of these particular Standard Model particles and components manifests as one of the specific configuration and relationships described by the UCP's newly discovered UCF! In other words, the Three Strong, Weak, Electromagnetic Forces describe different levels and configurations of the UCP's singular higher-ordered UCP's computation of the degree of any given particle (object) displacement across a given series of UF's frames! In that sense, there is no real "difference" between the UCP's computation of the degree of "displacement" of the Strong, Weak or Electromagnetic Forces operating within the nucleus or between the nucleus and its surrounding particles or between particles and other elements; In fact, the whole theoretical conceptualization of the very computational definitions of each of these multifarious Standard Model particles – including their mass, energy, localization and temporal values is viewed (for the first time) as one singular fully integrated computation by the UCP, rather than existing as "separate" and "independent" particles operating by different (Three) Strong, Weak or Electromagnetic Forces... No longer are the various Standard Model particles viewed as "independent" entities, nor do the Three Forces operating between them or uniting them seem as "separate" or "independent"; rather, the New "G-d's Physics" Paradigm's discovery of the singular higher ordered Universal Computational Formula completely unifies all of these apparently different subatomic particles and the Three Forces governing them as manifestations of different possible relationships described by this singular higher-ordered UCP UCF!

Indeed, it is suggested that just as the discovery of the "Periodic Table" provided a "blue-print" for the basic constitution of all possible chemical elements in Nature, just as Watson, & Crick discovery of the basic constituent elements of the DNA gave Science its basic understanding of the basic "building-bocks" of all Genetic-Biological organisms (and functions); so does "G-d's Physics" 21st Century Physics Paradigm's discovery of the new "Universal Computational Formula" (UCF) provides Theoretical Physics (and Science more generally) the basic understanding of all of Nature's basic (possible) plethora of subatomic particles and Four basic Forces, i.e., the Strong & Weak Forces, the Electromagnetic Force and the Gravitational Force! It is suggested that by using this newly discovered UCF we can find and identify all of the known "Standard Model" particles – and potentially additional yet undiscovered basic subatomic particles, e.g., based upon the precise interrelationships between any given particle's mass energy spatial and temporal values! This new UCF also integrates and unifies between the Three (Strong, Weak and Electromagnetic) Nuclear Forces (of the Standard Model and Quantum Mechanics) and the Gravitational Force (of General Relativity Theory) – simply because the Gravitational Force, alike these other Three Forces is computed by the singular higher-ordered UCF! As noted above, "G-d's Physics" New Paradigm offers a completely new and different theoretical account for General Relativity's "Gravitational Force", as well as for the Three Nuclear Forces, e.g., as stemming from the UCP's UCF computation of the four integrated and complimentary physical features of "space", "energy", "mass" and "time" – not as being "caused" by certain "massive objects" "curving "Space-Time", but rather as being produced by the UCP's simultaneous computation of all exhaustive spatial pixels comprising the entire physical universe; Specifically, what "appears" as General Relativity's "Gravitational Force" is the result of the UCP's computation of certain "regions" of each consecutive UF's frame/s to be comprised of "high-mass" regions which are therefore computed as "spatially-consistent" regions which remain relatively "constant" across a given series of UF's frames, as opposed to other regions constituting these series of UF's frames which may be defined as constituting "low-mass" regions which therefore do not appear "spatially-consistent" across a series of UF's frames! This according to "G-d's Physics" New Paradigm creates an appearance of the "curvature" of "Space-Time" around certain "massive objects"?! In much the same manner, "G-d's Physics" New Paradigm also offers an alternative new theoretical account for these "Three Forces" – not as being "caused" by any direct (or indirect) physical interactions between any of the "Standard Model" list of existing particles, but rather as being produced by the UCP's simultaneous computation of all exhaustive spatial pixels in the universe (for each consecutive UF's frame/s), thereby producing these "apparent" subatomic particle's associated "Three Forces"!?

It is perhaps important to highlight the unique new (expansive, higher-ordered) perspective offered by "G-d's Physics" New 21st Century Paradigm – shedding a complete new light upon the complete unification of the Four basic Forces based on the operation of the singular, higher-ordered UCP; First, as we've already seen, due to the *simultaneity* of the UCP's computation of all exhaustive spatial pixels in the universe for each consecutive UF's frame/s and the discovery of "G-d's Physics" New "A-Causal Computation" Paradigm – then this principally negates the very possibility of the existence of any direct (or even indirect) physical interaction/s between any two (or more) exhaustive spatial pixels existing either in the same- or different- UF's frames! This implies that there cannot exist any "material-causal" physical interaction/s between any of the subatomic elementary particles that are currently assumed to "transfer" the effects of Three (out of four) Forces – the

Weak, Strong and Electromagnetic! As noted previously, this principle negation of the existence of any direct (or indirect) "material-causal" physical interaction/s between any two or more particle/s (or exhaustive spatial pixels) is most apparent when we take into consideration the complete "dissolution" of the entire physical universe (e.g., and all of its exhaustive spatial pixels and subatomic particles) "in-between" any two consecutive UF's frame/s – which negates the very possibility of the existence of any such physical interactions or effects transferred across any two consecutive or non-consecutive UF's frames! Hence, the basic "material-causal" assumption underlying Relativity's explanation of the curvature of Space-Time as "caused" by its direct physical interaction with certain "massive objects" (as evinced in Einstein's Equations), as well as underlying the current "material-causal" Quantum, Standard Model explanation of the other (three) Forces – Strong, Weak and Electromagnetic as being "carried by" certain elementary particles being transferred between particles is strictly negated by the New "G-d's Physics A-Causal Computation" Paradigm! Instead, based on "G-d's Physics" New Paradigm's discovery (and description) of the manner in which the singular higher-ordered UCP simultaneously computes all exhaustive spatial pixels comprising the entire physical universe (for each consecutive UF's frame/s) – e.g., through the UCP's "Universal Computational Formula" (and based on the UCP's new computational definitions of the four basic physical features of "space" and "energy", "mass" and "time" associated with two of its Computational Dimensions) offers an entirely new (and fascinating) way of viewing each of these Four Forces as arising from simultaneous and integrated computation of this singular higher-ordered UCP!

In other words, the manner in which "G-d's Physics" New Paradigm unifies between the "Three Forces" and the "Gravitational Force" is based on its discovery of the singular higher-ordered UCP's simultaneous computation of all of the physical universe's exhaustive spatial pixels based on its unitary "Universal Computational Formula" (UCP) which completely unified between the four basic physical features of "space" and "energy", "mass" and "time"; According to this New "G-d's Physics" Paradigm theoretical framework, both the "Gravitational Force" and the "Three (other) Forces" represent *"apparent, phenomenal and transient*

Forces" which are computed together by the UCP's UCF for each of the universe's consecutive UF's frames based on the UCP's Universal Computational Formula!

5.   G-d's Physics New "Expansive-Unifying" Science:

We must realize (at this point) that the New "G-d's Physics" Paradigm not only is capable of unifying between Relativity Theory (RT) and Quantum Mechanics (QM) and also explain all of the unexplained physical phenomenon which could not be explained by the Old "Material-Causal" Paradigm underlying both of these RT & QM Models – including offering an alternative theoretical explanation for "dark-matter" and "dark-energy" assuming to comprise up to 95% of all of the mass and energy in the universe (which could not be detected empirically to date despite numerous attempts to do so...) Perhaps even more significantly, it offers a completely new "Expansive-Unifying" Scientific Theoretical Model of the universe! This is because in contrast to the Old "Material-Causal" Paradigm of 20th Century Physics underlying both RT & QM – which explained any physical phenomenon in the universe as being "caused" by a more basic "reductionistic" direct physical interaction between a given set of relativistic or quantum elements, the New "G-d's Physics" Paradigm of 21st Century Theoretical Physics forces us to expand and unify any such relativistic or quantum phenomenon based on the operation of the singular higher-ordered UCP! Once we realize based on two of the profound new theoretical postulates of this New "G-d's Physics" Paradigm called: the "Computational Invariance Principle" and its associated "Universal Consciousness Reality" – that the entire physical universe only exists as a "transient", "phenomenal" "appearance" of the real underlying "Universal Consciousness Reality" (UCR) [2]pixels in the universe (for each consecutive UF's frame/s), as well as exists "alone" without the presence of any physical universe "in-between" any two consecutive UF's Frames; our whole basic understanding and conceptualization of the origin- nature- sustenance- and evolution- of the entire physical universe alters in a very fundamental manner: We realize that all exhaustive spatial pixels comprising the entire physical universe – including all subatomic "particles", as well as all Quantum or Relativistic phenomena and laws, including those Four basic Forces of Nature "dissolve" and "cease to exist" "in-between" any two consecutive UF's frames! We realize that all such exhaustive spatial pixels of the universe and all of their associated manifestations of subatomic "particles", and all of the associated basic physical features of "space", "energy", "mass" and "time" – including the Four Forces of Nature exist only as "phenomenal", "transient" "manifestations" of the singular higher-ordered Universal Consciousness Principle (UCP) which alone exists both during its extremely rapid (e.g., "$c^2.h$" = 1.36^{-50} sec') computation of each consecutive UF's frame/s, as well as solely exists "in-between" any two such consecutive UF's frames in which the entire physical universe "dissolves" back into the singularity of this UCP!

Indeed, those two (far reaching) theoretical postulates of the "Computational Invariance Principle" and its associated "Universal Consciousness Reality" assert that since only this UCP exists constantly (and uniformly) both "during" it's extremely rapid production of the series of UF's frames – e.g., computing simultaneously all exhaustive spatial pixels' four basic physical features (of "space" and "energy", "mass" and "time") and solely exists "in-between" any two consecutive UF's frames, whereas all exhaustive spatial pixels comprising the entire physical universe (i.e., including all of their four basic physical features of "space", "energy", "mass" and "time" and all of their associated subatomic "particles", "wave", etc. and also the Four basic Forces) exist only "during" each consecutive UF's frame/s but "dissolve" back into the singularity of this singular higher-ordered UCP; therefore, only this singular UCP may be regarded as "real" ("computationally-invariant"), whereas all exhaustive spatial pixels comprising the entire physical universe (and their four basic associated physical features) may only be regarded as "transient", "phenomenal" "manifestations" of this singular higher-ordered unitary Universal Consciousness Reality, which exists constantly and continuously both during its manifestation as the physical universe's exhaustive spatial pixels as well as existing solely and singularly "in-between" any two consecutive UF's frames! Therefore, the new discovery of the "G-d's Physics" New Paradigm is that the entire physical universe – including its four basic Forces and all of its comprising Quantum and Relativistic phenomena and laws exist only as manifestations of this singular higher-ordered UCR! Hence, "G-d's Physics" New Paradigm's complete unification- not only of RT and QM, of the four basic physical features of "space" and "energy", "mass" and "time" (as indicated in one of the Special Issue's previous articles), but also of the Four basic Forces (Strong, Weak, Electromagnetic and Gravitational) all ensue from its discovery of the ("wondrous") "Universal Computational Formula" (UCR) describing the unfathomable rapid integrated and simultaneous computation of this singular higher-ordered UCP (or UCR) all exhaustive spatial pixels comprising the entire physical universe for each consecutive UF's frame/s!

Not less significant is the amazing theoretical implication of this New "G-d's Physics" discovery of the Universal Computational Formula – is the realization that since there cannot exist any "material-causal" direct physical interactions between any two exhaustive spatial pixels existing either in the same- or different- UF's frame/s, therefore the very existence of these apparent Four basic Forces of Nature merely represent specific UCP computations associated with the Universal Computational Formula, e.g., rather than exist as an "objective-material" reality (since, as noted above, it completely "dissolves" in-between any two consecutive UF's frames!); and as a matter of fact its existence may only be accounted for through the UCR's own intrinsic propensities which include "Ten-Hierarchical Laws of Manifestations" – of which the UCP's UCF represents the "lowest Dimension"! Indeed, the real significance of this New "G-d's Physics" Paradigm is its discovery of this singular higher-ordered UCP's intrinsic propensities which include:

a. **The UCP's "Multi Spatial-Temporal Reservoir" & Associated "Dynamic-Equilibrium Moral Principle":** According to this New "G-d's Physics" Paradigm the UCP is also associated with a "Multi Spatial-Temporal Reservoir" which contains all "past", "present" and multiple possible "future/s" for each Individual Human Consciousness (human-being) based on his/her "moral-choice/s" at any given moment – based upon which the UCP selects one of multiple possible "future/s"! This is due to the fact that from the singular higher-ordered computational perspective of the UCP all Individual Human Consciousness comprise integral parts of this UCP, and therefore any "immoral-choice" by one (given) Individual Human Consciousness directed towards another Individual Human Consciousness automatically instigates a proportional "reaction" computed by this singular UCP aimed at "balancing" and "correcting" any such "moral imbalance" caused by one Individual Human Consciousness inflicting "pain/ suffering" upon another Individual Human Consciousness. (A "Trampoline Metaphor" was given wherein a "metal-bar" placed upon this Trampoline's "elastic sheath" connecting two points along this sheath – wherein one point "choses" to "inflict-pain" upon the other point and "pushes" this metal-bar against the "other point" (e.g., another Individual Human Consciousness), then this would inevitably "cause" a reaction of the metal-bar to "press back" and inflict a proportional "pain/ suffering" upon the first point which chose to inflict "pain/ suffering" on the second point!) Hence, according to "G-d's Physics" New Paradigm, the UCP contains the "Dynamic-Equilibrium" Moral Principle's "intrinsic-tendency" to "correct" and "counter-balance" any "immoral-choice" selected by one Individual Human Consciousness against another Individual Human Consciousness – by selecting one of multiple possible UF's contained in the UCP's "Multi Spatial-Temporal Reservoir" for each Individual Human Consciousness based on its "moral choice/s" at any given point in time. (Noteworthy is the fact that according to this new "Dynamic-Equilibrium" Moral Principle, the UCP's selection of one of multiple possible future/s for each Individual Human Consciousness based on its action/s regarding another given Individual Human Consciousness also operates for "*positive* moral-actions" according to which carrying out of a "good moral choice" by one Individual Human Consciousness towards another Individual Human Consciousness also brings about the UCP's selection of one "positive" future/s from all possible future/s to remunerate that Individual Human Consciousness which chose to carry out a benevolent "good moral action" towards another Individual Human Consciousness...)

b. **The UCP's "Reversed-Time Goal Hypothesis":** According to "G-d's Physics" New 21st Century Paradigm, the UCP's whole computation of the series of UF's frames comprising the evolution of the entire physical universe – is geared towards bringing about an ultimate state of "Moral, Spiritual & Physical Perfection" from its initial UF's frame/s to its latter UF's frames! Indeed, according to this "UCP's Reversed-Time Goal Hypothesis" the entire evolution of the physical universe – i.e., including its evolution of progressive forms of "inanimate" matter, then "animate": "plants" and "animals" leading up to the appearance of Human Beings is all "directed" and computed by the singular higher-ordered UCP from the ultimate "Goal" of complete "Moral, Spiritual and even Physical Perfection" (termed: "Geula" in Jewish Tradition) – "back" towards all of "past" "present" and multiple possible "future/s" UF's that would lead to this ultimate "Geula" Perfected State! This means that rather than the physical universe being "caused" by a random initial "material-causal" "Big-Bang" nuclear event supposed to have created all of the suns, Galaxies, "matter" and "energy" in the universe – which was negated by the New "G-d's Physics" Paradigm's discovery of the *simultaneous UCP's computation of all exhaustive spatial pixels* in the universe for each consecutive UF's frame/s and the complete "dissolution" of the entire physical universe "in-between" any two consecutive UF's frame/s; and contrary to Darwin's "Natural Selection Principle's" assumed "material-causal" evolution of all Biological forms based on a random "material-causal" direct physical interaction/s between an array of given organisms and their environment which "causes" a particular "genetically mutated" organism to "survive" amidst "challenging environmental conditions", thereby selecting that particular ("fittest") organism to "survive" and pass on its genetic information to its descendants; the New 21st century "G-d's Physics" Paradigm asserts that since the UCP simultaneously computes all exhaustive spatial pixels in the universe for every consecutive UF's frame/s (and completely "dissolves" the entire physical universe back to itself "in-between" any two such consecutive UF's frame/s), therefore there cannot exist any such "material-causal" physical interactions between any given organism/s and its direct environment therefore negating Darwin's "Natural Selection Principle" – instead pointing at the UCP's mentioned "Reversed-Time Goal Hypothesis" describing the whole evolution and computation of the universe based on the UCP's directed ultimate Goal of "Geula" (Perfected Moral, Spiritual and Physical State, previously delineated)! This means that rather than the physical universe evolving "randomly" (and "haphazardly"), in fact the whole evolution, sustenance and even origination of the entire physical universe – is entirely dependent upon the UCP's "driving" the universe towards the manifestation of the "most expansive" form of Human Consciousness (from the "inanimate" material form through animate "plants", "animals" and ultimate Human forms of expansive Consciousness) and ultimately towards the expression and manifestation of the Redemptive "Geula" State in which there will exist a complete Harmony, Peace and Recognition of the singular higher-ordered "Good-Will" (and "Free-Will") UCP which incessantly and continuously creates- dissolves and recreates and evolves every exhaustive spatial pixel in the universe as well as the entirety of the cosmos towards this Perfected "Geula" State!

c. **The UCP's "Collective Human Consciousness Focus Hypothesis at the Jewish "Rosh-Hashana" New Year!**
Another (surprising) facet of the New "G-d's Physics" Paradigm's discovery of the UCP's sole continuous (simultaneous) computation of all exhaustive spatial pixels in the universe – is it's unique "Critical-Prediction", e.g., differentiating it from the corresponding predictions of the Old "Material-Causal"

Paradigm predicting that the accelerated expansion of the physical universe is "Non-Continuous" occurring at the Jewish New Year's ("Rosh-Hashana") – due to another (intrinsic) aspects of the UCP which is called: the "Collective Human Consciousness Focus Hypothesis"; As noted above, we reached the inevitable theoretical conclusion that the entire universe may only be regarded as a "transient", "phenomenal" "manifestation" of the singular higher-ordered UCP! Moreover, we realized that there cannot exist any "real" "material-causal" physical interactions between any two (or more) exhaustive spatial pixels existing either in the same- or other- UF's frame/s due to the simultaneity of the UCP's computation of all exhaustive spatial pixels comprising any single (or multiple) UF's frame/s and the complete "dissolution" of the entire physical universe "in-between" any two consecutive UF's frames) So, we also must reach the inevitable theoretical conclusion wherein the origination- sustenance- "dissolution" and evolution of the whole material universe – including its empirically validated accelerated expansion of the entire physical universe – cannot be the result of any such "material-causal" (direct or even indirect) physical interaction/s between any material entities or any two or more exhaustive spatial pixels, but may only de derived from this singular higher-ordered operation and intrinsic characteristics of this singular higher-ordered UCP! Indeed, as part of the abovementioned (and previously delineated) new "G-d's Physics" Paradigm's discovery of this singular higher-ordered UCP's intrinsic characteristics the UCP's "Non-Continuous Accelerated Expansion of the Universe at the Jewish "Rosh-Hashana" (New Year) uniquely serves as one of a few Critical Prediction/s differentiating it from the corresponding predictions of the Old "Material-Causal" Model's Relativistic and Quantum Predictions! Simply put, this New "G-d's Physics" "Non-Continuous Accelerated Expansion of the Universe at the Jewish "Rosh-Hashana" Critical Prediction posits that since the singular higher-ordered Universal Computational/ Consciousness Principle (UCP) can be affected by a "Collective

Human Consciousness Focus (Hypothesis)"- wherein the collective focus of Millions of Jews at the Jewish Rosh-Hashana upon this singular higher-ordered Universal Consciousness Principle (or Reality) – i.e., "G-d"(!) brings about this "Non-Continuous Accelerated Expansion" of the universe at this "special time interval"!

Alongside this specific "Critical Prediction", "G-d's Physics" New Paradigm called for an urgent empirical validation of at least one more unique "Critical Prediction" that is associated with this New Paradigm (and differentiates it from the predictions of both RT and QM: This relates to the greater number of times that a relatively "more massive" particle (such as the Muon) is predicted to be measured across a series of (minimal) "Fine-Temporal Measurements" (FTM) within an Subatomic Accelerator, relative to the number of corresponding FTM at which a relatively "less-massive" particle such as an electron)! This is due to "G-d's Physics" New Paradigm's novel computational definition of the "mass" of any given particle (or object) as computed by the UCP as the number of "consistent-object" values across a given number of FTM! This implies that a relatively "more massive" Muon particle should be detected or measured across a greater number of UF's frames relative to the number of times that a "less-massive" electron particle would be measured across the same number of FTM within a given Accelerator! Likewise, it was predicted that since the UCP continuously "creates" (computes), "dissolves" "re-computes" (and evolves) every exhaustive spatial pixel in the universe, e.g., through its creation of a series of consecutive UF's frames, therefore another unique (third) "Critical-Prediction" of "G-d's Physics" New Paradigm is that "in-between" any two consecutive UF's frames it will not be possible to measure the existence of any subatomic "particle" (e.g., since the whole entire physical universe "dissolves" in-between" any two consecutive UF's frames) – but that only "during" each of the UCP's extremely rapid ("c^2/h" = 1.36^{-50} sec') series of UF's frames it may be possible the existence of any given subatomic particle/s!

Indeed, Twenty-first Century Theoretical Physics (and Science, more generally) reaches an entirely new theoretical understanding of the origin- sustenance- dynamics and evolution- of the entire physical universe based on the discovery and necessary empirical validation of the New "G-d's Physics" (CUFT) Paradigm: The universe was not created by an initial "Big-Bang" nuclear event, nor does it evolve through the direct physical interactions of "massive objects" and their assumed "curvature of Space-Time"; nor is the universe's accelerated expansion "caused" by any (non-existent) "dark-matter" or "dark-energy" – but rather is brought about by the singular higher-ordered UCP's operation which (as we've seen) is also associated with the "Collective Human Consciousness" at the Jewish "Rosh-Hashana" special "time-interval"! This entirely new theoretical understanding of "G-d's Physics" Paradigm views the origin- "dissolution" sustenance- and evolution- of every exhaustive spatial pixel in the universe (as well as of the whole universe) as solely determined by the operation of the singular higher-ordered Universal Computational/Consciousness Principle (or Reality) which computes and sustains the universe at the incredible rate of "c^2/h" = 1.36^{-50} sec'(!), wherein "in-between" any two such consecutive UF's frames the entire physical universe "dissolves" back into the singularity of this UCP! Therefore, the new "G-d's Physics" theoretical understanding is that every exhaustive spatial pixel in the universe (and the entirety of the universe) exists only as a "transient", "phenomenal" "manifestation" of this singular higher-ordered "Universal Consciousness Reality" (UCR) which solely exists both "during" its simultaneous computation of all exhaustive spatial pixels in the universe for each consecutive UF's frame/s and also singularly exists "in-between" any two consecutive UF's frames (without the presence of any physical universe)! Indeed, since the whole origin- sustenance- evolution- and basic nature of the entire physical universe (including all of its exhaustive spatial pixels) is that it only exists as such a "transient", "phenomenal" *"manifestation"* of the singularly existing "Universal Consciousness Reality" – therefore, the existence of all of the subatomic particles and their Three (e.g., out of Four) corresponding basic Nuclear Forces (Strong, Weak & Electromagnetic) may also only be regarded as existing "transiently" and "phenomenally", i.e., existing only "during" each consecutive UF's frame's (and being computed and "sustained" by the singular UCP) as a manifestation of the singular UCR! Moreover, since we've already seen in this article that the UCP's sole and singular computation of the entire array of all existing subatomic particles is carried out through the UCP's (newly discovered) "Universal Computational Formula" (UCP) therefore also it was evinced that the UCP's computation of the Four basic Forces are all derived from this singular higher-ordered UCP's computation of the four basic physical features of "space", "time", "energy" and "mass" for all exhaustive spatial pixels comprising the entire physical universe for each consecutive UF's frame/s!

Perhaps most significantly, the discovery of the New 21st Century's "G-d's Physics" Paradigm brings about a fundamental theoretical conceptual "metamorphosis" – wherein no longer Theoretical Physics (and Science, more generally) seeks to explain any Relativistic or Subatomic (Quantum) phenomenon, entity or force – based on any "material-causal" (direct or indirect) physical interactions between any material or physical entities; but rather acknowledges that the Four basic Forces of Nature and all of its existing array of subatomic particles, the entire origin- sustenance, "dissolution" and re-computation and evolution of the entire physical universe may only be explained based on the discovery of the UCP's intrinsic characteristics and features such as its basic "Dynamic-Equilibrium Moral Principle" – which selects one of multiple possible "future/s" for each Individual Human Being based on his/her moral choice/s at any given point in time! And the

UCP's "Reversed-Time Goal Hypothesis" wherein the entire origination sustenance and evolution of the physical cosmos is all "directed" and "computed" by this singular higher-ordered Universal Computational/Consciousness Principle's (UCP) ultimate goal of producing a "Perfected World" – Morally, Spiritually and Physically in which the most expansive form of Consciousness existent, e.g., of Human Beings will acknowledge and appreciate the singular existence of this UCP (termed: "Geula"). Twenty-first Century Physics (and Science) has therefore entered an entirely new and (fascinating) era in which it acknowledges the singular, existence and operation of a "Good-Will" and "Free-Will" Universal Consciousness Reality which drives the entire origination- sustenance- and evolution into this ultimate "Geula" Perfected World, e.g., from its inception onwards through its progressively refined and more expansive manifestations of inanimate, animate: plants, animals and Human Beings – up until its ultimate "redemptive "Geula" State World…

Dedication: This article is dedicated to the Lunbavitecher Rebbi and to the Alter-Rebbi, Rabi Schneur-Zalman – who's date of passing occurs today (כ"ד טבת) and to Mamonides (whose date of passing occurred a few days ago כ טבת), and to the upliftment of my dear Beloved Diseased Mother's Soul Dr. Tirza Bentwich/ Zailer); May this Ne "G-d's Physics" Paradigm of 21st Century Physics uplift Humanity towards its ultimate Mission and Goal of creating a "Geula" Perfected World!

6.   References

Bentwich, J. (2012a) "Harmonizing Quantum Mechanics and Relativity Theory". *Theoretical Concepts of Quantum Mechanics*, Intech (ISBN 979-953-307-377-3), Chapter 22, pp. 515-550.

Bentwich, J. (2012b) "Theoretical Validation of the Computational Unified Field Theory". *Theoretical Concepts of Quantum Mechanics*, (ISBN 979-953-307-3773), Chapter 23, pp. 551-598.

Bentwich, J. (2013b). "The Theoretical Ramifications of the Computational Unified Field Theory". *Advances in Quantum Mechanics* (ISBN 978-953-51-1089-7), Chapter 28, pp. 671-882.

Bentwich, J. (2013c). The Computational Unified Field Theory (CUFT): A Candidate Theory of Everything. *Advances in Quantum Mechanics* (ISBN 978-953-51-1089-7) Chapter 18, pp. 395-436.

Bentwich, J. (2015). The Computational Unified Field Theory (CUFT): A Candidate 'Theory of Everything'. *Selected Topics in Application of Quantum Mechanics* (ISBN 978-953-51-2126-8) Chapter 6.

Bentwich, J. (2014) *What if Einstein was Right? Amazon Kindle Book Store.*

Bentwich, J. (2015). On the Geometry of Space, Time, Energy, and Mass: Empirical Validation of the Computational Unified Field Theory. *Unified Field Mechanics: Natural Science Beyond the Veil of Spacetime (Proceedings of VIGIER IX Conference, Morgan State University, USA, 16-19 November 2014).*

Bentwich, J. (2016) The 'Computational Unified Field Theory': A Paradigmatic Shift. *Research & Reviews: Journal of Pure & Applied Physics.*

Bentwich, J. (2017a) The Computational Unified Field Theory: Could 'Dark Matter' & 'Dark Energy' be "Superfluous"? *SciFed Journal of Quantum Physics Special Issue.*

Bentwich, J. (2017b) The Computational Unified Field Theory: Explaining the Universe from "Without". *SciFed Journal of Quantum Physics Special Issue.*

Bentwich, J. (2017c). The Computational Unified Field Theory: A New 'A-Causal Computation' Physics. *SciFed Journal of Quantum Physics Special Issue.*

Bentwich, J. (2017d). The 'Computational Unified Field Theory' (CUFT) May Challenge the 'Big-Bang Theory'. *SciFed Journal of Quantum Physics Special Issue.*

Bentwich, J. (2017e). Can the 'Computational Unified Field Theory' (CUFT) Challenge the Basic Laws of Conservation? *SciFed Journal of Quantum Physics Special Issue.*

Bentwich, J. (2017f). The Computational Unified Field Theory (CUFT): Time "Reversal" May be Possible. *SciFed Journal of Quantum Physics Special Issue.*

Bentwich, J. (2017g). The Computational Unified Field Theory (CUFT) Transcends Relativity's Speed of Light Constraint. *SciFed Journal of Quantum Physics, Special Issue.*

Bentwich, J. (2017h). The Computational Unified Field Theory's New Physics: Transcending Space, Time and Causality. *SciFed Journal of Quantum Physics Special Issue.*

Bentwich, J. (2017i). A "Supra-Spatial-Temporal Universal Consciousness Reality". *Research & Reviews: Journal of Pure & Applied Physics, Special Issue: The Computational Unified Field Theory (CUFT)- A Paradigmatic Shift in 21st Century Physics.*

Bentwich, J. (2017j). A New Science: An Infinite Omniscient Dynamic-Equilibrium Universal Consciousness Reality. *SciFed Journal of Quantum Physics Special Issue.*

Bentwich, J. (2017k). The Computational Unified Field Theory (CUFT) Challenges Darwin's 'Natural Selection Principle'! *SciFed Journal of Quantum Physics Special Issue.*

Bentwich, J. (2017l). The Computational Unified Field Theory (CUFT) Challenges the Second Law of Thermodynamics. *SciFed Journal of Quantum Physics Special Issue.*

Bentwich, J. (2017m). The Computational Unified Field Theory (CUFT): An Empirical & Mathematical Validation of the 'Computational Unified Field Theory'. *SciFed Journal of Quantum Physics Special Issue.*

Bentwich, J. (2017n). The Computational Unified Field Theory (CUFT) New Science; *SciFed Journal of Quantum Physics Special Issue.*

Bentwich, J. (2018a). Review: The Computational Unified Field Theory (CUFT) New Universe: *The Global Journal of Science Frontier Research, Vol. 18 (8-A), Special Issue.*

Bentwich, J. (2018b). The Computational Unified Field Theory (CUFT): What is "Time"? *The Global Journal of Science Frontier Research, Vol. 18 (8-A), Special Issue.*

Bentwich, J. (2018c). The Universal Consciousness Reality's Camouflage: The Physical Universe! *The Global Journal of Science Frontier Research, Vol. 18 (8-A), Special Issue.*

Bentwich, J. (2018d). The Computational Unified Field Theory (CUFT) Epilogue: Can Human Consciousness Affect the Cosmos? *The*

Global Journal of Science Frontier Research, Vol. 18 (8-A), Special Issue.

Bentwich, J. (2018e). Testing the Computational Unified Field Theory's (CUFT) Differential-Critical Predictions: The Higgs-Boson Particle May Not Exist Continuously! *The Global Journal of Science Frontier Research, Vol. 18 (8-A), Special Issue.*

Bentwich, J. (2018f). The Double-Faceted Universal Consciousness Reality: A Theoretical Review. *The Global Journal of Science Frontier Research, Vol. 18 (8-A), Special Issue.*

Bentwich, J. (2018g). Letter to the Editor: Dark Matter May Not Exist. *The Global Journal of Science Frontier Research, Vol. 18 (8-A), Special Issue.*

Bentwich, J. (2018h). The Computational Unified Field Theory's (CUFT) Epilogue: Possible Reversal of the Arrow of Time and Abolishment of Death. *The Global Journal of Science Frontier Research, Vol. 18 (8-A), Special Issue.*

Bentwich, J. (2019a). The Computational Unified Field Theory's (CUFT) New Universe. *The Global Journal of Science Frontier Research, Vol. 19 (6), Special Issue.*

Bentwich, J. (2019b). The Computational Unified Field Theory's (CUFT) Goes Beyond the 'Standard Model': "G-d's Physics"?!. *The Global Journal of Science Frontier Research, Vol. 18 (8-A), Special Issue.*

Bentwich, J. (2019c). A Call for Cosmologists & Experimental Physicists: Empirical Validation of the 'Computational Unified Field Theory' (CUFT) New Paradigm through "Time-Sensitive" Astronomical and Subatomic Measurements. *The Global Journal of Science Frontier Research, Vol. 19 (6), Special Issue.*

Bentwich, J. (2019d). The 'Computational Unified Field Theory' (CUFT): Redefining Mass, Gravity & the Physical Universe. *The Global Journal of Science Frontier Research, Vol. 19 (6), Special Issue.*

Bentwich, J. (2019d). Astronomical Validation of the Computational Unified Field Theory (CUFT) "Critical Prediction" & Resolution of the "Universe's Accelerated Expansion Rate Enigma" (UAERE).*The Global Journal of Science Frontier Research, Vol. 19 (6), Special Issue.*

Bentwich, J. (2019e) Urgent Call for Empirical Validation of the Computational Unified Field Theory's (CUFT) New 21st Century 'A-Causal Computation' (ACC) Paradigm. *Acta Scientific Applied Physics, Volume 1(1).*

Bentovish (Bentwich) J. (2020a) **'G-d's Physics'**. In Press. *iUniverse Publication.*

Bentovish (Bentwich), J. (2020b). 'G-d's Physics' (CUFT) New "Atom" & Purposeful Universe! *Advances in Theoretical & Computational Physics. Volume 3 (2),* p. 50-58.

Bentovish (Bentwich), J. (2020c). An Urgent Need for "G-d's Physics" New 21st Century Paradigm's Empirical Validation. *Advances in Theoretical & Computational Physics. Volume 3 (2),* p. 59-65.

ב"ה

G-d's Physics: Its "Time" for "Geula"!

Jehonathan Bentovish, Ph.D.

Note: Dr. Bentovish is seeking scientific collaboration and validation of this New CUFT's 'G-d's Physics' Paradigm's empirical "critical predictions" involving precise Astronomical /Cosmological Measurements as well as time-sensitive Accelerators validations.

Dr. Bentovish (Bentwich) e-mail is: drbentovish@gmail.com.

1. Science's Sole "Mandate": Discovery of Truth!

The development of Science represents a relatively "new" phenomenon along Humanity's pursuit- or inquiry- to discover "Truth", e.g., dated perhaps to Descartes famous "Philosophical Inquiries", roughly 250 years ago! Interestingly, Descrates, considered by many is the "Father" of the "Scientific Method" – was primarily preoccupied with discovering "Truth" through philosophical-introspective inquiries. Indeed, Humanity's quest to find "Truth" begun through Religious and Philosophical Schools of Thought – only relatively recently leading to the rapid evolution of Science as an effective "objective" means to unravelling deeper facets of the "physical reality"… It is likely that the great advantage and strength of Science – over "Philosophy", e.g., as far as the "objective" inquiry into the nature of the "physical reality" – stems from its insistence upon quantifiable empirical data, which can be verified (and replicated) "objectively", i.e., by different observers (regardless of their language, origin, or "personal beliefs"); And that this "objective-empirical" data is accompanied and based upon "logical-inferences" aimed at deriving the most logical and feasible theoretical Model or explanation for any given set of empirically observed phenomena (or data); This "objectivity" and "rational-basis" of all Scientific investigation represents Science's greatest "strength" – e.g., as far as unravelling the underlying "Truth" or "reality" underlying our "physical universe"… It circumvents any personal or even "collective" – "biases" (or "preconceived ideas") by placing a very simple two-fold criteria for the judgement of any given Scientific Model or Paradigm (e.g., guiding Science at a particular point in time):

a. Can a given "Standard Scientific Paradigm" explain a given set of known empirical phenomena (in a satisfactory "logical" manner)?

b. This "Standard Scientific Paradigm" (e.g., accepted within a given Scientific discipline at a certain point in time) "consistent" logically (e.g., does not possess any "intrinsic logical or theoretical inconsistencies")?

Indeed, the great Philosopher of Science, Thomas Kuhn (1962) postulated that whenever any given Scientific discipline reaches a point (in time) in which the answer to these two critical criteria for a satisfactory "Standard Scientific Paradigm" are *negative* – then this calls for a "Paradigmatic-Shift" towards a "New Scientific Paradigm" which can satisfy a third criteria (in addition to satisfying the first above mentioned two criteria for any satisfactory Scientific Paradigm):

c. The "New Scientific Paradigm" has to able to explain all of the known empirical phenomena in the field, explain any existing "theoretical inconsistencies" (in the "Old Standard Paradigm") (e.g., criteria a & b); and in addition, this "New Paradigm" needs to predict certain new unique "Critical Prediction/s" that cannot be accounted for by the "Old Paradigm?!

A very good example for Kuhn's rigorous analysis of the "Structure of Scientific Revolutions" (1962) was Einstein's revolutionizing of 19th Century "Newtonian Classical Mechanics" (and Maxwellian Theory): His "New Relativity Theory Paradigm" was able to resolve any apparent "theoretical inconsistencies" that seemed to exist between "Newtonian Classical Mechanics" and "Maxwellian Electromagnetic Theory", it replicated all known empirical phenomena – and it also identified a unique "Critical-Prediction" that differentiated it from the corresponding prediction of Newton's Classical Mechanics, e.g., regarding the much higher value of Mercury's Perihelion's curvature around the Sun (due to its curvature of "Space-Time")! Indeed, immediately upon Eddington's (well-known) empirical verification of Einstein's New "Relativity Theory" Paradigm's "Critical-Prediction", Einstein's "New Relativity Paradigm" was accepted as the New appropriate Paradigm for 20th Century Theoretical Physics (later on joined by the discovery of subatomic Quantum Mechanics).

We now stand at an equivalent "historic-juncture" along the upward evolution of Science – i.e., at a clear point in which the two primary "pillars" of 20th Century Physics' Old "Material-Causal" Paradigm, (i.e., Relativity Theory and Quantum Mechanics) seem to "contradict" each other, and in which this Old "Material-Causal" Paradigm cannot explain where up to 95% of all the "matter" and "energy" in the universe exist! (Termed: "dark-matter" and "dark-energy" and assumed to account for the accelerated expansion of the universe – but which cannot be directly detected or measured experimentally, despite numerous attempts to do so...) True, Thomas Kuhn identified the natural "human-resistance" to "change"- or "alter"- the "Old Paradigm" in favor of a New (unknown) Paradigm, which characterizes these "trying times" of a new "Paradigmatic-Shift"... But, nevertheless, since Science's sole "mandate" and "advantage" over mere "philosophical inquiries" is its strict insistence upon satisfying the two-fold (abovementioned) basic criteria for the acceptance of any Scientific Paradigm, the current "Paradigmatic-Crisis" of 20th century Theoretical Physics cannot continue to exist as the state of affairs of 21st Century Physics – calling for an urgent and immediate "Paradigmatic-Shift" towards the New "Computational Unified Field Theory" (CUFT, lately termed as: "G-d's Physics") as the New satisfactory Paradigm for 21st Century Physics – e.g., provided that its unique "Critical Prediction/s" are validated empirically! Needless to say, that if a "negative" situation arises in which, Science "refuses" or "obstructs" the discovery, empirical validation and ultimate "acceptance" of such a "New Paradigm" (such as the New "G-d's Physics" tentative Paradigm for 21st Century Theoretical

Physics) – e.g., due to its own "biases", "political-reasons" or any other reason/s; then the sole "mandate" given to Science (by Humanity) to investigate- and advance- (ever closer) to discovering "Truth", shall be removed from Science to any other "vehicle/s of Knowledge" – such as "Religion" and "Philosophy", so that Humanity may reach its "ultimate Goal" of "knowing Truth"!

2. The New "G-d's Physics" (CUFT) Paradigm of 21st Century Physics!

Perhaps, the best "starting-point" to briefly describe "G-d's Physics" New 21st Century Paradigm is to outline the basic "Material-Causal" assumption underlying the Old "Material-Causal" Paradigm of 20th Century's Relativity Theory (RT) and Quantum Mechanics" (QM): Succinctly stated, this basic "Material-Causal" assumption states that the nature, dynamics (or even origin) of any "macroscopic-relativistic" or "microscopic-quantum" phenomenon – strictly based on studying its constituting element's direct (or indirect) physical interactions: Thus, for instance, General Relativity Theory posits that it is the presence of certain "massive-objects" that "causes" the "curvature" of "Space-Time", and that this "curved Space-Time" also determines (or "causes") the "travelling-pathways" of these "massive" (and other "less-massive") objects, thereby de facto determining the continuous accelerated expansion of the physical universe, e.g., as portrayed by Einstein's famous Equations; Similarly, Quantum Mechanics posits that it is the direct physical interaction/s between a given subatomic "probe" element and a corresponding subatomic "target's probability wave-function" that "causes" the "collapse" of this "probability wave-function" into a singular "complimentary" ("energy-space", or "time-mass") value/s! But, once again, since it was shown (previously) that this Old "Material-Causal" 20th Century Paradigm of RT & QM has reached a state of a "Paradigmatic-Crisis" which calls for an immediate "Paradigmatic-Shift", therefore, the discovery of the New "G-d's Physics" Paradigm negated this basic "Material-Causal" Assumption, i.e., based on its discovery of a singular higher-ordered "Universal Computational/ Consciousness Principle" (UCP) which simultaneously computes all exhaustive spatial pixels in the universe for each consecutive "Universal Frame" (e.g., at the incredible rate of "c^2/h" = 1.36^{-50} sec')!

This is because a key assumption of the New "G-d's Physics" (CUFT) Paradigm is that since this singular (higher-ordered) UCP simultaneously computes all exhaustive spatial pixels comprising the entire physical universe (for each consecutive UF's frame/s), therefore there cannot (in principle) exist any direct (or even indirect) "material-causal" physical relationship/s between any two (or more) exhaustive spatial pixels existing either in the same- or other- UF's frame/s (comprising the entire physical universe at any minimal time-point)! Moreover, since according to this New "G-d's Physics" Paradigm, the entire physical universe "dissolves" "in-between" any two consecutive UF's frames back into the singularity of the UCP, therefore there cannot be any "transference" of any physical "effect" or "interaction" across any two consecutive UF's frames – therefore (once again) there cannot exist any direct or indirect physical interaction between any two (or more) exhaustive spatial pixels existing across different UF's frames! Indeed, this New "G-d's Physics" Paradigm has also been termed: an "A-Causal Computation" Paradigm, since it negates the very possibility of the existence of any physical interaction/s – either at the relativistic or quantum levels. Instead, the New "G-d's Physics" Paradigm postulates that this singular (higher-ordered) UCP possesses three "Computational-Dimensions", e.g., "Framework" ('frame' vs. 'object'), "Consistency" ('consistent' vs. 'inconsistent') and "Locus" ('global' vs. 'local') – two, out of which (Framework and Consistency) produce the four basic physical features of 'space' and 'energy', 'mass' and 'time'; Essentially it is postulated that the UCP's simultaneous computation of each exhaustive spatial pixel in the universe – for "object" – 'consistent' vs. 'inconsistent' computational measures yields their individual "mass" and "time" values; whereas the UCP simultaneous computation of each exhaustive spatial pixel's "frame" – 'consistent' vs. 'inconsistent' computational measures produces their "space" and "energy" physical features (correspondingly). In fact, for the first time in Physics history's theoretical conception of the physical reality, the New "G-d's Physics" Paradigm completely unified between these four basic physical features of "space" and "energy", "mass" and "time" as "integral-complimentary" secondary computational features of the UCP's singular simultaneous computation of each of the universe's comprising exhaustive spatial pixels – i.e., based on its discovery of a singular "Universal Computational Formula" (UCF) which describes the UCP's extremely rapid computation of each consecutive UF's frame/s exhaustive spatial pixels!

Universal Computational Formula (UCF):

$$\left\{ \frac{\text{י}c^2}{h} \right\} \quad \text{UF's} \{ \text{א...מ...ת} \} \qquad \frac{s \quad * \quad e}{t \quad * \quad m}$$

wherein the singular higher-ordered UCP – represented by the Hebrew letter "Yud" ("י") simultaneously computes all exhaustive spatial pixels in the universe comprising each consecutive Universal Frame/s (UF's) which already exist in a "potential-from" within the UCP's "Supra Spatial-Temporal Reservoir" of all "past", "present" and multiple possible "future/s" UF's (represented by the Hebrew letters from "א through "מ" to "ת)" depending on the Moral Choice of each Individual Human Consciousness – as computing and integrating these four basic physical features of "space" and "energy", "mass" and "time", at the incredible rate of: "c^2/h" = 1.36^{-50} sec'!

Interestingly, this new UCF – not only completely unifies between these four basic physical features (of "space", "energy", "mass" and "time"), but also resolves the apparent fundamental "theoretical inconsistency" that seem to exist between RT & QM, by integrating their key properties as secondary integral components of this singular (higher-ordered) UCF! Thus, for instance, RT's "Energy-Mass Equivalence" ("$E = Mc^2$") is embedded within the UCF's "Relativistic Format", e.g., as a "special limiting case" (which necessitates further empirical and theoretical investigation):

Likewise, the key Quantum Heisenberg's "Uncertainty Principle's" "complimentary-pairs" simultaneous measurement constraint (e.g., of "space" and "energy", or "time" and "mass" simultaneous subatomic measurement constraint set by Planck's constant) – have been (surprisingly) found to constitute "special-cases" embedded within the UCF's "Quantum Format:

Therefore, the new singular higher-ordered theoretical framework of the UCP's Universal Computational Formula completely integrates the four basic physical features of "space" and "energy", "mass" and "time", as well as the fundamental components of both RT & QM as integral elements of this singular UCP's extremely rapid, simultaneous computation of all exhaustive spatial pixels in the universe, e.g., for each consecutive UF's frame!

But, as significant as this new realization of the New 21st Century "G-d's Physics" Paradigm may be – e.g., fully integrating those four basic physical features of "space" and "energy", "mass" and "time" (for the first time in Physics' history!) and satisfactorily rectifying the two primary "pillars" of the Old "Material-Causal" (20th Century Physics), namely: RT & QM; Perhaps even more profound are some of the additional "Theoretical Postulates" of this New "G-d's Physics" Paradigm including: its "Computational Invariance Principle" and "Universal Consciousness Reality" postulates: In a nutshell, these profound additional theoretical postulates assert that since only the singular higher-ordered "Universal Computational/Consciousness Principle" (UCP) may be considered as "computationally-invariant", e.g., remains constant and continuous both "during" its sole computation of each exhaustive spatial pixel's four basic above mentioned physical features, as well as solely exists "in-between" any two consecutive UF's frames (e.g., without the presence of any physical universe – which "dissolves" back into the singularity of the UCP); whereas the entire physical universe (and every exhaustive spatial pixel comprising it) may only be deemed as "computationally-variant", e.g., existing only "during" each consecutive UF's frame/s (as solely computed by the UCP) but "dissolving" back into the singularity of the UCP "in-between" any two consecutive UF's frames; therefore, the "Computational-Invariance Principle" postulates that only this singular ('computationally-invariant') UCP may be regarded as "real" – i.e., continuously existing as the basis for all exhaustive spatial pixels of the universe while transcending it altogether when existing solely "in-between" any two consecutive UF's frames, whereas the four basic physical features of "space" and "energy", "mass" and "time" (as well as the whole physical universe they comprise at each of its exhaustive spatial pixels) may only be regarded as a "transient", "phenomenal" manifestation of this singular "Universal Consciousness Reality"! Indeed, closely related to this "Computational Invariance Principle" postulate is the "Universal Consciousness Reality" theoretical postulate which points out that since only this singular UCP exists "uninterruptedly" and "continuously" – both "during" its computation of each exhaustive spatial pixel in the universe for each consecutive UF's frame/s, and also "in-between" any two consecutive UF's frames in which it solely exists (without the presence of any accompanying physical universe), therefore there only truly exists this one singular "Universal Consciousness Reality" (UCP) – which manifests as the physical universe "during" each consecutive UF's frame/s and remains without the presence of the physical universe "in-between" any two consecutive UF's frames!

Indeed, these profound "Computational-Invariance" and "Universal Consciousness Reality" theoretical postulates have also led to the discovery of a series of additional postulates that completely alter Science's basic understanding of the "physical reality" – and what transcends and embeds this (merely) "physical" reality within it which is a detailed characterization of this singular higher-ordered "Universal Consciousness Reality" (UCR): Thus, for instance, the UCR's intrinsic "characterization" revealed that it contains a higher-ordered "Supra Spatial-Temporal Reservoir" containing all "past", "present" and multiple possible "future/s" UF's frames – which are based on the "Moral-Choice/s" that each Individual Human Consciousness (e.g., person) makes at any point in time… This is due to this UCR's intrinsic "propensity" to strive towards "balancing" any "Immoral-Imbalances" (or "injustices") due to its "unitary" nature- and composition- of all such "Individual Human Consciousness" as "integral-parts" of its singular existence! Indeed, the "Trampoline-Metaphor" has been utilized which demonstrates and explicates this "singular-unitary" nature- and tendency- of this singular higher-ordered "Universal Consciousness Reality" (UCR) to "balance" any "Moral-Imbalance" "disturbing" the "unitary-nature" of this singular UCR, e.g., by creating a series of UF's in which the "inflicting-pain/suffering" Individual Consciousness (which is likened to a given point along the Trampoline sheath which pushes an "Iron-Bar" against another given point representing another "suffering" Individual Consciousness – then this will inevitably "cause" a "reaction" in which this "Iron-Bar" would have to retract and "inflict-pain/suffering" upon that Individual Consciousness which initially inflicted pain/suffering upon the other Individual Consciousness, thereby "correcting" this "Immoral-Imbalance")... Hence, according to this New "G-d's Physics" Paradigm, the whole progression and evolution of the UCR's singular production of the entire physical universe – is driven by the UCR's "intrinsic-properties" which includes this basic "Dynamic-Equilibrium" Moral Principle, as well as a few other basic propensities – previously delineated termed: the UCR's Ten Laws of Hierarchical Manifestation"; These include such basic intrinsic properties as its inherent "Good-Will", "Free-Will" and ultimate driving force towards a "Perfected State" (Morally, Physically and Spiritually) of the world and universe in which all Human Beings would recognize their inseparability from this singular higher-ordered (all embracing) UCR and function accordingly (as will be further elaborated upon in the last segment of this article).

3. Theoretical Ramifications of the New "G-d's Physics" 21st Century Paradigm

Indeed, the discovery of this New "G-d's Physics" Paradigm for 21st Century Theoretical Physics brings about a profound change in our basic understanding of the origin- nature- evolution- and ultimate "Goal" of the UCR's singular higher-ordered reality: No longer is the universe assumed to originate in an initial "random" nuclear event, since there cannot have occurred such a nuclear explosion that would entail a direct physical interaction between two or more exhaustive spatial pixels in an assumed "first" 'Universal Frame' – which "caused" the creation of certain powerful physical effects (between multitude exhaustive spatial pixels) across the "Second", "third", fourth" etc. UF's frames (such as the creation of suns, galaxies, space, energy, etc. This is because as mentioned above (and previously), according to the

New "G-d's Physics" Paradigm, there cannot exist any such direct or even indirect "material-causal" physical interactions between any (two or more) exhaustive-spatial pixels existing either in the same- or different UF's frames, e.g., due to the "simultaneity" of the singular higher-ordered UCR's computation of all exhaustive spatial pixels in any given UF's frame/s, and the complete "dissolution" of the entire physical universe "in-between" any two such consecutive UF's frames! Therefore, there cannot exist any "transference" of any physical effect or direct physical interaction/s also across any series of UF's frames, thereby negating the basic "Big-Bang" Model! Similarly, this New "G-d's Physics" Paradigm also negates (in principle) "Einstein's Equations" fundamental "Material-Causal" assumption, wherein it is assumed that it is the presence of certain "massive objects" that "cause" the curvature of "Space-Time", and that it is this "curved Space-Time" that determines (or "causes") the "travelling pathways" of these "massive objects" (and other "non-massive" objects)! This is, once again, due to "G-d's Physics" negation of the very possibility of the existence of any direct or even indirect "material-causal" physical interactions between any two (or more) exhaustive spatial pixels in the universe (existing wither in the same- or different- UF's frame/s due to the simultaneous UCR's computation of all exhaustive spatial pixels in the universe for every consecutive UF's frame/s (and the complete "dissolution" of the entire physical universe "in-between" any two consecutive UF's frames). Because the UCR simultaneously computes all such exhaustive spatial pixels comprising the entire physical universe (for each consecutive UF's frame/s), therefore there cannot exist Einstein's Equations' assumed "material-causal" (direct or indirect) physical interactions between certain "massive objects" "causing" the "curvature" of Space-Time, nor the possibility of such "curved Space-Time" determining the "travelling-pathways" of any given "massive/non-massive" objects in the universe!

Instead, the New "G-d's Physics" Paradigm postulates that the evolution of the universe is solely governed by the UCR's singular (above mentioned) "Ten Laws of Hierarchical Manifestation" – which are not "constrained" or "directed" by any such "material-causal" physical interactions (laws, or effects)! Another "Cinematic-Film Metaphor" has been illustrated which demonstrates the possibility of a scenario in which apparently "cause and effect" "material-causal" interaction/s depicted within a given Cinematic Film progression are seen to arise from the ("higher-ordered") perspective of the "Film's Director"! In order to best explain this "G-d's Physics" New Paradigm's "Cinematic-Film" Metaphor explication of apparently "material-causal" effects or interactions, lets first review the basic depiction of this Cinematic-Film Metaphor's explanation of the manner in which the singular higher-ordered UCR computes the (above mentioned) four basic physical features of "space" and "energy", "mass" and "time": Imagine an extremely fat "jet-plane" "zooming" through the screen in a particular Film; if we were to ask the simple question: "does this jet-plane" possess any intrinsic "energy" or "velocity"? despite the appearance of such "high-velocity" depicted by this "supersonic jet's" depiction across a given series of Cinematic-Film Frames – upon further examination of this jet's positioning across a series of Cinematic Film Frames, it will be discovered that there truly does not exist any "velocity" or "energy" value to this (supersonic) "jet-pane"! This is because the appearance of such "energy" or "velocity" associated with this jet-plane simply arises from the computation of the degree of its displacement across a series of "film-frames"... Likewise, the apparent "space" value (e.g., "spatial-dimensions") of any given object in the film can be computed as the number of "consistent" spatial pixels comprising that object across a given series of film-frames; Similarly, Similarly, the "mass" value of any given "object" (appearing in the film) may be computed as the number of times that any such given object is being presented "consistently" (e.g., in terms of its "internal composition") across a series of film-frames (for instance, in such a manner that it's perceived "density" or "hue" is computed as a function of the number of consecutive frames in which that object appears "consistently"!) Finally, we can compute any given object's "temporal" value as a computation of the number of "changes" (e.g., inconsistent presentations) of that object's "internal-composition" across a given series of film-frames (e.g., "spatial-dimensions")... Note that this "Cinematic-Film Metaphor" coincides (almost perfectly) with the above (and previously) mentioned "dynamics" of the UCR's (or UCP's) computation of the four basic physical features of "space" and "energy", "mass" and "time" as being computed based on two of the

UCP's "Computational Dimensions" of "Framework" (frame/object) and "Consistency" (consistent/inconsistent) which produces these four basic apparently "physical" features!

Indeed, the manner in which this New "G-d's Physics" (CUFT) Paradigm is capable of offering an alternative new theoretical explanation for Relativity's (and QM's) apparently "material-causal" physical relationships – was also demonstrated utilizing another aspect of this "Cinematic-Film Metaphor": imagine a film depicting a given "Mercury-Ball" hitting a "Glass-Jar" filled with water – "causing" those water to be "spilled" on the floor... Apparently, it seems as if it is the "impact" of the "Mercury-Ball" upon the "Glass-Jar" which "causes" its waters to be spilled across the floor; But, upon further reflection, we find out that at none of this "film's scenario's" comprising film-frames can there exist any direct or indirect "physical interaction" between the "Mercury-Ball" and the "Glass-Jar" ("filled with water")! This is simply because at each of these ensuing (individual) film-frames, both the "Mercury-Ball" and the "Glass-Jar" are being presented "simultaneously" as comprising integral parts of the same frame! This means that at none of these "film-frames" can there exist any direct (or even indirect) physical interaction/s between these "Mercury-Ball" and "Glass-Jar" elements! All that really exist is their depiction at ever closer "spatial-proximity" until their "conjoining", e.g., being presented adjacent to each other, then followed by film frame/s depicting the "spillage" of the water on the floor... This gives us (the viewers of the film) the "impression" as if it was the "impact" of the "Mercury-Ball" upon the "Glass-Jar" which "caused" the "spillage" of the water on the floor... So, through this secondary aspect of the "Cinematic-Film Metaphor" we can understand that despite the appearance of an apparent "cause" and "effect" physical interaction/s between two given objects being depicted across a series of 'film-frames', truly this arises only from the "Film's-Director's" arrangement of the series of film-frames depicting ever closer proximity between these two given ("Mercury-Ball" and "Glass-Jar") in ever closer "spatial-proximity" "leading up" to the presentation of a "broken Jar" and "spilled-water"... Hence, this "Cinematic-Film Metaphor" was utilized in order to illustrate that what is regarded by Relativity's "Einstein's Equations" to represent a basic "Material-Causal" physical relationship/s between certain "massive-object/s" and their "curvature" of "Space-Time" (and conversely, assuming that it is this "curved Space-Time" which "causes" or "determines" these "massive" and other "less-massive" objects' "travelling-pathways"; may in fact, be the result of the singular higher-ordered UCR's (or UCP's) "simultaneous" computation of a series of Universal Frames" (UF's) depicting certain apparent physical relationships between the presentation of "massive" and "less-massive" objects – which arises from the UCR's (UCP's) complete integration of the four basic physical features of "space" and "energy", "mass" and "time" as secondary computational properties of the UCP's simultaneous computation of each exhaustive spatial pixel in the universe across a series of consecutive UF's frames (as indicated above and previously)!

In much the same manner, this New 21st Century "G-d's Physics" Paradigm also was shown to challenge- negate- embed- and transcend- Quantum Mechanics (QM's) fundamental "Material-Causal" assumption wherein it is assumed that it is the direct physical interaction between the subatomic "probe" and corresponding "target's probability wave function" that "causes" the "collapse" of the target's "probability wave function" into a single "complimentary" ("space/energy" or "mass/time") value... Once again, due to the New "G-d's Physics" Paradigm's insistence upon the "simultaneity" of the UCP's (UCR's) computation of all exhaustive spatial pixels in the universe (for each consecutive UF's frame/s), therefore it negates the very possibility of the existence of any such direct physical interaction between the subatomic "probe" and "target's (assumed) probability wave function" – nor the possibility of its "collapse" into a single (complimentary) "space/energy" or "mass/time" value (as "caused" by such "impossible" direct physical interaction)! Instead, the New "G-d's Physics" Paradigm posits that this singular higher-ordered UCP/UCR simultaneously computes all "single spatial-temporal" ("particle"), "multiple spatial-temporal" ("wave") and "exhaustive" (e.g., all exhaustive spatial pixels comprising the entire Universal Frame for any consecutive frame)! This higher-ordered "exhaustive" theoretical framework of the New "G-d's Physics Paradigm" was indeed shown to completely integrate QM and

RT as integral elements found within the UCP's singular "Universal Computational Formula" (UCF) and also resolve their apparent "theoretical inconsistency".

What's important to note is that this New "G-d's Physics" Paradigm completely alters and transcends the Old "Material-Causal" Paradigms basic assumption wherein the explanation of any "macroscopic" (relativistic) or "microscopic" (quantum) phenomenon, law or relationship can be simply explained based on such a phenomenon's "fragmentation" into smaller constituting elements or direct physical interactions which supposedly "explain" that phenomenon; i.e., such as in the case of the abovementioned "Einstein's Equations" assumed explanation of the dynamics of the universe's evolution based on the direct physical interaction/s between certain given "massive-objects" and their "curvature" of "Space-Time", or QM's assumed explanation of any subatomic target's measured (complimentary) "space-energy" or "mass-time" ("collapsed") value as a result of its direct physical interaction/s with the corresponding subatomic "probe" element. But, as we've already seen, based on the New "G-d's Physics" Paradigm's insistence that any such direct (or even indirect) physical interactions are made "impossible" due to the "simultaneity" of the UCP's/UCR's computation of each exhaustive spatial pixel/s in the universe (for each consecutive UF's frame/s, and the complete "dissolution" of all such exhaustive spatial pixels back into the singularity of the UCR), therefore the New "G-d's Physics" Paradigm points at the singularity of this UCR – and its intrinsic "propensities" represented by its "Ten Laws of Hierarchical Manifestation" which govern and determine the entire physical origination- sustenance- and evolution! Thus, for instance, it was shown that instead of the "randomly" assumed "Big-Bang" nuclear event which is assumed to have created all of the suns, galaxies, planets, space, energy etc. the entire physical universe is being continuously created- "dissolved" re-created- and evolved- (at an unfathomable rate of "c^2/h" = 1.36^{-50} sec') based on its intrinsic tendency towards manifesting an ever more "conscious" forms of Physical and Biological composition" i.e., from inanimate to animate: plants, animals and ultimately Human-Beings as part of the UCR's ultimate "Goal" of a "Perfected" Physical, Moral and Spiritual World and Universe – i.e., "termed: "Geula" in the

Jewish Tradition" (thereby also negating replacing Darwin's "Natural Selection Principle" with "G-d's Physics" purposefully directed manifestation of ever more conscious Physical and Biological forms leading up to Human-Being's Individual Human Consciousness and ultimately to its manifestation of the Perfected "Geula" State, as will also be delineated further below).

4.   Is Science Still Fulfilling its "Mandate" for Discovering "Truth"?!

As discussed above (and previously), the sole "mandate" given to Science (by Humanity) is to discover "Truth" – i.e., initially conceived as pertaining to the discovery of the "physical reality" and "physical universe"! The basic (powerful) "Scientific Method" – which seemed to "favor" the "Scientific Investigation" over (for instance) "Philosophical Inquiry" stems from the "Scientific Methodology" of basing its investigation upon the collection of "objective", "replicable" "empirical data" – accompanied by rigorous "logical reasoning", "modeling" and establishing of acceptable "Scientific Paradigm/s" which conforms to Kuhn's (abovementioned finely described) "criteria" for a valid Scientific Paradigm! This means that whenever Science reaches an apparent "dead-end" in terms of its acceptable "Standard Scientific Paradigm" – due to the appearance of basic "theoretical-inconsistencies" found between its basic "pillars" (e.g., such as between 20th Century's RT & QM!) and its principle inability to explain a series of given empirical phenomena (i.e., such as the currently assumed "dark-matter" and "dark-energy" purely hypothetical concepts which are postulated to account for up to 95% of all the "mass" and "energy" in the universe – but yet cannot be directly measured or verified despite numerous attempts to do so!); this points at a "Paradigmatic-Crisis" calling for an immediate "Paradigmatic-Shift" from the "Old Standard Paradigm" toward a "New Paradigm" that can resolve those apparent "theoretical inconsistencies" (between the "pillars" of the Old Paradigm), replicate all known physical phenomena, laws etc., and also predict new "Critical Prediction/s" which differentiate it from the predictions of "Old Standard Paradigm" – which need to be validated empirically!

Well, it is clear that the New "G-d's Physics" Paradigm of 21st Century Theoretical Physics satisfies all of these "stringent" criteria (based on Kuhn's well-established and acceptable analysis of the "Structure of Scientific Revolutions", 1962) – having been shown capable of resolving the apparent "theoretical inconsistencies" between RT & QM, replicating all of their major phenomena and laws, embedding- and transcending- key Relativistic and Quantum laws and relationships within its singular higher ordered "Universal Computational Formula" etc. The only "final" element necessary to justify the acceptance of this New 21st Century "G-ds Physics" Paradigm – is the empirical validation of one of its multiple "Critical Predictions" (which differentiate it from the corresponding predictions of either RT or QM!):

a. The "Non-Continuous Accelerated Expansion Rate" of the Universe at the Jewish "Rosh-Hashana" (New Year) Time Interval!

As outlined and delineated (extensively) previously, one of the unique "Critical-Predictions" of the New "G-d's Physics" Paradigm is its prediction that due to its postulated "Collective Human Consciousness Focus Hypothesis" (CHCFH) which hypothesizes that at any time-interval in which there exists an intense "Collective Human Consciousness Focus" upon the singularity of the higher-ordered Universal Consciousness Reality (UCR or UCP), e.g., through prayers etc., then this can produce an effect manifesting as a significant increase in the UCR's "accelerated expansion rate" of the universe; In fact, this unique "Critical Prediction" of the New "G-d's Physics" Paradigm offers an alternative explanation for the Old Paradigm's (purely hypothetical abovementioned) theoretical concepts of "dark-matter" and "dark-energy" which cannot be verified empirically but yet are assumed to be responsible for the empirically observed accelerated expansion rate of the universe! This is because instead of those "superfluous" (i.e., "non-existent!) "dark-matter" and "dark-energy" purely hypothetical concepts which were assumed to explain the accelerated rate of expansion of the universe; the New "G-d's Physics" account of this empirically observed accelerated expansion of the universe stems from the singular higher-ordered UCP's/UCR's accelerated increase in the number of additional exhaustive spatial pixels comprising each consecutive UF's frame! Specifically, to the extent that Cosmologist, Astronomers etc. accurately measure and validate this unique "Critical Prediction" of "G-d's Physics" New Paradigm indicating that at the special (two days) time interval of the Jewish New Year ("Rosh-Hashana) – i.e., this year it occurred on the 19th and 20th of October (2020) indicating that indeed the accelerated rate of the universe's expansion has increased "non-continuously" "during" these two days of the Jewish "Rosh-Hashana" (at which time Millions of Jews all around the World have prayed and focused solely upon this singular higher-ordered "Universal Consciousness Reality", i.e., "G-d"!) then this would inevitably prove that the New "G-d's Physics" Paradigm must be accepted as the New Paradigm for 21st Century Physics! *It is quite disappointing (and indeed "surprising") that despite numerous "Urgent Calls" for all Astronomers, Cosmologists and Empirical Physicists to empirically validate this unique "Critical Prediction" of this New "G-d's Physics" Paradigm during each year's Jewish "Rosh-Hashana" special time-interval – now, already for three consecutive years!? No such empirical validation has taken place!??*

b. Greater Number of "Fine-Temporal Measurements" (FTM) for "More-Massive" Particle/s Than "Less-Massive" Particles!

Another unique "Critical-Prediction" of the New "G-d's Physics" Paradigm regards the greater number of "Fine-Temporal Measurements" (FTM) (e.g., minimal time-point Subatomic Accelerators sampling measurement of the incredibly rapid rate of the UCP's ("c^2/h" = 1.36^{-50} sec') computation of the series of UF's frames) – of relatively "more massive" particles (such as the "Muon") then "less-massive" particles (such as the "electron") across a given FTM time interval! This is due to the New "G-d's Physics" Paradigm's UCP's computational definition of the "mass" value of any given particle as the number of "object-consistent" presentations of that particle across a given series of UF's frames; Consequently, any Subatomic Accelerator's FTM's "sampling" of a certain number of UF's should result in a much greater number of FTM measurements in which a relatively "more massive" (for instance "Muon") particle should be measured, relative to the number of FTM measurements of a relatively "less-massive" particle (such as the "electron") across the same FTM time-interval measured... *Once again multiple official public requests and calls for Empirical Physicists to carry out (and validate) this unique "Critical Prediction" have been delivered – but to no avail!??*

So, we find ourselves in an "impossible situation" for Science (in general): one the one hand, Science received a "mandate" to investigate- and discover- "Truth" – solely contingent upon its reliance upon the firm foundations of "objective gathering of empirical data" and its "stringent" analysis based on logical reasoning to arrive at a certain "Standard Scientific Paradigm" which can best explain all of this gathered empirical data, facts and phenomena) – e.g., as described by Kuhn's fine analysis of the evolution of any Scientific Discipline; and on the other hand, it seems that Science (or rather "scientists") are "resisting" to acknowledge the current appearance of Kuhn's clear definition of a "Paradigmatic-Crisis" in 20th Century Physics Old "Material-Causal" Paradigm and its ensuing (inevitable) necessary "Paradigmatic-Shift" into a satisfactory New ("G-d's Physics") Paradigm for 21st – including their ("obstinate") "unwillingness" to empirically validate the unique "Critical Predictions" of this New "G-d's Physics" Paradigm! True, Kuhn himself acknowledged that this special "Paradigmatic-Shift" phase is characterized (and often accompanied) by some "conflicts" and "difficulties" (e.g., because "scientists" are, after all, simply "human-beings" who are often reluctant to "let go" of their old ideas and assumptions etc. and embrace new "broader" ideas and understandings) – but still, they must realize that the only "mandate" given to Science (by Humanity) to discover "Truth" – is based on their unwavering "commitment" to investigating the true nature of the "physical reality" and "physical universe" – based on those fundamental stringent criteria that Kuhn identified (and Descartes was probably their first proponent), namely: "objective" data and its "logical reasoning interpretation and construction of certain "Standard Paradigm/s" – which have to "give-way" to "New Paradigm/s" capable of resolving any "theoretical inconsistencies" found within any "Old-Standard Paradigm", explaining "unexplained phenomena" (according to the "Old Paradigm/s") – and especially, empirical validation of any unique "Critical Prediction/s" of any "New Paradigm", which differentiate it from the corresponding prediction/s of the "Old Paradigm"!

Therefore, the current "impossible predicament" of Science must change immediately: Physics – and specifically Cosmologists, astronomers and Experimental Physicists must rush and validate the New 21st Century "G-d's Physics" Paradigm's "Critical Prediction/s" (as mentioned above and extensively previously); or else, it is likely that the special "mandate" given to Science (by Humanity) to investigate and discover "Truth" – would "pass" onto other "forms" of advanced Human Investigation/s and Knowledge, "demanded" by Humanity's incessant "quest" to discover "Truth"!?

5.   Fulfilling Science's & Humanity's "Goal": "Geula Time"!?

Indeed, the discovery of this profound New "G-d's Physics" 21st Century Paradigm points at the existence of a new higher-ordered "Universal Consciousness Reality" (UCR) which solely produces the entire physical universe (at the incredible rate of "c^2/h" = 1.36^{-50} sec') as an extremely rapid succession of "Universal Frames" (UF's) comprising all exhaustive spatial pixels in the universe (for each such minimal time-point) – with the entire physical universe "dissolving" "in-between" any two successive UF's frames! This profound new discovery of the New "G-d's Physics" Paradigm, alongside the (abovementioned) "Computational Invariance Principle" and associated "Universal Consciousness Reality" (UCR) brought about a new (and profound) realization wherein the existence of the entire physical universe (and all of its constituting exhaustive spatial pixels) may only be regarded as representing a "transient", "phenomenal" manifestation of the singular "computationally-invariant" reality of the UCR – which exists "consistently" and "uniformly" both "during" its (simultaneous) computation of all exhaustive spatial pixels comprising each consecutive UF's frame, and also (solely) exists "in-between" any two consecutive UF's frames! Therefore, "G-d's Physics" New Paradigm's profound realization that the physical universe does not exist as a "solid" "consistent" reality – but rather as a "transient", "phenomenal" "manifestation" of the singular higher-ordered "Universal Consciousness Reality" (UCR); and in fact, that the entire physical universe is being continuously "computed", "dissolved"- re-computed- and evolved- (at the incredible rate of "c^2/h" = 1.36^{-50} sec') by this singular higher-ordered UCR completely alters our basic conception and understanding of the physical universe (e.g., as well as our own important role as Human-Beings possessing an Individual Human Consciousness within it)! No longer is the universe conceived as "randomly" created by an initial "Big-Bang" nuclear event, nor as being evolved based on either macroscopic Relativistic direct physical interactions (between certain "massive-objects" assumed to "cause" the "curvature of Space-Time" etc.), nor as driven by direct subatomic physical interactions/ between a given "probe" and corresponding "target's probability wave function" which is assumed to "cause" the "collapse" of this "target's probability wave function" into a singular complimentary "space/energy" or "time/mass" value)... Nor is the universe "drifting aimlessly" into an ever increasing "greater Entropy" inevitable dissolution (based on the Second Law of Thermodynamics)... Nor is the "Biological Evolution" of the species "caused" by direct physical interactions between certain organism/s (e.g., which "genetically mutate" "randomly") and their environment – which "causes" the "survival of the fittest"?!

Instead, the New "G-d's Physics postulates that the (continuous) "origination" (or computation), "dissolution", re-computation- and evolution of each exhaustive spatial pixel comprising the entire physical universe is solely "guided" and "determined" by that singular higher-ordered "Universal Consciousness Reality" (UCR)'s intrinsic properties, e.g., including its "Ten Laws of Hierarchical Manifestation" – which also include" the UCR's "Good-Will", "Free-Will", "Dynamic-Equilibrium" Moral Principle etc., and its overarching "Reversed-Time Goals Hypothesis" (RTGH) which states that this singular higher-ordered UCR computes the whole evolution of the physical universe from its "Ultimate Final Goal" of reaching a "Perfected" – Physically, e.g., including the "abolishment of death" (see previous publication)!, Morally, e.g., the existence of a World and Universe in which all Individual Human Consciousness (Human-Beings) function and operate based on their realization of their complete (and mutual) "unity" and "inseparability" from this singular, higher-ordered UCR – which would bring about a fundamental change in their behavior such that it would be as "inconceivable" for any ("sane") Human Being to "inflict pain" by its "right hand" upon its "left hand"; in the same manner it would become completely "inconceivable" for any Individual Human Consciousness (Human Being, individual) to "inflict pain/suffering" upon another Human-Being due to Humanity's fundamental realization that all Human-Beings are "inseparable" from the singular higher-ordered "UCR" (and therefore form "integral-inseparable segments" of this singular UCR, and form each other!); And Spiritually – this UCR's ultimate "Perfected" State (e.g., termed: "Geula" in the profound Jewish Tradition) implies that all Human-Beings would recognize the singular existence of this higher-ordered UCR – of which Human-Beings and the entire physical cosmos are only "transient", "phenomenal" and "inseparable" elements, which would therefore increasingly manifest a basic sense of "recognition", "awe", "gratitude" (and "reverence") towards that Singular, Higher-Ordered, All-Goodness, All-Giving UCR, i.e., "G-d"!

Indeed, Science and Humanity is reaching a "pivotal-point" along its incessant development in which they "desperately" needs to undergo a basic fundamental "Paradigmatic-Shift" from its Old "Material-Causal" Paradigm of 20th Century Physics towards the much broader "exhaustive" New "G-d's Physics" Paradigm – which discovered the existence of a singular, higher-ordered "Universal Consciousness Reality" (UCR) that continuously computes- "dissolves"- re-computes and evolves every exhaustive spatial pixel in the universe (at an unfathomable rate); and which directs the World and Humanity towards a Physically, Morally and Spiritually Perfected "Geula" State – in which the most advanced form of Physical, Biological and Moral development, (e.g., "Human-Beings") reach a condition in which they (collectively) recognize the singularity of this higher-ordered UCR, its "Reversed-Time Goal Hypothesis" incessant "driving" of the Universe (from its "inception" and continuously with each consecutive UF's frame/s) towards this Physically, Morally and Spiritually "Perfected-Geula" Ultimate (and "eternal") State! Towards the discovery of this Ultimate Truth" – did Science receive its "mandate" from Humanity, and regardless of "scientist's" willingness (or "unwillingness") to recognize, embrace and advocate this singular, higher-ordered "Ultimate-Truth" – Humanity must reach this Perfected "Geula" State, i.e., especially during these "troubling" and "trying" times of the Covid-19 Pandemic (which seem to "challenge" many of the old "Material-Causal" Old Paradigm's basic assumptions), and in which Humanity is groping for a "Just", "Morally", "Physically" and "Spiritual" "New Reality": It's "Time" for "Geula"!

Dedication: This article (as well as all of the other articles in this Special Issue) are dedicated to my Great Lubavitcher Rebbi, my dear Father, Prof. Zvi Bentwich, my dear beloved diseased Saintly mother, Dr. Tirza Bentwich (daughter of Yitzchak), my dear beloved wife, Shulamit Bentovish, my two sons: Shoham and Nethanel Yossef and daughter Neomi Tirsa Shulamit, my eldest brother Issac and all of my extended family; To my Grandfather Yossef Bentwich and Great Grandfather Zvi Herbert Bentovish (Bentwich); It is also dedicated to Mr. Brian Fisher. It is dedicated (more generally) to all "True Scientists" who fight to discover "Truth" – no matter how "inconvenient" or "hard" the Journey to its discovery may be, for the sake of uplifting Humanity to its ultimate "Goal" of "Geula" and a Truly Perfected World which recognizes, acknowledges and adorns that Singular Higher-Ordered "Universal Consciousness Reality", i.e., "G-d"!

ב"ה

"G-d's Physics": On the True Nature of "Dark-Energy" & "Dark-Matter"

Jehonathan Bentovish (Bentwich), Ph.D.

Note: Dr. Bentovish is seeking scientific collaboration and validation of this New CUFT's 'G-d's Physics' Paradigm's empirical "critical predictions" involving precise Astronomical /Cosmological Measurements as well as time-sensitive Accelerators validations.

Dr. Bentovish (Bentwich) e-mail is: <u>drbentovish@gmail.com</u>.

Abstract

Twenty-first Century Theoretical Physics is in a state of a "Paradigmatic-Crisis" wherein the two pillars of the Old "Material-Causal" Paradigm (Relativity Theory & Quantum Mechanics) seem "inconsistent" and up to 95% of all the energy and mass in the universe cannot be directly accounted for, e.g., deemed as "Dark-Energy" and "Dark-Matter"?! Indeed, the quest for a satisfactory answer for these two primary conundrums: resolving the basic RT-QM inconsistency and explaining what precisely comprises these (purely hypothetical) "Dark-Matter", "Dark-Energy" concepts are most likely the most important topics – to be resolved by any (satisfactory) 21st Century Physics' "New Paradigm"! Fortunately, such a New "Computational Unified Field Theory" (CUFT), lately termed: "G-d's Physics" Paradigm provides satisfactory answers for these two critical fundamental issues; "G-d's Physics" was shown to resolve the apparent RT-QM "theoretical inconsistency" based on the discovery of a new singular higher-ordered "Universal Computational/ Consciousness Principle" (UCP) which *simultaneously* computes every exhaustive spatial pixel in the universe at the incredible rate of "c²/h" = 1.36^{-50} sec', creating an extremely rapid series of "Universal Frames"

(UF's) comprising the entire physical universe at every "minimal time-point"! Specifically, this New "G-d's Physics" Paradigm explains the fundamental nature of "Dark-Matter" and "Dark-Energy" in a completely new manner – i.e., as representing the operation of the singular higher-ordered UCP's "A-Causal Computation"! Hence, instead of "Dark-Matter" and "Dark-Matter" comprising actual "material" (hypothetical) elements, the New 21st Century "G-d's Physics" Paradigm explains these constructs as merely a manifestation of the singular higher-ordered UCP's accelerated addition of exhaustive spatial pixels for each consecutive UF's frame/s. Viewed in this new light, the real "cause" for the universe's accelerated expansion – is not found in any "material" or "physical" entities, but is rather contingent upon the successive simultaneous computation- "dissolution" re-computation and evolution of each exhaustive spatial pixel in the universe at the incredible rate of "c^2/h" = 1.36^{-50} sec'!

1. Introduction: Twenty-First Century's New "G-d's Physics" Paradigm

Twenty-first Century Theoretical Physics finds itself in a state of a "Paradigmatic-Crisis" as characterized by the famous Philosopher of Science, Thomas Kuhn in his analysis of the "Structure of Scientific Revolutions" (1962); This is because according to Kuhn, any scientific discipline undergoes alternating phases of "Standard Science" in which a given discipline follows the guidelines of a particular accepted "Standard Paradigm" which allows the research within that discipline to advance and evolve; Followed by an inevitable "Paradigmatic-Shift" phase/s in which those same "guidelines" and basic "assumptions" underlying the given discipline are questioned, challenged and transcended – due to the appearance of certain "theoretical inconsistencies" found between (different) "pillars" of that discipline, as well as the discovery of certain enigmatic empirical phenomena – which cannot adequately be explained or accounted for by that given "Standard Paradigm"... This calls for the discovery of a "New Paradigm" which seems to be able to resolve these (apparent) "theoretical inconsistencies" found within the Old "Standard

Paradigm", explain in a satisfactory manner those "unexplained phenomena" (by the Old Paradigm) – and ultimately predict a new unique "Critical-Prediction" that significantly differs from the prediction/s of the Old "Standard Paradigm", i.e., which if verified empirically "crowns" the New Paradigm as the new satisfactory paradigm for that scientific discipline (within a given point in time).

This is precisely what happened 101 years ago, when Albert Einstein discovered (General) Relativity Theory, which was shown capable of resolving the principle "theoretical inconsistencies" found between RT and QM, could offer an alternative explanation for the previously assumed ("non-existent") "Ether" concept, and ultimately predicted a unique "Critical-Prediction" regarding the far greater "curvature" of Mercury's perihelion travelling pathway around the Sun (e.g., relative to the Old Newtonian "Classical Mechanics" Paradigm's reduced perihelion's curvature value); Thus, when Eddington confirmed Einstein's General Relativity's greatly "increased" Mercury's perihelion's curvature value – "overnight", Einstein's RT was immediately accepted as the New acceptable Paradigm for 20th century Physics! In much the same manner, it is suggested that the current state of 21st Century Theoretical Physics has reached an "equivalent" state of a "Paradigmatic-Crisis" which inevitably calls for a (similar) "Paradigmatic-Shift"! This is because the Old "Material-Causal" Paradigm of 20th Century underlying both Relativity Theory (RT) and Quantum Mechanics (QM) has also reached a state in which there seem to exist basic "theoretical inconsistencies" between Relativity's strict "Speed of Light Constraint" set on the transmission of any signal (or information) across Space-Time and QM's empirically validated phenomenon of "Quantum Entanglement" which suggests that the subatomic measurement of one "entangled particle" seems to determine (or affect) the other "entangled particle's" complimentary s' (space/energy or time/mass) measured value "instantaneously", thereby apparently violating RT's strict "Speed of Light Constraint"!? Likewise, the (purely) hypothetical concepts of "Dark-Matter" and "Dark-Energy" which are assumed to account for up to 95% of all of the mass and energy in the physical universe – cannot be detected or measured "directly", despite numerous attempts to do so!? Fortunately, there is a New (alternative) more expansive Paradigm termed: the "Computational Unified Field Theory" (CUFT) lately also called: "G-d's Physics" Paradigm, which has been shown capable of resolving this apparent "theoretical inconsistency" between RT & QM, offer an alternative theoretical explanation for "Dark-Matter" and "Dark-Energy" (e.g., delineated in this article) and has also identified several (unique) "Critical Predictions" differentiating this New "G-d's Physics" Paradigm from the Old "Material-Causal" Paradigm's corresponding predictions;

But, before delving into the depths of this New "G-d's Physics" Paradigm for 21st Century Physics, let us portray the gist of the Old "Material-Causal" Paradigm underlying both RT and QM – so that we can better understand the differences between this Old "Material-Causal" Paradigm and the New "G-d's Physics" (CUFT) Paradigm: According to the Old "Material-Causal" Paradigm of RT & QM, every macroscopic (relativistic) or microscopic (quantum) material phenomenon (entity or law etc.) can be explained based on its direct physical interaction with another material component: ***

The primary Theoretical Postulates of this New "G-d's Physics" Paradigm include:

a. **The "Universal Computational/Consciousness Principle" (UCP)"**

One of the key primary theoretical postulates of the New "G-d's Physics" Paradigm arises from its discovery of a singular higher-ordered "Universal Computational/Consciousness Principle" (UCP) which is hypothesized to *simultaneously compute* every exhaustive spatial pixel in the universe at the incredible rate of "c^2/h" = 1.36^{-50} sec'(!) thereby creating an extremely rapid series of "Universal Frames" (UF's) comprising the whole physical universe (at any given "minimal time-point"); According to this new UCP theoretical postulate, "in-between" each two such consecutive UF's frames, all exhaustive spatial pixels comprising the entire physical universe "dissolve" – back into the singularity of the UCP! This means that the whole universe is being continuously computed ("created"), "dissolved",

"re-computed" and evolved at the incredible rate of "c^2/h" =1.36⁻
[50] (sec')!

b. **An "A-Causal Computation" Paradigm:**

Immediately ensuing from the discovery of this singular (higher-ordered) UCP by this New "G-d's Physics" (CUFT) Paradigm is the recognition of its "A-Causal Computation" characterization: Since the UCP is assumed to "simultaneously" compute all exhaustive spatial pixels in the universe, therefore there cannot exist any "material-causal", e.g., "cause" and "effect" physical relationship/s between any two (or more) exhaustive spatial pixels existing either in the same- or other- Universal Frame/s (UF's)! Moreover, since the whole entire universe "dissolves" (back into the singularity of the UCP) "in-between" any two consecutive UF's frame/s, therefore there also cannot be any "transference" or any "physical effect/s" "passing" across any two (or more) UF's frames! Therefore, any (apparent) "material-causal" physical relationship/s that seem to exist between any two (or more) exhaustive spatial pixel/s existing wither in the same- or different- UF's frame/s must be explained through the New "G-d's Physics" "A-Causal Computation" Paradigm, e.g., rather than through the Old "Material-Causal" Paradigm's basic assumption;

c. **The UCP's Computation of the Four Basic Physical Features:**

According to this New "G-d's Physics" Paradigm, the UCP is assumed to simultaneously compute each exhaustive spatial pixels' four basic physical features of "space" and "energy", "mass" and "time" based on the operation of three "Computational Dimensions", including: "Framework" (frame/object), "Consistency" (consistent/inconsistent) and "Locus" (global/local); Specifically, the four possible combinations of "Framework" and "Consistency", namely: "Frame" – "consistent" ("space") & "inconsistent" ("energy"), "Object" – "consistent" ("mass") and "inconsistent" ("time") are computed as secondary computational properties computed by these four UCP's combinations of two (of its three) Computational Dimensions (e.g., "Framework" and "Consistency"); Indeed, this entirely new conception of the four basic physical features of "space" ("frame-consistent"), "energy" ("frame-inconsistent"), "mass" ("object-consistent") and "time" ("object-inconsistent") for the first time completely unifies those four physical features as different complimentary secondary computational properties of the UCP singular simultaneous computation of each exhaustive spatial pixel in the universe (e.g., at the unfathomable rate of "c^2/h" = 1.36^{-50} sec')!

d. **The "Universal Computational Formula":**

Indeed, this complete (new) full integration of these four basic physical features of "space" and "energy", "mass" and "time" is best represented within "G-d's Physics" newly discovered "Universal Computational Formula" (UCF) which describes the manner in which this singular higher-ordered UCF simultaneously computes each exhaustive spatial pixel in the universe:

Universal Computational Formula (UCF):

$$\left\{ \frac{{}^{\prime}c^2}{h} \right\} \quad \text{UF's } \{ \text{ת...מ...א} \} \qquad \frac{s \; * \; e}{t \; * \; m}$$

wherein the singular higher-ordered UCP – represented by the Hebrew letter "Yud" ("י") simultaneously computes all exhaustive spatial pixels in the universe comprising each consecutive Universal Frame/s (UF's) which already exist in a "potential-from" within the UCP's "Supra Spatial-Temporal Reservoir" of all "past", "present" and multiple possible "future/s" UF's (represented by the Hebrew letters from "א through "מ" to "ת)" depending on the Moral Choice of each Individual Human Consciousness – as computing and integrating these four basic physical features of "space" and "energy", "mass" and "time", at the incredible rate of: "c^2/h" = 1.36^{-50} sec'!

Interestingly, this new UCF – not only completely unifies between these four basic physical features (of "space", "energy", "mass" and "time"), but also resolves the apparent fundamental "theoretical inconsistency" that seem to exist between RT & QM, by integrating their key properties as secondary integral components of this singular (higher-ordered) UCF! Thus, for instance, RT's "Energy-Mass Equivalence" ("$E = Mc^2$") is embedded within the UCF's "Relativistic Format", e.g., as a "special limiting case" (which necessitates further empirical and theoretical investigation). Likewise, the key Quantum Heisenberg's "Uncertainty Principle's" "complimentary-pairs" simultaneous measurement constraint (e.g., of "space" and "energy", or "time" and "mass" simultaneous subatomic measurement constraint set by Planck's constant) – have been (surprisingly) found to constitute "special-cases" embedded within the UCF's "Quantum Format".

e. **"G-d's Physics" New UCP's "Dynamic-Equilibrium Moral Principle" & "Supra Spatial-Temporal Reservoir"!**

Another profound discovery made through this New "G-d's Physics" Paradigm regards its unravelling of the UCP's higher-ordered "Supra Spatial-Temporal Reservoir" which contains all "past", "present" and multiple possible "future/s" – dictated by the "Moral-Choice/s" made by each Individual Human Consciousness (Human Being) at any given point in time based on the UCP's intrinsic "Dynamic-Equilibrium" Moral Principle; According to "G-d's Physics" New Paradigm, one of the intrinsic properties of this singular higher-ordered UCP it its "Dynamic-Equilibrium: Moral Principle which stems from the singularity and basic unity of all exhaustive spatial pixels in the universe with this singular UCP – specifically all of all Individual Human Consciousness entities with this this singular UCP! This "inseparability" of all Individual Human Consciousness (Human Beings) from the singular higher-ordered UCP "explains" the UCP's basic tendency towards "balancing" or "correcting" any "Moral Imbalance" created by an "Immoral Choice" affected by any given Individual Human Consciousness towards any other Individual Human Consciousness, which is the essence of this newly discovered UCP's "Dynamic-Equilibrium" Moral Principle; A "Trampoline-Metaphor" was given wherein there is a "Metal-Bar" placed upon a "Trampoline-Sheath", e.g., connecting two given points along this Sheath; whenever a situation arises wherein one of these two given "points" (Individual Human Consciousness) makes an "Immoral Choice" to inflict "pain"/"suffering" upon the other "point" – by pressing that "Metal-Bar" against the other "point" (Individual Human Consciousness), then this would "automatically" set in motion the "opposite balancing effect" of the first "point" suffering the same degree (and intensity) of pain/suffering as experienced by the other "point", e.g., based on its "Immoral-Choice": This represents the UCP's "Dynamic-Equilibrium" Principle, wherein whenever there is an "Immoral Choice" made by one Individual Human Consciousness towards another Individual Human Consciousness, then due to the UCP complete "unity"- and "inseparability" of all of its constituting Individual Human Consciousness ("points" along the "Trampoline's Sheath"), any such "Immoral Choice" inevitable leads to a "correcting" or "balancing" act of the UCP to create an "equivalent situation" in which that Individual Human Consciousness that inflicted "pain" or "suffering" upon another Individual Human Consciousness – would have to "suffer" or experience "pain" as did the other Individual Human Consciousness; That is (according to "G-d's Physics"

New Paradigm) unless that Individual Human Consciousness which "inflicted pain/suffering" makes a "Teshuva" (e.g., feels "remorse" for its "wrongdoing", asks "forgiveness" from the person that has suffered from its "immoral action/s" and towards that singular higher-ordered "Universal Consciousness Reality", and makes a principle "decision" to "not repeat" any such "immoral action/s")... In that case, the UCP may consider this "teshuva" as "rectifying" the "Immoral-Balance" created by that Individual Human Consciousness "Immoral-Choice"; It's important to note that the UCP's selection of one of multiple possible UF's future's for each Individual Human Consciousness' "Moral/Immoral Choice/s" at each point in time operates both for "good/moral" choices as well as for "negative/immoral" choices... Thus, according to this New "G-d's Physics" Paradigm, the selection of one of multiple possible UF's future/s for each Individual Human Consciousness is determined by its Moral/Immoral Choice/s at any given point in time – which obviously "baffles" our own limited Human understanding (and conception) of this singular higher-ordered UCP's "infinite" computing capabilities (i.e., which has to computed for each of the almost eight Billion Human Beings currently living, at any given point in time the precise UF's future/s – coupled with other Individual Human Consciousness towards which it has made "Moral/Immoral Choice/s" that would "rectify" or "balance" any "Immoral Balance" created by its choice/s as well as receive "remuneration" for any "Moral Choice/s" it made towards other Individual Human Consciousness)!

f. **The "Computational Invariance Principle" & "Universal Consciousness Reality"!**

Another two key (profound) new theoretical postulates of the New "G-d's Physics" Paradigm are the "Computational Invariance Principle" and associated "Universal Consciousness Reality" (UCR) postulates; According to the "Computational Invariance Principle" and accompanying "Universal

Consciousness Reality" postulates, since only the UCP exists consistently ("computational-invariant") both "during" its computation of each consecutive UF's frame (simultaneously computing each exhaustive spatial pixel's four basic physical features for each consecutive UF's frame/s) and also solely exists "in-between" any two consecutive UF's frame/s (in which the whole physical universe "dissolves" back into the singularity of the UCP), whereas those four basic physical features only exist "during" each consecutive UF's frame/s (as solely computed by the UCP for each exhaustive spatial pixel) but cease to exist (and "dissolve" back into the singular UCP) "in-between" any two such consecutive UF's frames, therefore only this singular higher-ordered UCP may be regarded as "real" whereas those four basic physical features of the entire physical universe may only be regarded as "phenomenal", "transient" manifestations of this singular UCP!

g. **A "Reversed-Time Goal Hypothesis" UCP's "Geula-Directed" Universe!**

The culmination of "G-d's Physics" New paradigm is its "Reversed-Time Goal Hypothesis" which posits that the whole origination, creation, and evolution of the entire physical universe is computed by the singular higher-ordered UCP (or "Universal Consciousness Reality") based on its "Intrinsic Goal" to bring the whole universe towards a "Perfected Geula State" (e.g., "Geula" denotes the Jewish Faith's term for such a "redemptive" State of "Moral", "Spiritual" and even "Physical" Perfection)! Indeed, according to this New "G-d's Physics" Paradigm, this singular higher-ordered UCP (or UCR) whole continuous (simultaneous) origination, ("dissolution"), sustenance and evolution of every exhaustive spatial pixel in the universe (as well as the evolution of the entire physical universe) has been "planned" to express ever more "expansive" physical (e.g., inanimate), biological (e.g., animate: plants, animals and human-beings) leading to the ultimate "Goal" of creating the most advanced form of "Individual Human Consciousness" (e.g., human-beings) – ultimately realizing the complete "oneness" of all creation and its sole dependence (and "gratitude" etc.) towards this singular higher-ordered "All-Goodness" UCR existence, i.e., the "Morally", "Spiritually" and even "Physically" "Perfected" State of "Geula"!

2. "G-d's Physics" New Paradigm's Revision & Transcendence of Relativistic & Quantum Models

We thus see that some of the most basic fundamental assumptions of the Old "Material-Causal" Physics Paradigm of 20th Century RT & QM are completely challenged, revised and indeed "transcended" through the discovery of the New 21st Century "G-d's Physics" (CUFT) Paradigm! No longer can we regard the universe as being originated by an initial "Big-Bang" nuclear event – since this is based on the Old "Material-Causal" Paradigm's basic assumption wherein it is through the direct physical interaction/s between certain exhaustive spatial pixels (within the universe) that a given physical phenomenon can be explained: Based on "G-d's Physics" New "A-Causal Computation" Paradigm which asserts that it is not possible (in principle) for any direct (or even indirect) physical interaction/s to exist between any two (or more) exhaustive spatial pixels in the universe (e.g., existing wither in the same- or different- "Universal Frame/s) due to the simultaneity of the UCP's computation of all exhaustive spatial pixels comprising any given UF's frame/s, and the complete "dissolution" of all exhaustive spatial pixels in the universe "in-between" any two consecutive UF's frame/s; therefore the New "G-d's Physics" Paradigm negated the basic "Material-Causal" assumption underlying the "Big-Bang" Model, wherein it was the direct physical interaction/s between a set of exhaustive spatial pixels in the "first" UF frame, as part of the initially assumed "nuclear event" – which "caused" the creation- and expansion of all suns galaxies, matter and energy in the universe – in the subsequent UF's frames!? But, since there cannot exist any such direct (or even indirect) physical interactions between any two (or more) exhaustive spatial pixels existing either in the "first", "second", "third"... "Nth" UF frame/s, nor can there be any "transference" of any "material" entity, effect or phenomenon across any two subsequent UF's frame/s (due to the complete "dissolution" of all exhaustive spatial pixels comprising the entire physical universe "in-between" any two such consecutive UF's frames), therefore the basic "Material-Causal" assumption underlying the "Big-Bang" Model was negated and rejected by the New "G-d's Physics" Paradigm of 21st Century Theoretical Physics;

Likewise, General Relativity's famous "Einstein's Equations" were also negated based on "G-d's Physics" New "A-Causal Computation" Paradigm – which negates the very possibility of the existence of any "material-causal" direct (or even indirect) physical interactions between any two (or more) exhaustive spatial pixels! This is because according to Einstein's Equations, the presence of given "massive" objects – "causes" a curvature of "Space-Time", and conversely this "curved Space-Time" "causes" (or determines) the travelling pathways of these "massive" (and other "less-massive") objects. But, since "G-d's Physics" New "A-Causal Computation" Paradigm's insists upon the "simultaneity" of the UCP's computation of all exhaustive spatial pixels in the universe (for each consecutive UF's frame/s), and since the entire physical universe "dissolves" "in-between" any two consecutive UF's frame/s, therefore there cannot exist any such "material-causal" direct or indirect physical interactions between the presence of certain "massive-objects" and their "curvature of Space-Time" – at any single or multiple UF's frames; Nor can there exist any such "material-causal" physical relationship/s between the "curvature of Space-Time" and the determination of these "massive" or other "less-massive" objects! This is simply because there cannot exist any "material-causal" physical interaction/s between any two (or more) exhaustive spatial pixels in the same- or different- UF's frame/s! Ensuing from this New "G-d's Physics" negation of the very possibility of the existence of any "material-causal" (direct or indirect) physical interaction/s between any two (or more) exhaustive spatial pixels, e.g., existing either in the same- or different- UF's frames, this New "G-d's Physics" Paradigm also challenged and negated the "Second law of Thermodynamics": This is because according to the "Second Law of Thermodynamics", the level of "Entropy" in any given physical system must "increase" as a function of the "passage of time"... But, this "Second Law of Thermodynamics" is also based on the basic "Material-Causal" assumption wherein there exists a "material-causal" physical interaction between the "state of Entropy" in a given UF's frame/s (n) and an "increase" in its corresponding "state of Entropy" in any subsequent UF's frame/s (n+1...n+m)?! However, this would entail the existence of a "material-causal" physical relationship/s between the given state of Entropy found within all of the exhaustive spatial pixels of a given Physical System in a particular UF's frame/s and the corresponding state of Entropy (within those exhaustive spatial pixels) found at a subsequent later UF's frame/s?! But, we've already seen that any such "material-causal" physical interaction/s between any two (or more) exhaustive spatial pixels existing either in the same- or other UF's frame/s is negated by the UCP's simultaneous computation of all exhaustive spatial pixels for each consecutive UF's frame/s, and the complete "dissolution" of the whole universe "in-between" any two consecutive UF's frames! Therefore, according to this New "G-d's Physics" Paradigm the Second Law of Thermodynamics is negated – instead, pointing at the "A-Causal Computation" characteristics of the UCP's simultaneous computation of all exhaustive spatial pixels comprising each consecutive UF's frame/s!

Yet another instance in which this New "G-d's Physics" Paradigm completely revises our basic theoretical understanding of the manner in which this singular higher-ordered UCP simultaneously computes all exhaustive spatial pixels in the universe is its principle negation- and rejection- of the Old "Material-Causal" Paradigm's Quantum Mechanical theoretical account of the "collapse" of the subatomic "target's (assumed) probability wave function" – as "caused" by its direct physical interaction with another corresponding subatomic "probe" element; Once again, since this probabilistic interpretation of QM assumes that there exist a direct physical interaction between a given subatomic "probe" element and a corresponding subatomic "target's probability wave function", e.g., which "causes" the "collapse" of the "target's probability wave function" into a singular "complimentary (space/energy, mass/time) value", then this is negated by the New "G-d's Physics" insistence upon the "simultaneity" of the UCP's computation of all exhaustive spatial pixels in the physical universe (for each consecutive UF's frame/s)! Instead, the New "G-d's Physics" Paradigm posits that this singular higher-ordered UCP simultaneous computation of all exhaustive spatial pixels (for each consecutive UF's frame/s) also includes all "*single* spatial-temporal *particle*", "*multiple* spatial-temporal *wave*", and "*exhaustive* spatial-temporal *Frame*" computational measures, and that the apparent "collapse" of the "probability wave function – really represents the UCP's alternate computation of such "*single* spatial-temporal *particle*" or "*multiple* spatial-temporal *wave*" entities embedded within its exhaustive simultaneous computation of all exhaustive spatial pixels comprising the entire physical universe (for each consecutive UF's frame/s)... Additionally, the apparent "collapse" of the "target's probability wave function" into a single "complimentary" (space/energy, mass/time) value – truly represents merely the complimentary computational characteristics of the UCP's computation of each exhaustive spatial pixel's "Frame"- "consistent" ("space") or "inconsistent" ("energy") and "Object" – "consistent" ("mass") or "inconsistent" (time") four basic physical features (as described above and previously).

Indeed, the New "G-d's Physics" theoretical conceptualization of the physical universe – as existing only "transiently" and "phenomenally", as a mere manifestation of the singular higher-ordered "Universal Computational/Consciousness Reality" (UCP) completely revises our basic understanding of the origin- sustenance- and evolution- of every exhaustive spatial pixel in the physical universe as well as its entirety! The universe was not "created" by an initial "Big-Bang" nuclear event, but is rather being continuously simultaneously computed, "dissolved", re-created and "evolved" for each of its constituting exhaustive spatial pixels by this singular higher-ordered UCP! In fact, according to this New "G-d's Physics, the whole conception of the universe's "origination" – so many Billions of times per second, what's "sustaining" and "evolving" every exhaustive spatial pixel within it (as well as the entire cosmos) is only the singular higher-ordered "Universal Consciousness Reality" – which possesses certain intrinsic properties and characteristics, including:

a) The UCP's "Dynamic-Equilibrium" Moral Principle (delineated above).

b) The UCP's "Reversed-Time Goal Hypothesis" – "Geula" Directed Universe! (delineated above)

c) The UCP's "Good-Will" and "Free-Will" Characteristics: As preciously delineated, it is hypothesized that characterizing this singular, higher-ordered UCP are two basic fundamental properties, e.g., the UCP basic "Good-Will" to create "life", sustain and evolved it, to sustain and evolved the universe towards its ultimate "Perfected Geula State" (Morally, Spiritually and even Physically) ; and the complete "Free-Will" of this singular higher-ordered UCP – i.e., "unbound" by any of the apparent "physical laws" that it has organized the physical reality to appear to abide and operate through… Indeed, this complete "Free-Will" and "Good-Will" fundamental characteristics of this singular higher UCP are directly implied from the complete "dissolution" of the entire physical universe between one UF's frame and the subsequent UF's frame, and principle impossibility of the existence of any direct or indirect physical interaction between any two (or more) exhaustive spatial pixels existing either in the same- or different- UF's frames! This means that the UCP Itself is "unbound" by any "material-causal" physical laws – and in fact, that the entire existence- continuity- and evolution- of each and every exhaustive spatial pixel in the universe is only a manifestation of this singular higher-ordered "Good-Will" (and "Free-Will") characterization…

3. Deciphering 21ˢᵗ Century Physics' "Dark-Matter" & "Dark Energy" Enigma

We thus see that some of the most basic fundamental assumptions of the Old "Material-Causal" Physics Paradigm of 20th Century RT & QM are completely challenged, revised and indeed "transcended" through the discovery of the New 21st Century "G-d's Physics" (CUFT) Paradigm! No longer can we regard the universe as being originated by an initial "Big-Bang" nuclear event – since this is based on the Old "Material-Causal" Paradigm's basic assumption wherein it is through the direct physical interaction/s between certain exhaustive spatial pixels (within the universe) that a given physical phenomenon can be explained; Nor can we (any longer) explain the subatomic "complimentary" ("space/energy" or "mass/time") properties of any subatomic "target's" (assumed "probability wave function") as determined by its direct physical interaction/s with another corresponding subatomic "probe" element – which "causes" the "collapse" of the target's (assumed) "probability wave function"; this is (once again) due to the New "G-d's Physics" Paradigm's negation of the very possibility of the existence of any direct (or even indirect) physical interaction between at least two (or more) exhaustive spatial pixels existing either in the same- or different-UF's frame/s, e.g., due to the simultaneity of the UCP's computation of all exhaustive spatial pixels comprising any single UF frame (and the complete "dissolution" of the entire physical universe "in-between" any two consecutive UF's frames); Likewise, the Relativistic conception of the fundamental dynamics determining the evolution of the physical universe – as described by "Einstein's Equations" was also negated, since it is based on the same basic "Material-Causal" assumption wherein it is assumed that it is the direct physical interaction between certain "massive objects" and "Space-Time" which "causes" the "curvature" of "Space-Time", which (in turn) determines (or "causes") the "Travelling-Pathways" of these "massive" and other "less-massive" objects!

But, this means that "G-d's Physics" New Paradigm challenges-negates- and transcends- all of the basic theoretical constructs associated with the Old "Material-Causal" Paradigm – including its principle negation of the (purely hypothetical) existence of "Dark-Matter" and "Dark-Energy", e.g., which is assumed to comprise up to 95% of all of the mass and energy in the physical universe!? This is because, once again, these (purely hypothetical) theoretical constructs) of "Dark-Matter" and "Dark-Energy" are based on the fundamental "Material-Causal" assumption, i.e., assuming that it is the direct physical interaction/s between these "Dark-Matter" and "Dark-Energy" (hypothetical) entities and the various galaxies, stars etc. which "causes" these various components of the physical universe to be "expunged" or "propelled" in such a manner which increases the entire physical universe's "accelerated rate of expansion"… But, as we've already seen, due to "G-d's Physics" New Paradigm's insistence upon the UCP's "simultaneous" computation of all exhaustive spatial pixels in the universe (for each consecutive UF's frame/s), and the complete "dissolution" of the entire physical universe "in-between" any two consecutive UF's frame/s, therefore there cannot exist any such direct (or even indirect) physical interaction/s between any such (purely hypothetical) "Dark-Matter" and "Dark-Energy" and any other single/multiple exhaustive spatial pixel/s in the universe, hence negating the very existence of "Dark-Matter" or "Dark-Energy", i.c., as "causing" the accelerated expansion of the physical universe!

Nevertheless, 21st Century Theoretical Physics New "G-d's Physics" Paradigm 20th must provide an alternative (satisfactory) theoretical explanation for the "true nature" of the previously hypothesized "Dark-Matter" and "Dark-Energy" purely hypothetical constructs; Indeed, akin to Einstein's "discarding" of the (purely hypothetical) "Ether" concept assumed by Newtonian Physics to pervade the entire physical universe – which has led to discovery of 20th Century Physics' (then) "New Paradigm" of Relativity Theory, the New 21st Century "G-d's Physics" Paradigm replaces the (purely hypothetical) "Dark-Matter" and "Dark-Energy" concepts with the discovery of the singular higher-ordered Universal Computational/Consciousness Principle (or Universal Consciousness Reality); Based on the unravelling of the singular, higher-ordered UCP (UCR), which continuously (and simultaneously) computes- "dissolves"- re-computes and evolves- every exhaustive spatial pixel in the universe, e.g., for each consecutive UF's frame at the "unfathomable" rate of "c^2/h" = 1.36^{-50} sec' (!) the New "G-d's Physics" Paradigm; alongside some of the other key "Theoretical Postulates" (outlined above) such as the "Computational Invariance Principle" and associated "Universal Consciousness Reality", which indicate that only the singular higher-ordered "Universal Consciousness Reality" (UCR) that exists both "during" its sole computation of every exhaustive spatial pixel's four basic physical features (of "space" and "energy", or of "mass" and "time") and also solely exists (without the "presence" of any physical universe "in-between" any two consecutive UF's frames) – indicating that only this singular higher-ordered UCR may considered as "real", "continuous" and "constant" (e.g., "computationally-invariant"), whereas the existence of the entire physical universe may only be deemed as a "transient-phenomenal" manifestation of this singular

"Universal Consciousness Reality"; The New "G-d's Physics" Paradigm reveals the real origin- ("dissolution"-) sustenance- and evolution- of each exhaustive spatial pixel in the universe, as well as of the accelerated expansion of the entire physical universe – as solely produced by this singular higher-ordered UCP/UCR! Indeed, when we begin realizing that the whole existence- "dissolution"- re-computation- and evolution- of every exhaustive spatial pixel in the universe is solely dictated and governed by this singular higher-ordered UCR, and that in fact the entire physical universe does not exist as an "objective-independent" "material reality", but rather represents a "transient-phenomenal" manifestation of this singular, higher-ordered UCR; the real sole and singular "unchanging" UCR – which manifests within the physical universe "during" each consecutive UF's frame, and solely remains (without the physical universe) "in-between" any two consecutive UF's frames is being realized!

Indeed, several previously published articles pointed at "G-d's Physics" New Paradigm's realization of the fact that the whole entire physical universe is nothing but a manifestation of this singular higher-ordered UCR – e.g., that the entire physical universe (with all of its multifarious physical phenomena and exhaustive spatial pixels) does not exist as an "independent (objective) reality", but is rather only a "transient-phenomenal manifestation" of this singular higher UCR! Hence, even the "tiniest" apparent "material components" of the physical universe (including all subatomic particles, components etc. as indicated by the "Standard Model") merely represent "transient-phenomenal" computations (e.g., manifestations) of the singular, higher-ordered UCR! None of the subatomic rudimentary particles and sub-particles etc. exists as an "objective-independent reality" – in fact their only "transient-phenomenal" existence is completely dependent upon- produced- "dissolved"- "re-produced- and evolved- solely by this singular higher-ordered UCR, so that we may state that none of these subatomic elements "exists" as a "real-independent" entity (or "reality"), but rather only represents a "transient-phenomenal" manifestation of this sole and singular UCR! This implies that the whole physical universe – i.e., from its "tiniest" subatomic particles, or entities to its largest "relativistic" phenomenon of the accelerated expansion of the universe can (no longer) be regarded as originating- existing or evolving based on mere physical or material (direct or indirect) interactions, but is rather solely dependent upon the singular higher-ordered UCR: its characteristics, features and basic "driving" tendencies! Indeed, since it was indicated that this singular higher-ordered UCR's manifestation of the entire physical universe is "driven" towards its "Ultimate-Goal" of a "Perfected State" (termed in the Jewish Tradition: "Geula")- "Morally", "Spiritually" and even "Physically" (e.g., with the possible abolishment of "death") based on the "UCR's Reversed-Time Goal Hypothesis", therefore the New "G-d's Physics" 21st Century Paradigm points at the existence of a "New Atom" – i.e., comprising the continuous (and incessant) computation carried out by this singular higher-ordered UCP/UCR of every exhaustive spatial pixel in the universe, and "Purposeful Universe" – e.g., a universe that has been originated- "dissolved- recomputed and evolved from its very conception solely towards the manifestation of ever more "expansive" manifestations of "Consciousness" (from the basic "inanimate" forms through "animate": "plants", "animals" and "Human-Beings" – leading up to the "expanded form of Human Consciousness" which is "inseparable" from the UCR) and ultimately towards the UCR's "Ultimate Goal" of "Geula": a "Perfected" Spiritual, Moral and Physical State of the universe, in which the singularity of the UCR as comprising and manifesting throughout the whole universe in all of these inanimate, animate" plants, animals and Human-Beings forms, highlighting its basic fundamental "Good-Will", "Peace", "Harmony" and "Goodness" features...

Indeed, viewed from such a high and profound new "G-d's Physics" Paradigm's theoretical perspective, the "enigma" of the "true nature" of "Dark-Matter" and "Dark-Energy" is deciphered: according to this New "G-d's Physics" Paradigm the true nature of "Dark-Matter" and "Dark-Energy" does not comprise any detectable "material" entity, but rather comprises this singular higher-ordered UCR's incessant and continuous "drive" towards Its Ultimate "Geula" State, which manifests though its accelerated addition of the number of exhaustive spatial pixels comprising each consecutive UF's frame/s – specifically at such special "Collective Human Consciousness Focus" times as the Jewish "Rosh Hashana" (New Year) interval, in which Millions of Jews collectively focus on this "Universal Consciousness Reality" ("G-d"!); which brings about a "non-continuous" increase in the UCR's accelerated expansion of the universe (e.g., a "non-continuous" increase in the UCR's accelerated increase in the number of additional exhaustive spatial pixels to each consecutive UF's frame/s!) Hence, one of several unique "G-d's Physics" New Paradigm's "Critical Predictions" – which has been called for (multiple times!) is the measurement of a "Non-Continuous Accelerated Expansion" of the physical universe at the Jewish "Rosh-Hashana" special time interval, which was predicted to increase the universe's accelerated rate of expansion beginning at each Jewish "Rosh-Hashanna" New Year!

4.   A Call for Validating "G-d's Physics" New 21st Century Paradigm's "Critical Predictions"!

Indeed, "G-d's Physics" New Paradigm's discovery of the "true nature" of "Dark-Matter" and "Dark-Energy" – not as comprising any "material" entity, but as representing the continuous (simultaneous) computation of the UCP simultaneously of every exhaustive spatial pixel in the universe (for each consecutive UF's frame); And specifically, of the UCP's accelerated addition of the number of exhaustive spatial pixels comprising each such consecutive UF's frame/s – which undergoes a "Non-Continuous Acceleration" at each Jewish New Year ("Rosh-Hashana"), e.g., due to "G-d's Physics" postulated "Collective Human Consciousness Focus" (as delineated previously) – constitutes one of several unique "Critical Predictions" differentiating this New "G-d's Physics" Paradigm from the (corresponding) predictions of the Old "Material-Causal" Paradigm;

a)   "G-d's Physics" Critical Prediction: The "Universe's Non-Continuous Accelerated Expansion During Rosh-Hashana" (Jewish New Year) (UNCAE-RH):

As stated above (and delineated previously), according to "G-d's Physics" New Paradigm's "Collective Human Consciousness Focus Hypothesis" whenever there is a "Collective Human

Consciousness Focus" upon the singular higher-ordered "Universal Computational/Consciousness Principle" (UCP) – i.e., such as predicted during the "Jewish New Year's ("Rosh-Hashana") two-day special time-interval in which Millions of Jews from around the world focus single-mindedly and pray (intensely) to this singular higher-ordered UCP ("G-d"!), then this may bring about a "Non-Continuous Accelerated Expansion of the Universe"! This means, that during this "special time" of the Jewish "Rosh-Hashana", "G-d's Physics" predicts that there will be a "non-continuous" significant increase in the universe's observed accelerated rate of expansion, i.e., relative the accelerated rate of the universe's expansion measured prior to the (specific) Rosh-Hashana time-interval (which is predicted to continue at the same "new increased accelerated rate" throughout the new Jewish Year)! It is important to note that there has been a repeated call for all Cosmologists and Astronomers – consistently (now) for the past three years during "Jewish-New Year: Rosh-Hashana" to empirically test this unique "Critical Prediction" of the New "G-d's Physics" – but to date, no such empirical measurement has been carried out?! As stated in one of the last articles published, Science's sole "Mandate" – as Humanity's designated "vehicle" for "discovering Truth" is to advance Humanity's knowledge and understanding of the physical reality (and beyond) based on the fundamental "Scientific Method", e.g., initially laid out by Descartes and subsequently crystalized through Thomas Kuhn's famous analysis if "The Structure of Scientific Revolutions" (1962); That is, to advance the Scientific knowledge within a given Scientific discipline based on the collection of "objective-empirical" data and associated acceptable "logical inference" methodology in order to validate a given "Scientific Standard Paradigm" – which has been proven to best "fit" and "explain" this given plethora of empirical data and phenomena etc. However, when Science (subsequently) reaches the "limitations" of any such "Standard Paradigm" (within a given Scientific discipline), i.e., manifest in the appearance of basic "theoretical inconsistencies" within the pillars of that given "Standard Paradigm", and additionally there exists a series of "unexplained" empirical phenomena or data – that cannot be adequately explained (or accounted for) by that "Standard Paradigm"; then Kuhn states that Science must undergo a fundamental "Paradigmatic-Shift" from the "Old Standard Paradigm" to a "New Paradigm", which is shown capable of resolving these apparent "theoretical inconsistencies" and can also adequately explain these "unexplained empirical phenomena"!

Well, 21st Century Theoretical Physics has reached such a "pivotal point" along its "historic" development – of an urgent need for a fundamental "Paradigmatic-Shift" from the Old "Material-Causal" Paradigm of 20th Century's Relativity Theory and Quantum Mechanics to the New "G-d's Physics" Paradigm! And the only manner in which (according to Kuhn's famous and widely accepted analysis) is based on its empirical validation of such unique "Critical Predictions" differentiating this New "G-d's Physics" Paradigm from the corresponding predictions of either Relativity Theory or Quantum Mechanics, e.g., which could not account for this "G-d's Physics" predicted "Universe's Accelerated Non-Continuous Expansion During 'Rosh-Hashana'"! Therefore, for Science to "retain" and "justify" it's "stature" as Humanity's designated "vehicle" for exploring and discovering the "true" nature of the physical universe (and of Humanity's special "role" within it) – it must (expediently) carry out these necessary empirical measurements validating this unique "Critical Prediction" of the New "G-d's Physics", as well as all other (below delineated) unique "Critical Predictions"!

b) "G-d's Physics" Critical Prediction: "Disappearance of the Physical Universe "In-Between" Any Two Consecutive "Universal Frames"!?

Another (rather) "surprising" and "fascinating" unique "Critical Prediction" of "G-d's New Paradigm regards the "disappearance" of the physical Universe "in-between" any two consecutive "Universal Frames"!? This is because according to this New "G-d's Physics" Paradigm, the UCP simultaneously computes all exhaustive spatial pixels comprising the entire physical universe for each consecutive "Universal Frame" (UF) – whereas "in-between" any two consecutive UF's frames, the entire physical universe "dissolves" back into the singularity of this higher-ordered UCP!? This means that if we were to measure the existence of any given subatomic particle (such as the "electron" or "Muon" particles) "in-between" any two consecutive UF's frames, we would "fail" to detect them at the "minimal temporal gap" "in-between" any two consecutive UF's frames!? Since according to the New "G-d's Physics" Paradigm, the rate at which this singular higher-ordered UCP (simultaneously) computes the extremely rapid series of UF's frames is given through "G-d's Physics" New Paradigm's discovered "Universal Computational Formula" (mentioned above) as "c^2/h" = 1.36^{-50} sec'! Therefore, another unique "Critical Prediction" of "G-d's Physics" New Paradigm is that "in-between" any two consecutive UF's frames, e.g., computed at the unfathomable extremely rapid rate of "c^2/h" = 1.36^{-50} sec', the measurement of any given subatomic particle (such as the "electron" or "Muon") would fail to detect them – whereas "during" each consecutive UF's frame/s these* (or any other) subatomic particle/s could be easily detected or measured!

c) "G-d's Physics" Critical Prediction: Greater Number of Universal Frames (UF's) Detecting The Presence of "More Massive" Particles than for "Less Massive" Particles!

*In fact, due to "G-d's Physics" New Paradigm's unique new computational definitions of the four basic physical features of "space" and "energy", "mass" and "time" – as representing different UCP's computations of "Frame"- "consistent" or "inconsistent", or "Object" – "consistent" or "inconsistent" values for each of the exhaustive spatial pixels comprising any subsequent UF's frame/s; another closely associated "Critical

Prediction" of the New "G-d's Physics" Paradigm predicts that there will be a greater number of UF's frames at which a relatively "More Massive" particle (e.g., such as the "Muon") would be detected, then at which a "Less Massive" particle (such as the "electron")!? This is specifically due to the UCP's computational definition of "mass" as the number of times in which any given "object" is presented "consistently" across a given series of UF's frames – which implies that a relatively "More Massive" particle such as the "Muon" would necessarily be measured across a greater number of UF's frames, than a relatively "less massive" particle such as the "electron"!?

Taken together, these two recent "Critical Predictions" of the New "G-d's Physics" Paradigm predict that when we measure (and compare) the presence of a relatively "More Massive" Muon particle to that of the "Less Massive" electron particle (through the "Fine-Temporal Measurements of a Subatomic Accelerator), we would find that:

1) There will be a greater number of UF's frames at which the "More Massive" Muon particle would be detected than at which the "Less Massive" electron particle would be detected!;

2) That for both of these Muon and electron particles – and in fact pertaining to any other subatomic particle/s, these subatomic particles could NOT be detected "in-between" any two subsequent UF's frames (e.g., due to the "dissolution" or disappearance" of the entire physical universe "in-between" any two consecutive UF's frames back into the singularity of the UCP!)

5.   Theoretical Implications: True Nature of "Dark-Matter" & "Dark-Energy"!

We thus reach the culmination of our quest to discover (and "unravel") the "True Nature" of "Dark-Matter" and "Dark-Energy"; Twenty-first

Century Theoretical Physics is undergoing a basic "Paradigmatic-Shift" from the Old "Material-Causal" Paradigm underlying Relativity Theory and Quantum Mechanics to the New "G-d's Physics" Paradigm! This is due to the "Paradigmatic-Crisis" characterizing the "fissures" and "theoretical inconsistencies" found between these two "pillars" of the Old (20th Century) "Material-Causal" Paradigm (as characterized by Kuhn's famous analysis of the "Structure of scientific Revolutions", as stated above) – leading up to the identification- and ultimate empirical validation- of particular "Critical Predictions" differentiating this New "G-d's Physics" Paradigm from the Old "Material-Causal" Paradigm! Indeed, the empirical validation of any one of the three "Critical Predictions" specified in this article (and previously called for – for three consecutive years, without any Astronomer or Cosmologist taking on to carry out an empirical validation of the "Universe's Non-Continuous Accelerated Expansion During Rosh-Hashana"!) is necessary and in fact "critical" for Science retaining and "justifying" its sole "mandate" to advance Humanity's "objective-quest" to discover the "True Nature of the universe and physical reality...

Based on the theoretical discovery of Twenty-first Century Theoretical Physics' New "G-d's Physics" Paradigm – which negated the possibility of the existence of any direct (or even indirect) physical interactions between any two (or more) exhaustive spatial pixels existing either in the same- or different- UF's frame/s, the basic "Material-Causal" assumption of the Old Paradigm underlying both Relativity Theory and Quantum Mechanics has been negated and rejected! Hence, it was shown that since the singular higher-ordered UCP simultaneously computes all exhaustive spatial pixels in the universe (for each consecutive UF's frame/s) therefore the physical universe may have not been originated or "caused" by an initial "nuclear event", nor is it "propelled" by the direct physical interactions between certain "massive objects" and their "curvature" of "Space-Time" (and conversely the determination of such "massive"/"non-massive" objects based on this stipulated "curvature of Space-Time"), e.g., as assumed by General Relativity's "Einstein's Equations"! Likewise, the Old "Material-Causal" assumption underlying Quantum Mechanics – i.e., wherein the determination of any subatomic "target's complimentary" (space-energy or mass-time) values is assumed to result from the direct physical interaction of the subatomic target's assumed "probability wave function" with a corresponding subatomic "probe" element which "causes" the "collapse" of this hypothetical "target's probability wave function" into a single "complimentary" ("space/energy" or "mass/time") value has been negated and rejected by the New "G-d's Physics" Paradigm.

Instead, the New "G-d's Physics" Paradigm stipulates that the singular higher-ordered UCP simultaneously computes all of the universe's exhaustive spatial pixels for each consecutive Universal Frame – e.g., giving rise to the four basic physical features of each of these exhaustive spatial pixels (across a series of UF's frames); Significantly, this New "G-d's Physics" has been shown capable of resolving the apparent "theoretical inconsistency" that seems to exist between Relativity Theory and Quantum Mechanics, e.g., through its discovery of the UCP's "single spatial-temporal *particle*", multiple "spatial-temporal *wave*" computational measures – which are embedded within the UCP's simultaneous computation of all exhaustive spatial pixels comprising any single or multiple UF's frames! Moreover, this New "G-d's Physics" Paradigm was shown to "replicate" or account for all major "Relativistic" or "Quantum" phenomena – and more significantly also offer a satisfactory alternative explanation for the "unexplained" phenomenon of the accelerated expansion of the physical universe, and decipher the "true nature" of "Dark-Matter" and "Dark-Energy"! Simply stated, in the same manner that this New "G-d's Physics" Paradigm has rejected and negated all of the Old "Material-Causal" assumed theoretical constructs assuming that there exists direct physical interaction/s between any two (or more) exhaustive spatial pixels (e.g., including the above mentioned "Big-Bang" Model, Einstein's Equations' "Material-Causal" assumption, Quantum Mechanics' "probabilistic interpretation" etc.) – so does this New "G-d's Physics" Paradigm negate the existence of "Dark-Matter" or "Dark-Energy" as a "real" "material entity"!? Indeed, in much the same manner in which Einstein discarded 19th Century Physics' ("purely hypothetical") "Ether" concept as "superfluous", i.e., "non-existent" – since it could not be detected empirically (despite numerus attempts to do so), so does the New "G-d's Physics" Paradigm, so does the New "G-d's Physics" Paradigm negate the existence of a "Dark-Matter" or "Dark-Energy", e.g., as any "material" element which "causes" the accelerated expansion of the physical universe (also due to the failure of Physics to directly detect or measure the existence of any such "purely hypothetical" "Dark-Matter" or "Dark-Energy" despite numerous failed attempts).

Instead, the New "G-d's Physics" Paradigm offers a new alternative (and exciting) theoretical explanation of the "true nature" of "Dark-Matter" or "Dark-Energy": Succinctly stated, that would relate to- or point at- the operation of the singular higher-ordered "Universal Consciousness Reality" (UCR) which simultaneously computes every exhaustive spatial pixel in the universe at the incredible rate of "c^2/h" = 1.36^{-50} sec'!) The empirically observed accelerated rate of the universe's expansion – is not due to any "material" substance such as "dark-matter" (or "dark-energy") but is rather the result of the singular higher-ordered "Universal Consciousness Reality's" (UCR) accelerated addition of the number of exhaustive spatial pixels comprising each consecutive UF's frame/s! More specifically, this UCR's (or UCP's) accelerated addition of the number of additional exhaustive spatial pixels (e.g., added to each subsequent UF's frame/s) is stipulated to be connected with the Jewish New Year's ("Rosh-Hashana") "special time interval" – based on "G-d's Physics" additional "Collective Human Consciousness Focus Hypothesis" (CHCFH); According to this new "Collective Human Consciousness Focus Hypothesis" (CHCFH) whenever there is a focus of a significant multitude of Individual Human Consciousness upon this singular higher-ordered UCR (UCP) this brings about a significant "non-continuous" increase in the UCR's rate of accelerated expansion of the physical universe! Therefore, it was predicted that at every consecutive Jewish New Year ("Rosh-Hashana") there will be a detectable "non-continuous" increase in the universe's recorded "Accelerated Rate of Expansion"! To the extent that this unique "Critical Prediction" of the New "G-d's Physics" Paradigm will be validated empirically, then this will unequivocally lead to the recognition of this New "G-d's Physics" as the New 21st Century Scientific Paradigm (e.g., as the fulfillment of this unique prediction cannot be explained or accounted for by either of the Old "Material-Causal" Paradigm's Relativity Theory or Quantum Mechanics Models)!

Indeed, some of the far reaching (and exciting) theoretical ramifications of this New "G-d's Physics" Paradigm of 21st Century Theoretical Physics is associated with the unravelling of the "true nature" of "Dark-Matter" or "Dark-Energy" which is the UCR's "driving" of the entire physical universe towards its Ultimate Goal" of the (Physically, Morally and Spiritually) "Perfected" "Geula State" (e.g., previously delineated); According to this new stipulated "G-d's Physics" "UCR's Reversed-Time Goal Hypothesis", the UCR possesses an "Ultimate Goal" of bringing our own world (and the entire physical universe) to a "Morally", "Spiritually" and even "Physically" "Perfected" State of "Geula" – i.e., a state in which this singular, higher-ordered, "unitary" UCR will be recognized (and experienced) by all Individual Human Consciousness (human-beings) which means that Humanity will recognize the singularity and unity of all creation, its complete and sole dependence upon the operation and sole existence of this singular higher-ordered UCR; subsequently, there could not exist any (acceptable) manifestations of "Immoral Actions" of one Individual Human Consciousness against another Individual Human Consciousness – e.g., based on the UCP/UCR's (earlier discovered and above mentioned) "Moral Dynamic-Equilibrium" Principle (which "balances" and "corrects" any such "Immoral Balance"); This "Perfected Geula State" will also be characterized by Humanity's recognition, gratitude and collective focus upon this singular higher-ordered UCR – being recognized for its "Goodwill", "Free-Will" Striving towards such a Perfected "Geula" State... (It may also be characterized by the "Perfection" of even the "Physical" existence – with the possible "Abolishment of Death" based on Science's and Humanity's higher-understanding of the true nature of "Time" (including the viable possibility of "time-reversal") and it's "Inseparability" from this singular, all exhaustive UCR!) So, it seems that the acceptance of this New "G-d's Physics" Paradigm of 21st Century Physics may indeed bring about the beginning of this Ultimate "Geula State" – with Science's acceptance of the singularity of the UCR's origination, sustenance, and Ultimate "Geula" Goal of this singular higher ordered UCR!

Dedication: This article is dedicated to my beloved wife, Shulamit and my sons: Shoham and Nethanel and daughter Neomy Tirza

Shulamit, may each one of them he bring Light to this World in their unique special way. Amen!

6.   References

Bentwich, J. (2012a) "Harmonizing Quantum Mechanics and Relativity Theory". *Theoretical Concepts of Quantum Mechanics*, Intech (ISBN 979-953-307-377-3), Chapter 22, pp. 515-550.

Bentwich, J. (2012b) "Theoretical Validation of the Computational Unified Field Theory". *Theoretical Concepts of Quantum Mechanics*, (ISBN 979-953-307-3773), Chapter 23, pp. 551-598.

Bentwich, J. (2013b). "The Theoretical Ramifications of the Computational Unified Field Theory". *Advances in Quantum Mechanics* (ISBN 978-953-51-1089-7), Chapter 28, pp. 671-882.

Bentwich, J. (2013c). The Computational Unified Field Theory (CUFT): A Candidate Theory of Everything. *Advances in Quantum Mechanics* (ISBN 978-953-51-1089-7) Chapter 18, pp. 395-436.

Bentwich, J. (2015). The Computational Unified Field Theory (CUFT): A Candidate 'Theory of Everything'. *Selected Topics in Application of Quantum Mechanics* (ISBN 978-953-51-2126-8) Chapter 6.

Bentwich, J. (2014) *What if Einstein was Right? Amazon Kindle Book Store.*

Bentwich, J. (2015). On the Geometry of Space, Time, Energy, and Mass: Empirical Validation of the Computational Unified Field Theory. *Unified Field Mechanics: Natural Science Beyond the Veil of Spacetime (Proceedings of VIGIER IX Conference, Morgan State University, USA, 16-19 November 2014).*

Bentwich, J. (2016) The 'Computational Unified Field Theory': A Paradigmatic Shift. *Research & Reviews: Journal of Pure & Applied Physics.*

Bentwich, J. (2017a) The Computational Unified Field Theory: Could 'Dark Matter' & 'Dark Energy' be "Superfluous"? *SciFed Journal of Quantum Physics Special Issue.*

Bentwich, J. (2017b) The Computational Unified Field Theory: Explaining the Universe from "Without". *SciFed Journal of Quantum Physics Special Issue.*

Bentwich, J. (2017c). The Computational Unified Field Theory: A New 'A-Causal Computation' Physics. *SciFed Journal of Quantum Physics Special Issue.*

Bentwich, J. (2017d). The 'Computational Unified Field Theory' (CUFT) May Challenge the 'Big-Bang Theory'. *SciFed Journal of Quantum Physics Special Issue.*

Bentwich, J. (2017e). Can the 'Computational Unified Field Theory' (CUFT) Challenge the Basic Laws of Conservation? *SciFed Journal of Quantum Physics Special Issue.*

Bentwich, J. (2017f). The Computational Unified Field Theory (CUFT): Time "Reversal" May be Possible. *SciFed Journal of Quantum Physics Special Issue.*

Bentwich, J. (2017g). The Computational Unified Field Theory (CUFT) Transcends Relativity's Speed of Light Constraint. *SciFed Journal of Quantum Physics, Special Issue.*

Bentwich, J. (2017h). The Computational Unified Field Theory's New Physics: Transcending Space, Time and Causality. *SciFed Journal of Quantum Physics Special Issue.*

Bentwich, J. (2017i). A "Supra-Spatial-Temporal Universal Consciousness Reality'. *Research & Reviews: Journal of Pure & Applied Physics, Special Issue: The Computational Unified Field Theory (CUFT)-A Paradigmatic Shift in 21st Century Physics.*

Bentwich, J. (2017j). A New Science: An Infinite Omniscient Dynamic-Equilibrium Universal Consciousness Reality. *SciFed Journal of Quantum Physics Special Issue.*

Bentwich, J. (2017k). The Computational Unified Field Theory (CUFT) Challenges Darwin's 'Natural Selection Principle'! *SciFed Journal of Quantum Physics Special Issue.*

Bentwich, J. (2017l). The Computational Unified Field Theory (CUFT) Challenges the Second Law of Thermodynamics. *SciFed Journal of Quantum Physics Special Issue.*

Bentwich, J. (2017m). The Computational Unified Field Theory (CUFT): An Empirical & Mathematical Validation of the 'Computational Unified Field Theory'; *SciFed Journal of Quantum Physics Special Issue.*

Bentwich, J. (2017n). The Computational Unified Field Theory (CUFT) New Science; *SciFed Journal of Quantum Physics Special Issue.*

Bentwich, J. (2018a). Review: The Computational Unified Field Theory (CUFT) New Universe: *The Global Journal of Science Frontier Research, Vol. 18 (8-A), Special Issue.*

Bentwich, J. (2018b). The Computational Unified Field Theory (CUFT): What is "Time"? *The Global Journal of Science Frontier Research, Vol. 18 (8-A), Special Issue.*

Bentwich, J. (2018c). The Universal Consciousness Reality's Camouflage: The Physical Universe! *The Global Journal of Science Frontier Research, Vol. 18 (8-A), Special Issue.*

Bentwich, J. (2018d). The Computational Unified Field Theory (CUFT) Epilogue: Can Human Consciousness Affect the Cosmos? *The Global Journal of Science Frontier Research, Vol. 18 (8-A), Special Issue.*

Bentwich, J. (2018e). Testing the Computational Unified Field Theory's (CUFT) Differential-Critical Predictions: The Higgs-Boson Particle May Not Exist Continuously! *The Global Journal of Science Frontier Research, Vol. 18 (8-A), Special Issue.*

Bentwich, J. (2018f). The Double-Faceted Universal Consciousness Reality: A Theoretical Review. *The Global Journal of Science Frontier Research, Vol. 18 (8-A), Special Issue.*

Bentwich, J. (2018g). Letter to the Editor: Dark Matter May Not Exist. *The Global Journal of Science Frontier Research, Vol. 18 (8-A), Special Issue.*

Bentwich, J. (2018h). The Computational Unified Field Theory's (CUFT) Epilogue: Possible Reversal of the Arrow of Time and Abolishment of Death. *The Global Journal of Science Frontier Research, Vol. 18 (8-A), Special Issue.*

Bentwich, J. (2019a). The Computational Unified Field Theory's (CUFT) New Universe. *The Global Journal of Science Frontier Research, Vol. 19 (6), Special Issue.*

Bentwich, J. (2019b). The Computational Unified Field Theory's (CUFT) Goes Beyond the 'Standard Model': "G-d's Physics"?!. *The Global Journal of Science Frontier Research, Vol. 18 (8-A), Special Issue.*

Bentwich, J. (2019c). A Call for Cosmologists & Experimental Physicists: Empirical Validation of the 'Computational Unified Field Theory' (CUFT) New Paradigm through "Time-Sensitive" Astronomical and Subatomic Measurements. *The Global Journal of Science Frontier Research, Vol. 19 (6), Special Issue.*

Bentwich, J. (2019d). The 'Computational Unified Field Theory' (CUFT): Redefining Mass, Gravity & the Physical Universe. *The Global Journal of Science Frontier Research, Vol. 19 (6), Special Issue.*

Bentwich, J. (2019d). Astronomical Validation of the Computational Unified Field Theory (CUFT) "Critical Prediction" & Resolution of the "Universe's Accelerated Expansion Rate Enigma" (UAERE).*The Global Journal of Science Frontier Research, Vol. 19 (6), Special Issue.*

Bentwich, J. (2019e) Urgent Call for Empirical Validation of the Computational Unified Field Theory's (CUFT) New 21st Century 'A-Causal Computation' (ACC) Paradigm. *Acta Scientific Applied Physics, Volume 1(1).*

Bentovish (Bentwich) J. (2020a) **'G-d's Physics'**. In Press. *iUniverse Publication.*

ב"ה

"G-d's Physics" New 21ˢᵗ Century Paradigm: A Complete Integration of "Space" & "Energy", "Mass" & "Time"!

Jehonathan Bentovish, Ph.D.

Note: Dr. Bentovish is seeking scientific collaboration and validation of this New CUFT's 'G-d's Physics' Paradigm's empirical "critical predictions" involving precise Astronomical /Cosmological Measurements as well as time-sensitive Accelerators validations.

Dr. Bentovish (Bentwich) e-mail is: drbentwich@gmail.com.

1. Introduction: 20ᵗʰ Century's Physics Old "Material-Causal" Paradigmatic Crisis

"No better destiny can be allotted to any Physical Theory than that it becomes a "Special-Case" in a broader theoretical understanding!" – is Einstein's famous reply to a question posed to him over 100 years ago regarding the "fate" of his Relativity Theory, i.e. would it "prevail" as the governing Theory in Physics?! Indeed, the great Einstein (considered as one of two greatest scientists the world has ever known!) was "humble" enough to admit (and even "foresee") the future evolution of Physics (and Science, more generally) – as leading to the inevitable further "expansion" of our Scientific understanding, which would (somehow) include his Relativity Theory (and subsequent Quantum Mechanics) as "Special-Cases" within a broader, more exhaustive New Theoretical Understanding! Einstein himself was "bold" enough to "question" and indeed "challenge" the former acceptable "Classical-Mechanics" Newtonian Paradigm (and subsequent Maxwellian Electromagnetic Theory) – discarding the "purely hypothetical" "Ether" concept which was assumed to pervade the entire physical universe, but could not yet be detected despite numerous attempts to do so (e.g., including

the famous "Michelson-Morley" experiment that failed to detect the existence of this "purely hypothetical" Ether element)! Einstein realized then- and indeed called for- discarding this "Ether" concept as "superfluous" (i.e., "non-existent") and went on to develop his General Theory of Relativity – which included the former "Newtonian Classical Mechanics" as a "Special-Case"!

We currently stand, it seems, at an "equivalent critical-juncture" along the inevitable evolution of Science, wherein the Old "Material-Causal" Paradigm of 20th Century Physics underlying both Relativity Theory (RT) and Quantum Mechanics (QM) seems to have reached a "parallel" fundamental "Paradigmatic-Crisis" calling for a similar (higher) "Paradigmatic-Shift" towards the New 21st Century "G-d's Physics", e.g., also called: the "Computational Unified Field Theory", CUFT, named after Einstein's "bold" quest to find such a "Unified Field Theory" that would resolve the apparent "contradiction" between these two pillars of 20th Century Physics (RT & QM)! This is because as described by the famous philosopher of Science, Thomas Kuhn, the evolution of any scientific discipline can be characterized through an alteration between phases which he termed as "Standard Science", in which the scientific inquiry is based on the assumptions of a given "Standard Paradigm", and phases of a "Paradigmatic-Shift" – in which the basic assumptions underlying the Old "Standard Paradigm" do not suffice (any longer) to explain a series of new phenomena, as well as due to the appearance of basic "theoretical inconsistencies" in the very foundations of that Old Paradigm! This seems to precisely characterize the state of 20th Century's Old "Material-Causal" Paradigm, in which there exists key unexplained phenomena such as the empirically observed accelerated expansion of the physical universe – which cannot be accounted for, except through the "purely hypothetical" existence of "dark-matter" and "dark-energy" which are assumed to account for up to 95% of all the mass and energy in the universe, but yet cannot be detected directly experimentally (despite numerous attempts to do so, alike the "Ether" concept)!? Indeed, alike Einstein's discarding of the "Ether" concept as "superfluous" (due to the inability to detect it experimentally), the New "G-d's Physics" (CUFT) Paradigm also stipulated those "purely hypothetical" "dark-matter" and "dark-energy" are "superfluous" (i.e., "non-existent"!) Additionally, the apparent basic "theoretical inconsistency" that seems to exist between Relativity Theory and Quantum Mechanics, e.g., due to RT's insistence upon a strict "Speed of Light Barrier" for the transmission of any signal across space and time, as opposed to QM's discovery of the "Quantum-Entanglement" phenomenon which indicates that the subatomic measurement of one "entangled-particle" instantaneously" determines the "complimentary-properties" of the other "entangled-particle", e.g., wherein these two "entangled-particles" are separated by a distance greater than can be traversed by a light signal! Indeed, according to Kuhn's fine analysis of the "Structure of Scientific Revolutions" (1962), this "impossible state" of 21st Century Physics clearly calls for a "Paradigmatic-Shift" from the Old "Material-Causal" Paradigm of 20th Century's RT & QM towards the New "G-d's Physics" (CUFT) Paradigm – provided that this New "G-d's Physics" (CUFT) Paradigm can resolve these apparent "theoretical inconsistencies" that seem to exist between RT & QM, satisfactorily offer an alternative explanation for the otherwise "unexplained" accelerated expansion of the physical universe (based on its discarding of those "dark-matter", "dark-energy" purely "hypothetical" concepts as "superfluous"!); and most importantly, provide at least one unique "Critical Prediction" that differentiates this New "G-d's Physics" Paradigm from the corresponding predictions of the Old "Material-Causal" 20th Century Paradigm of both RT & QM!

Indeed, in over forty scientific peer-reviewed articles and Textbooks, this New "G-d's Physics" (CUFT) Paradigm was shown capable of resolving this apparent "theoretical inconsistency" that seem to exist between RT & QM, e.g., based on it's (surprising) discovery of a singular higher-ordered "Universal Computational/Consciousness Principle" (UCP) – which simultaneously computes every exhaustive spatial pixel in the universe at the incredible rate of "c^2/h" = 1.36^{-50} sec', giving rise to an extremely rapid series of "Universal Frames" (depicting the entire physical universe at every such "minimal time-point" UF's frame/s)... Moreover, this New "G-d's Physics" Paradigm was also shown capable of replicating all major Relativistic and Quantum phenomena and laws, and also offered an alternative new theoretical explanation for the empirically observed accelerated expansion of the physical universe: In a nutshell, this new alternative explanation for the universe's observed accelerated expansion rate is explained through this singular higher-ordered "Universal Computational/Consciousness Principle" (UCP) accelerated addition of the number of exhaustive spatial comprising each consecutive UF's frame/s! In fact, this hypothetical new explanation of the accelerated expansion of the entire physical universe – also provided (with another additional "Collective Human Consciousness Focus Hypothesis" at the Jewish "Rosh-Hashana" New Year special "time-interval) one of the unique "Critical-Predictions" of this New "G-d's Physics" Paradigm, which was called for the immediate empirical validation of all Cosmologists and Astronomers! So far, unfortunately, no Cosmologist or Astronomer has reported carrying out this extremely important empirical validation of the New "G-d's Physics" Paradigm for 21st Century Physics!? It is indeed important to mention it is precisely those "bold" attempts of individual Experimental Physicists – to validate the "Critical Prediction/s" of any New Scientific Paradigm – like Eddington's famous "bold" expedition to measure (and indeed validate) Einstein's new "Critical Prediction" regarding the increased value of Mercury's Perihelion curvature – that "crowned" Relativity Theory as the New Paradigm for 20th Century Physics (replacing and embedding the Old Newtonian Paradigm as a "Special-Case" within its broader Theoretical Model)! Indeed, it is therefore of critical importance that such new "bold" Experimental Physicists, Astronomers, Cosmologists similarly attempt to verify one of multiple unique "Critical Predictions" of this New "G-d's Physics" (previously delineated), including the "Non-Continuous Accelerated Expansion of the Universe" at the Jewish "Rosh-Hashana" special (Collective-Human Consciousness Focus) time interval, as well as an empirical verification of the greater number of "Fine-Temporal Measurements" (FTM) instances in which a relatively "more-massive" subatomic particle (such as the "Muon" particle) would be measured relative to the number of instances that a relatively "less-massive" particle (such as an electron) would be measured (e.g., across the same given time-interval). Such empirical validations of either of these unique "Critical Predictions" of the New "G-d's Physics" Paradigm would similarly "crown" this New "G-d's Physics" Paradigm as the New appropriate Paradigm for 21st Century Theoretical Physics!

2. The New 21ˢᵗ Century "G-d's Physics" (CUFT) Paradigm

Since the aim of the current article is to highlight one of the amazing new discoveries of this New "G-d's Physics" Paradigm – i.e., regarding the complete unification of the four basic physical features of the entire physical universe of "space" and "energy", "mass" and "time"; it is first important to just outline the gist and basic theoretical postulates of the New "G-d's Physics" Paradigm: One of the primary discoveries made by "G-d's Physics" is the existence of a singular higher-ordered "Universal Computational/Consciousness Principle" (UCP) which simultaneously computes every exhaustive spatial pixel in the universe at the incredible rate of "c^2/h" = 1.35^{-50} sec'(!), which produces an extremely rapid rate of "Universal Frames" (comprising all of the spatial pixels in the universe at every such "minimal time-point")… "In-between" every two consecutive UF's frames the entire universe (and all of its comprising exhaustive spatial pixels) "dissolve" back into the singularity of the UCP! The simultaneity of the UCP's computation of all exhaustive spatial pixels in the universe (for each consecutive Universal Frame, UF) brought about the realization that "G-d's Physics" portrays a New "A-Causal Computational" Paradigm – i.e., which negates the very possibility of any "material-causal" direct physical interaction between any two (or more) exhaustive spatial pixels existing either in the same- or other UF's frame/s!? This is because since this singular (higher-ordered) UCP simultaneously computes all of the exhaustive spatial pixels in the universe there cannot exist any direct physical interaction/s between any two (or more) exhaustive spatial pixels existing in the same UF's frame; Moreover, since the entire physical universe "dissolves" "in-between" any two consecutive UF's frames back into the singularity of the UCP, there cannot be any transference of any "material" or "physical" entity (or "effect") across any two consecutive UF's frame/s!

In addition, the New "G-d's Physics" Paradigm posits that this singular (higher-ordered) UCP possesses three "Computational Dimensions", e.g., "Framework" (frame/object), "Consistency" (consistent/inconsistent) and "Locus" (global/local) – two out of which (Framework and Consistency) are responsible for the UCP's computation of the four basic physical features of "space", "time, "energy" and "mass"! Essentially, the New "G-d's Physics" Paradigm postulates that the UCP computes for each exhaustive spatial pixel in the universe (simultaneously) either it's "Object" – "consistent" ("mass") or "inconsistent" (time") values or its "Frame" – "consistent" ("space") or "inconsistent" ("energy") values based on the UCP's computation of the degree of "consistency" or "inconsistency" in a given object across a given series of UF's frames, or the degree of "consistency" or "inconsistency" of that object – relative to the entire "Universal Frame" (coordinates), once again, across a series of UF's frames! Indeed, since the UCP simultaneously computes both the "Object"-"consistent"/"inconsistent" and the "Frame"-"consistent"/"inconsistent" physical features (for each exhaustive spatial pixel in the universe for each consecutive UF's frames), this has led to the discovery of a singular "Universal Computational Formula" describing the UCP's (extremely rapid) computation of all of these (four) basic physical features (of "space and "energy", "mass" and "time") in an integrated manner (as further described below); Interestingly, "G-d's Physics" New Paradigm not only discovered the existence of this singular higher-ordered UCP which simultaneously computes all exhaustive spatial pixels in the universe (e.g., for each exhaustive spatial pixel at each consecutive UF's frame/s) – but also pointed at the existence of all "past", "present" and (multiple possible) "future/s" UF's frames within the UCP's "Multi Spatial-Temporal Reservoir"! Surprisingly, according to this New "G-d's Physics" Paradigm, the "selection" of which of multiple possible UF's frames would be computed by the UCP – i.e., at each given presentation of the "present" UF frame is determined by the "moral-choice" of each individual Human-Being (at any given point in time), based on the discovery of a novel "Dynamic-Equilibrium" Moral Principle (characterizing this singular higher-ordered UCP), which seeks to "balance" (or "correct") any "moral-imbalance" created by an "immoral act" executed by one "Individual Human Consciousness towards another Human-Being (as will be further delineated below);

3. "G-d's Physics" New "Universal Computational Formula"!

In order to fully appreciate "G-d's Physics" New 21st Century breakthrough in Theoretical Physics – and specifically it's complete unification of these four basic physical features of "space" and "energy", "mass" and "time" (which is the highlight of this article), we first need to understand the basic principle difference between the Old "Material-Causal" Paradigm of 20th Century Physics – underlying both Relativity Theory (RT) and Quantum Mechanics (QM): The basic assumption underlying both RT & QM is the Old (20th Century) Paradigm's "Material-Causal" Assumption; Basically, this "Material-Causal" Assumption posits that any physical phenomenon can be explained simply based on a finite series of direct physical interactions between a given set of material elements! In this manner, RT sought to explain the origin- and evolution- of the entire physical cosmos based on the direct physical interaction/s of given series of "massive" objects and their "causal" effect of curving (the "fabric" of) "Space-Time", or conversely explain the whole existence and dynamics of the subatomic reality based on the direct physical interactions between a subatomic "probe" and corresponding subatomic "target's probability wave function – which "causes" the "collapse" of that subatomic target's (assumed) "probability wave function "elements; But, based on the "G-d's Physics" New 21st Century Paradigm's discovery of the singular higher-ordered Universal Computational/Consciousness Principle (UCP) posited to **simultaneously compute** every exhaustive spatial pixel in the universe, e.g., for each consecutive Universal Frame/s (UF's), then this "Material-Causal" basic assumption is strictly negated! This is because this simultaneous UCP computation of all exhaustive spatial pixels in the universe for each consecutive UF's frame/s prohibits and negates the very possibility of the existence of any such direct physical interaction/s between any two (or more) exhaustive spatial pixels existing either in the same- or different UF's frame/s! Moreover, since the whole physical universe is posited to "dissolve" "in-between" any two such consecutive UF's frame/s, therefore there cannot also exist any direct "physical interaction" or even any "transference" of any "material" or "physical" element/s "across" any two consecutive UF's frame/s!

Therefore, the New "G-d's Physics" Paradigm (of 21st Century Physics) completely negates the basic "Material-Causal" assumption underlying both RT & QM - instead calling for a fundamental revision of our basic understanding of the origin- nature- dynamics- and evolution- of the entire physical cosmos! Nevertheless, it is important to note that the New "G-d's Physics" Paradigm does not negate the key phenomena described either by RT or QM – but rather explains them in a completely different manner, based on its much broader and more exhaustive theoretical understanding: Perhaps the best "starting-point" to describe the principle difference between this New "G-d's Physics" Paradigm and the Old "Material-Causal" paradigm (underlying both RT & QM) is by delineating "G-d's Physics" novel (and profound) analysis of the four basic physical features of "space", "energy", "mass" and "time": Unlike either RT or QM in which these four basic physical features are conceptualized as existing "separately" or "independently" of each other – albeit there exist certain "inter-relationships" (e.g., such as the unification of "space" and "time" as a four dimensional "Space-Time" continuum) or even certain "equivalences" (e.g., such as Relativity's famous "Energy-Mass Equivalence"), the New "G-d's Physics" Paradigm's "computational definitions" of each of those four basic physical features – as computed by a singular (higher-ordered) "Universal Computational/Consciousness Principle" (UCP) and its associated (novel) "Universal Computational Formula" (UCF) completely integrates these four basic physical features as comprising integral and in fact "inseparable" secondary computational by-products of this singular UCP's computation (and creation) of a series of Universal Frames!

In a nutshell, the New "G-d's Physics" Paradigm postulates that these four basic physical features of "space" and "energy" or "mass" and "time" are computed simultaneously by the singular (higher-ordered) Universal Computational/Consciousness Principle (UCP) – for each exhaustive spatial pixels, comprising the (extremely rapid, e.g., "c^2/h"= 1.36^{-50} sec'!) series of Universal Frames (UF's) portraying the entire physical universe (at each such minimal "time-point"); This extremely rapid computation of the UCP of each consecutive UF's frames' exhaustive spatial pixels' four physical features (of "space" and "energy", "time" or mass") is associated with the UCP's three "Computational Dimensions" – specifically with two of them, namely: "Framework" ('frame' vs. 'object') and "Consistency" ('consistent' vs. 'inconsistent'); This is because the UCP's computation of any exhaustive spatial pixel's "frame"- "consistent" or "inconsistent" measures (across a series of UF's frames) produces that spatial pixel's "space" and "energy" values! And likewise, the UCP's computation of any given exhaustive spatial pixel's "object" – "consistent" or "inconsistent" computational measures (across a series of UF's frames) provides that pixel's "mass" and "time" values! It is obviously quite "stunning" or indeed almost "inconceivable" to fathom the complexity and "infinitude" of the UCP's "Intelligence" – capable of simultaneously computing each of the almost infinite exhaustive spatial pixels comprising the entire physical universe for each consecutive UF's frame/s; and for each of these exhaustive spatial pixels the UCP has to compute the degree of that spatial pixel's "degree of change" ("inconsistent") or "degree of lack of change" ("consistent") – both at the "object" level, i.e., the number of times that that given object is presented "consistently" across a series of UF's frames (regardless of its "location" relative to the coordinates of the entire UF's Frame/s)… What's perhaps even more profound is this New "G-d's Physics" Paradigm's realization that the UCP's simultaneous computation of each exhaustive spatial pixels' four basic physical features of "space" and "energy", or "mass' and "time" – as the UCP's computation of any given spatial pixel's "frame" – consistent or "inconsistent", or "object"- "consistent" or "inconsistent" measures points at the complete integration of these four basic physical features as "secondary computational measures" of the same (singular) UCP's simultaneous computation!

We can begin noticing this UCP's complete integration of these four basic physical features – simply based on their "complimentary" computational characterizations: since (once again) the computational definitions of the UCP's computation of an "object's" – "consistent" vs. "inconsistent" measures of "energy" and "space", or of an object's "frame" – "consistent" or "inconsistent" measures as its "mass" and "time" values; this means that the UCP's computation of each of these "complimentary" computational measures of "frame"- "consistent" (space) or "inconsistent" (energy) values implies that these "complimentary computational" ("frame"- or "object"-) measures does not exist "independently" of each other, but rather represents complimentary-integrated secondary computational measures of the same UCP's singular integrated computation! Likewise, the UCP's singular-integrated computation of any given "object's" – "consistent" ("mass") or "inconsistent" ("time") computational measures must also be completely integrated as the UCP's simultaneous computation of any such given "object's" – "consistent" ("mass") or "inconsistent" ("time") computational measures represent "complimentary-interdependent" stemming from the UCP's singular simultaneous computation of that given "object's" degree of "change" ("inconsistent": "mass") or "lack of change" ("consistent": "time")! It may be said that these UCP's simultaneous singular-integrated computation/s of any given "object's" – "consistent" ("mass") or "inconsistent" ("time"), or of any given object's "frame" – "consistent" ("space") or "inconsistent" ("energy") values may be likened to the "measurement" of a given "cup's" – "half full" or "half-empty" properties which are "interdependent" and really represent "complimentary measures" of the same "cup's liquid-filled reality"!?

In fact, as shown previously, the UCP's "singular-integrated" computation of each of these "object" – "consistent" ("mass") or "inconsistent" ("time"), or "frame" – "consistent" ("space") or "inconsistent" ("time") measures is seen as also being "interdependent" or represent different "secondary computational integrated measures" of the same UCP singular simultaneous "Framework" ("object"/"frame") & "Consistency" ("consistent" or "inconsistent") Computational Dimensions' integrated computation! As shown previously, this lead to the discovery of the singular fully integrated UCP's "Universal Computational Formula" (UCF) which portrays the profound (and elegant) full integration of the UCP's simultaneous computation of these four basic physical features

Universal Computational Formula (UCF):

$$\left\{ \frac{\text{`}c^2}{h} \right\} = \frac{s \ * \ e}{t \ * \ m}$$

wherein the singular higher-ordered UCP – represented by the Hebrew letter "Yud" ("י") simultaneously computes all exhaustive spatial pixels in the universe comprising each consecutive Universal Frame/s (UF's) which already exist in a "potential-from" within the UCP's "Supra Spatial-Temporal Reservoir" of all "past", "present" and multiple possible "future/s" UF's (represented by the Hebrew letters from "א through "מ" to "ת")" depending on the Moral Choice of each Individual Human Consciousness – as computing and integrating these four basic physical features of "space" and "energy", "mass" and "time", at the incredible rate of: "c^2/h" = 1.36^{-50} sec'! as can be seen from this "Univresal Computational Formula" (UCF), the UCP simultaneously computes an integrated and combined interrelationships between these two "Object-consistent (mass)/inconsistent (time) and Frame-consistent (space) / inconsistent (energy) computational pairs! As previously delineated, this complete integration between the four basic physical features of "space", "energy", "mass" and "time" – as secondary integrated computational properties of the UCP's singular (higher-ordered) computation stems from the fact that each of these four secondary computational physical features represents a particular facet of the same singular integrated UCP's computation represented by this Universal Computational Formula! Thus, for instance, we can notice that the UCP's computation of an "object's" – number of "consistent" ("mass") presentations necessarily increases, as a function of that object's (UCP's computation of) its "frame-inconsistent" ("energy") value! This is simply due to the fact that the greater the value of a given object's "frame-inconsistent" ("energy") computed by the UCP, e.g., which implies that the UCP computes a greater degree of "displacement" (relative to the entire UF's frame) across a series of such UF's frames; this necessarily entails that that "object-consistent" ("mass") value has to also increase (due the maximal stipulated displacement of any given object across two consecutive UF's frames!)

So, we find that, for instance, the close "interdependency" between the UCP's computation of any given object's "frame-inconsistent" ("energy") value and its computed "object-consistent" ("mass") value stems from the fact that the UCP simultaneous computation of each exhaustive spatial pixel comprises a singular-integrated process carried out by its three (and specifically two) "Computational-Dimensions", e.g., of "Framework" ("frame" or "object") and "Consistency" ("consistent" or "inconsistent")! Likewise, we find that the "special-case" of Relativity's dilation of "time" ("object-inconsistent") as a function of an increase in "mass" (object-consistent), simply due to the fact that these two "object-"consistent" ("mass") and "inconsistent" ("time") UCP's computations represent "complimentary" aspects of the same object's consistency, e.g., alike measuring the "complimentary" properties of a glass filled with a certain portion of water: if we increase that cup's ("half-full") water portion – we necessarily decrease its "half-empty" portion (and vice versa)! In the same manner, once we realize that the UCP's singular-integrated computation of any given object's "object-consistent"" "mass" value, we necessarily decrease it's "object-inconsistent": "time" value – hence "G-d's Physics" New Twenty-first Century Paradigm's elegant explanation of Relativity's discovered "dilation of time" for "massive" objects; and likewise for high-energy relativistic objects (which as shown above, is simply derived from the close "interrelationship" between an object's "frame-inconsistent" ("energy") UCP's computation and its integrated computation of that object's "object-consistent" ("mass") value!

In fact, we surprisingly find that this New "G-d's Physics" Paradigm likewise offers a new simple (and elegant) explanation that fully integrates Heisenberg's "Uncertainty-Principle's" "complimentary-pairs" of "space" ("frame-consistent") and "energy" ("frame-inconsistent"), or "mass" ("object-consistent") and "time" ("object-inconsistent") values – as constrained by Planck's constant! This is because, unlike the "Material-Causal" assumption underlying "Heisenberg's Uncertainty Principle's" Quantum Mechanical explanation for the apparent "inter-dependency" between the subatomic measurement of any given "target" element – e.g., of its "time" and "mass" value, or between its "space" and "energy" values (as mutually constrained by Planck's constant, i.e., wherein any increase in the subatomic measurement accuracy level for any one of these "complimentary-pairs" would inevitably lead to a "proportionate" decrease in the subatomic accuracy level of the other pair's component); which explains this "Uncertain Principle's" mutual-accuracy level constraint – as "caused" by the direct physical interaction between the subatomic "probe" element's and its corresponding subatomic "target's" "complimentary-pairs property", so that an increase in the "probe's" accuracy of one of these two complimentary-pairs property (e.g., such as an increased accuracy measurement of the probe's "spatial localization") – would inevitably "cause" a proportionate "decrease" in the corresponding target's complimentary-pair's other property (e.g., the target's "energy" value); Unlike this "Material-Causal" QM's explanation of Heisenberg's "Uncertainty Principle", the New "G-d's Physics" "A-Causal Computation" Paradigm posits that these subatomic "complimentary-pairs" interdependency arises – not as "Caused" by any direct physical interactions between the subatomic "probe" and "target" elements, but rather stems from the singular-integrated computation of the "Universal Computational/Consciousness Principle" (UCP): Specifically, from the "complimentary-exhaustive" computation of the UCP's two (out of three) Computational-Dimensions' "(mentioned above and previously) "Frame" – "consistent" ("space") and "inconsistent" ("energy"), or "Object" – "consistent" ("mass") and "inconsistent" ("time") computational combinations! In other words, in the same manner that when we look at (or even measure) the physical properties of a "half-full", "half-empty" cup of water, we cannot measure at the same time both the 'half-full' and 'half-empty' physical properties of the cup – but rather we can only focus on one of these "complimentary" physical properties; in the same manner, when we "focus" in a photograph – either on a given "object", or on its "setting", but not on both simultaneously (and in fact the greater the "focus" given to that given "object"- the more "diffuse" is the perception of its surrounding "setting"!); Likewise, it is suggested that these UCP's two "exhaustive-computational pairs" of either the object's "Frame"- "consistent" ("space") and "inconsistent" ("energy") computational measures, or of the (object's) "Object" – "consistent" ("mass") and "inconsistent" ("time") computational measures jointly and exhaustively define that object's given physical properties; e.g., so that when we increase our "focus" or "measurement accuracy" of a given subatomic "target's" – say "spatial" ("Frame-consistent") "space" localization measurement, we necessarily decrease that subatomic "target's" "energy" ("Frame-inconsistent") measurement accuracy! Simply because these two

Object- "consistent"/"inconsistent" computational measurements "exhaustively" define its "Object" Consistency (e.g., consistent/inconsistent) across a given series of UF's frames! (And likewise, the subatomic target's two "Object-consistent" "mass" and "Object-inconsistent" "time" computational measures exhaustively define it's "Object-Consistency" physical properties across a given series of UF's frames!)

Thus, the discovery of "G-d's Physics" New "Universal Computational Formula" brought about an entirely new conception and understanding of the complete unification and integration of the four basic physical properties of "space" ("Frame-consistent") and "energy" ("Frame-inconsistent"), or "mass" ("Object-inconsistent") and "time" ("Object-inconsistent") physical properties; not as existing "separately" or "independently" of each other, yet possessing certain physical "interrelationships"; But, rather as representing "secondary computational" features of the same integrated (singular higher-ordered) UCP which simultaneously computes all of these four possible combinations pertaining to any given object's "Frame" (consistent/inconsistent) or "Object" (consistent/inconsistent) physical features! Indeed, this completely new way of looking at- and understanding- the nature of the physical universe as being continuously computed- "dissolved" re-computed- and evolved- by this singular higher-ordered UCP entirely alters our basic theoretical understanding of the origin- nature- and evolution- of the physical universe... The four basic physical properties of "space" and "energy", "mas" and "time" cease to exist as "independent" physical properties, but are rather seen as integrated "exhaustive-complimentary" computations of the singular (higher-ordered) UCP simultaneous computation of every exhaustive spatial pixel in the entire universe (e.g., at the incredible rate of "c^2/h" – 1.36^{-50} sec'!) Moreover, this new "Universal Computational Formula" (UCF) also portrays the apparently "different" (and even "contradictory") properties of Relativity Theory (RT) and Quantum Mechanics (QM) as representing different aspects of the same integrated (simultaneous) computation of the singular higher-ordered UCP! As indicated above, this is clearly seen in the two Computational Formats" of the same "Universal Computational Formula" (UCF) – in which certain (key) features of both RT – such as the "Energy-Mass Equivalence", and QM's Heisenberg's "Uncertainty Principle's" can be seen as "special" (limiting) cases within the UCF's Relativistic or Quantum Formats! Indeed, alongside the empirical validation of this New "G-d's Physics" 21st Century Paradigm – e.g., based on it's unique "Critical Predictions" pertaining to the "Non-Continuous Accelerated Expansion of the Universe" on the Jewish New-Year ("Rosh-Hashana") (due to "G-d's Physics" postulated "Collective Human Consciousness Focus Hypothesis), and its predicted greater number of "Fine-Temporal-Measurements" (FTM) of relatively "more massive" subatomic particles (such as the "Muon") in comparison to the corresponding number of FTM of a relatively "less massive" particle (such as the electron) which would establish this New "G-d's Physics" Paradigm as the New satisfactory 21st Century Paradigm; in parallel to the necessary empirical validation of this New "G-d's Physics" Paradigm – which was called for multiple times but unfortunately experimental physicists have failed to test this unique "Critical Predictions" – as "bold" Eddington did 101 years ago, which allowed for Relativity Theory to be "crowned" as the New Paradigm for 20th century Physics (alongside QM at the subatomic level); there would need to be further scientific exploration of this novel discovered "Universal Computational Formula" – in terms of its broader theoretical conceptualization – within which RT's and QM's key "Energy-Mass Equivalence" and QM's Heisenberg's "Uncertainty Principle" exist as "special-cases" (e.g., as clearly envisioned by the great Einstein himself!)

4. "G-d's Physics" "Moral" Purposeful "Reverse-Time" Goal-Oriented Cosmos!

As "amazing" as this New "G-d's Physics" New 21st Century Physics Paradigm's discovery of the complete unification of the four basic physical features of "space" and "energy", "mass" and "time" (as "exhaustive-complimentary" secondary computational features of the singular higher-ordered UCP!); the profound nature of the "Theoretical Assumptions" of this New "G-d's Physics" Paradigm completely alter our basic understanding of the "origin"- nature- sustenance- "dissolution"- and indeed ultimate "Goal" of the evolution- of the entire cosmos (e.g., at the "unfathomable" rate of "c^2/h" = 1.36^{-50} sec'!) This is because the entire new theoretical framework of this New "G-d's Physics" Paradigm talks about the existence of "Ten Laws of Hierarchical Manifestation" of which the UCP's simultaneous computation of these four basic physical features, e.g., through this newly discovered "Universal Computational Formula" (UCF) – represents only the "lowest" "Law of Manifestation", which is indeed "contingent" and entirely "dependent" upon the other nine higher "Laws of Manifestation"! Thus, for instance, the New "G-d's Physics" Paradigm postulates that the UCP's simultaneous computation of all exhaustive spatial pixels' (in the universe) four basic physical features produces only the "present" Universal Frame (UF) – which is embedded- and indeed completely dependent- upon the UCP's possession of a higher-ordered ("Dynamic-Equilibrium") "Moral-Principle" and the existence of a complete "Multi Spatial-Temporal Reservoir" containing all "past", "present" and "multiple (possible) "future/s" UF's frames! This is because according to the New "G-d's Physics" Paradigm, this singular higher-ordered UCP possesses certain intrinsic propensities such as for instance it's intrinsic "Dynamic-Equilibrium" Moral Principle stemming from several "Computational Invariance Principle", "Universal Consciousness Reality" and "Inseparability Principle" theoretical postulates: According to the "Computational Invariance Principle" – only the "computationally-invariant" UCP, which exists both "during" each consecutive UF's frame's computation of all exhaustive spatial pixels (within each consecutive frame) as well as solely exists "in-between" any two consecutive UF's frames (e.g., without the existence of any physical universe)! Whereas the four basic physical features of the physical universe (described above: of "space" and "energy", "or "mass" and "time") exist only as "computationally-variant": "transient", "phenomenal" "manifestations" of this singular "Universal Consciousness Reality" (UCR or UCP) – because they only exist "during" each consecutive UF's frame/s (as solely computed by this singular higher-ordered UCP) but "dissolve" back into the singularity of the UCP (or UCR) "in-between" any two consecutive UF's frames (in which only this singular UCP exists)! Hence, the "Universal Consciousness Reality" (UCR) posits that there truly exists only one singular unitary "Universal Consciousness Reality" (UCR) which exists consistently and unitarily (without any intrinsic change!) both "during" it's computation of each exhaustive spatial pixel comprising the extremely rapid series of UF's frames, as well as solely exists "in-between" any two consecutive UF's frames, e.g., without the presence of any physical universe! Moreover, this singular unitary "Universal Consciousness Reality" (UCR) is also characterized by an "Inseparability Principle" and associated Moral "Dynamic-Equilibrium" Principle – essentially pointing at the exhaustive and singular composition of all exhaustive spatial pixels in the universe, as well as all Individual Human Consciousness (e.g., individual Human-Beings) as solely comprised from- and "inseparable" parts of this unitary "Universal Consciousness Reality" (UCR) – which manifests as this singular unitary UCR's intrinsic "Dynamic-Equilibrium" Moral Principle that strives to "balance" any "immoral-choice" taken by any Individual Human Consciousness (towards any other "Individual Human Consciousness")!

A "Trampoline-Metaphor" was utilized to demonstrate this intrinsic "Dynamic-Equilibrium" Moral Principle; imagine a "Trampoline-sheath" upon which a solid "metal-bar" is placed, e.g., "connecting" two specific points along this "Trampoline-sheath", and imagine that one of these "trampoline-sheath-points' (representing one Individual Human Consciousness) "chooses to "inflict pain" upon another "trampoline-point" (also representing an Individual Human Consciousness) – which would be represented by one of these points (called the "inflicting-pain" Individual Human Consciousness) "pushing" this "metal-bar" against the "other-point"?! Inevitably, this would lead to that "metal-bar" being pushed ("automatically") against the first "inflicting-pain" Individual Human Consciousness (right?); So, this simple "Trampoline-metaphor" is utilized to demonstrate the UCP's (or UCR's) intrinsic tendency to "balance" and "correct" any "moral-imbalance" created by one Individual Human Consciousness "choosing" to "inflict-pain" upon another "Individual Human Consciousness" – which inevitably leads this singular higher-ordered UCP (or UCR) to produce an "equivalent-situation" in which the "inflicting-pain" Individual Human Consciousness would have to "experience" the same "type" and "degree" of "pain"/"suffering" that it chose to inflict upon the other Individual Human Consciousness, at a subsequent certain UF's frame/s! This implies that the "moral-choices" taken by each Individual Human Consciousness at any given point in time "triggers" the UCP's "correction" process to bring about an equivalent situation that would allow the "inflicting-pain" Individual Human Consciousness to experience that "immoral-act's pain" – and hence "correct" its own Consciousness accordingly, leading (hopefully) to it's own "moral-remorse" and "moral-decision" to not repeat such "immoral actions", e.g., which in the Jewish-Wisdom and Tradition is called "Teshuva"!

So, we find out that according to the New "G-d's Physics" Paradigm of 21st Century Physics, there exist "multiple possible future/s" (stored within the UCP's "Multi Spatial-Temporal Reservoir") – one of which would be "selected" by the UCP based on the "moral/immoral choice/s" of any given Individual Human Consciousness at any given point in time... It is obviously "inconceivable" to even try and imagine (or comprehend) the "infinite complexity" or "Intelligence" required by this singular higher-ordered UCP (or UCR) in order to computed for each consecutive UF's frame/s all of the necessary "moral-corrections" for each of the almost eight Billion Individual Human Consciousness living on our "Earth" Planet – representing one of multifarious possible "future/s" for each such Individual Human Consciousness! Nevertheless, this new conception of the physical universe as representing only a "transient-phenomenal" manifestation of this singular higher-ordered UCP (or UCR) – driven by certain intrinsic "Dynamic-Equilibrium" Moral Principle definitely opens up a completely new and profound understanding of the nature, dynamics and even "ultimate Goal" of this singular Universal Consciousness Reality, i.e., of producing a "Morally-Perfected", "Spiritually-Oriented" Unitary "Geula" ("Redemption") State of the World and Universe! Indeed, one of the most profound new understandings and theoretical postulates of this New "G-d's Physics" Paradigm of 21st Century Physics was termed: the "Reversed-Time Goal Hypothesis" which postulated that this singular unitary UCR computes the (almost) infinite series of UF's frames – including all "past", "present" and "future/s" UF's frames, from the standpoint of its "ultimate future" State of complete "Moral, Spiritual and even Physical Perfection", (e.g., called: "Geula" in Jewish Tradition) – towards all "past", "present" and "future" UF's frames, i.e., so that all of this "infinite" progression of all "past", "present" and "future" UF's frames is directed towards reaching the pre-ordained Goal of the Perfected "Geula" State! Hence, for instance, following "G-d's Physics" principle negation- and rejection- of the Old "Material-Causal" 20th Century Paradigm's assumption whereby the physical universe was created by a "random" "Big-Bang" nuclear event and is gravitating towards an inevitable "dissolution" of all galaxies, suns, etc. (based on the "Second Law of Thermodynamics"), as well as of Darwin's "Natural Selection Principle" evolutionary theory – based on "G-d's Physics" New "A-Causal Computation" Paradigm indicating that there cannot exist any direct physical interaction between any two (or more) exhaustive spatial pixels existing either in the same- or other-UF's frames (thereby principally negating all such "Material-Causal" Models and assumptions etc.); Following this principle negation of the very possibility of the existence of any such "material-causal" physical interactions, the New "G-d's Physics" Paradigm posited that the singular UCR drives the evolution of all "inanimate", "animate": plants, animals and Human Beings – based on this "Reversed-Time Goal Hypothesis" aiming at the appearance of more conscious forms of Physical and Biological complexity – ultimately leading to the appearance of Human-Beings, and ultimately leading to their recognition and acceptance of this singular, higher-ordered Morally, Physically and Spiritually Perfected "Geula" State! In this "Geula" State of Science and Humanity, e.g., with the acceptance of this New "G-d's Physics" 21st Century Paradigm, there is a recognition of the singular and sole existence of the UCR, and its accompanying theoretical understandings of the "Dynamic-Equilibrium" Moral Principle and the important role of Individual Human Consciousness (Human-Beings) "moral-choices" and advancement of the recognition and awareness of this Perfected "Geula State", previously described in length…

5.   References

Bentwich, J. (2012a) "Harmonizing Quantum Mechanics and Relativity Theory". *Theoretical Concepts of Quantum Mechanics*, Intech (ISBN 979-953-307-377-3), Chapter 22, pp. 515-550.

Bentwich, J. (2012b) "Theoretical Validation of the Computational Unified Field Theory". *Theoretical Concepts of Quantum Mechanics*, (ISBN 979-953-307-3773), Chapter 23, pp. 551-598.

Bentwich, J. (2013b). "The Theoretical Ramifications of the Computational Unified Field Theory". *Advances in Quantum Mechanics* (ISBN 978-953-51-1089-7), Chapter 28, pp. 671-882.

Bentwich, J. (2013c). The Computational Unified Field Theory (CUFT): A Candidate Theory of Everything. *Advances in Quantum Mechanics* (ISBN 978-953-51-1089-7) Chapter 18, pp. 395-436.

Bentwich, J. (2015). The Computational Unified Field Theory (CUFT): A Candidate 'Theory of Everything'. *Selected Topics in Application of Quantum Mechanics* (ISBN 978-953-51-2126-8) Chapter 6.

Bentwich, J. (2014) *What if Einstein was Right? Amazon Kindle Book Store.*

Bentwich, J. (2015). On the Geometry of Space, Time, Energy, and Mass: Empirical Validation of the Computational Unified Field Theory. *Unified Field Mechanics: Natural Science Beyond the Veil of Spacetime (Proceedings of VIGIER IX Conference, Morgan State University, USA, 16-19 November 2014).*

Bentwich, J. (2016) The 'Computational Unified Field Theory': A Paradigmatic Shift. *Research & Reviews: Journal of Pure & Applied Physics.*

Bentwich, J. (2017a) The Computational Unified Field Theory: Could 'Dark Matter' & 'Dark Energy' be "Superfluous"? *SciFed Journal of Quantum Physics Special Issue.*

Bentwich, J. (2017b) The Computational Unified Field Theory: Explaining the Universe from "Without". *SciFed Journal of Quantum Physics Special Issue.*

Bentwich, J. (2017c). The Computational Unified Field Theory: A New 'A-Causal Computation' Physics. *SciFed Journal of Quantum Physics Special Issue.*

Bentwich, J. (2017d). The 'Computational Unified Field Theory' (CUFT) May Challenge the 'Big-Bang Theory'. *SciFed Journal of Quantum Physics Special Issue.*

Bentwich, J. (2017e). Can the 'Computational Unified Field Theory' (CUFT) Challenge the Basic Laws of Conservation? *SciFed Journal of Quantum Physics Special Issue.*

Bentwich, J. (2017f). The Computational Unified Field Theory (CUFT): Time "Reversal" May be Possible. *SciFed Journal of Quantum Physics Special Issue.*

Bentwich, J. (2017g). The Computational Unified Field Theory (CUFT) Transcends Relativity's Speed of Light Constraint. *SciFed Journal of Quantum Physics, Special Issue.*

Bentwich, J. (2017h). The Computational Unified Field Theory's New Physics: Transcending Space, Time and Causality. *SciFed Journal of Quantum Physics Special Issue.*

Bentwich, J. (2017i). A "Supra-Spatial-Temporal Universal Consciousness Reality". *Research & Reviews: Journal of Pure & Applied Physics, Special Issue: The Computational Unified Field Theory (CUFT)- A Paradigmatic Shift in 21st Century Physics.*

Bentwich, J. (2017j). A New Science: An Infinite Omniscient Dynamic-Equilibrium Universal Consciousness Reality. *SciFed Journal of Quantum Physics Special Issue.*

Bentwich, J. (2017k). The Computational Unified Field Theory (CUFT) Challenges Darwin's 'Natural Selection Principle'! *SciFed Journal of Quantum Physics Special Issue.*

Bentwich, J. (2017l). The Computational Unified Field Theory (CUFT) Challenges the Second Law of Thermodynamics. *SciFed Journal of Quantum Physics Special Issue.*

Bentwich, J. (2017m). The Computational Unified Field Theory (CUFT): An Empirical & Mathematical Validation of the 'Computational Unified Field Theory'; *SciFed Journal of Quantum Physics Special Issue.*

Bentwich, J. (2017n). The Computational Unified Field Theory (CUFT) New Science; *SciFed Journal of Quantum Physics Special Issue.*

Bentwich, J. (2018a). Review: The Computational Unified Field Theory (CUFT) New Universe: *The Global Journal of Science Frontier Research, Vol. 18 (8-A), Special Issue.*

Bentwich, J. (2018b). The Computational Unified Field Theory (CUFT): What is "Time"? *The Global Journal of Science Frontier Research, Vol. 18 (8-A), Special Issue.*

Bentwich, J. (2018c). The Universal Consciousness Reality's Camouflage: The Physical Universe! *The Global Journal of Science Frontier Research, Vol. 18 (8-A), Special Issue.*

Bentwich, J. (2018d). The Computational Unified Field Theory (CUFT) Epilogue: Can Human Consciousness Affect the Cosmos? *The Global Journal of Science Frontier Research, Vol. 18 (8-A), Special Issue.*

Bentwich, J. (2018e). Testing the Computational Unified Field Theory's (CUFT) Differential-Critical Predictions: The Higgs-Boson Particle May Not Exist Continuously! *The Global Journal of Science Frontier Research, Vol. 18 (8-A), Special Issue.*

Bentwich, J. (2018f). The Double-Faceted Universal Consciousness Reality: A Theoretical Review. *The Global Journal of Science Frontier Research, Vol. 18 (8-A), Special Issue.*

Bentwich, J. (2018g). Letter to the Editor: Dark Matter May Not Exist. *The Global Journal of Science Frontier Research, Vol. 18 (8-A), Special Issue.*

Bentwich, J. (2018h). The Computational Unified Field Theory's (CUFT) Epilogue: Possible Reversal of the Arrow of Time and Abolishment of Death. *The Global Journal of Science Frontier Research, Vol. 18 (8-A), Special Issue.*

Bentwich, J. (2019a). The Computational Unified Field Theory's (CUFT) New Universe. *The Global Journal of Science Frontier Research, Vol. 19 (6), Special Issue.*

Bentwich, J. (2019b). The Computational Unified Field Theory's (CUFT) Goes Beyond the 'Standard Model': "G-d's Physics"?!. *The Global Journal of Science Frontier Research, Vol. 18 (8-A), Special Issue.*

Bentwich, J. (2019c). A Call for Cosmologists & Experimental Physicists: Empirical Validation of the 'Computational Unified Field Theory' (CUFT) New Paradigm through "Time-Sensitive" Astronomical and Subatomic Measurements. *The Global Journal of Science Frontier Research, Vol. 19 (6), Special Issue.*

Bentwich, J. (2019d). The 'Computational Unified Field Theory' (CUFT): Redefining Mass, Gravity & the Physical Universe. *The Global Journal of Science Frontier Research, Vol. 19 (6), Special Issue.*

Bentwich, J. (2019d). Astronomical Validation of the Computational Unified Field Theory (CUFT) "Critical Prediction" & Resolution of the "Universe's Accelerated Expansion Rate Enigma"

(UAERE).*The Global Journal of Science Frontier Research, Vol. 19 (6), Special Issue.*

Bentwich, J. (2019e) Urgent Call for Empirical Validation of the Computational Unified Field Theory's (CUFT) New 21st Century 'A-Causal Computation' (ACC) Paradigm. *Acta Scientific Applied Physics, Volume 1(1).*

Bentovish (Bentwich) J. (2020a) **'G-d's Physics'.** In Press. *iUniverse Publication.*

The New 'G-d's Physics' (CUFT) Twenty-First Century Paradigm: A Morally Perfected ("Geula") Directed New Physical Universe!

Jehonathan Bentovish, Ph.D.

Dr. Bentovish is affiliated with Zefat Academic College, Zefat, Israel.

*Note: Dr. Bentovish is currently seeking the most appropriate leading Academic Institute to assist him in carrying-out further necessary empirical validation and Theoretical elaboration of his New Twenty-first Century New 'G-d's Physics' Paradigm.

Dr. Bentovish (Bentwich) e-mail is: drbentwich@gmail.com.

Abstract:

Twenty-first Theoretical Physics is undergoing a profound "Paradigmatic-Shift" from the Old "Material-Causal" Paradigm underlying both Relativity Theory (RT) and Quantum Mechanics (QM) to the New "G-d's Physics" ("Computational Unified Field Theory", CUFT) Paradigm; Based on the New 'G-d's Physics' Paradigm's discovery of a singular higher-ordered "Universal Computational/ Consciousness Principle" (UCP) which simultaneously computes every exhaustive spatial pixel in the universe at the incredible rate of "c^2/h" = 1.36^{-50} sec' the basic "Material-Causal" assumption underlying both Relativity's "Big-Bang" Model, "Einstein's Equations" and the purely hypothetical "dark-matter" and "dark-energy" concepts, and QM's assumed "collapse" of the subatomic target's "probability wave function" as "caused" by its direct physical interaction with another subatomic "probe" element are negated!

Instead, the UCP's "Ten-Laws of Hierarchical Manifestation" are delineated, including: the "Dynamic-Equilibrium" Moral Principle, which selects one of multiple possible "future/s" for each Individual Human Consciousness based on its "Moral Choice/s"! Indeed, based on several of these Laws, including: the "Computational Invariance Principle" indicating the only "transient", "phenomenal" nature of the entire physical universe which exists only "during" each consecutive "Universal Frame" (UF) solely computed by the singular UCP, but "dissolves" back into the UCP "in-between" any two such consecutive UF's frames; and the UCP's "Good-Will" propensity and its "Reversed-Time Goals Hypothesis" 'G-d's Physics' New Paradigm points at the Ultimate Goal of this UCP, namely: striving towards a Physically, Morally and Spiritually "Perfected" State of the World named: "Geula", indicating a complete "Harmony", "Peace" and a recognition (and gratitude) towards this singular higher-ordered "Unity" and "Good-Will" UCP!

1. Introduction: The New Twenty-First Century 'G-d's Physics Paradigm

Twenty-first century Theoretical Physics has undergone a major "Paradigmatic-Shift" – i.e., from the Old 'Material-Causal' Paradigm underlying Relativity Theory (RT) & Quantum Mechanics (QM) towards the New 'G-d's Physics' ('Computational Unified Field Theory', CUFT) Paradigm which was shown capable of resolving the apparent "theoretical inconsistency" between RT & QM, and also offer an alternative satisfactory explanation for certain key Old 'Material-Causal' unexplained physical phenomena, including: the "dark-matter" and "dark-energy" (purely hypothetical) concepts whose empirical validation failed (thus far) but which is supposed to account for up to 95% of all of the mass and energy in the universe!? As analyzed by Thomas Kuhn in his famous Book "On the Structure of Scientific Revolutions" (1962), Scientific investigation (and progress) within a given field shifts between phases of "Standard Science" in which the scientific inquiry within a given discipline is based on an acceptable "Standard Paradigm" possessing certain assumptions, laws and stipulations, followed by an inevitable "Paradigmatic-Shift" phase in which the Old 'Standard Paradigm' doesn't suffice (any longer) to explain certain key (new) phenomenon, in addition to which there usually arise particular "theoretical inconsistencies" within the very foundations of the Old 'Standard Paradigm'... Indeed, this was the case when Einstein came along (e.g., prior to his 1905 "Annus-Mirabelus" and the 1915 ultimate empirical validation of one of the "critical predictions" of his New "Relativity Theory" Paradigm); The two basic "pillars" of the Old 'Standard Paradigm' of "Newtonian Mechanics" and Maxwell's "Electromagnetic Theory" seemed "contradictory" of each other and a key assumption within Newtonian Mechanics associated with the existence of the "ether" concept (which was supposed to pervade the entire physical universe) could not be found empirically despite numerous attempts to do so!? This called for a "Paradigmatic-Shift" from the Standard Newtonian-Maxwellian Paradigm to 20th century "Relativity Theory" and subsequently also Quantum Mechanics' Paradigm"...

Indeed, we've now reached an equivalent "pivotal-point" along the development of Science, wherein these two "pillars" of 20th century Theoretical Physics seem "contradictory" of each other, and the key empirical phenomenon of the accelerated expansion of the universe – cannot be account for by the purely hypothetical concepts of "dark-matter" and "dark-energy" which are supposed to account for up to 95% of all the mass and energy in the physical universe, but cannot be empirically detected!? Now, as then, the Newly discovered "G-d's Physics" (Computational Unified Field Theory, CUFT) Paradigm is able to resolve this apparent "theoretical inconsistency" between RT & QM, embed the key elements of both Models within a singular "Universal Computational Formula" (UCF), and offer an alternative theoretical account for the accelerated expansion of the physical universe – while "discarding" the purely hypothetical concepts of "dark-matter" and "dark-energy" as "superfluous" (i.e., non-existent)!?

Universal Computational Formula (UCF):

$$\left\{\frac{{}^,c^2}{h}\right\} = \frac{s \ * \ e}{t \ * \ m}$$

As can be glanced from this transformative UCF, Succinctly stated, this New 'G-d's Physics' Paradigm is based on the discovery of a new singular, higher-ordered "Universal Computational/Consciousness Principle" (UCP) which simultaneously computes every exhaustive spatial pixel in the universe at the incredible rate of "c^2/h" = 1.36^{-50} sec'(!), thereby producing a series of "Universal Frames" (UF's) depicting the entire universe (at every such minimal "time-point")! According to this New 'G-d's Physics' (CUFT) Paradigm, the whole entire physical universe "dissolves" back into the singularity of this singular, higher-ordered UCP "in-between" any two consecutive UF's frames…

One of the key differences between this New 'G-d's Physics' (CUFT) Paradigm and the Old 'Material-Causal' Paradigm is its insistence upon the "simultaneity" of the UCP's computation of each exhaustive spatial pixel, e.g., for each consecutive UF's frame/s, which negates the very possibility of the existence of any direct physical interaction/s between any two (or more) exhaustive spatial pixels existing either in the same- or different- UF's frames! This is because, if indeed all exhaustive spatial pixels comprising the entire physical universe are *simultaneously* computed by the (singular, higher-ordered) UCP for each consecutive UF's frame/s then there cannot exist any such direct physical interactions taking place at any (single or multiple) UF's frame/s! Likewise, since according to his New 'G-d's Physics' Paradigm the entire physical universe "dissolves" "in-between" any two consecutive UF's frames, therefore there cannot also exist any such physical interactions, e.g., between any two (or more) exhaustive spatial pixels existing across different UF's frame/s! Nor can there be any "transference" of any "material" entity or effect across any two consecutive UF's frame/s!

This entirely new singular higher-ordered conception of the physical universe as being continuously computed, "dissolved", re-computed and evolved by the singular, higher-ordered UCP has led to the negation- and revision of some of the most basic 'Material-Causal' assumptions underlying both RT & QM: Thus, for instance, RT's assumed 'Big-Bang' nuclear explosion which supposedly "caused" the creation of all suns' galaxies, planets, 'mass' and 'energy' etc. in the universe was challenged and negated by this New 'G-d's Physics (CUFT) Paradigm, due to the principle impossibility of the existence of any such direct physical interaction/s between any two (or more) exhaustive spatial pixels in the first, second, third etc. UF's frames, comprising the 'Big-Bang' Model!? Instead, the New 'G-d's Physics' Paradigm stipulates that for each consecutive UF's frame/s, the singular, higher-ordered UCP simultaneously computes the four basic physical features of 'space' and 'energy', 'mass' and 'time' for each exhaustive spatial pixel comprising the entire physical universe – thereby in effect stating that the origination- "dissolution"- re-creation- and evolution of each exhaustive spatial pixel comprising the entire physical universe is an ongoing, continuous process produced solely by the singular higher-ordered UCP!

Likewise, the New 'G-d's Physics' Paradigm negated the basic 'Material-Causal' assumption underlying General Relativity's "Einstein's Equations", e.g., assuming that it is the direct physical interactions between certain "massive objects" and "Space-Time", which "causes" the "curvature" of this 'Space-Time', and conversely that it is this 'curved Space-time' which "causes" (or determines) the "travelling pathways" of these 'massive objects' (or other less massive objects); This basic Old 'Material-Causal' Paradigm's assumption is being negated and rejected by 'G-d's Physics' New Paradigm's insistence upon the simultaneity of the UCP computation of all exhaustive spatial pixels in the universe (for each consecutive UF's frame/s) and the complete "dissolution" of the entire physical universe "in-between" any two consecutive UF's frames! Therefore, there cannot exist any such direct physical interactions between any two (or more) exhaustive spatial pixels comprising the entire physical universe – hence negating the possibility of certain 'massive objects' "causing" the 'curvature of Space-Time', and conversely of such 'curved Space-Time' "causing" the particular 'travelling pathways' of these 'massive objects' (and other less massive objects)! As a matter of fact, the entire evolution of the physical universe – as originated by a (hypothetical) initial 'Big-Bang' nuclear explosion, subsequently evolved by Einstein's Equations – e.g., including the purely hypothetical "dark-matter" or "dark-energy" entities "causing" the empirically observe accelerated expansion of the universe etc. – is completely negated and rejected by the New 'G-d's Physics' Paradigm's insistence upon the continuous, simultaneous computation of the singular, higher-ordered UCP of each and every exhaustive spatial pixel in the universe for each consecutive UF's frame/s, and the complete "dissolution" of all of these universe's exhaustive spatial pixels "in-between" any two consecutive UF's frame/s!

In much the same manner, the New 'G-d's Physics Paradigm was shown to negate the Old 'Material-Causal' Paradigm's assumption underlying Quantum Mechanics: According to QM 'Material-Causal' assumption, any given subatomic target possesses a "probability wave function" prior to its subatomic measurement brought about through its direct physical interaction with another corresponding subatomic 'probe' element – which then "causes" the "collapse" of this 'probability wave function's multifarious values into a singular (complimentary 'space-energy', 'mass-time') value. But, as we've already seen, since the New 'G-d's Physics' Paradigm postulates that the singular higher-ordered UCP simultaneously computes all exhaustive spatial pixels comprising the entire physical universe (e.g., for each consecutive UF's frame/s), therefore the New 'G-d's Physics' negates the very possibility of any such direct physical interaction between any two such subatomic 'probe' and 'target' elements (i.e., at any single or multiple UF's frames); Likewise, QM's basic assumption regarding the dual nature of any such subatomic 'target' element – which can exist either as a 'particle' or as a 'wave' has been considerably revised by the New 'G-d's Physics' Paradigm based on its discover of the singular higher-ordered UCP; This is because this single, higher-ordered UCP is postulated to simultaneously all "exhaustive" spatial pixels comprising any given consecutive UF's frame – including: all 'single spatial-temporal' "particle" values and 'multiple spatial-temporal' "wave" values, as embedded within the exhaustive computational framework of the consecutive UF's frames (comprising all exhaustive spatial pixels of the entire physical universe for each 'minimal time point').

2. 'G-d's Physics' "Cinematic-Film Metaphor" & "Computational Invariance Principle"

We therefore realize that the New 'G-d's Physics' portrays an entirely new "picture" of the whole physical universe – not as "originated" by an initial nuclear "Big-Bang" explosion, but rather as being continuously computed- "dissolved", re-computed and evolved- by the singular higher-ordered UCP's computation of each and every exhaustive spatial pixel in the universe, e.g., for each consecutive UF's frame (at the incredible rate of "c^2/h" = 1.36^{-50} sec'!) In fact, this New 'G-d's Physics' Paradigm for 21st century Theoretical Physics revises in such a "dramatic" manner all of our previous Relativistic and Quantum Mechanical understanding of the physical universe, therefore in order to better understand how this New 'G-d's Physics' Paradigm offers an alternative explanation for the Old Relativistic and Quantum Mechanical Models (comprising the Old 'Material-Causal' Paradigm), let's quote the previously explicated two key theoretical postulates of this New 'G-d's Physics' Paradigm, namely: the "Cinematic Film Metaphor" and the "Computational Invariance Principle"; The 'Cinematic Film Metaphor' portrays the production of the physical universe through its metaphoric representation based on a standard 'Cinematic-Film' dynamics: in much the same manner in which the rapid presentation of a series of 'film-frames' gives us the "illusion" of a "real-life" scenario, the 'Cinematic-Film Metaphor' teaches us that it is possible for a similar scenario to exist wherein the singular higher-ordered UCP also computes a series of 'Universal Frames' (UF's) that give us the impression (or perception) of a "physical universe" scenario... In fact, this 'Cinematic-Film Metaphor' has been used to explicate the UCP's simultaneous computation of all exhaustive spatial pixels' – four basic physical features of 'space', 'energy', 'mass' and 'time', based on its two (out of three) Computational Dimensions, namely: 'Framework' and 'Consistency'; According to this 'Cinematic-Film Metaphor', in the same manner in which we could measure the "energy" value of say a "jet-plane" "zooming" through the (cinematic) film-screen, based on the computation of the "degree of displacement" of that 'jet-plane' object (relative to the entire screen-frame) across a series of film-frames, so it is suggested that the singular higher-ordered UCP computes the degree of "object-consistency" across a series of frames to determine each object's "energy" value! Indeed, according to 'G-d's Physics' New Paradigm, the four basic physical features which the UCP computes (simultaneously) for each exhaustive spatial pixel/s comprising the entire physical universe are based on the four possible combinations of its two 'Framework' (frame/object) and 'Consistency' ('consistent'/'inconsistent' Dimensions: Thus, 'energy' and 'space' value of (any given object) are computed by the UCP as the degree of that object's displacement relative to the entire "frame", such that "energy" is computed as a "frame-inconsistent" measure, whereas "space" is computed (by the UCP) as "frame-consistent" computational measure! Likewise, the UCP (simultaneously) computes the values of "time" and "mass" as the degree of "object" – "inconsistent" ("time") and "consistent" ("mass") computational measures. Interestingly, this 'Cinematic-Film Metaphor' possesses quite a few (striking) "similarities" (as well as a few distinct "differences") to the UCP's production of the physical universe: Thus, for instance, in the same manner in which all "past", "present" and "future" 'film-frames' are "stored" within the film's entire "dvd's reservoir" of pictures, so "G-d's Physics" (Computational Unified Field Theory) New Paradigm postulates that all "past", "present" and (multiple possible) "future/s" are "stored" within the UCP's "Multi-Spatial-Temporal Reservoir" of all of the universe's "past", "present" and (multiple possible) "future/s"! One "surprising" difference relates to the fact that unlike the 'standard film' in which all of the ("exhaustive") spatial pixels' "objects" comprising each film-frame are presented in the following consecutive UF – whereas due to the UCP's computational measure of the "mass" of any given (relativistic or quantum) object as the number of times that that particular 'object' is presented "identically" (consistently) across a given number of UF's frames! This implies that according to the New 'G-d's Physics' Paradigm, relatively "more massive" objects should be presented across a larger number of UF's frames than a relatively "less-massive" object! In fact, one of the unique "critical predictions" of the New 'G-d's Physics' (CUFT) Paradigm precisely relates to this greater number of times that a relatively 'more massive' object would be presented, relative to a 'less massive' object across a given number of UF's frames!

Next, we turn to 'G-d's Physics' significant additional "Computational Invariance Principle" theoretical postulate, which asserts that only the "computationally-invariant" 'Universal Computational/Consciousness Principle' (UCP)" exists constantly and continuously – both "during" its sole (simultaneous) computation of each exhaustive spatial pixel's four basic physical features (of 'space', 'energy', 'mass' and 'time') in the universe (for each consecutive UF's frame/s), and also solely exists 'in-between' any two consecutive UF's frame/s in-between" any two consecutive UF's frames; whereas the entire physical universe (and all of its constituent exhaustive spatial pixels) exists only "computationally-variant", i.e., only "during" each consecutive UF's frame/s (as solely being computed by this singular, higher-ordered UCP), but "dissolves" back into the singularity of the UCP "in-between" any two consecutive UF's frames! Therefore, asserts the 'Computational Invariance Principle' that only the 'computationally invariant' Universal Computational/Consciousness Principle (UCP) may be regarded as "real" or "constant", whereas the appearance of the entire physical universe (and every exhaustive spatial pixel comprising it) may only be regarded as "transient" and "phenomenal"! In fact, a closely related "Universal Consciousness Reality" (UCR) theoretical postulate suggests that since the entire physical universe (and all of its constituting exhaustive spatial pixels) may only be regarded as a "phenomenal", "transient" manifestation of the singular higher-ordered UCR, and since only this singular Universal Computational/Consciousness Principle (UCP) exists "constantly" and "continuously" ("computationally-invariant"), therefore we must reach the inevitable conclusion wherein there exists only one singular "Universal Consciousness Reality" – which manifests ('transiently' and 'phenomenally') "during" each consecutive UF's frame/s, and exists solely "in-between" any two consecutive UF's frame/s (with the "phenomenal" universe "dissolving" back into the singularity of this "Universal Consciousness Reality" 'in-between' any two such consecutive UF's frames!)

We therefore see that the New 'G-d's Physics' Paradigm brings us to an entirely new conception and understanding of the origination- sustenance- "dissolution"- and re-computation and evolution of each and every exhaustive spatial pixel in the universe; No longer can we regard the physical universe as being created by an initial "Big-Bang" nuclear explosion; nor can we consider the sustenance and evolution of the physical universe as being "caused" by any direct physical interactions between any (two or more) exhaustive spatial pixels – including through any direct physical interaction/s between certain 'massive-objects' and their (assumed) "curvature" of "Space-Time", or through the converse determination of these massive-objects' "travelling-pathways" by the "curvature of Space-Time", as evinced by Einstein's Equations; nor as evolved by the direct physical interaction between (purely hypothetical) "dark-matter" and "dark-energy" entities which are assumed to "expulse" the galaxies apart of each other – "causing" the accelerated expansion of the physical universe… Nor can we regard the subatomic realm as being enacted by the direct physical interactions between given subatomic "probe" and "target's probability wave function" – which "causes" the "collapse" of this "target's probability wave function" into a singular (complimentary) 'space-energy', 'mass-time' value!? Instead, the New 'G-d's Physics' Paradigm teaches us that the entire physical universe is being continuously "created", "dissolved", "re-created" and "evolved" at every minimal time-point at the incredible rate of "c^2/h" = 1.36^{-50} sec'! by the singular higher-ordered 'Universal Computational/Consciousness Reality' – with the entire physical universe "dissolving" back into the singularity of the UCP 'in-between' any two consecutive UF's frames! Indeed, this entirely new conception of the physical universe as representing only a "transient", "phenomenal" manifestation of the singular "Universal Consciousness Reality" which exists uniformly both "during" its sole (simultaneous) computation of each exhaustive spatial pixel for each consecutive UF's frame/s, and also solely exists "in-between" any two consecutive UF's frames – opens up an entirely new understanding (and various possibilities) for Twenty-first century Theoretical Physics!

3. "Multiple Future/s", "Multiple Past/s" & the Moral 'Dynamic-Equilibrium' Principle!

One of the key new understandings that arises from this New 'G-d's Physics' (CUFT) Paradigm is that the entire physical universe – does not exist "independently" of it's constant "origination" (e.g., "dissolution" and re-computation and evolution) by the singular higher-ordered Universal Computational/Consciousness Reality! In fact, as mentioned above, that each and every exhaustive spatial pixel comprising the entire physical universe – may only exist (and be regarded) as a mere "manifestation" of this singular higher-ordered "Universal Consciousness Reality" (UCR)! This is simply because the entire physical universe "dissolves" back into the singularity of the UCP (or UCR) "in-between" any two consecutive UF's frames! Therefore, according to the New 'G-d's Physics (CUFT) Paradigm, the entire series of UF's – of all "past", "present" and multiple possible "future/s" exist in a "potential-form" within one of the UCP's "Ten Laws of Hierarchical Manifestation" (previously delineated) – namely: the "Supra-Spatial-Temporal Reservoir"! Indeed, according to this New 'G-d's Physics' (CUFT) Paradigm, all past- present- and (multiple possible) "future/s" already exist within the UCP's 'Supra-Spatial-Temporal Reservoir', based on another one of the UCP's "Ten Laws of Hierarchical Manifestation", namely: the "Dynamic-Equilibrium" Moral Principle! According to this 'Dynamic-Equilibrium' Moral Principle, the UCP intrinsic "Inseparability Principle" – wherein all Individual Human Consciousness constitute integral "inseparable" parts of this singular unitary UCP (or UCR), and as part of the UCP's "Good-Will" additional Law of Hierarchical Manifestation, this singular UCP (UCR) constantly strives towards a state of Complete Unity and Harmony; this means that whenever any given "Individual Human Consciousness" choses an "Immoral-Choice" (e.g., inflicting "pain" or "suffering" upon another "Individual Human Consciousness", then this automatically set in motion a "correction-process" conducted by the UCP to restore the initial "Unity" and "Harmony" of the UCP, e.g., by inflicting the same degree of "suffering" or "pain" unto that Individual Human Consciousness which inflicted the pain (or suffering) – so that it remorse for its "wrong-doing", and "realize" the Oneness of Humanity with the UCP! Therefore, the "Dynamic-Equilibrium" Moral Principle postulates that the UCP's (or UCR's) computation through its Ten Laws of Hierarchical – leading up to the manifestation of each and every "past", "present" and multiple possible "future/s" is set in such a manner as to "restore Moral balance", to "correct" and "rectify" any "Moral Imbalance" caused by any Moral/Immoral Choice done by any Individual Human Consciousness towards another Individual Human Consciousness!

Previously the "Trampoline Metaphor" has been utilized to illustrate the operation of this 'Dynamic-Equilibrium' Moral Principle: imagine a 'Trampoline' in which a 'Metal-Bar' in placed on its 'Membrane' so that it connects two particular points on this 'Membrane'; if one of these given points (representing a specific Individual Human Consciousness) "decided" to "inflict pain" unto the other 'Individual Human Consciousness point – by pushing this 'Metal-Bar' against that other point (Individual Human Consciousness), then we know that "automatically" that Metal Bar would "bounce back" and "inflict-pain" (to the same degree) unto that Individual Human Consciousness that decided to 'inflict pain' unto the other Individual Human Consciousness... This 'Trampoline Metaphor', therefore portrays the 'UCP's Moral Principle which postulates that at any given moment in time, the UCP has to compute for each of the almost eight Billion Individual Human Consciousness all of its "Moral Choices" throughout their entire life and calculate for each of the Individual Human Consciousness that it interacted with, what "Moral Balance/s" should be made to "rectify", "teach" and "harmonize" each Individual Human Consciousness – whether it be the "inflicting-pain/suffering" Individual Human Consciousness, or the "inflicted/suffering" Individual Human Consciousness!

Thus far, the New 'G-d's Physics' Paradigm postulated based on this 'Dynamic-Equilibrium' Moral Principle, that within the UCP's 'Multi Spatial-Temporal Reservoir' there exists all of the 'past', 'present' and multiple possible "future/s" UF's frames, and that the Moral Choice of each Individual Human Consciousness determines the UCP's Moral-Balancing' selection of one of multiple possible "future/s", in order to "teach" that Individual Human Consciousness whatever "pain"/"suffering" that it inflicted upon another Individual Human

Consciousness. (It should be noted that the UCP's 'Dynamic-Equilibrium' Moral Principle also postulates that also for every good "Moral Choice" of any given Individual Human Consciousness towards any other particular Individual Human Consciousness, the UCP computes and creates an equivalent situation which would allow these two Individual Human Consciousness to experience the same degree of good Moral Choice that the Individual Human Consciousness that initiated the good Moral Choice upon the other Individual Human Consciousness would also have to receive such an equivalent good Moral Choice from the other Individual Human Consciousness that received the "present" or "good/joyful" Moral action!) It is also worthwhile to note that when we consider the Infinite "Intelligence" (and "Goodness") of this singular higher-ordered UCP, which has to consider and compute – for each Individual Human Consciousness (on the planet) all of its past "Moral/Immoral Actions" directed towards particular Individual Consciousness, and select one of multiple possible "futures" for each consecutive UF's frame/s that would satisfy the precise "lesson"/"remuneration" for each of the almost eight Billion Individual Human Consciousness ("paired" with each specific Individual Human Consciousness that either received or delivered to that Individual Human Consciousness "Moral/Immoral Action/s"), this is clearly represents and "unfathomable" Infinite Intelligent/Good UCP (UCR), which also inevitably leads us to a great sense of "awe", "wonder" (and "gratitude")! A new discovery made at this point – is that it may not only be the case that the UCP's "Multi Spatial-Temporal Reservoir" contains only multiple possible "future/s", but also multiple possible "past/s", also entirely depending upon the "Moral Choice" made by each Individual Human Consciousness at any given moment in time – and particularly upon its "remorse" for its past "wrong-doing", asking "forgiveness" for its Immoral act, and a "rectifying moral decision", i.e., not to repeat any such "wrong-doing", what's termed in the Jewish Faith as "Teshuva"! Indeed, since the UCP's intrinsic characteristic (comprising one of its Ten Laws of Hierarchical Manifestation) is its "Good-Will" to bestow Life, Harmony Peace and "Goodness" and its associated "Dynamic-Equilibrium" Moral Principle are all directed towards increasing the "awareness" and "goodness" of all Individual Human Consciousness, therefore it follows that in cases in which any given Individual Human Consciousness makes a Moral Choice of "Teshuva" (i.e., remorse for any 'wrongdoing', asking for forgiveness, and a "good moral decision" not to repeat any such Immoral Choice/s), then this rectifies the UCP's selection – not only of one "good" future (out of multiple possible future/s), but also rectifies that Individual Human Consciousness' related past! This is because for that Individual Human Consciousness' related Moral-Choice/s which are rectified by the new "Teshuva" (remorse, forgiveness and good moral decision not to repeat that particular "wrong-doing") – this "Teshuva" "corrects" and "alters" all those past "immoral action/s" that were related to the particular issue for which that Individual Human Consciousness made "Teshuva"!

In other words, according to the new discovery made in this paper and alongside "G-d's Physics" New Paradigm understanding of the UCP's selection of one of multiple possible "future/s" based on the "Moral/Immoral Choice" of each "Individual Human Consciousness" and the Dynamic Equilibrium Moral Principle, we realize that (in reality) the UCP's higher-ordered 'Supra Spatial-Temporal Reservoir' contains multiple potential "past/s" and multiple potential "future/s" – based upon the "present" selection of each Individual Human Consciousness' Moral Choice at this present "moment"! Strikingly, this is reminiscent of the Jewish famous Maimonides (Doctor, Philosopher and Saint) declaration that for each moment in time a Human Being is supposed to envision the whole world- as found in a "delicate" 'Dynamic-Equilibrium' state – in which one good (moral) action by this Individual Human Consciousness would "tilt" the "scale" of the world towards a "good outcome" or (G-d forbid) towards a "negative outcome"... It is also in line with the Jewish Chassidic recognition that whatever is done by a Human Being effects not only this physical world, but also certain higher realms (e.g., such as the UCP's "Ten Laws of Manifestation")...

4. The UCP's "Reversed-Time Goal Hypothesis": A Morally Perfected "Geula" State!

We therefore reach the culmination point of this New 'G-d's Physics' Paradigm for 21st century Theoretical Physics: we realize that there only exists one singular higher-ordered UCP (or UCR) which continuously creates- "dissolves"- re-creates and evolves every exhaustive spatial pixel in the universe, and that the existence of the entire physical universe may only be regarded as a mere "transient", "phenomenal" "manifestation" of the singular higher-ordered "Universal Computational/Consciousness Principle" (UCP) or "Universal Consciousness Reality" (UCR)! We acknowledge (and realize) that there cannot exist any real "cause" and "effect" direct physical interactions between any (two or more) exhaustive spatial pixels in the universe, since the UCP simultaneously computes all such exhaustive spatial pixels (existing in any single or multiple UF's frames), and that "in-between" any two consecutive UF's frames the entire physical universe "dissolves" back into the singularity of the UCP! Moreover, with 'G-d's Physics' discovery of the UCP's 'Ten Laws of Hierarchical Manifestation', e.g., including the central "Dynamic-Equilibrium" Moral Principle, we realize that (in truth) all "multiple possible past/s", present and "multiple possible future/s" – are determined and computed by the UCP based on each Individual Human Consciousness "Moral-Choice/s" at any given moment in time!

We have to place this new remarkable realization and understanding – within the "wider scope" of 'G-d's Physics' New Paradigm: that is, within 'G-d's Physics' discovery of the "Reversed-Time Goal Hypothesis", which essentially talks about the UCP's striving towards- and computing all (multiple possible) "past/s"- present and (multiple possible) "future/s" from the standpoint of its Ultimate Goal of a Physically, Morally and Spiritually "Perfected" World, called: "Geula" (in the Jewish-Chassidic) Tradition; the key notion is that the UCP's whole creation and "evolution" of the entire physical universe is geared towards- and is being continuously computed based on- the "Ultimate Goal" of "Geula"! Thus, it was previously shown in what manner the entire creation of the whole physical universe was not created by an "accidental" Big-Bang nuclear explosion, but rather has been precisely evolved by the UCP to allow the development and evolution of ever more "refined" and "conscious" forms of "inanimate" matter leading through the appearance of "animate" forms: plants, animals and Human-Beings – leading up to the "expanded" form of Human Consciousness (discussed previously, in which the Individual Human Consciousness identifies itself completely with the Universal Consciousness Reality) and collectively towards the Sate of "Geula": a Physically, Morally and Spiritually Perfected World!

This New 'G-d's Physics' theoretical understanding of the entire physical universe – in terms of its "pre-planned" and "directed" evolution by the singular higher-ordered Universal Consciousness Reality from its envisioned Ultimate "Geula" State towards all (multiple possible) "past/s", "present" and (multiple possible) "future/s" - provides Twenty-first century Theoretical Physics, and Science (and Humanity), more generally with an exciting new opening towards an entirely new ("uplifting") Existence and Prospects: no longer does Science regard the origination and development of the entire physical universe as occurring "by-chance", e.g., as "caused" by an initial random Big-Bang "nuclear explosion", and as "gravitating" towards an inevitable "dissipation" and "extinction" of all Life, galaxies, suns etc. (based on the "Second Law of Thermodynamics")... No longer does the evolution of the various forms of Life on our planet are likewise considered as "caused" by Darwin's "chance-mutations" and "Natural Selection Principle" (as delineated in a previous article): Instead, the New 'G-d's Physics' Paradigm is shown to unify all forces, all phenomena, all of the various aspects of the physical universe – based on the discovery of the singular higher-ordered "Universal Consciousness Reality" (UCR) which simultaneously computes all exhaustive spatial pixels in the universe through its incredible rapid ("c^2/h" = 1.36^{-50} sec'!) series of UF's frames; and the surprising and exciting new discovery realized by this New 'G-d's Physics Paradigm is that this singular UCR – which exists both "during" its simultaneous computation of each exhaustive spatial pixel in the universe comprising the rapid series of consecutive UF's frames, and also solely exists without the presence of any physical universe, evolves the entire physical universe – towards one Ultimate Goal of "Geula": A Physically, Morally and Spiritually "Perfected" State of the World! Therefore, this singular higher-ordered UCR has evolved the physical form of the universe to sustain Life on this planet and to evolve from inanimate "matter" to animate: plants, animals and Human-Beings; to evolve Humanity towards a more refined Moral and Spiritual State of "Geula", in which there will be a complete "awareness", "recognition" and "gratitude" towards the existence of this singular higher-ordered UCR, possessing the ('Ten Law of Hierarchical Manifestation') characteristics of "Good-Will", "Free-Will", the "Dynamic Equilibrium" Moral Principle etc... To bring Science (and Humanity more generally) towards a basic recognition of the "Oneness" and "Inseparability" of every exhaustive spatial pixel with this singular higher-ordered UCR – and therefore (even to a much greater degree) the Moral realization (based on an understanding of the UCP's Dynamic-Equilibrium' Moral Principle) that all Human-Beings are "inseparable" and in fact comprise "integral parts" of this singular higher-ordered UCR, and therefore that we must make good "Moral Choices" towards each other (as this also "selects" a particular single "good/positive" future out of multiple possible future/s for each one of us)! This would lead Science and Humanity towards the "Perfected" State of "Geula" in which this basic knowledge of the "Oneness of all Creation" – as originated and constantly sustained by the singular higher-ordered UCR, would prevail in the World, there would be no "wars" or "Immoral behavior", Peace, Harmony, and a deep sense of appreciation and Gratitude towards this singular "Good-Will" UCR would prevail! This "Perfected Geula" State of the World (e.g., whose initiation may be advanced by this New 'G-d's Physics Paradigm for 21st century Science) perfectly conforms with many of the Jewish Prophets vision and of Maimonides' proclamation that "at that time, the whole World would be occupied with the 'higher knowledge' of that Singular Higher (UCR) Reality: 'G-d'!

5. References

Bentwich, J. (2012a) "Harmonizing Quantum Mechanics and Relativity Theory". *Theoretical Concepts of Quantum Mechanics*, Intech (ISBN 979-953-307-377-3), Chapter 22, pp. 515-550.

Bentwich, J. (2012b) "Theoretical Validation of the Computational Unified Field Theory". *Theoretical Concepts of Quantum Mechanics*, (ISBN 979-953-307-3773), Chapter 23, pp. 551-598.

Bentwich, J. (2013b). "The Theoretical Ramifications of the Computational Unified Field Theory". *Advances in Quantum Mechanics* (ISBN 978-953-51-1089-7), Chapter 28, pp. 671-882.

Bentwich, J. (2013c). The Computational Unified Field Theory (CUFT): A Candidate Theory of Everything. *Advances in Quantum Mechanics* (ISBN 978-953-51-1089-7) Chapter 18, pp. 395-436.

Bentwich, J. (2015). The Computational Unified Field Theory (CUFT): A Candidate 'Theory of Everything'. *Selected Topics in Application of Quantum Mechanics* (ISBN 978-953-51-2126-8) Chapter 6.

Bentwich, J. (2014) *What if Einstein was Right? Amazon Kindle Book Store.*

Bentwich, J. (2015). On the Geometry of Space, Time, Energy, and Mass: Empirical Validation of the Computational Unified Field Theory. *Unified Field Mechanics: Natural Science Beyond the Veil of Spacetime (Proceedings of VIGIER IX Conference, Morgan State University, USA, 16-19 November 2014).*

Bentwich, J. (2016) The 'Computational Unified Field Theory': A Paradigmatic Shift. *Research & Reviews: Journal of Pure & Applied Physics.*

Bentwich, J. (2017a) The Computational Unified Field Theory: Could 'Dark Matter' & 'Dark Energy' be "Superfluous"? *SciFed Journal of Quantum Physics Special Issue.*

Bentwich, J. (2017b) The Computational Unified Field Theory: Explaining the Universe from "Without". *SciFed Journal of Quantum Physics Special Issue.*

Bentwich, J. (2017c). The Computational Unified Field Theory: A New 'A-Causal Computation' Physics. *SciFed Journal of Quantum Physics Special Issue.*

Bentwich, J. (2017d). The 'Computational Unified Field Theory' (CUFT) May Challenge the 'Big-Bang Theory'. *SciFed Journal of Quantum Physics Special Issue.*

Bentwich, J. (2017e). Can the 'Computational Unified Field Theory' (CUFT) Challenge the Basic Laws of Conservation? *SciFed Journal of Quantum Physics Special Issue.*

Bentwich, J. (2017f). The Computational Unified Field Theory (CUFT): Time "Reversal" May be Possible. *SciFed Journal of Quantum Physics Special Issue.*

Bentwich, J. (2017g). The Computational Unified Field Theory (CUFT) Transcends Relativity's Speed of Light Constraint. *SciFed Journal of Quantum Physics, Special Issue.*

Bentwich, J. (2017h). The Computational Unified Field Theory's New Physics: Transcending Space, Time and Causality. *SciFed Journal of Quantum Physics Special Issue.*

Bentwich, J. (2017i). A "Supra-Spatial-Temporal Universal Consciousness Reality". *Research & Reviews: Journal of Pure & Applied Physics, Special Issue: The Computational Unified Field Theory (CUFT)- A Paradigmatic Shift in 21st Century Physics.*

Bentwich, J. (2017j). A New Science: An Infinite Omniscient Dynamic-Equilibrium Universal Consciousness Reality. *SciFed Journal of Quantum Physics Special Issue.*

Bentwich, J. (2017k). The Computational Unified Field Theory (CUFT) Challenges Darwin's 'Natural Selection Principle'! *SciFed Journal of Quantum Physics Special Issue.*

Bentwich, J. (2017l). The Computational Unified Field Theory (CUFT) Challenges the Second Law of Thermodynamics. *SciFed Journal of Quantum Physics Special Issue.*

Bentwich, J. (2017m). The Computational Unified Field Theory (CUFT): An Empirical & Mathematical Validation of the 'Computational Unified Field Theory'; *SciFed Journal of Quantum Physics Special Issue.*

Bentwich, J. (2017n). The Computational Unified Field Theory (CUFT) New Science; *SciFed Journal of Quantum Physics Special Issue.*

Bentwich, J. (2018a). Review: The Computational Unified Field Theory (CUFT) New Universe: *The Global Journal of Science Frontier Research, Vol. 18 (8-A), Special Issue.*

Bentwich, J. (2018b). The Computational Unified Field Theory (CUFT): What is "Time"? *The Global Journal of Science Frontier Research, Vol. 18 (8-A), Special Issue.*

Bentwich, J. (2018c). The Universal Consciousness Reality's Camouflage: The Physical Universe! *The Global Journal of Science Frontier Research, Vol. 18 (8-A), Special Issue.*

Bentwich, J. (2018d). The Computational Unified Field Theory (CUFT) Epilogue: Can Human Consciousness Affect the Cosmos? *The Global Journal of Science Frontier Research, Vol. 18 (8-A), Special Issue.*

Bentwich, J. (2018e). Testing the Computational Unified Field Theory's (CUFT) Differential-Critical Predictions: The Higgs-Boson Particle May Not Exist Continuously! *The Global Journal of Science Frontier Research, Vol. 18 (8-A), Special Issue.*

Bentwich, J. (2018f). The Double-Faceted Universal Consciousness Reality: A Theoretical Review. *The Global Journal of Science Frontier Research, Vol. 18 (8-A), Special Issue.*

Bentwich, J. (2018g). Letter to the Editor: Dark Matter May Not Exist. *The Global Journal of Science Frontier Research, Vol. 18 (8-A), Special Issue.*

Bentwich, J. (2018h). The Computational Unified Field Theory's (CUFT) Epilogue: Possible Reversal of the Arrow of Time and Abolishment of Death. *The Global Journal of Science Frontier Research, Vol. 18 (8-A), Special Issue.*

Bentwich, J. (2019a). The Computational Unified Field Theory's (CUFT) New Universe. *The Global Journal of Science Frontier Research, Vol. 19 (6), Special Issue.*

Bentwich, J. (2019b). The Computational Unified Field Theory's (CUFT) Goes Beyond the 'Standard Model': "G-d's Physics"?!. *The Global Journal of Science Frontier Research, Vol. 18 (8-A), Special Issue.*

Bentwich, J. (2019c). A Call for Cosmologists & Experimental Physicists: Empirical Validation of the 'Computational Unified Field Theory' (CUFT) New Paradigm through "Time-Sensitive" Astronomical and Subatomic Measurements. *The Global Journal of Science Frontier Research, Vol. 19 (6), Special Issue.*

Bentwich, J. (2019d). The 'Computational Unified Field Theory' (CUFT): Redefining Mass, Gravity & the Physical Universe. *The Global Journal of Science Frontier Research, Vol. 19 (6), Special Issue.*

Bentwich, J. (2019d). Astronomical Validation of the Computational Unified Field Theory (CUFT) "Critical Prediction" & Resolution of the "Universe's Accelerated Expansion Rate Enigma" (UAERE).*The Global Journal of Science Frontier Research, Vol. 19 (6), Special Issue.*

Bentwich, J. (2019e) Urgent Call for Empirical Validation of the Computational Unified Field Theory's (CUFT) New 21st Century 'A-Causal Computation' (ACC) Paradigm. *Acta Scientific Applied Physics, Volume 1(1).*

Bentovish (Bentwich) J. (2020a) *'G-d's Physics'.* In Press. iUniverse Publication.

Bentovish (Bentwich), J. (2020b). 'G-d's Physics' (CUFT) New "Atom" & Purposeful Universe! *Advances in Theoretical & Computational Physics. Volume 3 (2),* p. 50-58.

Bentovish (Bentwich), J. (2020c). An Urgent Need for "G-d's Physics" New 21st Century Paradigm's Empirical Validation. *Advances in Theoretical & Computational Physics. Volume 3 (2),* p. 59-65.

"G-d's Physics": From Arbitrary Physical & Biological "Evolution" towards a Universal Consciousness Reality's (UCR) Directed Morally-Perfected ("Geula") Universe!

Bentovish (Bentwich) Jehonathan, Ph.D.

Dr. Bentovish is affiliated with Zefat Academic College, Zefat, Israel.

*Note: Dr. Bentovish is currently seeking the most appropriate leading Academic Institute to assist him in carrying-out further necessary empirical validation and Theoretical elaboration of his New Twenty-first Century New 'G-d's Physics' Paradigm.

Dr. Bentovish (Bentwich) e-mail is: <u>drbentwich@gmail.com</u>.

Abstract:

Twenty-first century Theoretical Physics is undergoing a major "Paradigmatic-Shift" from the Old "Material-Causal" Paradigm of Relativity Theory (RT) & Quantum Mechanics (QM) to the New "G-d's Physics" Paradigm; This New 'G-d's Physics' (Computational Unified Field Theory, CUFT) Paradigm has been published in over thirty peer-reviewed articles and Books and has been shown capable of resolving the apparent "theoretical inconsistency" between RT & QM; It also discovering the existence of a singular higher-ordered "Universal Computational/Consciousness Principle" (UCP) that simultaneously computes every exhaustive spatial pixel in the universe at the incredible rate of "c^2/h" = 1.36^{-50} sec'(!) giving rise to an incredibly rapid series of "Universal Frames" (UF's) comprising the entire physical universe (which "dissolves" back into the singularity of the UCP 'in-between' any two consecutive UF's frames!) This New 'G-d's Physics' Paradigm is also shown to challenge and negate key RT & QM 'Material-Causal' assumptions such as: the 'Big-Bang; Model, Einstein's Equations and the "collapse" of the probability wave function. This article evinces that the New 'G-d's Physics' Paradigm similarly negates Darwin's Natural Selection Principle (DNSP) dual 'Material-Causal' assumptions due to the simultaneity of the UCP's computation of all exhaustive spatial pixels for each consecutive UF's frame! Instead, the New 'G-d's Physics' Paradigm points at the UCP's singular, higher-ordered characteristics of the "Ten Laws of Hierarchical Manifestation" including: "Free-Will", "Good-Will", the "Dynamic-Equilibrium" Moral Principle and its selection of one of multiple "possible future/s" based on the Moral Choice/s of each Individual Human Consciousness (at any point in time); and the UCP's "Reversed Time Goal Hypothesis" which completely integrates between all Physical, Biological and Moral developments – pointing at the UCP's Ultimate "Geula" (e.g., Physical, Moral & Spiritual "Perfected State") Goal of the universe, towards which this singular "Universal Consciousness Reality" continuously advances the entire physical universe and Humanity!

1. Introduction: New 'G-d's Physics' Twenty-First Century Physics Paradigm

Twenty-first Century Theoretical Physics has discovered and accepted a New 'G-d's Physics' Paradigm (e.g., formerly also called" the "Computational Unified Field Theory", CUFT, see numerous peer-reviewed published scientific articles); This New 'G-d's Physics' Paradigm replaces the Old (20th Century Physics') 'Material-Causal' Paradigm underlying both Relativity Theory (RT) and Quantum Mechanics (QM); It's been shown capable of resolving the apparent "theoretical inconsistency" that seemed to exist between RT & QM, offer an alternative explanation for key unresolved empirical phenomenon such as the purely hypothetical "dark-matter" and "dark-energy" concepts, e.g., which were supposed to account for up to 95% of all the "mass" and "energy" in the universe – but which nevertheless could not be accounted for (or detected) empirically!? Indeed, 21st century Theoretical Physics stands at an "equivalent juncture" as did pre-Einstein's 1905 & 1915 Theoretical Physics, in a state in which the two primary "pillars" of Physics seem to "contradict" each other: e.g., based on RT's insistence upon a strict "material-causal" constraint imposed upon the transmission of any light signal across 'Space-Time' and determination of "positivistic definite" physical values for any relativistic 'Space-Time', 'energy-mass' phenomenon; as opposed to QM's insistence upon the possibility of "quantum-entanglement", indicating that it is possible for two such "entangled-particles" separated by a distance greater than that which could be "covered" by the Speed of Light being able to apparently "affect" each other's measurements (probabilistic) complimentary values, as well as its only "probabilistic" mathematical values attributed to any 'space-energy' or 'mass-time' complimentary values!? Fortunately, a fundamental "Paradigmatic-Shift" from the Old 'Material-Causal' Paradigm has been signified by the New 'G-d's Physics' Paradigm – which was shown capable of resolving this basic apparent "theoretical inconsistency" between RT & QM; The New 'G-d's Physics' Paradigm is based upon the discovery of a singular higher-ordered Universal Computational/Consciousness Principle (UCP) which simultaneously computes all exhaustive spatial pixels in the physical universe at the incredible rate of "c^2/h" = 1.36^{-50} sec'(!) giving rise to an extremely rapid series of "Universal Frames" (UF's) comprising the entire physical universe at every such minimal "time-point"... Moreover, according to this New 'G-d's Physics' Paradigm, "in-between" any two consecutive UF's frames, the entire physical universe "dissolves" back into the singularity of the UCP, e.g., so that there cannot be any "transference" of any material "entity" or "effect" across any two consecutive UF's frames!

This New 'G-d's Physics' (CUFT) Paradigm was shown to significantly revise our basic understanding of the origin- sustenance- "dissolution"- and evolution- of every exhaustive spatial pixel in the universe (as well as the whole universe), challenge, transform and transcend the Old 'Material-Causal' Paradigm account of the origination and dynamics of the universe: Thus, for instance, the New 'G-d's Physics' challenges Relativity's conception of the "Big-Bang" Model, which assumes that the entire physical universe was created by an initial 'Big-Bang' nuclear explosion – which gave-rise (or "caused") the creation of the various suns, planets, galaxies, energy, matter, etc. This is because if indeed, the singular higher-ordered UCP simultaneously computes all exhaustive spatial pixels in the universe comprising an extremely rapid ("c^2/h" = 1.36^{-50} sec') series of UF's frames, then for each such consecutive UF's frame, there cannot exist any direct physical interactions between any two (or more) exhaustive spatial pixels – i.e., including those assumed by the Big-Bang initial nuclear explosion! In other words since the UCP simultaneously computes all exhaustive spatial pixels comprising each consecutive UF's frame/s, then for each of these frames there could not have existed such an initial 'Big-Bang' nuclear explosion direct physical interaction! Moreover, since the entire physical universe "dissolves" 'in-between' any two consecutive UF's frames, there could not have been a "continuous physical effect" emanating from the further "expulsion" or "evolution" of the Big-Bang's initial creation of sun's, galaxies, mass and energy etc.! In much the same manner, this New 'G-d's Physics' Paradigm challenges and negates some of the most fundamental 'Material-Causal' assumptions underlying both RT and QM: such as "Einstein's Equations" basic premise whereby it is the presence of certain "massive objects" which "cause" the "curvature" of "Space-Time", and conversely it is this "curved Space-Time" which "causes" or determines the "travelling-pathways" of these 'massive' (and other 'non-massive') objects!? This is because if the singular higher-ordered UCP simultaneously computes all exhaustive spatial pixels in the universe for each consecutive UF's frame, then there could not be any "cause" and "effect" direct physical interaction/s between any 'massive objects' and 'Space-Time', which could "cause" any such "curvature of Space-Time" or conversely could affect the travelling-pathways of those massive/non-massive objects based on their direct physical interaction/s with "curved Space-Time"!? In much the same manner, the New 'G-d's Physics' Paradigm challenged and negated the existence of the "purely hypothetical" concepts of "dark-matter" and "dark-energy" as "superfluous", i.e., non-existent! This is once again, due to the principle impossibility of the existence of any direct physical interactions between such (purely hypothetical) "dark matter"/"energy" entities and their assumed "expulsion" of the universes' galaxies etc.! So, apart from the mere fact that no direct empirical proof for the existence of these purely hypothetical "dark-matter" and "dark-energy" concepts could be found thus far, the New 'G-d's Physics' Paradigm teaches us that these hypothetical concepts could not exist in principle, due to the simultaneity of the UCP's computation of all exhaustive spatial pixels in the universe for each consecutive UF's frame/s (and the complete "dissolution" of the entire physical universe back into the singularity of the UCP 'in-between' any two consecutive UF's frames)!

In much the same manner, the New 'G-d's Physics (CUFT) Paradigm indicates that the basic 'Material-Causal' assumption underlying Quantum Mechanics (QM) wherein it is assumed that it is the direct physical interaction between a given subatomic "probe" element and a corresponding subatomic "target's probability wave function" – which "causes" the "collapse" of the target's 'probability wave function' into a singular (complimentary) 'space-energy' or 'time-mass' value – is invalid!? This is because, once again, to the extent that this New 'G-d's Physics' Paradigm can be validated empirically (as shown and discussed previously and below), then its basic theoretical postulate wherein the UCP simultaneously computes all exhaustive spatial pixels in the universe for each consecutive UF's frame/s principally negates the existence of any direct physical interactions between any two (or more) exhaustive spatial pixels in the universe at any single or multiple UF's frames – including the possibility of any such direct physical interaction between the subatomic 'probe' and 'target's (probability wave function)! Likewise, the complete "dissolution" of the entire physical universe 'in-between' any two consecutive UF's frames also negates the possibility of any such direct physical interaction's "causing" the "collapse" of the probability wave function" across any two consecutive UF's frames! Therefore, the New 'G-d's Physics' Paradigm forces us to challenge and negate the basic 'Material-Causal' assumptions underlying both RT' Einstein's Equations' and QM's "collapse of the probability wave function" tenets. Instead, we arrive at a completely new understanding of the origin- sustenance- "dissolution" and evolution of the whole physical universe by the UCP which was shown to completely integrate, embed and indeed transcend the narrow constraints of the Old 'Material-Causal' Paradigm of RT and QM;

Thus, the New 'G-ds Physics' Paradigm was able to integrate the key elements of RT & QM within a singular higher-ordered "Universal Computational Formula" (which also possesses two Relativistic and Quantum Formats emphasizing the embedding of those key corresponding Relativistic and Quantum features, previously published):

Universal Computational Formula (UCF):

$$\left\{ \begin{array}{c} \text{\foreignlanguage{hebrew}{י}} c^2 \\ \\ — \\ \\ h \end{array} \right\} \quad \text{UF's } \{\text{ת}...\text{מ}...\text{א}\} \qquad \begin{array}{ccc} & = & s \; * \; e \\ \\ & & t \; * \; m \end{array}$$

(**Note**: herein the singular higher-ordered UCP – represented by the Hebrew letter "Yud" ("י") simultaneously computes all exhaustive spatial pixels in the universe comprising each consecutive Universal Frame/s (UF's) which already exist in a "potential-from" within the UCP's "Supra Spatial-Temporal Reservoir" of all "past", "present" and multiple possible "future/s" UF's (represented by the Hebrew letters from "א through "מ" to "ת)" depending on the Moral Choice of each Individual Human Consciousness – as computing and integrating these four basic physical features of "space" and "energy", "mass" and "time", at the incredible rate of: "c^2/h" = 1.36^{-50} sec'!)

Hence, the New 'G-d's Physics' Paradigm discovered an exhaustive new theoretical framework which indeed completely integrates the basic features of RT & QM within the singular higher-ordered UCP's Universal Computational Formula (as well as completely integrates the four basic features of 'space', 'energy', 'mass' and 'time' as secondary computational properties of the UCP's singular higher-ordered simultaneous computation of all exhaustive spatial pixels in the universe for each minimal time-point "c^2/h" = 1.36^{-50} sec'(!)

2. The New G-d's Physics Negation of Darwin's "Natural Selection Principle" (DNSP)!

According o the New 'G-d's Physics' Paradigm, the entire physical universe is being created- dissolved- re-created- and evolved- many billions of times each second simultaneously by the singular higher-ordered Universal Computational/Consciousness Principle (UCP), as an extremely raid series of Universal Frames (UF's)! Moreover, according to this New 'G-d's Physics' (CUFT) Paradigm, the entire physical universe completely "dissolves" back into the singularity of the UCP "in-between" any two consecutive UF's frames (including all of its exhaustive spatial pixels)! This implies that there cannot exist any direct physical interaction between any two (or more) exhaustive spatial pixels existing either in the same- or different- UF's frames; Furthermore, given the complete "dissolution" of the entire physical universe "in-between" any two consecutive UF's frames, there cannot exist any "transference" of any "physical effect" or (any) "material entity/ ies" across any two consecutive UF's frames! In this manner, the New 'G-d's Physics' Paradigm was shown to challenge and (in fact) negate all of the major assumptions of the Old 'Material-Causal' Paradigm (underlying both RT & QM): It was shown to negate the "Big-Bang" Model, assuming that the universe was created as "caused" by an initial "nuclear explosion", since there could not have been any direct physical interaction between any two (or more) exhaustive spatial pixels either in the "first", "second", "third", etc. UF's frames! Likewise, the New 'G-d's Physics' Paradigm was shown to negate the existence of the purely hypothetical concepts of "dark-matter" or "dark-energy" which are assumed to "cause" the accelerated "expulsion" (or expansion) of the physical universe, once again because there cannot exist any direct physical interactions between any two (or more) exhaustive spatial pixels (e.g., at- or between- any two consecutive UF's frames!) Similarly, it was shown to negate the basic "Material-Causal" assumption underlying RT's Einstein's Equations, e.g., assuming that certain "massive-objects" "cause" a "curvature" of 'Space-Time', and conversely that it is this 'curved Space-Time' which "causes" (or determines) the travelling-pathways of those and other less-massive objects…

So we see that the New 'G-d's Physics' Paradigm totally negates the very possibility of the existence of any direct physical interaction between any two (or more) exhaustive spatial pixels in any single- or multiple- UF's frames! We now come to 'G-d's Physics' New Paradigm's basic challenging, negation and indeed transformation of Darwin's fundamental "Natural-Selection Principle's" (DNSP) evolutionary Theory; according to DNSP, the gradual evolution of the various Biological Species is brought about by a combination of "Chance-Genetic Mutations" (CGM) in a particular organism "caused" by direct physical interactions between certain ultraviolet cosmic radiation with the genetic code of that particular organism; together with the given "Environmental Factors" direct physical interaction with that particular organism – i.e., as opposed to the direct physical interaction of other equivalent (same-species) organisms (which did not undergo the same CGM) that "causes" that particular CGM organism to "survive" better than the other equivalent species' organisms... Hence, DNSP is based on a "dual Material-Causal" assumptions structure wherein the "selection of the fittest" is "Caused" by: a) a direct physical interaction between ultraviolet radiation and the genetic-code of the mutated (CGM) particular organism; b) a direct physical interaction between that 'mutated' (CGM) and a given set of 'Environmental Factors' which "causes" the selection of that 'mutated' (CGM) particular organism to "survive" and "pass-on" its "superior" genetic-code to its descendants (as opposed to the other equivalent species' organisms which could not survive and therefore cannot pass their genetic information to any descendants, i.e., get "extinct")! But, based on the New 'G-d's Physics' Paradigm for 21st century Physics – which explicitly negates the very possibility of the existence of any such "direct physical interaction" between any two (or more) exhaustive spatial pixels existing either in the same- or any other- UF's frames, e.g., due to the "simultaneity" of the UCP's computation of all exhaustive spatial pixels in the universe for each consecutive UF's frame/s, and the complete "dissolution" of the whole universe "in-between" any two such consecutive UF's; therefore, the New 'G-d's Physics' Paradigm strictly negates DNSP's basic 'dual Material-Causal' assumptions – hence de facto negating the feasibility and validity of DNSP as "impossible"!?

Indeed, in order to better understand 'G-d's Physics' basic challenging- negation- and transcendence- of DNSP Old 'Material-Causal' (dual) assumptions nature, it is perhaps appropriate to mention 'G-d's Physics' New 21st century Paradigm's associated "Cinematic-Film Metaphor", which delineates certain aspects of the 'Computational Unified Field Theory's' (CUFT) description of the UCP's computation of the series of consecutive UF's frames: let's examine a standard 'Cinematic-Film' dynamics (and progression) – for instance, depicting a scenario in which a given "Glass-Jar" is being "impacted" by another "Mercury-Ball" which "causes" the "breakage" of that 'Glass Jar' and the "spillage" of its containing water unto the floor... the key point to be realizes is that despite the "appearance" of a direct "cause and effect" physical interaction between the 'Mercury-Ball's' impact upon the 'Glass-Jar' – which seems to have "caused" its 'breakage' (and water-spillage on the floor), when we closely examine the direct physical interaction between that 'Glass-Jar' and 'Mercury-Ball', for each consecutive Cinematic-Film frame/s, we are bound to realize that at no single or multiple UF's frame/s could there have existed any "direct physical interaction", and hence any "cause and effect" physical relationships between the 'Mercury-Ball' and the 'Glass-Jar'!? This is simply because for each (single or multiple) UF's frame/s, all of the exhaustive spatial pixels comprising each consecutive Cinematic-Frame/s are being simultaneously presented! Moreover "in-between" any two such consecutive 'Cinematic-Frames', there only exists the "pure light" so that there cannot really be any "transference" of any "material-entity" or any "physical interaction/s" or "physical effects" across any two consecutive Cinematic-Frames! So, we must realize that despite the "appearance" of a clear "cause and effect" direct physical relationship/s between the 'Mercury-Ball' and the 'Glass-Jar', in reality there does not (and cannot) exist any such direct physical "cause and effect" relationships between the 'Mercury-Ball' and 'Glass-Jar'! Instead, we reach the inevitable theoretical conclusion whereby it is only the "arrangement" of the consecutive 'Cinematic Film Frames' by the producer of the film that gives rise to out "subjective impression" of a "cause and effect" physical relationship between the 'Mercury-Ball' impact upon the (delicate) 'Glass-Jar', which seems to have "caused" its 'breakage' and consequent 'water-spillage'... Indeed, this 'Cinematic-Film Metaphor' assists us in fully realizing that in much the same manner that the apparent "direct physical interaction" between the 'Mercury-Ball' and the 'Glass-Jar' seem to have "caused" the 'breakage' of the 'Glass-Jar' (and 'spillage' of its constituent waters) – but in truth was found out to arise merely from the "arrangement" of the series of 'Cinematic-Film Frames' by the film's produce in such a manner wherein the "spatial-proximity" between the depiction of the 'Mercury-Ball' and the 'Glass-Jar' become closer and closer across the series of Cinematic-Film Frames; so it is suggested that the UCP's arrangement of the series of UF's depicting the "evolution" of any given "new species" merely arises from the presentation of certain changes in given 'Environmental Factors' and parallel presentation of certain "new organism's" appearance along a given series of UF's frames!?

Hence, we reach the amazing conclusion wherein the very basis for Darwin's Natural Selection Principle is negated and rejected by the New 'G-d's Physics' Paradigm which points at the simultaneity of the UCP's computation of all exhaustive spatial pixel in the universe for each consecutive UF's frame/s (thereby negating the possibility of the existence of any direct physical interactions between any two or more exhaustive spatial pixels in the entire physical universe), and also negates the possibility of the transference of any "physical effects" or any "material-entity" across any two such consecutive UF's frames (due to the "dissolution" of the entire physical universe "in-between" any two consecutive UF's frames!) Noteworthy is also the fact that not only this "second-later" of DNSP, e.g., assuming that it is based on the direct physical interaction between a given organism and its 'Environmental Factors' which determines which organism will "survive" and pass on its genetic information to its descendants and which organism will be "extinct" (and therefore could not pass on its genetic information) – is negated by the New 'G-d's Physics' Paradigm; Also the "first-layer" of the (abovementioned) DNSP is negated for the same principle reason by the New 'G-d's Physics' Paradigm: since according to 'G-d' Physics' Paradigm there cannot exist any direct physical interaction between any two (or more) exhaustive spatial pixels at any single- or multiple-UF's frames (and moreover then entire physical universe "dissolves" 'in-between' any two consecutive UF's frames thereby negating the possibility of any "physical" or "biological effect" across any two consecutive UF's frames), therefore the 'first-layer' of DNSP is also negated- assuming that it is the direct physical interaction between cosmic electromagnetic radiation and the genetic information of particular organism/s which "causes" the random "genetic-mutations" at such a particular organism that then "sets it" to the 'second-layer' of DNSP's 'Material-Causal' assumption, i.e., assuming that it is those "rare" (chance) "genetically mutated" organisms that are later on found to be those special organism/s that can actually "survive" amidst the "challenging" 'Environmental Factors', thereby giving rise the evolution of a new specie?! This is because, once again, based on the simultaneity of the UCP computation of all exhaustive spatial pixels in the universe for each consecutive UF's frame (and the complete "dissolution" of the entire physical universe 'in-between' any two consecutive UF's frames) we must reach the inevitable conclusion that there cannot exist any such "direct physical interaction" between any hypothetical "cosmic-electromagnetic rays" and any given organism's "genetic information" which then "Causes" a "mutation" in that particular 'genetic-information' (nor can there exist any "physical" or "biological effect" transferring any "changes" in the assumed 'genetic information' of a particular organism from one UF's frame/s to another!);

All that truly exists is, as illustrated by the fine "Cinematic-Film Metaphor", is a particular "arrangement" of the series of UF's frames by the Universal Computational/Consciousness Principle (UCP) in such a manner which gives us the perceived effect of a given "Biological Evolution"!? Just as we've seen through this 'Cinematic-Film Metaphor, that what seems to be a "cause" and "effect" direct physical relationship between the "impact" of the "Mercury-Ball" and the "shattering" of the "Glass-Jar", but in truth only arises from the "arrangement" of the Cinematic-Film Frames in such a manner in which the spatial-proximity of those two 'Mercury-Ball' and 'Glass-Jar' are presented in ever closer proximity in each consecutive frame – leasing up to the final frame which presents the "shattered" 'Glass-Jar' with the adjacent 'Mercury-Ball' (and the 'spilled-off' water on the ground...) So, it is suggested that the apparent "Biological-Evolution" stipulated by DNSP also arises merely from the "arrangement" of the series of UF's frames in such a manner that seems to associate between certain changes appearing perhaps in a given Environment ('Environmental Factors') and equivalent changes in a given organism, which give us the "impression" of a direct "cause" and "effect" physical relationship/s between them!? But, as we've already seen that no such direct physical interactions are possible between any two (or more) exhaustive spatial pixels existing either in the same- or different- Universal Frames (UF's), and moreover the entire physical universe "dissolves" 'in-between' any two consecutive UF's frames, therefore the New 'G-d's Physics' Paradigm explains the origination- "dissolution"- re-creation and evolution of each specific exhaustive spatial pixel throughout the entire physical universe – only based on the singular higher-ordered UCP's operation and characteristics, as explained and delineated previously.

3.   G-d's Physics: UCP's Complete Unification of "Physical", "Biological" & Moral Developments

In fact, in order to fully understand (and appreciate) 'G-d's Physics' New Paradigm's exhaustive theoretical framework – which completely integrates all "Physical", Biological" & "Moral" developments, we have to reexamine some of the basic tenets and theoretical postulates of the CUFT's including its complete unification of 'space', 'time', energy' and 'mass' – within a single "Universal Computational Formula" (UCF), e.g., as secondary computational features of the singular higher-ordered UCP's operation; according to 'G-d's Physics' singular 'Universal Computational Formula' (UCF) (and associated theoretical postulates) the UCP possesses three "Computational Dimensions" (e.g., "Framework", "Consistency" and "Locus") – two out of which ('Framework' and 'Consistency') compute together the four basic physical features of 'space' and 'energy', 'mass' and 'time', based on the UCP's computation for each exhaustive spatial pixel in the universe (simultaneously) of the degree of "change" ('consistent') or "lack of change" ('inconsistent') pertaining to each spatial-pixel's (entire) 'frame' or focusing of the 'object's characteristics across a given series of Universal Frames (UF's): Thus, the UCP's computation of space' 'and 'energy' stem from the UCP's computation of 'frame'- 'consistent' or 'inconsistent' measures across any given series of UF's frames, whereas the UCP's computation of 'time' and ;mass' represent the degree of 'object' – 'consistent' or 'inconsistent' measures across the same UF's series; Indeed, for the first time in Physics history the four basic physical dimensions of 'space', 'energy', 'mass' and 'time' are completely unified as integrative computational aspects of the singular higher-ordered UCP's simultaneous computation of all exhaustive spatial pixels in the universe comprising an extremely rapid (e.g., "c^2/h" = 1.36^{-50} sec'!) series of Universal Frames (UF's) depicting the whole physical universe! Thus far, only 'space' and 'time' (Space-Time), or 'energy' and 'mass' ("E = Mc^2") have been united, and likewise the "curvature" of "Space-Time" by Massive objects (as described in General Relativity's "Einstein's Equations"), and conversely the determination of these (and other) 'Massive' (and less massive) objects is assumed to be determined (or "Caused") by this 'curvature of Space-Time'; But this New 'G-d's Physics' (CUFT) Paradigm signifies the first complete unification of these four basic physical features of 'space', 'energy', 'mass' and 'time' as integral secondary computational properties of the singular higher-ordered UCP simultaneous computation of all exhaustive spatial pixels in the universe (for each consecutive UF's frame/s)! Moreover, due to another key "Computational Invariance Principle" postulate of the CUFT ('G-d's Physics') which asserts that only the "Universal Computational Principle" (UCP) remains "computationally invariant" (i.e., constant) – both "during" its computation of all exhaustive spatial pixels' four basic physical features (of 'space' and 'energy', 'mass' and 'time') comprising each consecutive UF's frame/s, as well "in-between" any two consecutive UF's frame/s (in which the entire universe "dissolves" back into the singularity of the UCP); whereas the entire physical universe (and each of its constituting exhaustive spatial pixels' four basic physical features) may only be considered as "computationally-variant", since it only exists "during" each consecutive UF's frame/s (as solely computed by the UCP) but "dissolves" (back into the UCP) "in-between" any two consecutive UF's frame/s – therefore deemed only as a "transient", "phenomenal" manifestation of the singular UCP; hence, this "Computational Invariance" Principle regards the whole entire physical universe as only a "transient", "phenomenal" manifestation of the singular existence of the UCP! This additional "Computational Invariance Principle" and its associated "Universal Consciousness Reality" theoretical postulate is important because it transforms our basic understanding (and appreciation) of the "independent existence" of the physical universe as a "Material-Causal" entity – governed by mere physical interactions (e.g, such as postulated by the abovementioned General Relativity Theory's curvature of 'Space-Time' by massive objects etc.);

We realize that the only entity that exists uniformly, continuously and constantly is the singular higher-ordered "Universal Consciousness Reality" (UCR) which exists "computationally invariantly" – both "during" its computation of every exhaustive spatial pixel comprising the entire physical universe, and also singularly (without the existence of any physical universe) "in-between" any two consecutive UF's frames; and therefore, that the whole existence of the physical universe cannot be explained (any longer) through any direct physical interactions – e.g., such as between 'Massive objects' and their assumed "curvature of Space-Time', or such as between the initially assumed "Big-Bang" nuclear explosion and its "creation" of "space", "energy", suns or galaxies, or indeed between DNSP's assumed dual 'Material-Causal' (direct physical) interaction between certain assumed electromagnetic rays and particular organism's "genetic information", or between that particular organism's and a given set of (challenging) "Environmental Factors" (which are both supposed to "cause" the "survival of the fittest"!?) Instead, we arrive at an entirely new and exciting theoretical account of the origin- "dissolution"- re-creation and evolution of each and every exhaustive spatial pixel comprising the entire physical universe, which is solely by the singularity of the UCP (or UCR)! Indeed, a series of over forty scientific 'peer-reviewed' articles and Books (see Bentwich References) indicated that since this singular higher-ordered UCR exists "computationally invariantly" – both during its production of every consecutive UF's frame/s depiction of the entire physical universe (constituting exhaustive spatial pixels) and also solely exists "in-between" any two consecutive UF's frames (whereas the entire physical universe only exists "transiently" and "phenomenally" "during" each consecutive UF's frame but "dissolves" back into the UCR "in-between" every two consecutive UF's frames); therefore the singularity of this

UCR – and its intrinsic characteristics are solely responsible for any physical, biological (and moral) laws, phenomena etc., including an alternative unitary explanation for the entire origination, sustenance and evolution of the entire physical universe!

Hence, 'G-d's Physics' New Paradigm for the first time completely integrates not only between the four basic physical features (of 'space', 'energy', 'mass' and time'), as well as between RT and QM (being seen as integral "special cases" within the CUFT's exhaustive computational framework) – but more importantly, between the apparently "different" aspects of Biological, Physical – and even Moral evolution of the entire physical universe!? Indeed, based on 'G-d's Physics' new discovery of the UCP's Ten Laws of Hierarchical Manifestation, which describe some of the UCP's intrinsic characterizations these apparent "separate" and "random" aspects of the universe's Physical, Biological and even Moral evolution are seen to be completely unified! Unlike the Old 'Material-Causal' Paradigm which assumes that the origination of the physical universe can be explained as being "caused" by an initial "random Big-Bang" nuclear explosion, which created "space", "energy", the various suns and galaxies etc.; and unlike DNSP equivalent dual 'Material-Causal' assumption wherein the evolution of all Biological forms and species can be explained merely based on the direct physical interactions between "cosmic electromagnetic rays" and the "genetic information" of particular organism/s which "causes" "random-mutations", which in turn produces a "survival advantage" for those "randomly mutated" organism/s in its direct physical interaction with a given set of 'Environmental Factors'; the UCP's Ten Laws of Hierarchical Manifestation posit that both the origination- sustenance- "dissolution"- and evolution of every exhaustive spatial pixel in the universe, i.e., including their "Physical", "Biological" or "Moral" aspects – is solely determined and directed by the singular higher-ordered UCP (or UCR) which exists both "during" its simultaneous computation of every exhaustive spatial pixel in the universe comprising each consecutive UF's frame, as well as solely exists "in-between" any two consecutive UF's frames! Succinctly stated, the New 'G-d's Physics' Paradigm posits that the UCP's characteristics of "Good-Will", "Free-Will", "Moral Dynamic-Equilibrium" Principle manifest as the underlying "driving" and determining factors for the Physical, Biological and Moral evolution of the entire physical universe towards the UCP's ultimate "Goal" of Perfection, e.g., termed: "Geula" in the Jewish-Chassidic Tradition! As previously described, the UCP's computation of all "past", "present" and "multiple-possible future/s" is carried out by its "Supra-Spatial-Temporal Reservoir" which contains all past, present and multiple possible future/s UF's frames; this UCP's computation is related to another one of the UCP's higher-ordered 'Ten Laws of Hierarchical Manifestation', namely: the Moral 'Dynamic-Equilibrium' Principle – which stems from the UCP's "Inseparability Principle"; Simply explained, this new 'G-d's Physics' "Dynamic-Equilibrium" Principle states that based on the UCP's 'Inseparability Principle' acknowledgement of the fact that all Individual Human Consciousness comprise integral parts of the Universal Consciousness Reality (and are not "separate" from it), therefore the singular higher-ordered UCP (or UCR) possesses an "intrinsic" property that strives towards "unity" and "harmony" between all of its constituent 'Individual Human Consciousness' – such that in any case in which this "Moral Unity" is violated, e.g., through any Immoral Choice made by one of its constituting 'Individual Human Consciousness' inflicting 'pain' or 'suffering' towards another 'Individual Human Consciousness'; then according to the UCP's 'Dynamic-Equilibrium Principle' this must necessarily lead to the UCP's "correction" of such a 'Moral-Imbalance' through the rectification brought about by the creation of an "equivalent situation" in which that "Individual Human Consciousness" which 'inflicted pain' upon the other "suffering" Individual Human Consciousness – would have to experience the same kind (and degree) of suffering itself (in order to learn and understand the UCP's Inseparability and Moral Principle)... Hence, the selection of one of multiple possible future/s found within the UCP's "Multi-Spatial-Temporal Reservoir" is carried out based on one of the UCP's Ten-Laws of Manifestation, i.e., the 'Dynamic Equilibrium' Moral Principle!

More generally, the UCP's other higher Laws of Hierarchical Manifestation include the UCP's innate tendency of 'Goodwill" – an intrinsic propensity to bestow Life, Happiness, Goodness and Giving; when coupled with the UCP's "Free-Will" Law of Hierarchical

Manifestation – which essentially states that since only the singular UCP (or UCR) exists continuously and "computationally invariantly" both "during" its simultaneous computation of all exhaustive spatial pixels in the universe comprising the series of consecutive UF's frames, and also solely existing "in-between" any two consecutive UF's frame, therefore that this singular higher-ordered UCP is not "constrained" or "limited" by any 'Material-Causal' laws etc. but is rather completely "free" to create- sustain and evolve every exhaustive spatial pixel in the universe according to its "Free-Will", and "Good-Will" propensities... Indeed, the UCP (or UCR) "Reversed-Time" Goal Hypothesis anchors the whole evolution of the entire physical universe in the UCP's ultimate Goal of "Geula", e.g., Physical, Moral and Spiritual Perfection! According to this "Reversed Time Goal Hypothesis" the UCP "arranges" and "drives" the whole evolution of the universe towards an Ultimate State of 'Geula' – a "Perfected State" of the world (and universe) in which there is complete Harmony, Peace, an Awareness of the Singular Existence of the UCR and a sense of Gratitude towards It; Towards that end, the singular higher-ordered UCR produces the whole universe – producing, sustaining and evolving the entire physical universe enabling the appearance of Life on our small planet; and in particular, "driving" the UF's depiction of "inanimate" matter, then "animate" Life: from "plants" through "animals" to "Human-Beings" – and towards the appearance of an "expanded" form of Consciousness (for specific Individual Human Beings whose own Individual Human Consciousness is "not separate" from the functioning of the singular Universal Consciousness, e.g., at the "waking state" of Consciousness); and ultimately towards the Physically, Morally and Spiritually Perfected State of "Geula" in which all Human Beings will realize their "inseparability" from that Singular Higher-Ordered Universal Consciousness Reality, a State in which also "Death" will be "Abolished" (e.g., with one "empirical" manifestation of such "Death Abolishment" possibility based on a "time-reversal" application of the basic principles of the New 'G-d's Physics' Paradigm, as described previously)... In that sense we see that there is no real "separation" between the UCP's origination and development of the entire physical universe – e.g., including its accelerated expansion of the universe as brought about by its accelerated addition of the number of exhaustive spatial pixels to each consecutive UF's frame/s (rather than as "explained" by the purely hypothetical "non-existent" concepts of "dark-matter" and "dark-energy"), and its evolution of all inanimate and animate Biological Forms, all being driven by the singular higher-ordered UCP towards Its Ultimate Goal of a Perfected "Geula" State!

We therefore reach an entirely new understanding of the whole physical universe – whose continuous origination- "dissolution", sustenance and evolution- is not "caused" by any direct physical interactions between any relativistic 'Massive objects' and their assumed "curvature of Space-Time", nor by the "collapse" of the subatomic target's "probability wave function" as "caused" by its direct physical interaction with the corresponding subatomic "probe" element; A New singular, higher-ordered UCR directed 'Geula' Perfected State (e.g., Physically, Morally and Spiritually) towards which the UCR continuously creates-dissolves- re-creates and evolves each and every exhaustive spatial pixel comprising the entire physical universe for each consecutive UF's frame! We can see that this singular higher-ordered UCR directs the entire evolution of the physical universe to manifest ever more Conscious forms – from "inanimate" matter: the creation of all suns, planets, galaxies – leading up to the special "Life-enabling" conditions manifest in our Planet, as well as the accelerated expansion of the physical universe (based on the abovementioned UCR's accelerated addition of the number of exhaustive spatial pixels comprising the whole physical universe with each consecutive UF's frame), which allows Science and Humanity to notice and be aware of the operation and singularity of this UCR!; and towards the Ultimate "Perfected Geula" State through animate: plants, animals, Humans – and up to the manifestation of Humanity's (and the universe's!) Ultimate Perfected (Physical, Moral and Spiritual) State! Hence, in stark contrast to DNSP and the Old 'Material-Causal' Paradigm's depiction of the origination of the universe as "caused" by a "random nuclear Big-Bang explosion", is governed by mere direct physical interactions between relativistic 'Massive-objects' and their 'curvature of Space-Time' (which in turn determines the "travelling pathways" of these and other non-massive' objects) or direct physical interactions between random subatomic probe elements and their corresponding subatomic 'target's probability wave function; and the further expansion of the physical universe based on (purely hypothetical) "dark-matter", "dark-energy" concepts – leading to an inevitable eventual "death" or "dissipation" of all suns, galaxies, Life etc., based on the "Second Law of Thermodynamics" which states that the level of Entropy must increase with time... Moreover according to DNSP dual level 'Material-Causal' Model, the evolution of Biological forms of life is also assumed to be brought about by "random", "purposeless" direct physical interactions between certain "cosmic rays" and particular organisms' "genetic code" which "causes" random "genetic-mutations" – that in turn transform this particular "genetically mutated" organism to "survive better" in its direct physical interaction with a given set of 'Environmental Factors' (then its other "peer-organisms"), thereby allowing it to evolve into a new species etc. In contrast, the New 'G-d's Physics' Paradigm advocates an entirely new (and exciting) theoretical perspective and understanding of the origination- sustenance ("dissolution") and evolution of the entire physical universe – as being constantly and continuously directed towards the UCR's (or UCP's) "Ultimate Goal" of manifesting ever more Conscious, Moral and Harmonious forms, e.g., from the inanimate material entities through animate: animals, plants and Human-Beings – and up to Humanity's full manifestation of a "Perfected Geula State" in which the Presence and "Inseparability" of every exhaustive spatial pixel in the universe, every rock, plant, animal and human-being from the constant and continuous creation- dissolution- re-creation and evolution of every such exhaustive spatial pixel from the UCP's singular existence; in which this "Geula State" manifests as a full appreciation of the Oneness of all Humanity and all Creation, and consequent Perfected Moral and Spiritual State of Harmony, Awareness of the UCP's singular higher-ordered Existence and associated deep sense of Gratitude and Appreciation... We therefore realize that instead of the universe being created "by chance" and its evolution being "random", e.g., including the "Random Genetic Mutations" which supposedly created Life and evolves it (as explained by the Old 'Material-Causal' Paradigm), the creation- sustenance- "dissolution" and continuous "evolution" of the entire physical universe may only be seen as a "phenomenal", "transient" manifestation of the singular "computationally-invariant" 'Universal Consciousness Reality' (UCR) – which exists both "during" its sole (simultaneous) computation of all exhaustive spatial pixels' (four basic physical features of 'space', 'time', 'energy' and 'mas') comprising each consecutive UF's frame, and also exists singularly "in-between" any two consecutive UF's frames! Indeed, due to the singular existence of this UCR, the complete dependency of the entire physical universe – including all Biological forms solely upon the continuous operation of this singular, higher-ordered UCR we realized that the whole creation, sustenance ("dissolution") and evolution of the entire physical universe and all of its Biological Forms is solely directed by the UCP towards a manifestation of a Perfected "Geula" State – Physically, Morally and Spiritually!

4.   References

Bentwich, J. (2012a) "Harmonizing Quantum Mechanics and Relativity Theory". *Theoretical Concepts of Quantum Mechanics*, Intech (ISBN 979-953-307-377-3), Chapter 22, pp. 515-550.

Bentwich, J. (2012b) "Theoretical Validation of the Computational Unified Field Theory". *Theoretical Concepts of Quantum Mechanics*, (ISBN 979-953-307-3773), Chapter 23, pp. 551-598.

Bentwich, J. (2013b). "The Theoretical Ramifications of the Computational Unified Field Theory". *Advances in Quantum Mechanics* (ISBN 978-953-51-1089-7), Chapter 28, pp. 671-882.

Bentwich, J. (2013c). The Computational Unified Field Theory (CUFT): A Candidate Theory of Everything. *Advances in Quantum Mechanics* (ISBN 978-953-51-1089-7) Chapter 18, pp. 395-436.

Bentwich, J. (2015). The Computational Unified Field Theory (CUFT): A Candidate 'Theory of Everything'. *Selected Topics in Application of Quantum Mechanics* (ISBN 978-953-51-2126-8) Chapter 6.

Bentwich, J. (2014) *What if Einstein was Right? Amazon Kindle Book Store.*

Bentwich, J. (2015). On the Geometry of Space, Time, Energy, and Mass: Empirical Validation of the Computational Unified Field Theory. *Unified Field Mechanics: Natural Science Beyond the Veil of Spacetime (Proceedings of VIGIER IX Conference, Morgan State University, USA, 16-19 November 2014).*

Bentwich, J. (2016) The 'Computational Unified Field Theory': A Paradigmatic Shift. *Research & Reviews: Journal of Pure & Applied Physics.*

Bentwich, J. (2017a) The Computational Unified Field Theory: Could 'Dark Matter' & 'Dark Energy' be "Superfluous"? *SciFed Journal of Quantum Physics Special Issue.*

Bentwich, J. (2017b) The Computational Unified Field Theory: Explaining the Universe from "Without". *SciFed Journal of Quantum Physics Special Issue.*

Bentwich, J. (2017c). The Computational Unified Field Theory: A New 'A-Causal Computation' Physics. *SciFed Journal of Quantum Physics Special Issue.*

Bentwich, J. (2017d). The 'Computational Unified Field Theory' (CUFT) May Challenge the 'Big-Bang Theory'. *SciFed Journal of Quantum Physics Special Issue.*

Bentwich, J. (2017e). Can the 'Computational Unified Field Theory' (CUFT) Challenge the Basic Laws of Conservation? *SciFed Journal of Quantum Physics Special Issue.*

Bentwich, J. (2017f). The Computational Unified Field Theory (CUFT): Time "Reversal" May be Possible. *SciFed Journal of Quantum Physics Special Issue.*

Bentwich, J. (2017g). The Computational Unified Field Theory (CUFT) Transcends Relativity's Speed of Light Constraint. *SciFed Journal of Quantum Physics, Special Issue.*

Bentwich, J. (2017h). The Computational Unified Field Theory's New Physics: Transcending Space, Time and Causality. *SciFed Journal of Quantum Physics Special Issue.*

Bentwich, J. (2017i). A "Supra-Spatial-Temporal Universal Consciousness Reality". *Research & Reviews: Journal of Pure & Applied Physics, Special Issue: The Computational Unified Field Theory (CUFT)- A Paradigmatic Shift in 21st Century Physics.*

Bentwich, J. (2017j). A New Science: An Infinite Omniscient Dynamic-Equilibrium Universal Consciousness Reality. *SciFed Journal of Quantum Physics Special Issue.*

Bentwich, J. (2017k). The Computational Unified Field Theory (CUFT) Challenges Darwin's 'Natural Selection Principle'! *SciFed Journal of Quantum Physics Special Issue.*

Bentwich, J. (2017l). The Computational Unified Field Theory (CUFT) Challenges the Second Law of Thermodynamics.*SciFed Journal of Quantum Physics Special Issue.*

Bentwich, J. (2017m). The Computational Unified Field Theory (CUFT): An Empirical & Mathematical Validation of the 'Computational Unified Field Theory'; *SciFed Journal of Quantum Physics Special Issue.*

Bentwich, J. (2017n). The Computational Unified Field Theory (CUFT) New Science; *SciFed Journal of Quantum Physics Special Issue.*

Bentwich, J. (2018a). Review: The Computational Unified Field Theory (CUFT) New Universe: *The Global Journal of Science Frontier Research, Vol. 18 (8-A), Special Issue.*

Bentwich, J. (2018b). The Computational Unified Field Theory (CUFT): What is "Time"? *The Global Journal of Science Frontier Research, Vol. 18 (8-A), Special Issue.*

Bentwich, J. (2018c). The Universal Consciousness Reality's Camouflage: The Physical Universe! *The Global Journal of Science Frontier Research, Vol. 18 (8-A), Special Issue.*

Bentwich, J. (2018d). The Computational Unified Field Theory (CUFT) Epilogue: Can Human Consciousness Affect the Cosmos? *The Global Journal of Science Frontier Research, Vol. 18 (8-A), Special Issue.*

Bentwich, J. (2018e). Testing the Computational Unified Field Theory's (CUFT) Differential-Critical Predictions: The Higgs-Boson Particle May Not Exist Continuously! *The Global Journal of Science Frontier Research, Vol. 18 (8-A), Special Issue.*

Bentwich, J. (2018f). The Double-Faceted Universal Consciousness Reality: A Theoretical Review. *The Global Journal of Science Frontier Research, Vol. 18 (8-A), Special Issue.*

Bentwich, J. (2018g). Letter to the Editor: Dark Matter May Not Exist. *The Global Journal of Science Frontier Research, Vol. 18 (8-A), Special Issue.*

Bentwich, J. (2018h). The Computational Unified Field Theory's (CUFT) Epilogue: Possible Reversal of the Arrow of Time and Abolishment of Death. *The Global Journal of Science Frontier Research, Vol. 18 (8-A), Special Issue.*

Bentwich, J. (2019a). The Computational Unified Field Theory's (CUFT) New Universe. *The Global Journal of Science Frontier Research, Vol. 19 (6), Special Issue.*

Bentwich, J. (2019b). The Computational Unified Field Theory's (CUFT) Goes Beyond the 'Standard Model': "G-d's Physics"?!. *The Global Journal of Science Frontier Research, Vol. 18 (8-A), Special Issue.*

Bentwich, J. (2019c). A Call for Cosmologists & Experimental Physicists: Empirical Validation of the 'Computational Unified Field Theory' (CUFT) New Paradigm through "Time-Sensitive" Astronomical and Subatomic Measurements. *The Global Journal of Science Frontier Research, Vol. 19 (6), Special Issue.*

Bentwich, J. (2019d). The 'Computational Unified Field Theory' (CUFT): Redefining Mass, Gravity & the Physical Universe. *The Global Journal of Science Frontier Research, Vol. 19 (6), Special Issue.*

Bentwich, J. (2019d). Astronomical Validation of the Computational Unified Field Theory (CUFT) "Critical Prediction" & Resolution of the "Universe's Accelerated Expansion Rate Enigma" (UAERE).*The Global Journal of Science Frontier Research, Vol. 19 (6), Special Issue.*

Bentwich, J. (2019e) Urgent Call for Empirical Validation of the Computational Unified Field Theory's (CUFT) New 21st Century 'A-Causal Computation' (ACC) Paradigm. *Acta Scientific Applied Physics, Volume 1(1).*

Bentovish (Bentwich) J. (2020a) *'G-d's Physics'.* In Press. *iUniverse Publication.*

Bentovish (Bentwich), J. (2020b). 'G-d's Physics' (CUFT) New "Atom" & Purposeful Universe! *Advances in Theoretical & Computational Physics. Volume 3 (2),* p. 50-58.

Bentovish (Bentwich), J. (2020c). An Urgent Need for "G-d's Physics" New 21st Century Paradigm's Empirical Validation. *Advances in Theoretical & Computational Physics. Volume 3 (2),* p. 59-65.